DANTE AND THE MIDDLE AGES

PUBLICATIONS OF THE FOUNDATION FOR ITALIAN STUDIES
UNIVERSITY COLLEGE, DUBLIN

General Editor: John C. Barnes

Dante and the Middle Ages: Literary and Historical Essays, ed. J. C. Barnes and C. Ó Cuilleanáin
Dante Comparisons: Comparative Studies of Dante and: Montale, Foscolo, Tasso, Chaucer, Petrarch, Propertius and Catullus, ed. E. Haywood and B. Jones
Dante Readings, ed. E. Haywood
Dante Soundings: Eight Literary and Historical Essays, ed. D. Nolan
Word and Drama in Dante: Essays on the "Divina Commedia", ed. J. C. Barnes and J. Petrie
J. Petrie, *Petrarch: The Augustan Poets, the Italian Tradition and the "Canzoniere"*
T. O'Neill, *Of Virgin Muses and of Love: A Study of Foscolo's "Dei Sepolcri"*
Italian Storytellers: Essays on Italian Narrative Literature, ed. E. Haywood and C. Ó Cuilleanáin

BELFIELD ITALIAN LIBRARY

Dante Alighieri, *Vita nuova*, ed. J. Petrie and J. Salmons
Lorenzo de' Medici, *Selected Writings*, ed C. Salvadori
Luigi Pirandello, *Il berretto a sonagli*, ed. J. C. Barnes

DANTE AND THE MIDDLE AGES

Literary and Historical Essays

Edited by

JOHN C. BARNES

and

CORMAC Ó CUILLEANÁIN

Published for
The Foundation for Italian Studies
University College, Dublin

IRISH ACADEMIC PRESS · DUBLIN

Publication of this book was assisted by grants from

The National University of Ireland
The Faculty of Arts, University College Dublin
The Istituto Italiano di Cultura, Dublin

Printed and bound by Antony Rowe Ltd, Chippenham, England

First published 1995

by

Irish Academic Press Ltd
Kill Lane
Blackrock
County Dublin
Ireland

A catalogue record for this book is available from the British Library

ISBN 0 7165 2527 5

© Foundation for Italian Studies, University College Dublin, 1995

PREFACE

The essays in this collection are based on lectures forming part of the annual Dante Series in University College, Dublin between 1987 and 1993. Its editors and contributors are a mixture of local scholars and visitors from abroad: Zygmunt Barański is a Professor of Italian Studies in the University of Reading; John Barnes is the Professor of Italian in University College, Dublin, where Yolande de Pontfarcy and Jean-Michel Picard are both Statutory Lecturers in French; Peter Biller is a Lecturer in History in the University of York; Teresa Hankey is a Reader in Classics in the University of Kent; Christine Meek is an Associate Professor of Medieval History in Trinity College, Dublin, where Cormac Ó Cuilleanáin is a Lecturer in Italian and where Clotilde Soave-Bowe was formerly a Lecturer in Italian; Deborah Parker is an Associate Professor of Italian in the University of Virginia; Christopher Ryan is a Professor of Italian in the University of Sussex; Diana Webb is a Lecturer in History in King's College, London.

The title *Dante and the Middle Ages* was that of the original lecture series, and contributors—historians and literary scholars—responded to it in a variety of ways. The historians are now placed first. Christine Meek scrutinizes Dante's experience of city-state life, politics and exile in the light of the general background of his day. Diana Webb pursues the theme of saints and pilgrims in Dante's Italy, identifying particularly the different layers in local pantheons, which often owed their development to secular as well as spiritual impulses. Peter Biller, examining Florentine culture around 1300 from the point of view of its engagement with demographic issues, discovers that its awareness in this area appears to have been remarkably high in comparison with Latin Christendom as a whole. These three historical essays are followed by three contributions which might be broadly situated in the history of ideas. Yolande de Pontfarcy reviews recent work on the origins of

Purgatory and maintains that Dante's conception of the afterlife may well have been influenced by two Latin texts of Celtic provenance. Christopher Ryan challenges the usual view that Dante's understanding of the Incarnation simply replicates that of St Anselm, arguing that in Dante's opinion the Incarnation was not necessary for redemption but was freely chosen by God, Who could have waived the requirements of justice. Zygmunt Barański draws on his reading of medieval Biblical exegesis in exploring Dante's debt to theories about God's communication with mankind by means of signs, and hints that the accepted view of the poet's ideology as broadly Aristotelian requires fundamental reassessment. Another historical window is opened by Clotilde Soave-Bowe, who surveys Dante's references to individual members of the Swabian dynasty and gives a detailed reading of the Manfred episode in *Purgatorio* III. Teresa Hankey, setting out to uncover some of the implications for the reader of the identity between Dante the allegorist and Dante the prophet, presents an object-lesson in reading as an intellectual activity and offers fresh insights into the prophetic roles of Dante and particularly his re-created character Virgil. John Barnes finds that, for a layman, Dante had a remarkably extensive knowledge of the liturgy, and considers the poet's use of that knowledge in the creation of liturgies of his own in the *Commedia*. The last two essays, chronologically speaking, reach out beyond Dante. Jean-Michel Picard weaves a cultural web which links Italy with Ireland both before and after Dante, and focuses on a fourteenth-century Italian visitor to St Patrick's Purgatory. Deborah Parker concludes a critical survey of nineteenth- and twentieth-century scholarship on Dante's early commentators with a plea for a new awareness of cultural tradition as such scholarship enters the era of the database.

The editors wish to record their gratitude to Brian Morrissey and the late Carene Comerford for help with the preparation of the pages that follow.

All Biblical references in English are to the New English Bible, and all references to the works of Dante are based on the following editions, which in the notes are indicated by the abbreviations shown here:

Vn	*Vita nuova*, edited by D. De Robertis (Milan–Naples, Ricciardi, 1980); also in D. Alighieri, *Opere minori*, 2 vols in 3 (Milan–Naples, Ricciardi, 1979–88), I, i, 27–247

Conv.	Convivio, edited by C. Vasoli and D. De Robertis = D. Alighieri, Opere minori, I, ii
DVE	De Vulgari Eloquentia, edited by P. V. Mengaldo, in D. Alighieri, Opere minori, II, 1–237
Mon.	Monarchia, edited by B. Nardi, in D. Alighieri, Opere minori, II, 239–503
	La "Commedia" secondo l'antica vulgata, edited by G. Petrocchi, 4 vols (Milan, Mondadori, 1966–67)
Epist.	Epistole, edited by A. Frugoni and G. Brugnoli, in D. Alighieri, Opere minori, II, 505–643
	Questio de Aqua et Terra, edited by F. Mazzoni, in D. Alighieri, Opere minori, II, 691–880

The following abbreviations are also used:

Inf.	Inferno
Purg.	Purgatorio
Par.	Paradiso
Enc. dant.	Enciclopedia dantesca, 6 vols (Rome, Istituto dell'Enciclopedia Italiana, 1970–78)
Aen.	Virgil, Aeneid
Pat. Lat.	Patrologiae Cursus Completus, Series Latina, edited by J. P. Migne, 221 vols (Paris, Migne, 1844–1963)
MGH	Monumenta Germaniae Historica inde ab Anno Christi Quingentesimo usque ad Annum Millesimum et Quingentesimum Auspiciis Societatis Aperiendis Fontibus Rerum Germanicarum Medii Aevi, edited by G. H. Pertz et al. (Hanover etc., 1826–)
MGH: Const.	MGH: Legum Sectio IV: Constitutiones et Acta Publica Imperatorum et Regum, edited by L. Weiland et al. (Hanover, Hahn, 1893–)
MGH: Epist. Pont.	MGH: Epistolae Saeculi XIII et Regestis Pontificum Romanorum Selectae, edited by C. Rodenberg, 3 vols (Berlin, Weidmann, 1883–94)
MGH: SS	MGH: Scriptores, 32 vols in 34 (Hanover, Hahn; Leipzig, Hiersemann, 1826–1934)
RIS	Rerum Italicarum Scriptores ab Anno Aerae Christianae Quingentesimo ad Millesimum Quingentesimum Quorum Potissima Pars

	Nunc Primum in Lucem Prodit, edited by L. A. Muratori, 25 vols in 28 (Milan, Società Palatina, 1723–51)
RIS2	*Rerum Italicarum Scriptores: raccolta degli storici italiani dal Cinquecento al Millecinquecento ordinata da L. A. Muratori, nuova edizione riveduta, ampliata e corretta*, edited by G. Carducci et al. (Città di Castello, Lapi; Bologna, Zanichelli, 1900–)
Nuova cronica	Giovanni Villani, *Nuova cronica*, edited by G. Porta, 3 vols (Parma, Fondazione Bembo/Guanda, 1990–91)

Unless stated otherwise, English translations of passages from the following works adhere to the versions indicated:

Vn	*La vita nuova (Poems of Youth)*, translated by B. Reynolds (Harmondsworth, Penguin, 1969)
Conv.	*The Banquet*, translated by C. Ryan (Saratoga, California, ANMA Libri, 1989)
DVE	*Literature in the Vernacular*, translated by S. Purcell (Manchester, Carcanet, 1981)
Mon.	*Monarchy and Three Political Letters*, translated by D. Nicholl and C. Hardie (London, Weidenfeld and Nicolson, 1954)
	The Divine Comedy, translated by C. S. Singleton, 3 vols in 6 (Princeton, Princeton University Press, 1970–75)
Epist.	*Dantis Alagherii Epistolae: The Letters of Dante*, edited by P. Toynbee, second edition (Oxford, Clarendon Press, 1966)
Aen.	*Virgil*, with an English translation by H. Rushton Fairclough, revised edition, 2 vols [Loeb Classical Library] (Cambridge, Massachusetts, Harvard University Press; London, Heinemann, 1967), I, 239–II, 365

Uncredited translations of passages from other works are by the author of the essay in question. The use of italics in quotations is almost always the initiative of the author of the essay, not of the editor of the text quoted. Exceptions are indicated as they occur.

CONTENTS

Preface   5

Dante's Life His Times
CHRISTINE MEEK   11

Saints and Pilgrims in Dante's Italy
DIANA M. WEBB   33

"Demographic Thought" around 1300 and Dante's Florence
PETER BILLER   57

The Topography of the Other World and the Influence of Twelfth-century Irish Visions on Dante
YOLANDE DE PONTFARCY   93

Paradiso VII: Marking the Difference between Dante and Anselm
CHRISTOPHER RYAN   117

Dante's Signs: An Introduction to Medieval Semiotics and Dante
ZYGMUNT G. BARAŃSKI   139

Dante and the Hohenstaufen: From Chronicle to Poetry
CLOTILDE SOAVE-BOWE   181

The Clear and the Obscure: Dante, Virgil and the Role of the Prophet
TERESA HANKEY   211

Vestiges of the Liturgy in Dante's Verse
    JOHN C. BARNES   231

Inferno, v. 73–142: The Irish Sequel
    JEAN-MICHEL PICARD   271

Dante's Medieval and Renaissance Commentators:
    Nineteenth- and Twentieth-century Constructions
    DEBORAH PARKER   287

Index of References to Dante's Works   305

Index of Names   307

DANTE'S LIFE IN HIS TIMES

Christine Meek

It is hoped that the title of this essay will not arouse expectations it is unable to fulfil. Although the broad outlines of Dante's life are known, the only part of it which is at all well documented is the period of his political activity from 1295 to 1301. He tells us a certain amount about his life in his own works, but these are not always easy to date or to interpret. Very little is known for certain about the first thirty years of his life, and there are many doubts about his whereabouts at various times during his twenty years of exile. This essay has no new information, nor even any new theories, to offer, and in fact will not be concerned with Dante's life in any detail. It will deal rather with broad areas of his experience—municipal life, politics, exile—in the light of the general background of his day.

Dante was, of course, born a Florentine, a member of an Italian *comune*. Florence was still quite small, though growing rapidly in the late thirteenth century. The second circle of walls begun in 1172 had enclosed only about 80 hectares, but the third circle enclosed 630 hectares. The population may have been nearing 100,000 in 1300, but had earlier been much lower.[1] Illustrations of Florence and other Italian cities of the period show narrow streets with tall buildings closely packed together, many with towers. Most of the things that come to mind when Florence is mentioned were still in the future, whether they be cultural achievements in art or literature or even the buildings most characteristic of Florence today. The Baptistery was there in Dante's day, the Bargello was begun about 1255 and Santa Maria Novella in 1246, but was in nothing like its present form. The Duomo was begun in 1296 and the campanile about 1334—not to be completed until well into the fifteenth century. The Palazzo della Signoria was begun in 1299 and Santa Croce, replacing earlier buildings, in 1294–95. Neither can have made much progress by the time of Dante's exile.[2]

But Florence itself was certainly growing rapidly in the late thirteenth century in population, economic activity and wealth. It was in this period that Florence decisively overtook old rivals like Pisa or Siena and established itself as the leading Tuscan *comune*. This was at the cost of some disruption to the old way of life. There were indeed new immigrants from the countryside and "sùbiti guadagni" ["sudden gains": *Inferno*, XVI. 73]. The city was indeed much larger than it had earlier been, though whether it had suffered the moral decline of which Dante has his great-great-grandfather Cacciaguida speak in *Paradiso* XV is more debatable. Florence was still quite an intimate society. It was still small enough for everyone to be baptized in the one font in San Giovanni (Dino Compagni, *Cronica*, II. 8), and Dante can ask in *Inferno* and *Purgatorio* whether there are any Florentines present in the expectation that if they are his contemporaries he will know them.

Italians of this period generally felt a great love for and pride in their city. There are a number of eulogies of Italian cities, often articulated in statistical terms. Bonvesin della Riva, although he was not a layman but a tertiary of the order of the Umiliati, shows this kind of civic pride in the city of Milan; in a chapter headed "in praise of Milan's fertility and abundance of goods" he lists the 30,000 oxen cultivating Milanese territory, the 115 parishes in the city alone, the 40,000 men Milan could put in the field, the city's 120 lawyers, 1,500 notaries, 28 physicians, 150 surgeons, 300 bakeries, 440 butchers, 150 inns, 80 blacksmiths and so on. There is a similar description of Padua in 1318 by Judge Giovanni de Nono, and, best-known of all, Giovanni Villani's famous description of the wealth and power of Florence in the year 1338 (*Nuova cronica*, XII. 94), where he not only lists the number of judges, inns, bakeries and suchlike, but also provides statistics quantifying the annual output of woollen cloth and the annual imports of grain, wine, cattle, pigs, goats and melons for the city's needs, as well as detailing the beauty of Florence's houses and churches. Dante's contemporary, the Dominican Remigio de' Girolami, lists the seven principal blessings bestowed on Florence as great wealth and population, a noble currency, a civilized way of life, the textile and armaments industries and noble buildings.[3]

Since many of Dante's pronouncements on Florence were written after his exile, when he was more concerned to condemn her political decisions and castigate her corruption than to praise her achievements, there are comparatively few direct expressions of affection for the city in his works. They are not, however, entirely lacking: he speaks of Florence as "la bellissima e famosissima figlia di Roma" ["Rome's most beautiful and famous daughter"] in *Convivio*, I. 3. 4, and in *Paradiso*, XXV. 5 as the "bello ovile ov' io dormi' agnello" ["fair sheepfold where I slept as a lamb"]. Obviously even his condemnations of Florence reveal how central his native city was in his concerns. In *De Vulgari Eloquentia*, when attempting to be more objective, he takes it for granted that everyone considers his birthplace the loveliest place under the sun and says, "Although I drank from Arno before I cut my teeth and although I love Florence so much that for that love I suffer an unjust exile [...]" and, "Although for my pleasure and for the charming of my senses there is no lovelier place in the world than Florence [...]",[4] even while recognizing that this might not objectively be true.

To live in an Italian *comune* did not mean to be a member of a peaceful merchant or artisan community. Although Florence was an active mercantile, banking and industrial society in the late thirteenth century, this was a relatively recent development. In its origins and earlier history the *comune* had been a place where members of landed families had had a leading role. They resided in the *comune* for at least part of the year, but drew their income from land in the surrounding countryside. They had a military training and outlook, very similar to that of the rural nobility. They were clannish with a strong sense of family solidarity and family honour, prone to quarrels and quick to avenge insults.[5]

Dante's own family pride is clear from the *Commedia*—from his exchange with Farinata degli Uberti in *Inferno* X, from his embarrassment when in *Inferno* XXIX a cousin, Geri del Bello, makes a threatening gesture, which Dante attributes to the family's failure to avenge his murder, and above all from his attitude to his ancestor Cacciaguida, whom he addresses with the honorific *voi* and makes one of the main characters in *Paradiso*. In fact there are chronological difficulties about Cacciaguida's alleged participation in the Second Crusade and his knighting by Emperor Conrad III, and it is improbable that Dante's family was noble. Dante's father, his uncle Brunetto and their father Bellincione were moneylenders. Another uncle declared himself to be a banker in 1270 and other relatives were either moneylenders or cloth manufacturers. Dante's forebears appear to have constituted one of the many families that rose through trade and banking in the second half of the thirteenth century, and the claim to nobility is an example of the contemporary tendency to glorify predecessors by alleging descent from Lombards or even Romans (as Dante himself does in *Inferno*, xv. 73–78).[6]

Little is known for certain of the first thirty years of Dante's life, though this period includes his relationship with Beatrice, her death and his early poetry, his marriage to Gemma, daughter of Manente Donati, of a minor branch of an important family, and Dante's education. Relatively little is known about the education available to the laity in thirteenth-century Florence, though other Tuscan *comuni* are known to have had teachers of Latin grammar and in some cases law, notarial studies, logic or medicine. Nor is it known what books were generally available. Dante refers to his reading Cicero's *De Amicitia* and Boethius's *De Consolatione Philosophiae*, but says that the latter was "little-known" ("non conosciuto da molti"; *Convivio*, II. 12. 2–4). Brunetto Latini seems to have been an important influence. According to Villani he was "the first to teach refinement to the Florentines and the art of speaking well" ("egli fue cominciatore e maestro in digrossare i Fiorentini, e farli scorti in bene parlare"; *Nuova cronica*, IX. 10). He may have gathered a circle of pupils and friends around him, or may have given formal lectures. In any case he exercised an influence through his writings, his translations and his example. There were also religious schools, especially that of the Franciscans at Santa Croce and that of the Dominicans at Santa Maria Novella. Dante is probably referring to these when he says he went "ne le scuole de li religiosi e a le disputazioni de li filosofanti" ["to the schools of the religious and the disputations of the philosophers": *Convivio*, II. 12. 7] after the death of Beatrice, when he was seeking the consolation of the "donna gentile", Lady Philosophy. Peter Olivi and Ubertino da Casale, of the Spiritual wing of the Franciscans, had been teaching in Santa Croce in 1287–89, and Remigio de' Girolami in Santa Maria Novella rather later. Since all of these had studied in Paris, Dante was in touch with Parisian teaching indirectly, even if the story that he studied there himself during his exile has to be relegated to the sphere of legend. Many books would also be available in the convents of the orders of friars, and there are parallels between some of Dante's ideas and those of contemporary mendicant thinkers, especially Fra Remigio de' Girolami.[7]

Tradition has it that Dante served in the Florentine forces in the campaign against Arezzo, which culminated in the victory at Campaldino in 1289. Although there is no documentary evidence of this, and references to military affairs in the *Commedia* (*Inferno*, XXI. 94–96, XXII. 1–9) and perhaps the *Vita nuova* (IX. 1) could bear other interpretations, service in the *comune*'s army is by no means improbable for a man of Dante's age and status. The obligation to serve as cavalry or infantry, according to means, was universal for adult males, often between extreme age limits, in Italian *comuni* from their earliest days. Dante was twenty-four in 1289 and thus of a very suitable age to serve in person.

The *comune*'s forces consisted of conscripts, but service was not necessarily performed unwillingly; it must have been regarded as part of municipal life.[8] Campaigns were usually brief—a few weeks in the summer or autumn—and fairly local. Florentine territory was still of modest extent and campaigns beyond the borders would still not be unduly far from the city itself. The campaign against Arezzo would be a good illustration of this.

Although military obligation was general, not everyone would be called upon to serve on any particular occasion. Service was organized on the basis of the *sesti* into which Florence was divided, and one or two *sesti* might be summoned for any particular campaign, as dictated by the numbers required. Thus the ordinary economic activities of the city would not be too seriously disrupted. Each *sesto* had both infantry and cavalry with special officials to determine who should have the obligation to serve as cavalry, or rather to maintain a horse for the service of the *comune*, since it was permitted to name a younger relative or other suitable deputy, instead of serving in person. Although service was obligatory and the forces were conscripts, they seem to have been paid and also to have received compensation for horses lost in the *comune*'s service. In some cases exemption could be purchased for particular campaigns, the money thus disbursed being used to pay substitutes. Conversely there were fines for failing to appear when summoned, or failure to provide the requisite arms and equipment. Selling a horse registered for municipal service rendered the owner liable to a heavy fine of £100 (more than a year's salary for, say, most municipal officials).

Armies of this period also included mercenaries, that is, non-Florentines serving Florence for pay, usually as cavalry. The practice of employing mercenaries certainly goes back to the very early thirteenth century and in all probability to the twelfth. There were mercenaries from Lombardy and Romagna on the Florentine side in the 1260 Montaperti campaign, though they were not very significant numerically and were recruited piecemeal. Some of them may have been exiled from their own *comuni*—they included Sienese.

The use of mercenaries increased after 1266 when a permanent Guelf army was maintained by the Guelf cities of Tuscany and Charles of Anjou, King of Sicily. Each member of the league had to maintain a proportion of this force, called a *tallia*, with the largest share falling to Florence. In the 1280s Florence seems to have been maintaining 500 cavalry on this basis. Not only did mercenaries become numerically, militarily and financially more significant, but they were raised in a different way from previously, no longer individually and piecemeal, but in organized troops under recognized commanders or constables. Although the troop led by each individual constable was usually quite small—25, 50, rarely as many as 100—these constables were the not-too-distant ancestors of the later Italian *condottieri*. They and their followers were often Provençal, Southern French or Catalan, but there were some Italians too, from Tuscany, Umbria, the March of Ancona, Emilia and Lombardy. There were also Italians who were virtually professional soldiers, such as Nello della Pietra de' Pannocchieschi (the husband of Pia de' Tolomei), the counts of Sarteano, the counts of Romena, Mainardo da Susinana and Uguccione della Faggiuola.

These mercenary forces supplemented and stiffened the citizen levies, but they did not replace them: the citizen element still continued, fighting beside the mercenary forces. Those selected for cavalry service had to keep a horse for the purpose, but received payment of forty florins per year, with an additional 10–15 *soldi* per day for time actually served. Five to six hundred men were liable for this service and sometimes more. The citizen forces, like the mercenaries, were usually cavalry; infantry was provided from levies in the *contado*. Both citizens and *contadini* are recorded as having fought in considerable numbers.

Thus, if Dante did indeed fight at Campaldino on 11 June 1289, he was one of a mixed force of mercenary and citizen cavalry. Florence provided 1,000 of the 1,600 cavalry that fought on the Guelf side. Four hundred of these were mercenaries, and this element was prominent in the campaign. The Florentines were led by the mercenary Amauri de Narbonne, who also commanded a personal troop of 100 cavalry, and the password at Campaldino was "Nerbona cavaliere"; but 600 of the cavalry were Florentines, and so were perhaps about 6,000 of the infantry. The army had left Florence on 2 June and returned in triumph on 23 July.[9]

This persistence of obligations by Florentines to personal military service continued in the early decades of the fourteenth century, and Florentine armies continued to be a combination of mercenaries, allies and citizen forces. Florentines fought in person against Henry VII in 1311–13, and with less happy results at Montecatini in 1315 and Altopascio in 1325, when they suffered heavy casualties. Dante's service at Campaldino would be part of a long and continuing tradition of military obligation and personal service to their *comune* by Florentines and other Italians of this period.

In 1295 Dante, then aged thirty, began an active participation in Florentine political life, in 1300 reaching the office of prior, the highest office open to Florentine citizens except for that of *gonfaloniere di giustizia*. Political office-holding was voluntary, unpaid and exclusive. Medieval Italian *comuni* had been run from their earliest days by their own members, holding office for fairly limited periods of time and managing to combine this with their own normal affairs, their businesses and livelihoods.[10] The Florentine priors held office for two months at a time and were required to leave their own homes and live in the public palace for that period, so that they would always be on hand to deal with municipal affairs. The priors obviously had to be in a position to do this. Since participation in politics was voluntary, Dante was not obliged to engage in political activity; he chose to do so.

Not everyone who might wish to hold political office, however, would be in a position to secure election.[11] The fact that Dante did hold office in 1295–1301 is an indication not only of interest in political life but also of a certain status in Florentine society. He belonged to a category of citizens perceived by their fellow citizens to be eligible for public office. In fact the basis of office-holding in this period was the guilds. The priors were the priors of the guilds, elected by various methods among guild members. Dante held office as prior of the guild of doctors and apothecaries. He did not actually practise as a doctor or apothecary; he had merely enrolled in the guild—at an unknown date—in order to be eligible for political office. Slightly earlier this would not have been permitted. Under the Ordinances of Justice of 1293 only those who had effectively practised the trade or business of their guild had been eligible for office, but in 1295 this regulation had been modified to extend eligibility to all those who were enrolled in a guild, whether or not they practised the trade in question.

If voluntary unpaid participation in politics is the positive side of Italian city-state life, factionalism is its negative side, and Dante inevitably became involved in Florentine factional struggles. Factions in Italian *comuni* date back to about 1200. In Florence they were traditionally dated from the murder of Buondelmonte de' Buondelmonti in 1216, when he jilted a lady to whom he had been betrothed as part of an attempt to settle a slightly earlier dispute among noble families. Despite the obvious legendary elements in it, the story is probably an accurate enough reflection of the world of nobles, family pride, insults and vendettas that gave rise to factions.[12] To these were added Guelf and Ghibelline elements. There were captains of the Parte Guelfa in Florence in the 1240s and probably other institutional elements as well. The Ghibellines had a similar organization and could function outside their *comune* as well as inside it if sent into exile. The Guelfs and Ghibellines were at the same time rival groups of noble families and the supporters of the Papacy and Charles of Anjou in the case of the Guelfs and of the Empire in the case of the Ghibellines. By the 1280s the Guelfs were victorious and the Ghibellines reduced to impotence in Florence, though not elsewhere; but new factions grew up, as happened in other cities.

In Parma there was a *pars nova* and a *pars antiqua*, in Ghibelline Arezzo the *secchi* and the *verdi*, in Orvieto the *malcorani* and the *befatti* and in Pisa the *raspanti* and the *bergolini*. In Pistoia and also in Florence there were the Blacks and the Whites, led in Florence by Corso Donati and Vieri de' Cerchi, respectively.[13] The rivalry between Corso Donati, a member of an ancient family but not a particularly wealthy man, and Vieri de' Cerchi, a very wealthy banker of a less ancient family, was probably largely personal, but they and their followers also took rather different lines at a time when there were important political decisions to be made. Although Dante had connections with both sides (his wife was a Donati and he was a friend of Forese Donati, but also a friend of Guido Cavalcanti, a great enemy of Corso Donati), he was a White. He entered political life in July 1295 when the Cerchi rose to prominence, and he temporarily disappears from the records late in 1296 or in early 1297, when the Donati got the upper hand, to reappear again when the Cerchi regained control in 1299. He then became involved in the disputes of the Florentine government and Pope Boniface VIII. The Whites were, of course, Guelf and as such faithful to the papal and Angevin alliance, but not expecting excessive demands to be made on them or excessive subservience to be required of them. This kind of moderate Guelfism was broadly in line with the policy of popes such as Gregory X or Nicholas III in the 1270s and 1280s or Benedict XI in 1303–04. But the pope they had to deal with was Boniface VIII, who was particularly demanding in the assistance he required from Florence and specifically in need of finance and forces for his attempts to achieve the reconquest of Sicily for the Angevins and, nearer home, the defeat of the Colonna family to strengthen the position of his own family, the Caetani. The Pope began to intervene more directly in Florentine political affairs in defence of a group of Florentine businessmen who had been condemned by the *comune* but enjoyed great influence at the papal Curia. Defending Florentine dignity and independence without arousing the Pope's suspicions about her loyalty and good faith was an almost impossible task. Eventually the Pope called in Charles of Valois, the brother of the French king. The Florentines certainly had the power to resist his entry into the city, but did not attempt to do so. The exiled Corso Donati and the Blacks took advantage of the opportunity to return to Florence by force and carry out a *coup d'état*.[14] From then onwards Florence remained in the hands of the Blacks, and Dante spent the rest of his life in exile.

He was apparently absent from Florence at the time of Charles of Valois's entry and never able to return. Although Dante himself appears to attribute his exile to his priorate, it seems to have been less the fact that he had been prior in 1300 than his attitude subsequently that sealed his fate. Some of his fellow priors were able to change sides and even hold office under the Blacks: Neri del Giudice was prior again in 1304, 1314, 1319 and 1323, and Noffo di Guido Bonafedi in 1304, 1314 and 1315. But in June 1301 Dante was the only councillor to speak against granting aid requested by the Pope, though many others voted against the proposal.[15] Had he been less wholehearted or more willing to compromise, perhaps he too could have remained in Florence.

Dante is the most famous exile of the Middle Ages, but by no means the only one. Other exiles—Brunetto Latini, Farinata degli Uberti, Guido Cavalcanti and many others—are mentioned in the

Commedia itself. Randolph Starn was able to list well over thirty exiled *poets* of the thirteenth and fourteenth centuries. Exile was a common phenomenon.[16]

What did exile mean in practice? What was the life of an exile like? In view of what has already been said about local patriotism and love of one's native city, exile, even in the most favourable circumstances, meant living somewhere other than the place where the exile most wanted to be. Exile was a personal disaster. For a medieval Florentine or Sienese or Bolognese there was nowhere else on earth to equal Florence or Siena or Bologna, and to be obliged to live elsewhere was in itself a punishment and a torment. There is a whole genre of exile poetry, based partly on classical exemplars, describing the miseries of the place of exile, the delights of home and the joy that would be experienced if return were ever possible. As Ser Pietro Faitinelli of Lucca wrote:

> S'io veggio in Lucca bella mio ritorno,
> che fi' quando la pera fie ben mezza,
> in nullo cuore uman tant' allegrezza
> già mai non fu, quant' io avrò quel giorno.
>   Le mura andrò leccando d'ogn' intorno
> e gli uomini, piangendo d'allegrezza;
> odio, rancore, guerra ed ogni empiezza
> porrò giú contra quei che mi cacciorno.[17]

[If I live to see my return to beautiful Lucca, which will be when the pear is overripe, never was there in any human heart such joy as I shall have on that day. I will go around licking all the walls and the citizens, weeping with joy; I will lay aside hatred, rancour, strife and anger towards those who exiled me.]

Exile, however, might vary considerably. It might be permanent or temporary, sudden or anticipated and well prepared for, penurious or cushioned and comfortable. Perhaps the mildest kind of exile was enforced residence in a particular place, in the way that Guido Cavalcanti was obliged to live in Sarzana in 1300, though in his case it led to his death. This kind of exile was often temporary and usually involved an orderly departure in agreement with the authorities in the home city. While the exile or *confinato* remained in the place assigned to him, he was likely to be able to live unmolested and enjoy the revenues of his property at home.

Other exiles too might have had time to make preparations and take some property with them. The Guelfs defeated at Montaperti returned to Florence and had—were perhaps even allowed—four days to make their preparations before the victorious Ghibellines entered the city.[18] Later Vieri de' Cerchi is said to have taken 60,000 florins to exile in Arezzo, and Vermiglio degli Alfani, although an exile at the time, was nevertheless in a position to make loans to Emperor Henry VII.[19]

Others were less fortunate. Driven into exile as a result of tumults and street fighting, they were lucky to escape with their lives and certainly had no chance to arrange their affairs or select valuables to take with them. Dante, of course, came into this category. Tradition has it that he was absent from Florence on an embassy when political upheavals there rendered his return impossible. Thus, although not in any physical danger, he had no chance to make preparations or arrange transfer of assets abroad—in any case his resources seem to have been modest. Certainly penury is an aspect of exile which he stresses in references in both the *Commedia* and the *Convivio*. Dante also came into the category of exiles who were subject to punitive measures by adversaries, death sentences, a price on his head and the confiscation and destruction of his property.[20]

Exiles faced a number of problems. They might be smarting from the humiliation of defeat, bitter about the precise circumstances which had led to their exile, conscious of themselves as victims of misfortune or injustice. They often had the practical problems of where to find a refuge and how to support themselves; and they also had to face the question of future relations with their own city, the possibility of return at some future date and the best policy to pursue in order to bring it about.

Finding a refuge might be no easy matter. An exile's city would no doubt have enemies who would be willing to receive him— Farinata degli Uberti went to Ghibelline Siena in 1258 and the Florentine Guelfs to Lucca after Montaperti—but to settle in an enemy city was likely to be regarded as an act of hostility by the authorities of one's home city. In any case it might not prove a permanent refuge. Political changes might compel an exile to move on. A number of Dante's fellow exiles from Florence congregated in Arezzo, but when the Ghibelline leader Uguccione della Faggiuola, who was *podestà* there, came to terms with the Pope, the White Guelf exiles either were driven out or felt it wiser to move elsewhere.[21] The treatment of exiles was often the subject of negotiations and diplomatic pressure between *comuni*. One city would request, or urge, or demand that another city should not receive its exiles, and treaties between cities often contained clauses regarding the treatment of their respective exiles.

Many exiles also had problems in supporting themselves and making a living. Those who had least difficulty were probably merchants, though their assets at home might have been lost. Since merchants normally travelled with their goods, they were accustomed to living abroad, sometimes for years on end. They could just as easily trade abroad from Bologna or Venice as from Florence or Siena, and sometimes had skills or connections which caused them to be welcomed in other cities. The merchants of Lucca are said to have been welcomed in Florence, Bologna and Venice when driven out of their own *comune* in 1314, because their skills in the manufacture of silk cloth could bring profit to their host cities. Enrico Sandei is said to have arrived in Venice in his shirt, but subsequently to have made a great fortune there.[22]

It may sometimes have been difficult to distinguish exiled merchants from merchants who lived outside their native cities for many years simply in the course of their trade. Certainly Lucca found it difficult to do so in the 1340s, when, after various previous amnesties, the *comune* offered tax concessions to exiled merchants and craftsmen who were prepared to return. Although the records are far from complete, some sixty-two individuals or families took up this offer. The *comune* later found, however, that in some cases the concessions had been granted improperly to men who had been absent but not exiles, while their families and kinsmen had been living tranquilly in the city.[23]

Another category which may have found it relatively easy to make a living in exile was that of nobles and soldiers who were prepared to serve as mercenary cavalry. A good example of such a man is Castruccio Castracani, who during his period of exile from 1300 to 1314, apart from an adventurous stay in England, apparently served as a mercenary in Flanders and in the forces of Can Grande della Scala of Verona and with Uguccione della Faggiuola in Pisa.[24] With the growing importance of mercenary forces and increased opportunities for such employment it can be difficult to distinguish mercenaries who were exiles from others who were not. The wandering adventurous career of Castruccio Castracani as an exile reads very like the wandering adventurous career of Uguccione della Faggiuola, a noble from the Massa Trabaia and lord of seventy-two castles, who served as captain or *podestà* of Arezzo, Gubbio, Forlí, Faenza and Imola, was vicar of Genoa for Henry VII, was summoned to Pisa as war captain after the Emperor's death, adding Lucca in 1314 but losing both Lucca and Pisa in 1316, so that he ended his career, in 1319, as a mercenary in the service of Can Grande della Scala.[25] The difference was that Uguccione della Faggiuola could always return home, while Castruccio Castracani until 1314 could not.

Despite the impression to the contrary that the example of Dante might create, exiles were not normally isolated individuals. Dante, like Farinata degli Uberti before him, had been exiled not as an individual but as a member of a party. In the Middle Ages men tended to act in groups rather than as individuals. Like groups with common interests within cities (the *popolo*, men engaged in a particular business or craft) or outside (merchants of a particular city living abroad), exiles too tended to form themselves into associations, a *communitas* or *universitas*. Thus the Whites of Florence, Lucca or Prato in exile or the Blacks of Pistoia, which was ruled by the Whites, formed associations, appointed officials such as *podestà*, captains and councils, had a common seal and a common treasury, raised armies for military operations, and appointed proctors for legal affairs and diplomatic negotiations. They were organized in precisely the same way as a party within a particular *comune* and could easily replace it if the opportunity arose. Other powers negotiated with the *pars extrinseca* of a *comune* on the same basis as they did with the *pars intrinseca*. Relations were influenced by political and diplomatic considerations, not by any legal differences. Organized exiles could form military and diplomatic alliances just as a party controlling a *comune* did.[26] Dante was involved in this kind of activity in the early years of his exile. He was with the other Whites, subscribing to the pact between the community of White Guelfs and their Ghibelline allies at San Godenzo in the Apennines in June 1302. If the letter is genuinely his, he wrote to the Cardinal of Prato in the name of the Whites in the spring of 1304, and later he wrote to Henry VII on behalf of "all the Tuscans everywhere who desire peace", though he had long before left "la compagnia malvagia e scempia" ["the evil and senseless company": *Paradiso*, XVII. 62] to form a party on his own.[27]

The numbers involved in such associations could be large. There were 382 Blacks exiled from Pistoia and 689 Whites exiled from Florence in 1301–02. Dino Compagni speaks of 3,000 Florentine exiles in the mid-thirteenth century and there were apparently 4,000 in 1323, when an amnesty was offered. Sometimes even higher figures are quoted: 1,500 families driven out of Ferrara when the d'Este took over in 1240, or 12,000 Lambertazzi partisans driven out of Bologna in 1274—a figure which seems improbably high, since it would mean that a third to a half of the population was in exile at the same time.[28]

Some exiles were accompanied by wives and children, though Gemma Donati apparently did not join Dante in exile. Legislation sometimes compelled children, especially sons, to join their fathers in exile when they reached a certain age. Other exiles had children born to them abroad. Fazio degli Uberti and Petrarch were both born in exile and Coluccio Salutati, later the Chancellor of Florence, grew up in exile in Bologna. Fazio degli Uberti has Florence lament:

> Vedove e pupilli e innocenti
> del mio sangue miglior van per lo pane
> per altrui terre strane
> con gran vergogna e con mortale affanno;[29]

[Widows and minors and innocents of my finest stock go seeking their daily bread in other people's alien cities with great humiliation and deadly suffering];

but in the 1320s exiles of Genoa were said to be living comfortably with their families, practising their trades and occupations just as they did at home.[30]

The most important decision an exile had to face was what attitude to adopt towards his home city. Exile was by no means always or necessarily permanent, and an exile might reasonably hope to return to his city at some future date. Whether or not he was able to do so would depend on the circumstances of his exile, his own attitude and activities while in exile, the attitude of the group ruling his city and the turn of events.

Assuming that the exile did wish to return home, he might adopt a policy of humble passivity, striving to do nothing that could cause offence, in the hope of being recalled. The most famous example of this attitude is well outside Dante's period, when Cosimo de' Medici was able to secure his recall to Florence in 1434 less than a year after he had been sent into exile. According to

Leonardo Bruni's fifteenth-century biography of the poet, Dante too attempted to obtain his recall by this method.

The alternative was the opposite extreme—seeking allies in order to return by force. This too could be successful: Corso Donati returned in the wake of Charles of Valois's expedition to Florence in 1301, and Castruccio Castracani returned to Lucca in 1314 helping Uguccione della Faggiuola to take the city by storm. Archbishop Ottone Visconti had ended fifteen years of exile from Milan in a similar way in 1277. The Florentine Whites attempted to enter Florence by force on 20 July 1304, though unsuccessfully.[31]

In such circumstances a ruling regime might well regard its exiles as a threat, especially since they were likely to have kinsmen and friends within the city who might serve as a fifth column. The ruling regime might therefore press its neighbours to expel its exiles, but was itself subject to pressure in their favour. Treaties often included clauses about the treatment of exiles. A city that made a treaty from a position of strength might be able to insist on their expulsion, but if it had suffered a defeat or been forced to sue for peace, it might be compelled to agree to the readmission of some or all of its exiles and even to the restoration of their property. In other cases a city might voluntarily invite the least dangerous of its exiles to return, in order to reduce the number of its enemies, to strengthen its economy or increase its population, or to improve its finances by commuting sentences of exile to fines. The amnesties and tax concessions offered by Lucca in the 1330s and 1340s seem to come into this category. On 2 September 1311 Florence offered an amnesty from which Dante was excluded, and on 19 May 1315 another amnesty which had no exclusions.[32] These seem to have been motivated by the *comune*'s hopes of improving its finances from the fines which the exiles were to pay on their return. Dante could, of course, have returned on this basis, had he been prepared to accept the implicit admission of guilt and do the required penance.

Exiles might also benefit from totally unexpected turns of events. The amnesty of 19 May 1315 was offered during the campaigning that led to Florence's defeat at Montecatini. In 1280 Cardinal Latino Malabranca, as legate of his uncle, Pope Nicholas III, tried to arrange pacifications of factions in the cities of Tuscany and Romagna, which did lead to the restoration of many Ghibelline exiles to Florence, though rarely to the full recovery of their property and position within the city. The reconciliation of factions and the restoration of exiles to their city was a major element in the policy of Emperor Henry VII.

In 1310 Dante's hopes were aroused by the announcement of Henry VII's expedition to Italy.[33] It is difficult to be sure how committed an imperialist he had been before this, though he had written in the *Convivio* (IV. 4. 6–7) that the Roman Empire was founded by God for the perfection of human life and possessed universal jurisdiction, so that

> Quasi dire si può de lo Imperadore [...] che elli sia lo cavalcatore de la umana volontade. Lo quale cavallo come vada sanza lo cavalcatore per lo campo assai è manifesto, e spezialmente ne la misera Italia, che sanza mezzo alcuno a la sua governazione è rimasa!
>
> (*Convivio*, IV. 9. 10)

> [One may describe the emperor (...) as the rider of the human will. How this horse careers about the field when it is without a rider is only too clear, especially in unhappy Italy, which is left without any government charged with its care.]

Now there seemed to Dante to be some possibility of universal imperial rule becoming a reality. He wrote in 1310:

> Behold now is the accepted time, wherein arise the signs of consolation and peace. [...] Rejoice, therefore, O Italy [...], for soon shalt thou be the envy of the whole world [...]; he is at hand who shall bring thee forth from the prison of the ungodly, and shall smite the workers of iniquity with the edge of the sword, and shall destroy them. [...] He will pardon all those who implore his mercy, since he is Caesar, and his sovereignty derives from the fountain of pity. His judgements abhor all severity [...]. Ye that groan under oppression, lift up your hearts, for your salvation is nigh at hand [...]. Awake, therefore, all of you, and rise up to meet your King, ye inhabitants of Italy, as being reserved not only as subjects unto his sovereignty, but also as free peoples unto his guidance.[34]

Henry's expedition was to end in failure and Dante's hopes in bitter disillusion. But was he alone in cherishing such hopes or were they widely shared? Few perhaps shared Dante's particular brand of intellectual imperialism, but some writers, jurists and notaries favoured imperial claims on an ideological level or had *some* hopes of Henry's expedition. Francesco da Garbagnate, an exiled Ghibelline who taught in the university of Padua, is said to have sold his books to purchase arms and horses and join the Emperor at Speier.[35]

When ambassadors were sent to Italy early in 1310 to announce the coming expedition, they seem to have aroused general enthusiasm among the populace of the *comuni* they visited. It is unclear whether this sprang from particular local hopes of a change of ruler or from general traditionalist sentiment in favour of the Emperor and almost superstitious hopes that he might indeed inaugurate a period of peace and prosperity. Traditional feudal loyalty also still counted for something. No doubt this was behind the favourable reception which the envoy Nicholas of Butrinto records the imperial ambassadors as receiving among the nobles of the Florentine *contado*, even those who were traditionally Guelf, and the alacrity with which many local lords, counts and castellans of Lombardy swore allegiance to Henry.[36] Even Filippo da Langusco, of Ghibelline traditions, who was in the delicate position of ruling traditionally Guelf Pavia, promised that his city would serve the Emperor "as its natural lord" and was unwilling to contemplate treachery to the Emperor, from whose predecessors his ancestors had received so many benefits, despite the problems that support for Henry VII might cause him.[37] The prospect of Henry's expedition was greeted with enthusiasm in Pisa; it aroused memories of the city's ancient Ghibellinism, which had coincided with the era of Pisa's greatest prosperity and glory. Monza and Vigevano had difficulty in replying to Henry's embassy, since they were ruled by Milan and its della Torre lords, despite the fact that juridically they were directly dependent on the Empire, but Vigevano did reply that it was willing to do anything for the Emperor, "for the said lord Emperor is its lord in all and for all." Vicenza, under Paduan domination for the previous fifty years, felt genuine enthusiasm for Henry VII, who might restore its ancient freedom. Exiles, too, were eager supporters of Henry VII for obvious reasons: his policy of pacification would be likely to lead to their readmission to their own *comuni*. Two Florentine Ghibelline exiles, Ugolino da Vico and Vermiglio degli Alfani, were among his earliest supporters even before the Italian expedition was seriously mooted, and Giovanni de' Cerchi, a Florentine White exile, was prominent in the pro-imperial movement in Pisa in 1310. Something like a hundred Lucchese Whites in Pisa, who had been in exile since 1301, swore fealty to Henry and offered him their service in person or by proxy in June and October 1310.[38]

Clearly the enthusiasm of subject cities or exiles for Henry's Italian expedition was by no means disinterested, and the element of calculation and self-interest is even clearer in the attitude of those in power in various *comuni*. Few cared to oppose the Emperor openly. Even Florence, the most committed opponent of imperial claims, advocated answering requests with fair words and was willing for her Tuscan allies to supply Henry with money and forces, provided he confirmed them in possession of the territory they actually held and did not insist on the readmission of exiles or interfere in their internal government. Men who were ruling *comuni* as lords were willing to recognize the Emperor, even if they were Guelfs like Ghiberto da Correggio of Parma or Riccardo da Camino of Treviso. A show of loyalty might bring rewards in the form of imperial grants or confirmations; outright opposition was a serious matter and any apparent lukewarmness might play into the hands of rivals and exiles, especially if they were Ghibellines.[39]

It is not certain whether Dante joined Henry VII's entourage in Italy or, if so, at what point he left it. Nor is it known when or in what circumstances he wrote *Monarchia*. Henry VII's expedition ended in failure and disillusion, but Dante remained faithful to imperial ideals and to the memory of Henry himself, reserving a place for him in Paradise (since he was not yet dead at the date the poem is set; *Paradiso*, xxx. 133–38) and castigating other emperors-elect for their neglect of Italy (*Purgatorio*, VI. 97–105). Dante himself resumed his life of exile, partly at the court of Can Grande della Scala, and died near Ravenna in the course of an embassy.

I am unhappily aware that in considering Dante and his experiences in the light of his times I run the risk of diminishing him; that in stating that in membership of a *comune*, in personal military service, in participation in political life and in exile he was sharing common experiences of the period I may have given the impression that he himself was commonplace. Many important aspects of his life were, of course, part of the common experience of men of a certain social level of the period, but this only serves to emphasize how extraordinary Dante himself was, and that a life which included many widely shared experiences resulted in his case in unprecedented and unparalleled literary achievements.

NOTES

1. J. C. Russell, *Medieval Regions and Their Cities* (Newton Abbot, David and Charles, 1972), pp. 42–45.
2. J.White, *Art and Architecture in Italy, 1250–1400* (Harmondsworth, Penguin, 1966), pp. 7–11, 24–25, 33–34, 172; R. A. Goldthwaite, *The Building of Renaissance Florence* (Baltimore–London, Johns Hopkins University Press, 1980), pp. 2–6.
3. J. K. Hyde, *Society and Politics in Medieval Italy* (London, Macmillan, 1973), pp. 154–58; D. Waley, *The Italian City Republics*, third edition (London–New York, Longman, 1988), pp. 101–07.
4. "Nos autem [...] quanquam Sarnum biberimus ante dentes et Florentiam adeo diligamus ut, quia dileximus, exilium patiamur iniuste [...]. Et quamvis ad voluptatem nostram sive nostre sensualitatis quietem in terris amenior locus quam Florentia non existat [...]" (*DVE*, I. 6. 3).
5. D. Waley, *The Italian City Republics*, especially Chapter 6.
6. E. Fiumi, "Fioritura e decadenza dell'economia fiorentina: I, Nobiltà feudale e borghesia mercantile", *Archivio storico italiano*, 115 (1957), 396–405 (pp. 399–401). J.Catto, "Florence, Tuscany and the World of Dante", in *The World of Dante: Essays on Dante and His Times*, edited by C. Grayson (Oxford, Clarendon Press, 1980), pp. 1–17 (pp. 7–9) takes a more favourable view of Dante's claims.
7. C. T. Davis, "Education in Dante's Florence", *Speculum*, 40 (1965), 415–35, also in his *Dante's Italy and Other Essays* (Philadelphia, University of Pennsylvania Press, 1984), pp. 137–65; S. Debenedetti, "Sui piú antichi *doctores puerorum* a Firenze", *Studi medievali*, 2 (1907), 327–51; G. A. Holmes, *Florence, Rome and the Origins of the Renaissance* (Oxford, Clarendon Press, 1986), pp. 74–88.
8. The following paragraphs are based on D.Waley, "The Army of the Florentine Republic from the Twelfth to the Fourteenth Century", in *Florentine Studies: Politics and Society in Renaissance Florence*, edited by N. Rubinstein (London, Faber, 1968), pp. 70–108; D. Waley, "*Condotte e condottieri* in the Thirteenth Century", *Proceedings of the British Academy*, 61 (1976), 337–71.
9. On the campaign and battle see H. L. Oerter, "Campaldino, 1289", *Speculum*, 43 (1968), 429–50.
10. D. Waley, *The Italian City Republics*, Chapter 3, especially pp. 46, 66–68.
11. J. M. Najemy, *Corporatism and Consensus in Florentine Electoral Politics, 1280–1400* (Chapel Hill, North Carolina, University of North Carolina Press, 1982), pp. 17–78. On Florentine political life in the thirteenth century generally, see R. Davidsohn, *Storia di Firenze* [1896–1927], translated by G. B. Klein and R. Palmarocchi, 8 vols (Florence, Sansoni, 1956–65), vols III and IV.
12. G. A. Holmes, *Florence, Rome and the Origins of the Renaissance*, pp. 164–67.
13. E. Peters, "*Pars, Parte*: Dante and an Urban Contribution to Political Thought", in *The Medieval City*, edited by H. A. Miskimin, D. Herlihy and A. L. Udovitch (New Haven–London, Yale University Press, 1977), pp. 113–40; J. Heers, *Parties and Political Life in the Medieval West* (Amsterdam–New York–Oxford, North–Holland, 1977), pp. 13–219; D. Waley, *The Italian City Republics*, Chapter 6.

14 G. A. Holmes, *Florence, Rome and the Origins of the Renaissance*, Chapter 7; R. Davidsohn, *Storia di Firenze*, IV, Chapter 1, "Bonifazio VIII e Firenze".
15 G. A. Holmes, *Florence, Rome and the Origins of the Renaissance*, pp. 174–78.
16 On exile in medieval Italy generally, see the valuable study by R. Starn, *Contrary Commonwealth: The Theme of Exile in Medieval and Renaissance Italy* (Berkeley–Los Angeles–London, University of California Press, 1982); J. Heers, *Parties and Political Life*, pp. 185–96; J. K. Laurent, "The Exiles and the Signory: the Case of Ferrara", *Journal of Medieval and Renaissance Studies*, 11 (1981), 281–97.
17 *Rimatori comico-realistici del Due e Trecento*, edited by M. Vitale (Turin, UTET, reprinted 1968), pp. 672–73.
18 R. Davidsohn, *Storia di Firenze*, II, 697–99.
19 R. Starn, *Contrary Commonwealth*, pp. 43, 55.
20 The proceedings against Dante are usefully described in R. Starn, *Contrary Commonwealth*, pp. 60–85.
21 R. Davidsohn, *Storia di Firenze*, IV, 763–64; J. Heers, *Parties and Political Life*, pp. 189–90.
22 G. Livi, "I mercanti di seta lucchesi a Bologna nei secoli XIII e XIV", *Archivio storico italiano*, fourth series, 7 (1881), 29–55 (pp. 35–37); T. Bini, *I lucchesi a Venezia* (Lucca, n. n., 1843), pp. 178ff; J. Heers, *Parties and Political Life*, pp. 190–92.
23 G. Livi, "I mercanti di seta lucchesi", pp. 38–47; C. E. Meek, *The Commune of Lucca under Pisan Rule, 1342–1369* (Cambridge, Massachusetts, Medieval Academy of America, 1980), pp. 57–58.
24 L. Green, *Castruccio Castracani: A Study of the Origins and Character of a Fourteenth-century Italian Despotism* (Oxford, Clarendon Press, 1986), pp. 39–51; D. Waley, *The Italian City Republics*, pp. 216–18.
25 P. Vigo, *Uguccione della Faggiuola, potestà di Pisa e di Lucca (1313–1316)* (Livorno, Vigo, 1879); C. E. Meek, "Della Faggiuola, Uguccione", in *Dizionario biografico degli italiani* (Rome, Istituto della Enciclopedia Italiana, 1960–), XXXVI, 804–08.
26 D. Waley, *The Italian City Republics*, pp. 214–16.
27 G. A. Holmes, *Florence, Rome and the Origins of the Renaissance*, p. 180; the letters referred to are *Epistole* I and VII.
28 R. Starn, *Contrary Commonwealth*, pp. 40–43, 45.
29 *Rimatori del Trecento*, edited by G. Corsi (Turin, UTET, 1969), p. 272.
30 R. Starn, *Contrary Commonwealth*, p. 46.
31 L. Green, *Castruccio Castracani*, pp. 51–56; R. Starn, *Contrary Commonwealth*, pp. 51–54; G. A. Holmes, *Florence, Rome and the Origins of the Renaissance*, pp. 180–81.
32 *Epistole* XII is Dante's response to this.
33 G. A. Holmes, *Florence, Rome and the Origins of the Renaissance*, pp. 191, 247–48.
34 "'Ecce nunc tempus acceptabile', quo signa surgunt consolationis et pacis. [...] Letare iam nunc miseranda Ytalia [...], que statim invidiosa per orbem videberis, [...] nam prope est qui liberabit te de carcere impiorum; qui percutiens malignantes in ore gladii perdet eos [...]. Ignoscet omnibus misericordiam implorantibus, cum sit Cesar et maiestas eius de Fonte defluat pietatis. Huius iudicium omnem severitatem abhorret [...]. Vos autem qui lugetis oppressi 'animum sublevate, quoniam prope est vestra salus'. [...]

Evigilate igitur omnes et assurgite regi vestro, incole Latiales, non solum sibi ad imperium, sed, ut liberi, ad regimen reservati" (*Epist.*, v. 2–19; *Epist.*, edited by P. Toynbee, pp. 58–61).

35 W. M. Bowsky, *Henry VII in Italy: The Conflict of Empire and City-state, 1310–1313* (Lincoln, Nebraska, University of Nebraska Press, 1960), p. 51, and, for other Italian exiles, pp. 26–27.
36 On Henry's reception generally, see W. M. Bowsky, *Henry VII in Italy*, pp. 28–42.
37 W. M. Bowsky, *Henry VII in Italy*, pp. 29–30; J. K. Hyde, *Society and Politics in Medieval Italy*, pp. 138–39.
38 L. Green, *Castruccio Castracani*, pp. 30, 38–39.
39 R. Starn, *Contrary Commonwealth*, pp. 54–59.

SAINTS AND PILGRIMS IN DANTE'S ITALY

Diana M. Webb

In the year 1300 an anonymous chronicler of Parma described the passage through his city of the crowds attracted to Rome by the Jubilee indulgence proclaimed by Pope Boniface VIII:

> Every day it seemed as if an army was passing along the Strata Claudia, in and out; and there came lords and ladies of France and other far-flung parts, with mounted escorts of forty or fifty or more; and all the houses on the Strata Claudia, both in the city and outside it, were for the most part taken up with guests, and they provided food and drink for money, and every day they were full of people.[1]

Dante may have been a pilgrim to Rome in 1300, and, with a characteristic sense of ironic juxtaposition, he likens the flow of fraudulent sinners under the whips of the demons to their appointed places of punishment in Malebolge to the system of traffic control which was used to regulate the crowds flocking across the Ponte Sant' Angelo to St Peter's (*Inferno*, XVIII. 28–33). The year of the Jubilee was, of course, the supposed date of the vision recorded in the *Commedia*, and Giovanni Villani also claimed to have received the inspiration for his Florentine chronicle from the spectacle of Rome in that year (*Nuova cronica*, IX. 36).

This was a special occasion, and it is not to be supposed that numbers as great were involved in Roman pilgrimage year in, year out. Nonetheless, of course, Rome always was a regular pilgrim goal, especially at Eastertide, and that of itself meant that the roads of Italy were seasonally traversed by sufficient numbers of penitents, or merely tourists, for the pilgrim to be a familiar sight. The Strata Claudia mentioned by the Parma chronicler formed part of one of the great highways of Europe. It had originated, under the name Via Emilia, as a Roman consular road; now the same name or names designated a major route by which the traveller from northwestern Europe, descending from the St Bernard or Mont Cenis pass, progressed through Piacenza, Parma, Modena, Bologna and Faenza, whence the Roman road continued down to the Adriatic coast at Rimini, or branched off along any one of a number of tributary routes across the Apennines to Tuscany, central Italy and Rome.[2] One of the most notable of these routes, which acquired the evocative name Via Francigena, conveyed the pilgrim from the vicinity of Parma across the mountains to Lucca, where he would pay his respects to the miraculous crucifix, the Volto Santo, which was itself very probably a product of the pilgrimage traffic. It was only natural that subsidiary shrines should spring up along the way to tap the passing trade.[3]

The roads helped to shape the cities they passed through. The Via Emilia still pursues a recognizable course through its cities, and bears its ancient name in Piacenza, Reggio Emilia, Modena and Faenza. The safe-keeping of the road was a matter of concern to urban governments. Early fourteenth-century legislation in Modena required the owners of land on the Strata Claudia to build houses along it, for the better security of pilgrims.[4] In Tuscany, the town of San Gimignano grew along the line of the Via Francigena, which visibly forms the roughly north–south axis of the settlement. These roads carried travellers of all sorts, whose business might not necessarily consist primarily of visits to shrines; nor was Rome the only destination of the pilgrim. Not only was the peninsula naturally traversed by pilgrims *en route* to the Holy Land, who might call at such shrines on the eastern seaboard as that of St Nicholas in Bari, but St James in Compostela and the saints of southern France, notably St Gilles and St Antony, had an Italian clientele. André Vauchez has emphasized the enduringly important part played by pilgrimage in the popular conception of sanctity in the Mediterranean region, and the lives of numerous Italian saints bear witness to the merit they were believed to have acquired from frequent pilgrimage. Among saints of this type who died in the thirteenth century we might note Raimondo "the Palmer" of Piacenza, who was unusual in turning his back on pilgrimage, at Christ's express command, in order to do good works in his native city; Bona of Pisa, called "Jacobipeta" by her biographer in token of her journeys to Compostela; Fazio of Cremona; and Antonio, surnamed "the Pilgrim", of Padua.[5]

It need then occasion no surprise that Dante responded to the visible presence of pilgrims in his Italy by scattering images derived from pilgrimage throughout his works. One of the most moving occurs in *Convivio*, IV. 12. 15, where the soul is likened to a pilgrim traversing an unfamiliar road and thinking that every house he sees must be the hostel. Others are still more homely. Beatrice tells Dante to conserve some remembrance of what she has been telling him about divine justice, even if only as a pilgrim returning from the Holy Land binds palm about his staff as a souvenir (*Purgatorio*, XXXIII. 73–78). In *Paradiso*, XXV. 17–18 she hails St James as "il barone/per cui là giú si vicita Galizia" ["the Baron for whose sake, down below, folk visit Galicia"]. In *Convivio*, II. 14. 1 Dante reports how the "Galaxy" (the Milky Way) was popularly known as "la Via di Sa' Iacopo" ["St James's Way"]. Had he himself been to Compostela, like his friend and fellow poet Guido Cavalcanti, whose mortal enemy Corso Donati tried to have him murdered while he was on pilgrimage to St James?[6]

At this point a note of linguistic caution must be sounded. We know that the word *peregrino* does not always signify a pilgrim, as opposed to a foreigner or stranger in general. Its evolution from those original Latin meanings to its more restricted modern connotation was not yet complete. When in *Purgatorio*, II. 63 Virgil courteously informs the souls newly arrived at the foot of the mountain that, far from being able to give them directions, he and Dante are "peregrin come voi siete", he is saying that they are strangers there themselves. In actuality, however, many if not most of those described as *peregrini*, especially when the word was used as a substantive rather than as an adjective, would have been pilgrims in the sense we now attach to the word, rather than merchants, ambassadors or church dignitaries, who were easily identifiable and describable in specific terms.

There is certainly no ambiguity when in the fortieth chapter of the *Vita nuova* Dante gives an explicit account of pilgrim terminology. He recalls seeing a group of pilgrims in the middle of Florence, and says he was struck by their air of preoccupation, which he realized could have nothing to do with the death of Beatrice, which was absorbing *him*, but meant rather that their thoughts were with their friends far away, of whom he and the Florentines knew nothing. This is the cue for the poem, ostensibly inspired by this sight, "Deh peregrini che pensosi andate"; but first Dante analyses the words commonly applied to pilgrims. He states that the term *peregrino* may be used generically to embrace those who go to Rome, Compostela or the Holy Land, though more strictly it signifies a pilgrim to Compostela, the others being respectively *romei* and *palmieri*.

This is neither the first nor the last appearance of the word in the *Vita nuova*. In the ninth chapter Love appears to Dante in the enigmatic guise of a scantily clad pilgrim whose perturbed aspect and downcast gaze will recur in the poet's "pilgrim" images: "Elli mi parea disbigottito, e guardava la terra" ["He seemed dejected and kept his gaze on the ground": *Vita nuova*, IX. 4]. Used as an adjective, the word reappears in the penultimate chapter, in the sonnet "Oltre la spera che piú larga gira", where Dante envisages "lo peregrino spirito" ["the pilgrim spirit"] gazing upon his lady beyond the Primum Mobile, that is, in Heaven itself (*Vita nuova*, XLI. 10–11). It is striking how at the climax of the *Commedia* certain of these "pilgrim" images from the closing chapters of the *Vita nuova* reappear, now reassorted into subtly different yet related contexts.

In between, we may note, the image of the traveller whose thoughts are with all he has left behind reappears (*Purgatorio*, VIII. 1–6), and the pilgrim weighed down by thought who passes along an unknown road is to be found in *Purgatorio*, XXIII. 16–18, thus recombining two of Dante's earlier images into one. At the summit of Paradise, Beatrice vanishes from his side and the old man to whom he finds himself talking directs his eyes upwards to where she sits in her place, gazing upon the face of Christ (*Paradiso*, XXXI. 64–72). Thus simultaneously the fortieth chapter of the *Vita nuova* and "Oltre la spera" are recalled: the pilgrim soul has attained his vision of his lady, but has learned that this is not the supreme vision that he has come for. On being informed that the old man is St Bernard, he feels the same stupefaction as someone "forse di Croazia" ["perchance from Croatia"] might feel when at last beholding the Veronica, the miraculous image of the face of Christ which was exhibited in Rome and is here (*Paradiso*, XXXI. 103–11) given its popular name, as it was not when mentioned in *Vita nuova* XL.

By this stage in his own imagined pilgrimage, Dante has met and conversed with several of the greatest of those who were universally regarded as saints: Peter, James, John the Evangelist, and last of all Bernard. He refers to several others; and to sing the praises of Francis and Dominic he calls upon two canonized saints of the future, Aquinas and Bonaventure. The saints are the exemplars of Christianity in word and in deed, in penitence and in faith, who have on earth shown what Christianity is; now radically detached from human existence, they can be moved by compassion for those still engaged on their earthly pilgrimage, as the Virgin, Lucy and Beatrice in turn have responded to Dante's own predicament; but they can also feel anger at the outrages committed in the world, not infrequently by and in the name of the Church. Themselves focused unwaveringly on Christ, it is their function, in so far as the narrative is concerned, to help the poet towards that same exclusive attachment.

It would be beyond the scope of the present study to attempt to elucidate Dante's attitude to popular religion in Italy in his day. We have seen that he was keenly aware of the phenomenon of pilgrimage, but this in itself does not tell us to what extent he participated in the emotions of the pilgrims he so sensitively observed. Of the swarming popular devotions to new saints which marked the Italian religious scene there is little trace in his writings, though it has been suggested that his presentation of Beatrice may have been influenced by the way in which the devotees of such notable holy women as Angela of Foligno or Clare of Montefalco described their heroines.[7] Of the many popular saints who were newly venerated in his lifetime he mentions only two, Pier Pettinaio of Siena and Zita of Lucca. Zita's name occurs in a context to which we shall return, while in *Purgatorio*, XIII. 124–29 Sapia gratefully acknowledges the efficacy of Pier Pettinaio's "sante orazioni" ["holy prayers"] in helping her towards salvation.

New-fangled saints such as these had made their way into the ranks of those to whom urban governments awarded public honours, a phenomenon to which Dante makes a few oblique and somewhat sardonic references. As an adult Florentine male, Dante must have shared in the compulsory rituals of homage to the patron saint of the *comune*, who in Florence was of course John the Baptist. He must have known that the *carroccio*, the ceremonial war-chariot of the city, was kept in his "bel san Giovanni", and that the Florentines sometimes marked the Saint's day by making raids on their enemies. Villani tells us that in 1290 and 1292 the *palio* for St John's Day was run to the walls of, respectively, Arezzo and Pisa (*Nuova cronica*, VIII. 140, 154). Dante may have witnessed the release of prisoners at the Baptist's altar, performed as a pious act at Easter, or the offering to the Saint of prisoners of war. These were commonplace manifestations of the civic cult, paralleled almost everywhere.[8] In 1315 Dante himself was offered the opportunity to return from exile on condition, *inter alia*, that he processed through the streets, robed as a penitent, to offer himself to Saint John. We know what his reaction to the terms of this offer was (*Epistole* XII).

In *Inferno*, XIII. 143–50 an unnamed Florentine suicide defines his city as the one which changed its first patron for the Baptist. As a result, he says, the disgruntled first patron, the god Mars, continued to vex the city with his art, and only the survival of a statue of him on the Ponte Vecchio protected Florence from outright ruin. Seen from the standpoint of Hell, the Florentines were still subjects of the destructive god of war. It is hardly to be thought that Dante intended any disrespect to St John by implying that he had no effective power over the city or that he chose not to exercise it. The issue, implicitly, was rather whether or not the Florentines had any right to invoke the Baptist's protection. Dante's veneration for the Saint seen in a true perspective is abundantly demonstrated in the *Commedia*.

When the poets leave the circle of Purgatory where avarice is purged and enter the circle of gluttony, they hear a voice praising the Baptist's abstemious diet of honey and locusts (*Purgatorio*, XXII. 151–54). In Heaven the Saint is pointed out to Dante sitting opposite Mary in the highest place, and described as one who "'l diserto e 'l martiro/sofferse, e poi l'inferno da due anni" ["endured the desert and martyrdom, and then Hell for two years": *Paradiso*, XXXII. 31–33]. This image of the Baptist as the type of the ascetic and martyr has also appeared earlier but with a bitterly ironic twist, which, although overtly at the expense of the Curia and the clergy, is indirectly at the expense of Florence. It was common, though by no means invariable, for the patron's image to appear on a city's coinage. The Baptist was depicted on the florin, and in *Paradiso*, XVIII. 133–36 the Eagle of Justice imagines the pastors of the modern church as excusing their neglect of Peter and Paul on the grounds of their ceaseless devotion to him who lived alone and was dragged to martyrdom as a result of Salome's dance. The jibe at Florence depends on its authorship of the coin that has corrupted the world. It is made more explicit in *Paradiso*, IX. 127–32, where, however, it is the fleur-de-lis, which appeared on the other side of the florin, which "ha disvïate le pecore e li agni,/però che fatto ha lupo del pastore" ["has caused the sheep and the lambs to stray, because it has made a wolf of the shepherd"]. It cannot have been pleasing to Dante to see the Baptist thus coupled with the hated Guelf emblem. One suspects that when he describes Florence to Cacciaguida as "l'ovil di San Giovanni" ["the sheepfold of St John": *Paradiso*, XVI. 25] it is more the expression of an ideal, or of a dream, than a description to which he felt its present inhabitants were entitled.

Paradise however has its own politics. If Florence has no right to boast of the patronage of the Baptist it is not merely, or even primarily, because of the debauching effects of the florin upon the world, but because of the city's leading role in opposition to the political purposes of God on earth. There are few places left unfilled in Paradise, but one of them is reserved for "l'alto Arrigo" ["lofty Henry": *Paradiso*, XXX. 137], who by the time Dante wrote the final *cantica* was dead, with his professed aim of pacifying Italy in ruins. Many of the Italian states, Florence foremost among them, had opposed him, invoking the Virgin and all the saints of Heaven, which to Dante can only have seemed a blasphemous absurdity.[9] The Italians, we might say, fought Henry in order to retain the right freely to go to war with one another in future, and to lead into their internecine battles their *carrocci*, adorned with the emblems of their particular saints. In theory at least, the code enjoined respectful treatment of a captured enemy *carroccio*, but that scarcely affected the fundamental illogic of this use of the members of the court of Heaven.

A Sienese account of the Battle of Montaperti, which took place on 4 September 1260, and in which Florence and the Guelfs of Tuscany met disastrous defeat at the hands of Siena and her Ghibelline allies, alleges that the Sienese made mock of Florence's local saints, Zenobius and Reparata. Zenobius was an ancient bishop of Florence and Reparata a third-century Syrian martyr who was popular in the early medieval Mediterranean world. The Sienese pointed out that they had not done the Florentines much good.[10] Now this account was written long after the event, in the fifteenth century, and is full of colourful elaborations, but such a detail might be thought to have the ring of truth about it. Clearly some saints were greater than others, and the greatest would command a universal respect that the lesser and the merely local could not match. No one would have claimed that the Sienese sneered at John the Baptist. Not merely might it have been both impolite and unwise to do so: their own cathedral baptistery was dedicated to him.

Whatever violence the use of the saints as political symbols in the conflict-ridden world of the city-states did to theological plausibility or coherence, it was a fact. The term "patron saint" can be misleading if we take it to mean that each city looked only to one saint. We have already seen the Baptist, Zenobius and Reparata mentioned as patrons (however unequal in prestige or presumed effectiveness) in Florence. Many cities had what André Vauchez has usefully termed a "pantheon".[11] It was not uncommon for the chief patron of the *comune*, who received the compulsory annual offerings from citizens and subject communities, to be a saint other than the dedicatee of the cathedral. This arrangement too is illustrated in Florence, where first Reparata and later the Virgin were patrons of the cathedral, the Baptist of the *comune*. The civic cult proves often to have been built up in layers, each city exhibiting its own stratigraphy. The earliest levels were commonly composed of early bishops and local martyrs, the latest, of members of the mendicant orders and their devotees. Strata were still being laid down in Dante's lifetime. The period of the extinction of Hohenstaufen rule in Italy and the establishment of the Angevin ascendancy was fruitful in producing new cults, some of which, however, owed less to political events than to the ongoing process by which the mendicant orders consolidated their place in urban life.

It was also possible for old cults to take on new or renewed meanings. The Sienese "pantheon" provides some examples. Its official version is illustrated in two masterpieces of civic art, the *Maestà* of Duccio, completed in 1311 and borne in triumph through the streets to its place in the cathedral,[12] and that of Simone Martini, painted in about 1315 on the end wall of the principal council chamber in the public palace of the *comune*.[13] The two Virgins differ in their appearance, the one being a Byzantine madonna, the other a French Gothic queen, but both are enthroned centrally amid a court of saints and angels. Foremost among the saints, kneeling on either side of the throne as suppliants for the well-being of Siena, are four ancient martyrs whose relics were claimed by the cathedral: Ansanus, Savinus, Victor and Crescentius. These were the bishop's saints. If we look at the Sienese statute of 1262 or at the vernacular statute that was compiled in 1309–10, we will find no mention of public honours for any of them, whereas we *will* find regulations for the honours that were to be paid to the Virgin as patron of the *comune*.[14]

The Virgin's patronage of the Sienese church was centuries old, and there could be no doubt that the Queen of Heaven would also be adopted by the political community. Her patronage acquired a more specifically political character, however, in the traditions which grew up around the Battle of Montaperti. Faced with the threat of Florence and the other Tuscan Guelfs, the Sienese, so it was said, had mounted a great penitential procession which had ended at the Virgin's altar in the cathedral, where she was offered the keys of the city and a notary solemnly recorded the transaction.[15] This chronicle account, as we have already had occasion to note, is late and has the ring of fictional elaboration about it. There can, however, be no dispute about the fact that a few days after the battle, on 8 September 1260, the Virgin was designated "defensatrix et gubernatrix" ["protector and ruler"] of Siena in the official record of the submission to the Sienese of the little town of Montalcino. This was the title which (in the masculine gender) was borne by the Nine who ruled Siena from 1287 to 1355.[16] The *Maestà* of Duccio, and perhaps even more that of Simone, must be seen in this context. The Virgin was ruler of Siena, and, as a fifteenth-century chancellor of the city put it, she had never been absent from the counsels of the republic.[17] The inscription on her throne in Simone's fresco expresses her concern for good and just government, while the Child, standing on her knee, holds a scroll with the words "Diligite iustitiam qui iudicatis terram" ["Love righteousness, ye that be judges of the earth"]—the opening words of the Book of Wisdom, which, we may recall, are spelled out by the souls of the just rulers in the Heaven of Mars (*Paradiso*, xviii. 91–93).

Dante is our witness, in his words to Farinata (*Inferno*, x. 85–87), to how bitterly Montaperti was remembered in Florence a generation and more later. If, as it seems, the battle may have done something to shape the cult of the Virgin in Siena, it had another, more transient, consequence there which is of some interest. The chronicler tells us that the German cavalry whom Manfred of Sicily had sent to Siena's aid called on the name of St George as they rode into battle.[18] This helps to account for what might otherwise seem the surprising fact that George appears in the text of the submission of Montalcino, and that in the 1262 statute he receives the most fulsome praises and the promise of concrete favours, such as official contributions to the rebuilding of the Sienese church of San Giorgio.[19] The chronicler further tells us that the Sienese used to hold a *festa* on St George's Day, re-enacting the story of the princess and the dragon. This was done for "a long time", but when the Sienese came to be on good terms with the Florentines again, the *festa* was removed from St George's Day and held instead at the Dominican church in memory of the Blessed Ambrogio Sansedoni.[20] Among the vernacular statutes of 1309–10 there is a rubric, dated 1306, concerning the celebration of Ambrogio's day and the provision of a *palio* for which a race was to be run according to Sienese custom.[21] By this time all references to George have vanished.

With the mention of Ambrogio Sansedoni, a notable preacher and founder of confraternities, we come to the new saints who in Dante's lifetime were pressing forward to share civic honours with those longer established. If the Dominicans of Siena succeeded in obtaining official recognition for Ambrogio, the Franciscans promoted Sapia's Pier Pettinaio to good effect. In 1289, the year of his death, the *comune* gave the Friars Minor 200 pounds towards the cost of a tomb with altar and ciborium to be built in his honour, and it is known from other documents that in 1296 the *comune* was participating in the celebration of his feast-day by the provision of a large quantity of wax candles.[22] This is a reminder that regulations formally enshrined in statute tell us only a part of what was done, or was supposed to be done, by the civic authorities in honour of saints. Records of conciliar deliberations may reveal what honours were annually or occasionally petitioned for, and granted or not, while account books record what expenditures were actually laid out on such objects.

For our present purpose, however, the real point of interest is the appearance of these new saints in the urban pantheon, which suggests the influence that the orders promoting them had in the ruling circles of the *comune*. Vauchez has described how the Servites, Augustinian Hermits and Carmelites also obtained recognition for their saints, and how in 1328–29 all the orders mobilized themselves to avert the threatened loss of these honours. In order to save money, the authorities had sought to ban official participation in a *festa* unless it was required "per formam statutorum".[23] This would of course have left the rituals of homage to the Virgin at the Feast of the Assumption (and also, presumably, Ambrogio Sansedoni's *palio*) intact; but clearly a great deal more had recently been done and was by now demanded.

A few years earlier another episode had occurred which implies the existence of other interests and even some faint hostility to these new cults. On 24 October 1326 the Consiglio Generale of Siena heard a petition which asked the Nine to be mindful of the fact that "our Lord, by the prayers and merits of the blessed Ansanus, the patron of this city, miraculously converted our ancestors, who at that time followed the perfidy of the devil, to the faith, after which he liberated us from divers perils." The Nine were asked, "on account of reverence for so great a saint", to decree, "as your predecessors have ordered for several other saints", that "his holy feast be devoutly celebrated in your city of Siena, all citizens ceasing from all servile work". The *podestà* or the vicar (Charles of Calabria's vicar was in the city at the time) and the other officials of the *comune* were to be bound to attend "cum luminariis decentibus" ["with befitting torches"]. Their offerings were to be converted by the clerk of works of the cathedral into ornaments for the Saint's most glorious body.[24]

Whatever the specific social, political or personal interests which may have motivated this petition, the rise of Ansanus to unambiguous recognition as a civic patron may be seen as a symptom of a pious antiquarianism which sought to emphasize the old saints who could be seen as emblems of the city's, and the locality's, historic identity. We may note in this context Villani's description of the solemn exposition (*inventio*) of Zenobius's relics that was performed in Florence in 1331 (*Nuova cronica*, XI. 169) and the decision of the rulers of Pistoia in 1337 that henceforth a procession was to be held on the eve of the feast of San Zeno, the patron of the cathedral, as was customarily done for San Jacopo, the patron of the *comune*.[25] San Jacopo's chapel and office of works were housed within the cathedral and dated back to the mid-twelfth century, as did his *opera*, clearly a lay institution, as its early fourteenth-century vernacular statutes indicate. As I have argued elsewhere, the springs of devotion to James at Pistoia, and to the Volto Santo at Lucca, were probably "popular" rather than clerical or rooted within the local ecclesiastical establishment.[26] It is tempting to regard both cults as offshoots of the pilgrimage traffic which crossed northern Tuscany on its way to and from Rome and to and from Compostela. However this may be, it was the duty of the bishop and his clergy to keep *their* saints—Zeno in Pistoia, Martin of Tours in Lucca—before the public eye and to obtain the cooperation of the rulers of the *comune* in ensuring that due reverence was observed towards them.

When Dante and Virgil in Hell observe the punishment inflicted on those who have trafficked in public office, they see a fearful demon ducking a sinner and informing his colleagues, "Ecco un de li anzïan di Santa Zita!" ["Here's one of St Zita's Elders!"], remarking further that he is going back to the same source of supply for more. The sinner, on trying to surface, is told gleefully that there is no room here for the Volto Santo, and that swimming here is not like it is in the Serchio (*Inferno*, XXI. 37–49). Dante had first-hand knowledge of Lucca. Is this unseemly treatment of the city and its cults a reaction simply to the notorious corruption of its public men—which Dante felt keenly because he himself had been accused of this offence—or also to Lucca's stance for much of his lifetime as one of the pillars, with Florence, of Tuscan Guelfism? For whatever reason, he was to come to think better of Lucca, as the poet Bonagiunta prophesies in *Purgatorio*, XXIV. 34–39. The mockery of his demons does, however, have the merit of alerting us to the fact that in Lucca we have another "pantheon", another many-layered structure.

The Volto Santo in Lucca received the compulsory offerings that in Florence were made to the Baptist or in Siena to the Virgin. The offerings due from Lucca's subject communities are minutely particularized in the *comune*'s statute of 1308.[27] Dante's demons, however, know that they can also identify the city by reference to a new saint, the serving-woman Zita, who died in 1272. She is mentioned only once in the 1308 statute, in a clause which provides for the safe-keeping of the city's two major churches on the vigils of their principal feast-days. This was done in order to prevent "maleficia et turpitudines" ["crimes and infamies"], including the rape or other molestation of women who were keeping vigil. The cathedral was to be so guarded on the eve of the feasts of St Martin and St Regulus, and also of the Exaltation of the Cross. The guard was to be provided by the consuls of the *contrada* of San Martino, but, significantly, was to be reinforced by officers of the *comune* on the eve of the feast of the Cross. The consuls of the *contrada* of San Frediano were to see to the safe-keeping of the church of that name on the eve of St Zita's Day.[28]

Who were these saints, who, to judge from this one clause, received special consideration from the city's rulers, or whose feasts, simply as a matter of fact, attracted larger crowds of the faithful? St Martin of Tours, we have noted, was the titular saint of the cathedral. St Regulus was a martyr whose relics had been brought to Lucca in the late eighth century by an extremely active bishop, to whom, in fact, legend attributed the acquisition of the Volto Santo. His feast-day (1 September) provided the occasion for an annual fair, at which races were run and gambling legally permitted. By the mid-twelfth century the Volto Santo had risen to a position alongside these old episcopal saints which made it necessary to divide the offerings made at the cathedral on certain days between the officers of the old *opera* of San Martino and the officers of the Opera Sanctae Crucis (the office of works of the Volto Santo).[29] The situation was very similar to that which obtained in nearby Pistoia.

The newcomer Zita lay in another church, San Frediano. Frediano had been a sixth-century bishop of Lucca. The church that bore his name lay to the north of the city, outside the Roman wall, and would have been passed by pilgrims approaching Lucca from that direction; it had a hospice in the late eleventh century. It had become Lucca's second baptismal church in about the year 1000, and later was a centre of the reformed canonical life, attracting papal patronage and (partly for that reason) the jealousy of the cathedral clergy. Much of the twelfth century was taken up in undignified wrangles between the two communities about the right to celebrate, and to enjoy the offerings, on the feasts of Martin, Regulus and Frediano—the saints, that is, of the bishopric.[30] In the mid-twelfth century San Frediano made a bid for a larger share in the pool of available offerings by promoting the cult of an improbable Anglo-Saxon royal saint, improbably called Richard, a choice which further highlights the long historic connection between Lucca and the pilgrimage routes from the north.[31] When in 1272 a devoted female parishioner of San Frediano died after a lifetime spent working in the household of the Faitinelli family, and performed a string of miracles which were duly notarized by a member of that family, it must have been welcome news to the canons.[32]

The 1308 statute says nothing about official offerings to Zita, or, for that matter, to Martin, Regulus or Frediano. Acts and offerings that were in fact regular and customary but did not have to do with the unique patron of the *comune* may often have been enshrined in statute, if at all, only as an afterthought. In the new edition of the Lucchese statutes that was prepared in 1331 reference is made to the custom of robing the image of St Martin and the Beggar at the cathedral at the *comune*'s expense. The garments were to be removed and given to the messenger of the *anziani*, who would in return offer a candle of one pound weight to the *operarius* of the Holy Cross, and would bear the garments around the streets on horseback for all to see.[33] This custom is said to have "obtained hitherto", but there is no mention of it in 1308, and no indication of how old it was. Obviously there were festivities on St Martin's Day. We know that Castruccio Castracani kept the feast in great state in 1325 after the Battle of Altopascio, parading his Florentine prisoners of war and the captured *carroccio* through the streets, and that in 1327 he played host to Lewis of Bavaria for the *festa* (Villani, *Nuova cronica*, x. 323; xi. 38).

The pantheon of Lucca seems to differ from that of Siena in several respects, thus reminding us that here as in other areas of Italian life and history every city exhibits its own profile. The Virgin plays no especially prominent part in the Lucchese pantheon, and the lack of a strong mendicant presence is noteworthy. Zita, associated with a collegiate church, is the only new saint to figure.

In the course of Dante's lifetime, however, another new cult was coming into being in Lucca, but it was of an ancient saint, albeit one who may never have existed. In July 1261 there were discovered in the church of Sant' Antonio in Lucca the relics of several alleged martyrs, foremost among them Paulinus, who was described in an accompanying inscription as "the first bishop of Lucca, and disciple of the apostle Peter". The discovery was welcomed with joy and celebrations which were, as it happened, graced by the presence in the city of the cardinal-legate Guala. In the narrative of the *inventio* we are told that the Lucchese had learned from the legend of the saint how the apostle Peter sent Paulinus to Lucca, "and how he preached and planted the faith, and faithfully baptized the Lucchese people; and how fondly he loved the city, and fervently prayed for it that God would augment the Lucchese people and preserve them in unity without division and deliver them from heretical pravity and defend the city from the hands of its enemies in perpetuity". The bishop ordered that the church where the relics had been found should henceforth be named San Paolino and that the Saint's day should be observed for ever.[34] The well-informed annalist Tolomeo of Lucca knew that St Peter had sent Paulinus to Lucca at the same time as he had sent Apollinaris to Ravenna and Syrus to Pavia.[35] Villani, however, who traces the name Lucca to the fact that it was the first city in Tuscany to receive the *lux* ["light"] of the faith, knows nothing about Paulinus, and (wrongly) describes San Frediano as the first bishop of the city (*Nuova cronica*, II. 12).

If Paulinus was a fabrication, he was one with a great deal of point. Clearly what I have termed "pious antiquarianism"—the desire, in this instance, to give Lucca a founding bishop with apostolic credentials on the model of Syrus and Apollinaris—might be seen as the decisive motive; but it is possible to suspect the strong influence of political circumstances. Ten months before the *inventio*, Lucca had suffered temporary shipwreck, along with Florence, at the Battle of Montaperti. "The state of Tuscany was totally transformed," wrote Tolomeo of Lucca, "because all of imperial Tuscany except Lucca and the Guelf exiles from Florence was converted to the Ghibelline party."[36] Lucca was now a refugee camp for Tuscan Guelfs, and there were numerous Lucchese prisoners in Siena,[37] one of whom, significantly, was among the first beneficiaries of the rediscovered Paulinus's miracles. Moreover, the Saint's prayers for his city were extremely pointed in the situation of the 1260s. Could it be that the bishop and the other sponsors of the *inventio* hoped to bolster the confidence of the populace in Lucca's Guelf stance by conjuring up a saint who emphasized linkage with St Peter and joined hands, so to speak, with Guala, Rome's current representative? Certainly it is hard to believe that the appearance of a saint with Paulinus's features had nothing to do with a situation in which Guelf Lucca momentarily stood alone.

This must in large part remain speculation; but there cannot be much doubt that there was an element of deliberation in the discovery of Paulinus which had to do precisely with his alleged apostolic connections. In the year 1900 a fire necessitated the restoration of the high altar of San Paolino. The work uncovered a sarcophagus with an inscription, seemingly authentic, which recorded an *inventio* of Paulinus and his companions in 1197, "in the time of Emperor Henry and of Cardinal Lord Pandulf and Bishop Guido". Paulinus is described as "bishop and martyr", but it is not specified that he was Bishop of Lucca, and, rather more importantly, no mention is made of St Peter. These, or so at least it seems, were additions to Paulinus's pedigree made in 1261.[38]

Was Paulinus, then, intended by his rediscoverers to be not merely Roman but Guelf? Certainly elsewhere in Italy the crisis of the 1260s helped to produce new or enhanced devotions with political point. In Parma, as in Siena, it was on the eve of the Feast of the Assumption that citizens and subject communities made their obligatory offerings. When Innocent IV wrote to the citizens in March 1250 to congratulate them on their recent victory over Emperor Frederick II, he was in no doubt that the credit should go to the Virgin, "your patron".[39] In 1264 the rise of a new associate patron for Parma was signalled when Urban IV solicited support for the Society of St Hilary. This was one of the Guelf vigilante organizations which sprang up in Italian cities during these years to spearhead the offensives against heresy and Ghibellinism. The saint of Poitiers, with his reputation as a hammer of heretics and his regional associations, was a very suitable candidate for preferment in the Italy of Charles of Anjou, who in fact extended his favour to the Society.[40] The Parma statute of 1266 refers to the suburb (*burgus*) of St Hilary, which was to be fortified in the Saint's honour.[41] In 1287 peace was made between Parma and Modena in the names of God, the Virgin, the Baptist and Saints Hilary and Geminianus, who stood as the particular patrons of the two cities.[42]

Hilary did not, of course, supplant the Virgin in Parma, but he survived the passing of the political situation which had brought him to prominence. In 1417 the revised *ordinarium* of the cathedral said of him that he "has been and is advocate of the city and people of Parma".[43] When in 1447 on the death of the Duke of Milan the revived republics of Parma and Milan entered into an alliance, Hilary and St Ambrose were depicted at the head of the text of the treaty.[44] Unlike Hilary, and like Ambrose, Geminianus of Modena was the ancient bishop-patron of his city; but all showed the usefulness of saints who could without too much impropriety be invoked in strictly political contexts as standing for one particular city. Geminianus's bodily presence in Modena had its own value, as was demonstrated when in 1287 his relics were brought out in an effort to get the city's factions to accept a peace initiative.[45] In the legislation enacted in 1306, when Modena briefly threw off the rule of the Marquis of Este, the Virgin received many compliments, but Geminianus was repeatedly invoked and honoured as the active defender of the city's liberty. Special celebrations were to be held on 26 January each year in commemoration of the *comune*'s liberation from the yoke of Pharoah (that is, the Este).[46] Alas for the vanity of human wishes, the Este were not gone for long, but when they returned they did not attempt to suppress the festivities of 26

January; rather they put it about that in fact they commemorated the Saint's triumph over Attila the Hun.[47]

It was common form to decree the annual celebration of a notable victory and the honouring of saints on whose feast-days such victories occurred. It was a curious chance that two battles which marked crucial stages in the establishment of Guelf and Florentine pre-eminence in Tuscany both took place on 11 June, St Barnabas's Day: first, the victory over the Sienese at Colle di Val d'Elsa in 1269, which was revenge for Montaperti, and then the defeat of the Aretines at Campaldino exactly twenty years later (Villani, *Nuova cronica*, VIII. 31, 131). In 1311 the Florentines received relics of Barnabas from no less a source than the papal court. They were sent by Clement V's nephew, Cardinal Arnaut de Pellegrue, who knew of Florence's devotion to the apostle, and they were installed in the altar of San Giovanni (*Nuova cronica*, x. 13). The political context may be readily established. Cardinal Pellegrue was his uncle's legate in Italy from early 1309 to late 1310. In the summer of 1309 the Florentines sent forces to aid Pellegrue in the defence of Ferrara against the Venetians, and Villani says that they were eagerly soliciting his favour. In August 1310 he came to Florence and was met by a grand procession headed by the *carroccio*. He was presented with the sum of 2,000 florins and obligingly absolved his hosts from the sentences of interdict and excommunication previously laid upon them by Cardinal Napoleone Orsini (*Nuova cronica*, IX. 115). The new Emperor entered Italy a month after Pellegrue visited Florence. If Dante in exile learned of these friendly contacts between his native city and the court of Avignon, he is unlikely to have thought that they boded well for the Pope's continued support of Henry VII.

So it was that Barnabas entered the Florentine pantheon. One idea of what this consisted of around the time of Dante's death is given in the preamble to the statute of the *podestà*, promulgated in 1325. The Baptist stands after Christ and the Virgin, and is the "precipuus patronus et defensor communis Florentie" ["principal patron and defender of the *comune* of Florence"]. There follow Peter and Paul, Philip and James, then Barnabas, Reparata, Zenobius and Miniato, the legendary martyr whose church stands on the hilltop overlooking the city.[48] The Baptistery possessed the arm of St Philip, brought there from Jerusalem in 1205, and the 1325 statute laid down regulations, in the first chapter of its fourth book, for the offering of candles both to the Baptist and to Philip, the value of which was to be converted into funds for the painting of *picturae* in the Baptistery. The old patron of the cathedral (Reparata) and the new patron of the Guelfs (Barnabas) both received the compliment on their feast-day of having foot-races run for a prize provided at the expense of the *comune*. Barnabas is described as "the protector and especial defender of the people and *comune* of Florence, and also of the Parte Guelfa". As there was no church of St Barnabas already in Florence, one was to be built, as "it is appropriate that the *comune* and people of Florence and the Parte Guelfa" should especially honour him. The building of such a church had several times been considered, in view of "the victories that the people and *comune* of Florence have had and hope to have"; now it was to be done (and was done), "in reverence to that same most holy Barnabas, and so that the Parte Guelfa may be exalted and receive no hurt, through the merits and prayers of the most holy apostle".[49]

If then Barnabas may be regarded, like Hilary in Parma and (perhaps) Paulinus in Lucca, as a Guelf saint, he is not the only Guelf saint to be mentioned in the 1325 statute. Florence's intimate relationship with the Angevin monarchy of Naples is expressed in the appearance of both Louis of Toulouse and Thomas Aquinas (canonized in 1317 and 1323 respectively) among the saints whose days were to be kept as public holidays, with shops and workshops closed.[50] Villani devotes a chapter to the canonization of Aquinas (*Nuova cronica*, x. 218), and the political context of both canonizations is well attested.[51]

If Dante venerated Thomas, however, it was not because he had the backing of Robert of Naples. For Dante, the saints are in Heaven; they have fought the good fight, but now they are detached from earthly concerns and totally absorbed in the contemplation of God. Their meaning for earth-dwellers is an exemplary and admonitory one. The living may learn from their lives and works what it is to be Christian, but they need not expect to enlist their support in their mundane quarrels. At the very highest level, St Peter condemns the use of the emblem of the keys on banners carried into battle against Christians (*Paradiso*, XXVII. 49–51). Justinian has earlier condemned the abuse by Ghibellines of another emblem which Dante held sacred, the imperial eagle (*Paradiso*, VI. 31–33). Henry VII, though assured of his place in Heaven, had, here and now, the task of establishing on earth the optimal conditions for the realization of human potentialities and the creation of human happiness, as Dante argued at length in *Monarchia*. (This of course Henry was not permitted to do.) To invoke the saints against him was, on the one hand, a sacrilegious absurdity, and, on the other, a confusion of two spheres which—as Dante had a persistent tendency to think and feel—were by God's own decree distinct.[52] This confusion his contemporaries were very understandably perpetrating all the time.

Only saints who could be imagined as actively concerning themselves with the ordinary accidents of human life were intelligible or congenial to the generality of the devout; and only saints thus conceived could serve the purposes of governments and rulers, though it was not necessarily saints exciting genuine popular devotion who were used as political symbols by urban regimes: the Virgin was the outstanding exception. Saints could be so used because they were always much more than saints. Their festivals punctuated the year, bringing with them holidays, fairs and markets, races and processions; and in a manner which must have been very widely—even if not very consciously—apprehended, they linked the present to the past. They helped to give city-state governments an aura of the legitimacy and continuity that they might well feel they lacked. In republics they could be put to work as surrogate monarchs, before whom the subjects of a still imperfectly conceived state could be required to bow the knee without expressing subjugation to a mere mortal. Thus our chancellor of mid-fifteenth-century Siena could claim that although over many centuries Siena had never known a lord, it had never lacked a prince, to wit, the Virgin.[53] The so-called despots in fact had not dissimilar reasons for upholding the civic cult when they took power. Blasphemy was commonly an offence punishable by the civic authorities. According to the rules laid down for Modena in the statutes published by the Este in 1420, not all blasphemy was equally expensive. It cost ten pounds to insult God or the Virgin, five pounds to blaspheme Geminianus, "almificum patronum nostrum antistitem" ["our protecting patron and bishop"], and three pounds for the rest.[54] The deity and the Virgin stood universally, Geminianus in a particularist sense in this city, for the authority of the lawgiver, and to show disrespect to them was to impugn that authority.

An imaginative aerial view of Dante's Italy, as indeed of his Europe, might show a network of shrines, between which men and women were constantly on the move, over distances both great and small. An ancient conception of pilgrimage saw the journey itself, the pilgrim's total renunciation of all his familiar ties, as the essential feature of his penance. As we have seen, Dante was poetically sensitive to the pilgrim's foreignness, his nostalgia and his insecurity. Not all visitors to shrines, however, came from faraway places. On the eve of the Feast of the Holy Cross in Lucca, the procession of citizens and representatives of subject communities who were required to do homage to the Volto Santo assembled before the church of San Frediano and made its way to the cathedral along a route which, it was believed, the holy image itself had followed when it first entered Lucca. To follow this path was also to affirm the relationship between the two churches and the spiritual unity of the city. The journey thus undertaken was neither individual nor voluntary, and in this it differed from much pilgrimage. To a greater extent than in most other parts of Europe, the constituent pieces in the mosaic of Italian shrines were autonomous political units, and this had the consequence that much ritual movement to these shrines expressed not so much penitence as obedience, although there were situations in which the line between the two was indistinct. If on the eve of the Battle of Montaperti the Sienese processed solemnly to the Virgin's altar and begged her to take on the governance of the city in their hour of need, they were expressing both.

Dante would doubtless have rendered willing homage to the Baptist when he beheld him in Paradise; but he would not do so at the behest of a Florentine government which clearly equated the demonstration of penitence before the altar of St John with acceptance of its own exercise of authority, on its own terms. Whatever outrages the Florentines committed in the name of their saint, the poet continued to see himself as a true lamb of the true sheepfold of St John, and to dream, even as he approached the climax of the *Commedia*, of returning to the font where he had received baptism. There he would take part in a ritual which would vindicate both his life and his work in the eyes of Florence and of the world, and reaffirm the centrality of that church in his life as in the lives of all Florentines. There he would receive the poet's crown, the ceremony in this setting giving recognition to the holiness of the poetic enterprise which had so consumed him over so many years (*Paradiso*, xxv. 1–9). And this (which was never to happen) would happen only when the Florentines had come to a proper understanding of the purposes, in Heaven and on earth, to which their saint and all the other saints were dedicated.

NOTES

1 *Chronicon Parmense*, edited by G. Bonazzi (*RIS2*, IX, ix), p. 81.
2 A. C. Quintavalle, *La Strada romea* (Milan, Silvana, 1976); A. C. Quintavalle, *Vie dei pellegrini nell'Emilia medievale* (Milan, Electa, 1977); R. Stopani, *La Via francigena in Toscana* (Florence, Salimbeni, 1984).
3 D. M. Webb, "The Holy Face of Lucca", *Anglo-Norman Studies*, 9 (= *Proceedings of the Battle Conference 1986*, edited by R. A. Brown [1987]), pp. 227–37. The Volto Santo was a Romanesque wooden crucifix, supposedly sculpted by Nicodemus to preserve his memories of the Saviour and brought miraculously by sea to Lucca in the eighth century.
4 *Statuta Civitatis Mutine* (*Monumenti di storia patria delle province modenesi: serie degli statuti*, I, 2 vols [1864]), II, 268: "Ad hoc ut peregrini transeuntes per stratam Claudiam securius ire possent ne valeant ab aliquo impedire [...] ibi debeant facere unam domum [...] et eam habitare vel habitari facere."
5 A. Vauchez, *La Sainteté en occident aux derniers siècles du Moyen Age* [1981], second edition (Rome, Ecole française de Rome, 1988), pp. 232–34, with references.
6 D. Compagni, *Cronica delle cose occorrenti ne' tempi suoi*, edited by G. Bezzola (Milan, Rizzoli, 1982), p. 92. On Dante's references to pilgrimage and the Jubilee, see P. Armour, *The Door of Purgatory: A Study of Multiple Symbolism in Dante's "Purgatorio"* (Oxford, Clarendon Press, 1983), especially pp. 144–85.
7 G. Holmes, *Florence, Rome and the Origins of the Renaissance* (Oxford, Clarendon Press, 1986), pp. 62–67, 119. For the belief that Dante himself visited Margaret of Cortona in 1289 and later represented her as Lucy, see R. Bell, *Holy Anorexia* (Chicago, University of Chicago Press, 1985), pp. 96, 204.
8 D. M. Webb, "Cities of God: The Italian City States at War", *Studies in Church History*, 20 (1983), 111–27. On civic cults in general, see H. Peyer, *Stadt und Stadt-Patron in mittelalterlichen Italien* (Zurich, Europa, 1955); A. Vauchez, "Patronage des saints et religion civique dans l'Italie communale à la fin du Moyen Age", in *Patronage and Public in the Trecento*, edited by V. Moleta (Florence, Olschki, 1986), pp. 59–80; D. M. Webb, "Saints and Cities in Medieval Italy", *History Today*, 43 (July 1993), 15–21.
9 W. Bowsky, "Florence, Henry of Luxemburg, King of the Romans, and the Rebirth of Guelfism", *Speculum*, 33 (1958), 177–203 (p. 201). See also *Epistole* VI, for Dante's belief in the divinity of Henry's mission.
10 *Cronaca senese conosciuta sotto il nome di Paolo di Tommaso Montauri*, edited by A. Lisini and F. Iacometti (*RIS2*, XV, vi), p. 212.
11 A. Vauchez, "La Commune de Sienne, les ordres mendiants et le culte des saints: histoire et enseignements d'une crise (novembre 1328–avril 1329)", *Mélanges de l'Ecole française de Rome*, 89 (1977), 757–67 (p. 757).

12 See J. White, *Duccio: Tuscan Art and the Medieval Workshop* (London, Thames and Hudson, 1979), pp. 80–134.
13 See A. Martindale, *Simone Martini: Complete Edition* (Oxford, Phaidon, 1988), pp. 14–17, 204–09.
14 *Il constituto del comune di Siena dell'anno 1262*, edited by L. Zdekauer (Milan, Hoepli, 1897) mentions George, as will be seen below, and also certain honours done to the Virgin (for example, p. 26, two candles must burn constantly before her altar). The annual festivities at the Feast of the Assumption, obviously long-established, are referred to in the sections on crime and punishment, where penalties are provided for misbehaviour: L. Zdekauer, "Il frammento degli ultimi due libri del piú antico constituto senese", *Bollettino senese di storia patria*, 1 (1894), 131–54 (pp. 149–50). A much fuller account of the regulations for the festivities appears in *Il constituto del comune di Siena, volgarizzato nel MCCCIX–MCCCX*, edited by A. Lisini, 2 vols (Siena, Lazzeri, 1905), I, 64–68. This vernacular statute was a translation of the collection produced, in Latin, between 1287 and 1295. The relationship between these statute collections seems to illustrate a trend towards putting a consolidated version of established custom down in writing.
15 *Cronaca senese*, pp. 201–02.
16 *Il Caleffo vecchio del comune di Siena*, edited by G. Cecchini, 3 vols (Siena, Lazzeri, 1931–40), II, 846. On the Nine, see in general W. Bowsky, *A Medieval Italian Commune: Siena under the Nine, 1287–1355* (Berkeley, University of California Press, 1981).
17 A. Dati, *Opera* (Siena, Nardi, 1503), p. CCXXXI.
18 *Cronaca senese*, pp. 209–10.
19 *Il constituto del comune di Siena*, pp. 54–55.
20 *Cronaca senese*, p. 222.
21 *Il constituto del comune di Siena, volgarizzato*, I, 85.
22 A. Vauchez, "La Commune de Sienne", p. 759.
23 A. Vauchez, "La Commune de Sienne", *passim*.
24 Siena, Archivio di Stato, Consiglio Generale 103, fols. 94 verso–97.
25 J. Fioravanti, *Memorie storiche della città di Pistoia* (Lucca, Benedini, 1758), p. 134.
26 D. M. Webb, "The Holy Face of Lucca", p. 234.
27 *Statuto del comune di Lucca dell'anno MCCCVIII*, edited by S. Bongi and L. De Prete (= *Memorie e documenti per servire alla storia di Lucca*, 3 [1867]), pp. 36–44.
28 *Statuto del comune di Lucca*, p. 12.
29 D. M. Webb, "The Holy Face of Lucca", pp. 228, 233.
30 D. M. Webb, "The Holy Face of Lucca", p. 233.
31 M. Coens, "Légende et miracles du Roi S. Richard", *Analecta Bollandiana*, 49 (1931), 353–97.
32 Zita's life and miracles are to be found in *Acta Sanctorum Aprilis*, 3 vols (Antwerp, Cnobarus, 1675), III, 497–527.
33 Lucca, Archivio di Stato, Serie degli Statuti 4, fol. 58 verso.
34 *Acta Sanctorum Iulii*, 7 vols (Antwerp, Moulin, 1719–31), III, 258–72.
35 Tolomeo of Lucca, *Historia Ecclesiastica a Nativitate Christi usque ad Annum circiter MCCCXII* (*RIS*, IX, cols 740–1249), col. 765.
36 *Die Annalen des Tholomeus von Lucca*, edited by B. Schmeidler (*MGH: Scriptores Rerum Germanicarum*, new series, VIII), second edition (1955), p. 144.
37 *Cronaca senese*, p. 219.

Saints and Pilgrims in Dante's Italy 55

38 The problems and controversies generated by the discoveries of 1900 are summarized by H. Delehaye in a review of pamphlet warfare on the subject in *Analecta Bollandiana*, 23 (1904), pp. 491–92. Paulinus's chief scholarly defender was P. Guidi: see for example his "La Chiesa di San Paolino", *Atti della Reale accademia lucchese di scienze, lettere ed arti*, 35 (1919), 3–111. A sceptical view was taken by F. Lanzoni, *Le origini delle diocesi antiche d'Italia* (Rome, Tipografia Poliglotta Vaticana, 1923), pp. 366–67.
39 I. Affò, *Storia di Parma*, 4 vols (Parma, Carmignani, 1792–95), III, 386–87.
40 E. Jordan, *Les Origines de la domination angevine en Italie* (Paris, Picard, 1901), p. 364; N. Housley, "Politics and Heresy in Italy: Anti-heretical Crusades, Orders and Confraternities, 1200–1500", *Journal of Ecclesiastical History*, 33 (1982), 193–208 (pp. 201–05).
41 *Ordinarium Ecclesiae Parmensis*, edited by A. Barbieri (Parma, Fiaccadori, 1866), p. 114.
42 *Chronicon Parmense*, pp. 50–51.
43 *Statuta Communis Parmae ab Anno MCCLXVI ad Annum circiter MCCCIV*, edited by A. Ronchini (Parma, Fiaccadori, 1857), p. 470.
44 A. Pezzana, *Storia della città di Parma*, 5 vols (Parma, Tipografia Ducale, Reale Tipografia, 1837–59), II, 555–56.
45 *Chronicon Parmense*, p. 52.
46 *Respublica Mutinensis (1306–07)*, edited by E. Vicini, 2 vols (*Corpus Statutorum Italicorum*, XI, xiv), II, 1, 99.
47 *Statuta Civitatis Mutine*, p. lxiv.
48 *Statuti della repubblica fiorentina*, edited by R. Caggese, 2 vols (Florence, Galileiana, 1910–21), II (*Statuto del podestà dell'anno 1325*), 1.
49 *Statuto del podestà*, pp. 303–05, 437, 439.
50 *Statuto del podestà*, pp. 95–96
51 A. Vauchez, *La Sainteté en occident*, pp. 92–93.
52 K. Foster, *The Two Dantes* (London, Darton, Longman and Todd, 1977) has numerous thought-provoking reflections on Dante's "dualism".
53 A. Dati, *Opera*, p. ccxxxv.
54 These statutes were printed in two parts, without title-page or pagination, in Modena in 1487–88. The passage referred to is in Book III, rubric xxvi.

"DEMOGRAPHIC THOUGHT" AROUND 1300 AND DANTE'S FLORENCE[1]

Peter Biller

"Demographic" here refers partly to that bundle of subjects which modern demographers regard as demography—overall population, sex-ratios, life-expectancy, marriage patterns—and partly to that peculiar mixture of disciplines, from biology to mathematics, which demographers bring to bear on their own discipline. The broader enquiry puts these questions: what did people in the thirteenth and early fourteenth centuries think on "demographic" issues, and how far did they have the concepts and vocabulary to think "demographically"?

The thesis that this existed as an area of thought in the Middle Ages is not put forward without difficulty. On the one hand, it runs against a strong historiographical trend: standard histories of demographic thought pass straight from the Greeks to the sixteenth century, bypassing medieval people, who, it is assumed, were capable of nothing more than blind reliance on an Old Testament emphasis on fertility, and were innumerate. On the other hand, there is clearly a possibility of anachronism in an attempt to demonstrate that "medieval demographic thought" existed. Here the devil's advocate would point to the danger of categorizing as an area of thought what may not have been so categorized then, or to the insidious verbal-conceptual misrepresentation which may occur when using modern words and phrases to describe the thought of people in the distant past—when using "demographic", for example, the first recorded English use of which is as recent as 1882.[2]

Although much of a general study of this theme would need to focus on north-western Europe, especially Paris, there are cogent reasons for turning towards Italy: in general, the level of numeracy there, and in particular some striking examples of demographic thought in Florence. The development of numeracy, especially in the thirteenth century, has been illuminatingly described by Alexander Murray, who has attributed much of it to the pressures of the fiscal and military needs of government.[3] Whether one looks at high or low levels of the application of numbers to people, it seems remarkably easy to find good examples in Italian milieux. For example, one may turn to treatises written by French, German or Italian inquisitors, and examine the treatment of the size of heretical groups, which was a matter of both practical and theologico-polemical concern. A treatise from south-eastern Germany of around 1266 contains the categories "few" and "many", whereas a treatise by a former Cathar and later Dominican, who came from Piacenza, contains a formidable array of precise numbers of different Cathar groups, variation in numbers through time, and an overall estimate of the numbers of Cathars in 1250: a unique exercise in the inquisitorial literature of this period.[4] Counter-examples, of necessity negative, could easily be given—the present writer is not aware of a distinctly Italian input into the decisions by the Strasbourg and Naples general chapters of the Franciscans to compile statistics of the Order—,[5] but more of the available information would support an impression of ready Italian numeracy at an ordinary level.

At a higher mathematical level, only one example occurs, but it is a very striking one: a new development in mathematics itself concerning the application of number to population—in this case animal population. Again, it is Italian. Leonardo of Pisa's *Liber Abaci* goes over many mathematical problems which are applied to practical questions in contemporary life. Many of these deal with trade and the exchange of different currencies, but there is also one problem which shows the application of number to a demographic theme, length of life: how long has a man lived if, after doubling his age and adding to it eleven-forty-thirds of his age and one year, he will have lived to one hundred?[6] In the midst of such briefly stated arithmetical problems, the innovation in mathematical thought appears in the—subsequently—famous rabbits problem. How many rabbits will you have at the end of a year if you begin with one pair, who produce two each month, who in turn...?[7] It can be put in other words: what is the formula for unlimited regular population expansion, disregarding mortality? Thought up in a crowded Italian city, this is a development of which one could easily make too much—but also too little, for Leonardo's text indicates wider natural experimental rather than mathematical interest in the problem. He writes that someone (*quidam*) had put a pair of rabbits into a place enclosed by walls to see how many pairs would be produced in one year.[8] Unfortunately no more details are given— and in the present undeveloped state of scholarship on Leonardo one cannot totally exclude the possibility of a literary rather than contemporary source for this experiment.

Florence stands out among Italian cities which might demand attention in a study of medieval demographic thought, because of several remarkable examples of expression of thought by Florentines on population themes. This essay will be devoted, firstly, to a brief survey of the principal features of three of these, and then, secondly, to an exploration of their sources. The examples range from the early thirteenth century to the 1340s. Although the enquiry is about the presence of these ideas among Florentines in general, not in Dante alone, the exploration of their sources will be restricted to Florence in the period before Dante's exile.

Chronologically, the first of the examples comes from Salimbene (1221–87), and from an account he gave of *trufatores*, mockers or jokers, which has recently been borrowed by Umberto Eco.[9] In one anecdote Florentines are talking about a Dominican, John of Vicenza, and the possibility that he might come to Florence. "For God's sake, he must not come here," say the Florentines, "for we have heard that he raises the dead, and we are so many that there is no room for us in the city!" The other anecdotes in Salimbene's text show Florentines—clearly lay Florentines—watching friars, talking, joking and in one case watching someone fall over on an icy street. Salimbene describes such scenes in his own remarkably pliant and verbally inventive Latin, but as he wrote he was hearing these jokes in his mind in the vernacular. In the sentence which follows "no room for us in the city" he praises the sound of the Florentines' words in their own *ydioma*.[10] Here, then, is a rare glimpse, set in the 1230s, of the tart vernacular conversation of ordinary Florentines, where, significantly, one of the few examples given embodies a demographic thought, the notion of overpopulation. The way it is formulated suggests that bystanders will have shared this idea virtually as a commonplace.

In the second example one moves from the crudities of the Florentine man in the street to the writings of a self-consciously learned layman, Dante, whose demographic allusions or statements are briefly listed here. The *Convivio* contains some treatments of groups in terms of fractions or proportions—one-tenth, one to a thousand, and a breakdown of literate or illiterate people into the very broad terms of more or less in numbers; it also contains a set-piece discussion of the very traditional theme of the ages (*aetates*) of man.[11] Here the principal point of interest is that one of Aristotle's *Parva Naturalia* is cited in relation to variation in the span of these ages.[12] In the *Commedia* some of the interest lies in the appropriateness of a poet coming from such a crowded city as Florence depicting such a crowded counterpart as Hell, and to some extent Purgatory—teeming with crowds, the most usual commonplace being "piú di mille" ["more than a thousand"].[13] The population of a particular moral category in Dante's afterlife may refer directly to an estimate about a particular group in the world of the living, most obviously in the case of followers of particular heretical groups—higher numbers than Dante-*personaggio* might believe (*Inferno*, IX. 127–29). This is underlined by, for example, allusions to the population in specified areas of the Italy of the living (*Inferno*, XVIII. 59–61; *Paradiso*, IX. 43–44) and an evocative recollection of the Roman two-way pedestrian traffic system for crowd control during the Jubilee of 1300 (*Inferno*, XVIII. 28–33).

Framing these crowds are the opening line of the *Commedia* and the final systematic discussion of Florence in the central cantos of *Paradiso*. In the first line Dante asks the reader to work out what is half our life-span. Here, even if the mental arithmetic might have been stretching, the reference to a Biblically allotted life-span is commonplace. This cannot be said of the demographic elements in the discussion of Florence in the Cacciaguida cantos. There, among the answers about Florence which are given to Dante-*personaggio* by his ancestor in order to establish a series of contrasts between Florence in the first half of the twelfth century, the good former time, and the Florence of 1300, three of the points made are specifically demographic. In the first place, Florence's population is related to older and more recent city walls, and a ratio is given of one to five between the numbers of inhabitants at the two points in time represented by Cacciaguida and Dante (*Paradiso*, XVI. 46–48). Secondly, the age of first marriage for girls has gone out of control

"Demographic Thought" and Dante's Florence 61

by 1300; that is to say, earlier it was higher and now, in 1300, it is lower (*Paradiso*, XV. 103–05). Thirdly, in Cacciaguida's day Sardanapalus, figure of lust, had not yet shown what could be done in the bedroom, and houses were not empty of family—plausibly, though not necessarily, a statement that by 1300, though not at an earlier date, certain forms of sexual activity were being directed towards, and were resulting in, lack of offspring.[14]

These points come from a broader picture of the good former time which has long been the subject of acute scholarly debate.[15] Prominent have been the vexed question of parallels between the passage as a whole and passages in Giovanni Villani and Riccobaldo of Ferrara, and the context of earlier Florentine historiography written to the greater glory of Florence, the literary genre of descriptions of cities containing praise of cities for size and wealth, and specific examples of praise of Florence for its abundance of population,[16] where Dante's originality in praising the poor, small and simple rather than the wealthy and large stands out in relief. There is no contribution here to the solution of the puzzle of possible literary analogues, merely a reminder of the prominence of these three points in this crucial passage in the *Commedia*, their sharpness, and Dante's preference for a less numerous city and a high marriage age for girls, together with a (possible) reference to birth-control.

The chronicle of Giovanni Villani (*c*.1280–1348) provides the third example of Florentine demographic thought. Concerned with the *realities* of population and economy, scholars have quarried Villani's statistical information on 1336–38 and debated its reliability.[17] Here the theme is not Villani's reliability, but the capacity for thought about demographic matters demonstrated by a second lay Florentine, a man connected with the world of business, and one who did not aspire to Dante's absorption of academic natural philosophy and theology. If one sets aside the famous "good former time" passage (*Nuova cronica*, VII. 69. 18–39) and the 1336–38 statistics (XII. 91–94), one is still reading a text which is impregnated with population themes. A comparison of the first three books with the earlier *Chronica de Origine Civitatis* shows that population material of various sorts has been overlaid onto the *Chronica* by the time of Villani's text.[18] Villani adds Old Testament population history, including the effect of polygamy in bringing about rapid increase, and God's punishment on David for counting the people of Israel and Judah.[19] There is the effect of the agricultural fertility or healthiness of a spot on population increase.[20] There is the notion of evaluating a particular size of a city in the terms of a given historical period—"good for those times" ("buona città secondo il tempo d'allora": II. 5. 6–7), and the suggestion of 22,000 as the figure for Florence's men-at-arms at the time of Totila (III. 1. 77–79).

Florence is obviously central to Villani's outlook, and it is only for Florence that he produces his most sophisticated demographic measure, his annual estimate of the sex-ratio at birth, and a population estimate, 90,000 (*Nuova cronica*, XII. 94. 20–34). He does look beyond Florence, in the first instance to nearby cities, for example, Pisa,[21] and he relates mortality in battle to the total population sizes of Florence and Siena.[22] The geographical range can be much wider. Going beyond the Alps, he provides a proportional estimate for mortality from famine in Germany in 1316.[23] He compares Europe with the rest of the world—it is the most populated part of the world—,[24] and he talks about Saracen population,[25] and the large numbers of the Mongols.[26] Several aspects of the figures he supplies are striking. There is a concern for precision, reflected, for example, in his providing a qualifying adverbial phrase to indicate that a figure is an approximation,[27] or in his indication of a gap between belief and fact: at first it was thought that 3,000 had died in the 1333 flood, but in fact the figure was 300 (XII. 1. 160–64). This concern for precision may partly explain his leaning towards proportions and fractions: while he may provide an overall figure for mortality or population, at the same time he may say that population was a quarter of what it was to be later,[28] or that mortality was at least one per family.[29] Here his statements suggest observation of deaths by family or estimating population movements by changes in the area enclosed by wall circuits (IV. 2, V. 7–8, VIII. 99). Again, Villani puts certain categories beside his descriptions and figures of illness and mortality: male and female, young and old, rich and poor, town and country (XII. 1. 160–63, XII. 33. 1–5, XII. 114. 10–24). Eventually the potential of this juxtaposition is realized in a simple breakdown of a mortality figure, when Villani states that the mortality had more effect on one or several of these categories, which he specifies (XIII. 84. 1–12).

The Bible and contemporary religions and sects supply some of the vocabulary and concerns. Already noted in Villani's text are the

"Demographic Thought" and Dante's Florence 63

presence of Old Testament population history, David's census, and the (ultimately) Augustinian notion of a relation between polygamy and rapid population increase. This notion is imported elsewhere into discussion of the size of the Saracen population.[30] There is passing reference to teaching the procreative purpose of marriage (*Nuova cronica*, v. 21. 58–65), and Villani's provision of a number of followers of the heretic Dolcino—three thousand—recalls both earlier Italian concern to count heretics and Dante's concern with their number (*Nuova cronica*, IX. 84. 13–15; *Inferno*, IX. 127–29). There is biological knowledge, with Villani's references to the natural terminus of generation in women and to Sarah's supernatural passing of that limit,[31] and there is astrology: population issues are often brought into relation with planetary conjunctions.[32]

Witticisms of the street, a businessman's chronicle, a religious poem: what lay behind the demographic thoughts expressed in them?

First, beyond common human experience, what demographic facts pressed distinctively upon Florentines? Theirs was a city subject to expansion in numbers from immigration and a city which planned and built a wider circuit of walls to encompass anticipated expansion of population. Precisely how norms or changes in other demographic areas, such as life-expectancy or marriage patterns, came over to Florentine eyes is not usually clear, though the haggling of the *sensali* (marriage brokers), who are praised in the sermons of the Dominican Giordano of Pisa,[33] could clearly have been in the mind of someone writing about marriage age and dowry. It may not be known how archaic was the practice, noted by Villani, of the baptizing rector at San Giovanni casting different beans for female and male babies, but clearly this practice might impress upon observers other than Villani the notion of sex-ratio at birth. Resources of manpower in city and *contado* were clearly brought to many people's attention by fiscal and military needs or demands. Further, there was the entry into Florence of demographic facts from further afield. Here one must remember the conditions which rendered Florence an extraordinarily good centre for news, firstly its being at the centre of the international networks of Florentine companies. Thus the geographical span of Villani's demographic data recalls the north-western European span of Florentine companies, whether on a matter of information, such as a mortality estimate for Germany in 1316, or of debate, such as Villani's concern with the size of the Saracen population, which is reminiscent of writing on this issue by those at the French court who were concerned with the recovery of the Holy Land. Secondly, there were the even wider networks of the mendicant convents; these are discussed more fully below.

Information was coming over in varying degrees, being absorbed and refracted in the minds of Florentines. Famous are the statistics provided by Villani about the elementary education of those minds—8,000 to 10,000 boys and girls learning to read, 1,000 to 1,200 learning the abacus and algorism, 550 to 600 learning grammar and logic (*Nuova cronica*, xii. 94. 34–39)—, and frustrating the lack of evidence by which to estimate the quality and effectiveness of this education. Does one derive too positive a picture from the 700 vernacular sermons delivered to Florentine audiences by Giordano of Pisa in the first decade of the fourteenth century? These sermons contain casual references both to mathematics (for example, to the use of three and one seventh in relation to circles),[34] and to reading (*leggere* as well as listening to sermons as an act of piety),[35] which seem to imply high assumptions on Giordano's part about the education of his audience.

What may be said more broadly about those features of the culture of these Florentines which encouraged generalizing thought about population? George Holmes has been a persuasive exponent of a view of Florentine culture in this period where, once one excludes later developments of the fourteenth and fifteenth centuries, one sees the period around 1300 as markedly provincial and removed from the centres of thought. In 1973 Holmes examined the elementary education of merchants, and the education of notaries in composition and Latin rhetoric—the strand of lay culture. Juxtaposed with this was the other principal strand, Scholastic culture, trickling into Florence through several figures who had studied in Paris and taught and preached at the Dominican and Franciscan convents of (respectively) Santa Maria Novella and Santa Croce. In Holmes's most recent and expanded account of Florentine culture, the exposition of sources of lay culture gives a central place to a summary of the contents of popularizing, vernacular, encyclopaedic works, in particular those of Brunetto Latini; and another theme also appears, that of interchange between Florence and Bologna.[36]

"Demographic Thought" and Dante's Florence

It would seem profitable to borrow this model for the present enquiry, looking first at vernacular didactic works, secondly at the "Bologna connection", and leaving until last the more substantial theme of the mendicants. Among works in the first category examined here there is no question about the relevance of one, *Li Livres dou tresor*,[37] written by the author who, in Villani's words, "fue cominciatore e maestro in digrossare i Fiorentini" ["began the process of civilizing the Florentines": *Nuova cronica*, IX. 10. 28–29], Brunetto Latini. There is less certainty, however, about the specifically Florentine (as opposed to Tuscan or Italian) relevance of two others. These are a natural-philosophical encyclopaedia, intended for a vernacular-reading audience, written in 1282 by Ristoro of Arezzo,[38] and the representation and elaboration of Aristotelian moral philosophy in Giles of Rome's treatise *De Regimine Principum*, which was available in an Italian version by 1288, and in French almost certainly by the late thirteenth century.[39] Ristoro and Giles are imported here because the scholarship devoted to hunting Dante's sources has long argued for the high probability that at least one Florentine knew them.[40]

Listed here are the principal observations or generalizing propositions about population themes which were put over in these simplifying vernacular works. *Li Livres dou tresor*, which Brunetto brought to Florence in 1266, provides a geography which transmits a view of this world as divided into inhabited and uninhabited parts, and the further notion of degrees of populousness, in this case of cities: cities in India are described as "bien peuplees" (*Tresor*, I. 122. 16, 19). There is no special emphasis in these commonplaces. Brunetto does not omit entirely, nor does he underline, the *mirabilia* favoured by his geographical source, Solinus. He includes some marvels of early gestation and brevity of life (I. 122. 21). This sort of material, which was present in other encyclopaedic works, perhaps in part catered for some people's taste for a cross between *Tales of the Fantastic* and *The Guinness Book of Records*; if so, it may tell one little about what was in the minds of others of more sober outlook. More significant is the fact that Brunetto's most obvious addition to his source is a piece of well-conceived population history. Where Britain may once have been uninhabited, Brunetto introduces the suggestion that this changed after population increase led to emigration: "Et por ce jadis i fu la fins des terres habitees, jusc'a tant que les gens crurent et multepliierent et k'il passerent en un ille ki est en mer [...] la grant Bretaigne" ["And for this reason the inhabited lands once ended there, until the peoples grew and multiplied and crossed to an island in the sea, Great Britain": I. 123. 24].

Nor is there any special emphasis in Brunetto's Old Testament history, which includes the longevity of the patriarchs and a comment on Sarah's great age when bearing a child (*Tresor*, I. 20. 6, I. 21. 1, I. 40. 1; I. 25. 1)—both also found in Villani. As for marriage, Brunetto conveys its theological history—marriage as a precept in the old law and virginity praised in the new law (I. 18. 2)—but without the usual population context of this history (variation depending on a scarcity or sufficiency of people). When transmitting material from the *Summa de Vitiis et Virtutibus* of the Lyons Dominican William Peraldus, however, there is more of interest: after emphasizing the procreative purpose of marriage, Brunetto goes on to underline the ideal of parity between marriage partners, including parity of age: "k'il se marie a son pareil de linage de cors et d'aage" ["may he marry his equal in lineage, body and age": *Tresor*, II. 77. 3].

Ristoro of Arezzo's treatise again provides an account of the "disposizione della terra", part inhabited, part uninhabited (*La composizione del mondo*, I. 20, 23; II. 3), but more systematically than that of *Li Livres dou tresor*. It pays attention to natural death and life-span: a "tempo e vita diterminata" ["allotted time and life"] for every animal, "LXX anni per natura, e piú e meno" ["seventy years by nature, and more and less"] for man. Averroes is cited on the terminus of growth at the age of thirty-five; greater life-span is explained by "buona complessione" as well as good care (I. 22). Heavenly bodies are connected with epidemics and plagues, and Ristoro conveys very powerfully the sense of revolutionary change in regions over long periods of time, from city to forest, forest to city (VII. 4. 3).

Giles of Rome's treatise has attracted the attention of scholars hunting for Dante's sources because of some remarkable parallels, among which, of importance to the current theme, are the presence of Sardanapalus as a figure of lust,[41] and the notion of a house without offspring not being perfect (*Del reggimento de' principi*, II. 1. 3). Some of the rich demographic material of Aristotle's *Politics* is transmitted. There is political demography—comparing the utility of many or few among the rich, the "gente di mezzo" ["middling folk"], and the poor (III. 2. 30). There is the theme of marriage

"Demographic Thought" and Dante's Florence

systems—a comparison of monogamy with polygamy, where Giles adds a reference to Saracens and other religions. There is the proposition that polyandry leads to female sterility or lower fertility, based on the observation that prostitutes are more sterile than other women (II. 1. 7). The most significant element, however, is a theme which has also been noticed in *Li Livres dou tresor*: attention to marriage age. Where parity of age was the ideal transmitted by Brunetto, what Giles upholds, in his reworking of Book VII of the *Politics*, is a suitable age in both sexes, which does not include a low age. He points out four dangers of low age at marriage: the generation of imperfect children; inclining women to intemperance; the physical danger to women when giving birth at too young an age; and enfeeblement of men through engaging in sexual relations too early. A man should not take a wife "essendo nel tempo di troppa giovanezza, ned infino che l'uno e l'altro, cioè la moglie e 'l marito, non sono in tempo convenevole" ["being of too youthful an age, nor until the one and the other, that is, the wife and the husband, are of a suitable age"]. The ages which Giles upheld were probably intended to be minima. "E dovemo sapere che a la femmina conviene avere diciotto anni e all'uomo ventuno, innanzi ch'ellino sieno in congiungimento naturale" ["And we must know that for a woman the suitable age is eighteen years and for a man twenty-one, before they are in natural union": II. 1. 13]. Here, by omission, something very different from Aristotle's eighteen and thirty-seven is achieved, an ideal of "tempo convenevole" in which there is a very small gap between the sexes.

"We must allow for a considerable intellectual interchange between Florence and the University of Bologna," George Holmes has written.[42] Here one has on the one hand Nancy Siraisi's recreation of the intellectual world of a circle of academic physicians in Bologna in the late thirteenth and early fourteenth centuries, men whose interests mingled medicine and Aristotle's moral philosophy. On the other hand, there are the particular Florentine contacts remarked upon by Holmes, beginning with Taddeo Alderotti, who came from Florence and married a Florentine, and continuing with the Florentine links (or origins) of Taddeo's pupils.[43]

The present significance of the physicians is twofold. First of all, there were the demographic commonplaces of the standard textbooks of a doctor's training.[44] These included schemes of the *aetates* of man,[45] the discussion of regional variation of human life-span in Avicenna's *Canon of Medicine*,[46] and the wide range of considerations on various aspects of human reproduction, fertility, sterility and avoidance of conception, in the *Canon* and other works. Secondly, there were the emphases of works of the Florentine scholars in Bologna themselves. In the *expositiones* of the earliest of the group, Taddeo, one finds a *quaestio* which refers to one of Aristotle's *Parva Naturalia* and debates his opinion about regional variation in life-span; elsewhere in Taddeo one finds a lengthy treatment of the *aetates* of man.[47]

Bartholomew of Parma was a lecturer in astronomy in Bologna in 1297. Demographic facts are considered in his works, as in those of other astrologers, not just in relation to particulars—an individual at a certain time—but also in relation to longer periods of time and to groups or sub-groups of people. Thus Bartholomew envisages considerable illness and mortality among men in general, or among human groups: among *young* men and women; or among a particular social group, men "villis et servilis conditionis, ut artificum et rusticorum" ["of base and servile condition, such as that of artisans and peasants"], or in the "vulgus" ["masses"]; or a high incidence of miscarriages. The suggestion here is that the conceptualizations of astrological works, already briefly encountered in Ristoro, may have disseminated generalizing and analytic habits of thought about population data—a demographic cast of mind of the sort found in Villani.[48]

Absent from George Holmes's account is a discussion of possible influences from north-eastern Italy. Further enquiry concerned with centres of "demographic" thought could turn in that direction—to Padua, for example, because of the academic attention paid by Engelbert of Admont and Pietro d'Abano to the theme of life-span;[49] and to Venice, because of Marco Polo. Villani knew the latter's work, and cites it as one of his sources at the end of the chapter in which he writes about the enormous size of the Tartar population.[50]

The teaching and preaching of the religious probably constituted the principal means by which ideas were disseminated and stimulated in Florence during this period. Among these religious, one easily forgotten group needs to be briefly recalled: heretical *magistri*. A point which stands out in the general picture one has of thirteenth-century Italian Catharism is that a far greater part was played in Italian cities than in France by debate and polemical discussions, which could and did involve literate laymen. Such debate probably brought about a wide diffusion of Cathar themes. Cathars had a long history in Florence, and varied evidence attests to their continuing presence there. Thus in a deposition made to the inquisitor Bernard Gui one encounters a casual reference to residence with a Cathar and meeting a number of *credentes* in Florence in 1300; and one also needs to consider the implications of the fact that the two most prominent late thirteenth-century preachers in Florence were concerned with the Cathars.[51] The danger posed by the Cathar Church could stimulate thought about relative numbers, while, more directly, Cathar teaching of the illicitness of marriage and procreation could stimulate general thought about marriage and population. In fact there is some (slight) evidence suggesting attention to conception and conservation of the human race, stimulated by Cathars in Florence, as well as discussion of the relative numerical sizes of Church and sect; such evidence is summarized later in this essay.

Far more visible, and more demonstrably important, were the mendicant friars, in particular the Franciscans at Santa Croce and the Dominicans at Santa Maria Novella. These convents were part of two extraordinarily far-flung and busy international networks, and were therefore first of all receivers and disseminators of news. Travel to and information about eastern lands is an immediate example. In his account of one traveller in the Far East, the Franciscan John of Pian di Carpine, Salimbene emphasizes news—a John who was indefatigable in talking about the Mongols, having his book read, and expanding and expounding particular points—and, of more immediate relevance to Florence, Salimbene tells of Gerard of Prato being sent from Santa Croce to journey to the Mongols.[52] In the slightly later case of Ricoldo of Monte Croce, returning to Santa Maria Novella in 1301, there is a friar bringing back travel information which includes a high population estimate for a distant people—about 200,000 for the Saracens living in Baghdad.[53]

Some of the friars in these convents had studied in Paris. The foundations of a view of their diffusion of ideas were laid by Martin Grabmann and Lorenzo Minio-Paluello, and later built upon by scholars such as Charles Davis and George Holmes.[54] David d'Avray has added to this view a rich, condensed account of Florence as one of the two principal preaching centres after Paris.[55] Expositions of this view have concentrated on the following themes. Dante writes that he attended lectures and disputations at the schools of the religious, probably the schools of these convents. In the libraries of these convents were manuscripts which contained the higher learning in question. One way of examining the flow of ideas into Florence, therefore, is to look at these manuscripts, and they may be studied partly through a catalogue of the manuscript books which were at Santa Croce in this period,[56] and partly through the Aristotle manuscripts of around 1300 which *may* have been at Santa Croce at that time.[57] Another way is to look at the presence of some learned figures in these convents, men who in some cases, through their education in Paris or absorption of Parisian learning, and their writing or preaching in Florence, acted as personal conduits of such learning. These are mainly preachers, like Remigio de' Girolami and Servasanto of Faenza, though the relevance of others who stayed more briefly at these convents, such as Peter of John Olivi and Tolomeo of Lucca, has also been suggested. Some scholars have attempted to demonstrate parallels or possible influence, for instance of Remigio on Dante.

David d'Avray argues that "in the thirteenth and into the fourteenth centuries the Dominican and Franciscan convents must have been the major centres for the diffusion of ideas into the city."[58] In the remainder of the present essay this view will be adopted as the basis for an examination of the books in the library at Santa Croce and some of the surviving writings of the four mendicants mentioned above.[59] Two questions will be considered: how far these friars and their books brought the common stock of academic texts and ideas about population themes into the city, and how far they displayed distinct developments or emphases in their handling of those themes.

When one surveys both the books written before or shortly after 1300 which Davis has established were then in Santa Croce and also the Aristotle manuscripts which, though later in Santa Croce, were not necessarily there around 1300, one finds the following. There are certain standard works of canon law: Gratian's *Decretum* and Gregory IX's *Libri Quinque Decretalium* (referred to below as *Decretals*), with glosses, together with Huguccio (Uguccione of Pisa) on Gratian and Bernard of Parma on the *Decretals*. In theology there are certain standard works which are commentaries on, compendia of, or related to, Peter Lombard's *Libri Quatuor Sententiarum* (referred to below as the *Sentences*), and these include copies of William of Auxerre's *Summa Aurea*, St Bonaventure's commentary on the *Sentences*, and in addition a recent compendium of the *Sentences* prepared by Gerard of Prato while lector in Florence. Among the moral works written by or attributed to Aristotle there are the *Politics* and *Economics*; among the natural works, the *Parva Naturalia* and Averroes's epitomes of these; among standard works of reference, finally, the *Magnae Derivationes* of Huguccio.

The first point to note in this list is that it includes most of the standard texts which offered material for demographic reflection in arts, theology and canon law faculties. Self-evidently, the lengthy legal treatment of marriage in the *Decretum* and *Decretals*, together with their glosses and commentaries, as well as the theological treatment of marriage in Book IV of the *Sentences*, together with commentaries on these and compendia of them, paraded a host of demographic themes. Of these the least observed, perhaps, is the encouragement provided by Distinction 33 in Book IV of the *Sentences* to discuss polygamy, marriage and virginity in terms of the history of God's population (or simply population in general), and variations through history in scarcity or abundance of people. Furthermore, in Distinction 20 of Book II, the discussion of the population of Paradise if man had not sinned offered a "counter-factual conditional" which allowed commentators not only the opportunity to introduce natural philosophical material on population, but also the licence to discuss it with some freedom. Aristotle's *Politics* again held up a wealth of demographic themes, concepts and vocabulary, including the relation between lives and deaths in a stable population, the notions of ideal population, overpopulation and control of population, and intense discussion of ideal ages at marriage. Aristotle's little natural tract *De Longitudine et Brevitate Vitae* provided a model of systematic discussion of life-span, according to nature or contingency, comparatively (of human and animal, and, among humans, of male and female) and region by region.

Secondly, when reflecting on these standard texts one should bear in mind a comment made by Elizabeth Eisenstein in connection with the intellectual impact of printing: the denser juxtaposition of many standard texts can be a stimulus to further, and new, thought. This comment may be applied to earlier accumulations of books.[60] Consider the following examples, which illustrate both the Santa Croce books and the possible results of their convergence on particular themes. First of all, the opportunity to juxtapose different texts on age at marriage seems obvious. There are the sections in the *Decretum* and the *Decretals* which deal with minimum age, Huguccio's commentary on this part, which refers to the *physici*, introducing the theme of medical opinion on age of maturity,[61] and Aristotle's systematic discussion of ideal ages of marriage in Book VII of the *Politics*. If one turns to one widely diffused early commentary on the *Politics*, not known to have been in the Santa Croce library, namely Peter of Auvergne's continuation of St Thomas's commentary, one finds that Peter breaks away from the mode of literal commentary and into something more independent. He notes the discrepancy between the ages upheld by Aristotle and those in the laws (that is, canon law); he points to legal concern with the common good as justification for the difference; and he introduces a point ultimately derived from Aristotle's *De Longitudine et Brevitate Vitae* to explain the differences between the sexes in age at marriage.[62] In Peter's case the convergence of texts seems to provoke a certain fizz in thought about this topic. Could convergence of the Santa Croce texts have provoked a similar fizz in the mind of a friar reading in that library—or, more indirectly, in the mind of a layman made aware of this theme through a sermon and also through vernacular works which upheld parity in age between the sexes (Brunetto) or attacked low age at marriage (Giles)?

Another example is the theme of the theological history of population, which is brought up in a large number of canon-legal and theological texts. *Gaudemus in Domino* (on polygamy), in Gregory IX's *Decretals*, and Distinction 33 in Book IV of the *Sentences* bring up or thoroughly discuss variations in relation to paucity or expansion of human population: marriage as a precept, virginity not preferred and polygamy permitted when there were few people; marriage as an indulgence, virginity preferred, polygamy no longer permitted when population had expanded.[63] Gerard of Prato's compendium preserves only the outline of this: marriage was a precept, he writes, only when there was a paucity of men, therefore men are not now bound by it.[64] In William of Auxerre's *Summa Aurea*, however, where material from Distinction 33 is imported into a discussion of marriage in Paradise, it is expanded, and Gerard's implied premiss—that there is now a sufficiency—is spelled out in suggestively strong language: the people of God has now expanded throughout the world, and countless marriages nowadays generate a sufficiency of children of God.[65] The theme of variation through time here cedes primacy of place to the current sufficiency of population, and this notion was open to crystallization in an appropriate phrase. Of incalculable significance, here, is what William of Moerbeke's Latin translation of the *Politics* meant for the meeting of words and concepts in Western minds, when it presented those minds not only with discussions but also with a neat phrase for "overpopulation": "excessus multitudinis".[66]

What might these texts have suggested to a friar observing the crowded streets outside the walls of Santa Croce? Slightly later a Dominican, Giordano of Pisa, addressed a Florentine audience and told it that "i santi" (by which he meant Scholastic authorities) say that "al mondo hae gente troppa" ["there are too many people in the world"]. One is tempted to suggest that one of the things lying behind his sermon is precisely such a convergence of texts and observation of contemporary population pressure.[67]

A third example of convergence of texts concerns the question of avoidance of conception. The Augustinian *Aliquando* was present both in the *Decretum* and in Peter Lombard's *Sentences*.[68] In addition, clarification of this dense and ambiguous text was provided in Santa Croce by Huguccio's commentary. Huguccio posits three cases: some married people act in order to avoid conceiving, he writes, going on to distinguish this from abortion, and spelling out that such intentions prior to marriage would annul it.[69] The *Decretals* of 1234 represent a later stage of explicitness in thought about this, where such a "contraceptive" intention prior to marriage is cast in a possible form of words: "I contract with you provided that you avoid the conception of offspring."[70] These texts could, perhaps, have converged with the discussion of ways of controlling population in the *Politics*—and, outside Santa Croce, with the theme of "case" which, lacking "famiglia", were not perfect (Giles).

A fourth example comes from St Bonaventure. The presence in Santa Croce of his commentary on Book II the *Sentences* made available, among other demographic items, a phrase which was clumsy but useable in the area of thought about "sex-ratio": in the passage on Distinction 20, the question is asked, with regard to human population in Paradise had man not sinned, "whether there would have been an equal multiplication of men and women".[71] The lengthy answer goes through variations in ratio: more, less, or one to one where all were married. It refers to the question of sex-determination as a *magna quaestio* among natural philosophers and doctors. It concludes with the notion of variation, that in the hypothetical case the ratio would have been one to one, whereas in reality there is no fixed determination of number of those to be generated in either sex. Alongside this, William of Auxerre's *Summa Aurea* must have diffused, via a question on monogamy, the notion that God ordained the production of more males than females, partly in relation to God's will to provide among males, in addition to the married, those who were to be rulers, teachers, and virgins in the Church (William seems to have envisaged more male than female religious celibates).[72] Here there is an obvious convergence. There is the presence in Santa Croce of texts producing vocabulary for the "sex-ratio", the notion of contrasts in the ratios of different times (the pre- and post-lapsarian worlds), the practice of the rector at San Giovanni in Florence, at least by 1336–38, listing baptized babies by sex, and finally, Villani's attempt to provide ranges of annual figures for the "sex-ratio" in Florence.

So far the present discussion has centred on books which, apart from Gerard of Prato's *Breviloquium*, were not written in Florence—widely diffused standard texts, copies of which were, or probably were, at Santa Croce. The discussion now moves on to four figures who lived and worked at Santa Croce and Santa Maria Novella. Remigio was sometime lector of Santa Maria Novella and a prominent preacher in Florence, living there for most of the time between 1260 and his death in 1319.[73] Another prominent preacher, the Franciscan Servasanto of Faenza—"the greatest moralist of the thirteenth century"—, received orders between 1244 and 1260, and preached in Italian cities, principally in Tuscany and especially in Florence, where he spent most of his life and died, probably around 1300.[74] In the other two cases the connection with Florence is slighter: the French Spiritual Franciscan Peter of John Olivi was lector in Florence in 1287–89,[75] while Tolomeo of Lucca was prior of Santa Maria Novella in 1301–02.[76] One needs to distinguish degrees of plausibility for the diffusion in Florence of ideas contained in the writings of these four men. On the one hand there seems little reason to doubt the closest of relations between surviving manuscripts of the sermons of Servasanto and Remigio and sermons which were actually delivered in Florence in the decades up to 1300.[77] Behind these stand Remigio's treatise *Contra Falsos Ecclesie Professores*, which Davis has suggested was intended to supply material for sermons,[78] and Servasanto's *Summa de Poenitentia* and *Liber de Exemplis Naturalibus*—also works designed to furnish materials for preachers.[79] In studying these works one is still quite close to sermon collections and the diffusion of ideas in Florence through the delivery of sermons. The cases of Olivi and Tolomeo are rather different. Examined here are two of Olivi's *quaestiones* on marriage, which, in their formulation, relate to academic commentaries and questions on Book IV of the *Sentences*. One was probably written by 1283. No more is invoked here to link ideas in these *quaestiones* with Florence than Olivi's presence at Santa Croce in 1287-89.[80] The works of Tolomeo of Lucca which are discussed here—his *Exaemeron* and his continuation of St Thomas's *De Regimine Principum ad Regem Cypri*, completed near 1300—are again writings principally linked with Florence only through Tolomeo's period at Santa Maria Novella.[81]

The sermon materials may conveniently be examined first. An immediately notable feature of Servasanto and Remigio is their repeated concern with the Cathars, whose persistence in Florence at this time has already been noted.[82] There are two themes of demographic interest. Both Remigio's marriage sermon and Servasanto's on the text *Nupcie facte sunt* contain references to heretical views—more fully developed by Servasanto. "In recent times some have been leaving the faith," he says, "forbidding marriage [...]. It is manifest that all those who condemn marriage are in error." Earlier he defends marriage, as natural, as necessary for conserving the species, and so on.[83] Implied are the outlines of Cathar preachers' diffusion of their ideas in Florence at this time, and also mendicant preachers' holding up for examination, in front of Florentine audiences, the relationship between contrasting heretical and orthodox approaches to marriage and procreation, and the impact of these on the continuation of the human race.

Another point about heresy appears very sharply in Remigio's *Contra Falsos Ecclesie Professores*. A polemical point made against heretical sects was a comparison of the large size and unity of the Church against the small size and divisions of heresy. It is a stock point which may be found, for example, in one earlier Italian layman's treatise against heresy, the *Liber supra Stella* of the Piacentine nobleman Salvo Burci, and in one earlier Italian Dominican text, Moneta of Cremona's treatise against Cathars and Waldensians.[84] Remigio picks up this polemical charge and inserts it into his odd and interesting schema of the Church having and knowing the seven liberal arts. The Church has arithmetic; arithmetic is concerned with multitude; there is prophesy of the numerous and innumerable multitude which will be in the Church, and the Church has this multitude; the church of the infidels cannot be said to be the Church. To support this, Remigio then provides a notably precise citation of a text on the Cathars by Rainier Sacconi—Remigio specifies both its date of composition (1250) and Sacconi's career first as a Cathar and then as a Dominican—, before adopting a statistical item from it: in the whole world, counting Cathars of both sexes, there are not 4,000 of them. Sacconi's basis for this statement is also given: the computation had been made several times among the Cathars themselves.[85] What is distinctive in Remigio's deployment of this stock polemical theme is his almost exclusive emphasis on number rather than unity, his unique concern, and success, in digging out a precise figure, and his setting of his contrasting magnitudes—less than 4,000 Cathars against the Church's multitude—within a consideration of the liberal art of arithmetic. While Remigio's point would lead a polemicist to underline how *few* heretics there were, writing on heresy which had the aim of warning of the danger it posed would lead a writer to underline how *many* there were. If one views *few* and *many* as opposite ends of a register, then one might place Villani's estimate of Dolcino's followers somewhere in the middle—a fairly neutral expression by a man interested in statistics?—and Dante's emphasis on larger numbers over at one end. All three share a concern with number.

A feature of Servasanto's writings is his concern with *aetates* and life-span. What is usually shown is a preacher's commonplace, the topos of the brevity of life, or interest in the length of life of individuals.[86] Servasanto had a very wide knowledge of Aristotle's works, and of academic medicine, and it is therefore not surprising to see him displaying it on the question of death and life-span: he discusses the consumption of *humidum radicale*, he uses the image of a burning candle for life and death, and he cites Aristotle's tract on life-span.[87] In the midst of this there is one point of unusual

"Demographic Thought" and Dante's Florence

interest: attention to age at marriage. Servasanto selected for entry into his *Liber de Exemplis Naturalibus* a text which dealt with a far-off people, situated within the confines of Germania, the Frisians. This particular people is ideal in several ways. It is a *gens libera*, subject to no king. It observes chastity in a wonderful way, punishes indecencies heavily, and keeps its sons and daughters chaste until the completion of adolescence. Therefore, when this people hands its offspring over in marriage, there is generation of robust offspring.[88] The presentation of an ideal which combines liberty, chastity and late age at marriage is ultimately reminiscent of Tacitus's *Germania*. Its more immediate source is a Franciscan encyclopaedia (or perhaps, more correctly, compendium of natural philosophical knowledge for preachers), Bartholomaeus Anglicus's *De Rerum Proprietatibus*, composed around 1240.[89] Servasanto's text at this point is almost identical to the text which is found in early printed editions of Bartholomaeus. It is possible, therefore, that what Servasanto put in the *Liber de Exemplis Naturalibus* was an exact copy of the reading in the (unknown) manuscript which he used.

At this stage, the significant point is that a friar working in Florence and producing a compilation of preachable materials should have chosen this particular text for inclusion. The next stage was Servasanto's reworking of and selection from this passage in a sermon on St Agnes, at a point where Servasanto holds up the Saint's virginity against the morals and practices of his own times. He writes:

> The virgins of our times are never like that [St Agnes]; they are corrupted before they are ready. [...] It is necessary to hand them over in marriage before they reach the time of puberty, to avoid their being debauched, perhaps, before they are handed over to their husbands. The Christian girls among the Frisians are not like that. For this Frisian people is wonderfully zealous for chastity, and punishes very severely any of either sex who transgress. The Frisians therefore keep their daughters in their houses for a long time, nor do they allow them to marry before almost thirty; and for this reason they [these Frisian daughters] do not, like our girls, generate weak and little children, but strong and big ones, as is proved by experience.[90]

Servasanto has selected and omitted. Political liberty no longer appears. The chastity and marriage age of girls alone are at issue, not of both sexes. The pressures behind this selection could be simultaneously the exigencies of a sermon about a female virgin and contemporary social practice. Inserted is a detail not found in Bartholomaeus, one which would have been a commonplace of social practice in Servasanto's milieu: that of families keeping daughters "in their houses". Servasanto's other sermons make it clear that "here and now" is in Italy north of Rome; "our Italians flee the ultramontanes"; merchants travel across the Alps; "Who except a fool would go to France via Rome?" Most of his references are in fact to Florence.[91] It is this part of Italy which is invoked, then, when he refers to "our" girls. What he has to say about these girls of his time and area is that they are handed over in marriage very early, and that they generate weak offspring. The first of these factors is linked to lack of chastity, and not, as in Dante (*Paradiso*, XV. 103–05), to dowry. As the opposite of contemporary practice both Servasanto and Dante choose to exemplify the ideal of later marriage in a remote people. The remoteness is geographical in Servasanto, far away in north-western Europe, but chronological in Dante, far away in much earlier, smaller and chaster Florence.

Unlike Dante, but like Villani, Servasanto mentions a precise figure for marriage age in his remote ideal. Servasanto's number is not present in Bartholomaeus's description of the Frisians, though it is one of four numbers given in Bartholomaeus's earlier discussion *de aetatibus*, when he is looking at what is meant by "completion of adolescence": the twenty-first year, or up to the twenty-eighth, or up to the thirtieth, or up to the thirty-fifth (*De Rerum Proprietatibus*, VI. 1). What was the significance of thirty? Servasanto had considerable knowledge of written sources on periods of life and life-span, though the present writer has not encountered in his works a knowledge of the discussion of marriage age in the *Politics*. On this point, however, he was not copying. Perhaps he was simply choosing a very high number to underline the contrast—possibly, in a mental world of white and black, ideal and its opposite, a rounded figure which was double the norm of practice in the social and geographical milieu in which he and his audience lived.

It is also difficult to be sure about the meaning of his reference to "experience" showing the robustness of Frisian offspring. Physical robustness of the Germani in general was a literary commonplace—perhaps sufficiently well known to his audience to supply the mental framework of their observation of actual men from northern Europe. What is clear, however, is the special significance of a great Franciscan preacher working in Florence and noting the low age at marriage of girls in "our times", as opposed to an ideal which he located in a people of north-western Europe.

One of Servasanto's favourite topoi is the superior morality of animal as opposed to human behaviour, and on at least two occasions he uses this to make a point about sex in marriage. In one sermon, there is the fishes' ideal of conjugal continence and no adultery, whereas the opposite is the case among human beings: "In fact there is more adulterous or incestuous coitus than lawful; more against nature than through the natural act."[92] The point about sex against nature in marriage is spelled out more fully in another sermon: "Beasts come together for generation, to conserve the species, man generally for the pleasure of the flesh [...]. A beast in the carnal act does not alter the mode of nature but, apart from a few, observes it; but men more often change the mode of nature, and do not observe it with their wives."[93] Evidence survives of this theme also being tackled by a later Dominican preacher, Giordano of Pisa, in a sermon in which he said that "è dato il matrimonio a potere usare, e sodisfare alla natura secondo Iddio, e non se ne trova quasi nel centinaio uno che ben l'osservi" ["marriage is given to enable people to use and satisfy nature in accordance with God's will, but out of a hundred scarcely one is found who observes it well"].[94] An analogous statement is made much later again in a vernacular sermon by St Bernardino of Siena, who said, when preaching about marriage, "Of a thousand marriages, I believe nine hundred and ninety-nine are the devil's." Noonan has interpreted this as a reference to the practice of one form of sin against nature, contraceptive *coitus interruptus*, and it is one of the texts he uses to suggest that this "was the kind of contraceptive behaviour most frequently encountered" in the thirteenth to fifteenth centuries.[95] We may apply Noonan's interpretation of St Bernardino's text to Giordano's and Servasanto's sermons, and Noonan's conjecture about contraceptive behaviour to the audiences to which these sermons were delivered. In Giordano's case this means applying the suggestion specifically to thought and practice among the Florentines to whom Giordano addressed his words, in the vernacular, at Santa Maria Novella on 5 August 1304.

The third author is Peter of John Olivi. Of his two *quaestiones* on marriage, one is significant only for a brief point about the relationship between vocabulary and mentality, and consciousness about "birth-control". A clarifying analogy may be modern England, where the *Oxford English Dictionary* may be used to trace the rise and fall, the succession and the diffusion, of various words and phrases for "birth-control" in the English language—and this history of words may then itself be used to trace the history of a developing contraceptive mentality. Material exists for a parallel study of the use of words and phrases in medieval Latin. Such a study would point to the ubiquity of phrases which were ambiguous or cumbersome: "poisons of sterility", "sin against nature" (in marriage or among the married), "abuse of the act", "act in order to avoid offspring".[96] It would then move on to Olivi's contribution, the use of the slightly odd phrase "proli procurando impeditivo", and suggest that this is a development both semantically and—in the suggestive directness and compactness of "impeditivo"—in mentality.[97]

Olivi's other *quaestio*, a comparison of virginity and marriage which is unremarkable in its formulation of questions on Distinction 33 of Book IV of the *Sentences*, contains material whose significance is more concrete. In a long discussion of the relative value of marriage and virginity—the conclusion to which is of course the conventional one that virginity is preferable—a first point of interest is the sheer number and range of the arguments deployed, including material from Aristotle. Among the arguments *pro* marriage are multiplication as a contribution to the common good—which is opposed to the private good of the virgin—, the productive use of human seed, and the greater dignity of being the origin of many. Olivi's treatment of the stock contrast of earlier and later populations is fuller than usual. Of greatest interest, however, are the emphases of Olivi's arguments *contra* marriage, within the framework of the conventional thesis that procreation is a lesser good. The multiplication of corrupt men is not in itself as great a good as the contemplation of one man. Although offspring may be desired in itself, rightly and with natural desire, because offspring is in itself and absolutely a certain good, one should ponder what disadvantages the generating person incurs through procreating and conserving offspring. When one has weighed the sufficient multiplication of the human race—sufficient, that is, to complete the number of the elect—, one will think that, in the context both of the time and of divine will, having offspring connotes something ill, not good, or at best an imperfect good. For a poor man having corn is a good, but pressing on with agriculture is laborious. More space would be needed for an exhaustive exposition of the full meaning, implications and nuances of this very long *quaestio*, but what stands out rapidly is its erosion, within certain population conditions—contemporary conditions—, of a simple theological statement of the good of offspring.

The fourth example is Tolomeo of Lucca, whose *Exaemeron* (xv. 11) is of some interest in that it shows the use of material from epitomes of Roman science and Aristotle on life-span. Rather more significant is his continuation of St Thomas's *De Regimine Principum*, particularly two chapters of it where he reworks some themes from the *Politics* concerning ideal constitutions and comments on them with some independence. First, he reproduces Aristotle's description of the constitution proposed by Hippodamus, and Aristotle's criticism of Hippodamus for proposing a determined number of people for the polity. "We can see this error," writes Tolomeo; " [...] we cannot give a determined number to a polity, because a people in it increases according to the amenity of the place or the repute of the region." After describing the demographic fact of life, population increase, and alluding to immigration, Tolomeo goes on to the relationship between size of population and prestige. "Again," he writes, "we see cities which are judged to be more famous and powerful the more they abound in people." There is a possible emphasis—one of detachment—in Tolomeo's leaving this to the judgement of others. But his commentary takes a very sharp turn after he has expounded Aristotle's account of the Spartan constitution, in particular Sparta's adoption of a law to encourage the birthrate—a law which provided that there should be no military service for the father of three sons and no taxes imposed on the father of four sons. His commentary incorporates a stock Old Testament theme for comparison: although there was a curse on sterility and polygamy was permitted to increase generation, this was only a temporary concession. After repeating Aristotle's criticisms, Tolomeo goes further. It is right that in the republic one should receive honour and be rewarded for such displays of *virtus* as fighting, counselling and ruling. Generating, however, should not be rewarded in the republic. "For," writes Tolomeo witheringly, "even a *vilis homo* may possess more generative power" (*De*

Regimine Principum Continuatio, IV. 11, 15). Tolomeo's category "vilis homo" seems to be more a social one than a moral one, and it is clear that his attack on the notion of generating being meritorious and worthy of reward in the republic goes beyond the original discussion in the *Politics*.

A study of demographic thought in Latin Christendom as a whole shows the thirteenth and early fourteenth centuries to be a period of considerable development. Parts of the *Sentences* and two of Aristotle's works provided some of the vocabulary and concepts of demographic thought. In theology and arts faculties the formal lecturing, expounding and raising of questions on these texts could be the occasion of further concentration on and exploration of demographic themes. Internal and external religious threats—Cathar rejection of procreation and Islamic upholding of polygamy—provoked reflection, part of which could be demographic, and also comparative thought about size and numbers. Within Latin Christendom, there was a growing pressure of population, and some expression of a sense of overpopulation. Predominant in the view of more remote regions, in a knowledge of geography which was extending the size of the known world and Europe's awareness of distant populations, was wonder at the sheer size of those distant populations, in particular those of mainland China. This coalesced with a nearer concern with the recovery of the Holy Land, much of the literature concerning which took as one of its central themes the population basis of Islamic armies, and the population problem of recolonizing an eventually reconquered Holy Land. Together these strands of thought were producing by the early fourteenth century a view of the Western Christian population as small compared to the rest of the world—one-tenth or one-twentieth. Population thought at this time was beginning to resemble a very early map—crude, initially laughable, but no longer entirely based on religious symbolism, and containing a recognizable outline of a part of the earth.

What was Florence's place in this? Whether one looks at the presence of standard texts or of information about distant populations, it is immediately clear that Florence shared in much of this thought. Closer examination, however, shows that Florence was much more than a microcosm. Demographic thought was present in Florence in a quite dense and ramified form, and in

Florence it displays distinctive features. There are notable examples of attention to marriage age, expressions of a sense of overpopulation, erosion of the notions that largeness in a city and fertility are unquestioned goods, and (possibly) concern with "contraceptive" sexual acts in marriage.

Ultimately, what impresses is the sheer range and density of this thought. The most striking examples are population estimates by Florentines or in Florence. Well known is Dante, referring to Florence in the early twelfth century and Florence in 1300 as being in the ratio of 1:5. Equally well known is Villani, who attributes 90,000 mouths to Florence. Hitherto unnoticed is Giordano of Pisa, preaching at Santa Maria Novella on 15 November 1304 and comparing a Biblical population figure with the current figure for Tuscany: "Di Moises si legge che pur egli solo volea fare ogni cosa di reggere e di guidare tutto il popolo [= 600,000 arms-bearing men], ch'era piú due volte che tutta Toscana" ["One reads of Moses that he alone wished to do everything pertaining to governing and guiding the whole people, which was twice the population of all Tuscany"].[99] The intent of Giordano's sermon was a point about Moses, not Tuscany, so that the immediate interpretation is that he was using his assumption of his audience's knowledge of the population of Tuscany to direct its minds towards a specific Biblical population figure. From Salimbene's wisecracking bystanders to Giordano's attentive congregation, one senses the presence of many unknown and unnamed Florentines, whose demographic awareness seems to have been remarkably high, and who were given, like Dante, to measuring the spiritual and moral realms against their very concrete sense of this world and its inhabitants.

NOTES

1 This essay, which is a by-product of research for a general study of medieval demographic thought, is dedicated to the memory of Fr Conor Martin; see n. 62. The largest debt incurred has been to David d'Avray, who has supplied much help and advice; see nn. 55, 77, 79 and 83. Further help, from Christopher Tyerman and Richard Smith, is acknowledged in nn. 80 and 99.
2 See its entry in the *Oxford English Dictionary*.
3 A. V. Murray, *Reason and Society in the Middle Ages* (Oxford, Clarendon Press, 1978), Chs 7–8.

4   The Passau Anonymous, cited here from a later recension edited by J. Gretser, in *Maxima Bibliotheca Veterum Patrum*, edited by M. de La Bigne, 27 vols in 28 (Lyons–Geneva, Anissonii, 1677–1707), xxv, 263–64. The theme is analysed by D. Kurze, "Häresie und Minderheit im Mittelalter", *Historische Zeitschrift*, 229 (1979), 529–73. Rainier Sacconi, *Summa de Catharis et Leonistis seu Pauperibus de Lugduno*, edited by F. Sanjek (= *Archivum Fratrum Praedicatorum*, 44 [1974]), p. 50. For later Florentine use of Sacconi's figures, see below and n. 85.

5   For these figures, see G. Golubovich, "Series Provinciarum O. F. M. Saec. xiii–xiv", *Archivum Franciscanum Historicum*, 1 (1908), 1–22 (pp. 19–20).

6   *Il Liber Abbaci di Leonardo Pisano*, edited by B. Boncompagni (= vol. I of *Scritti di Leonardo Pisano*, 2 vols [Rome, Tipografia delle Scienze Matematiche e Fisiche, 1857–62]), p. 177.

7   *Il Liber Abbaci*, pp. 283–84.

8   "Quidam posuit unum par cuniculorum in quodam loco, qui erat undique pariete circundatus, ut sciret, quot ex eo paria germinarentur in uno anno."

9   U. Eco, *Il nome della rosa* (Milan, Bompiani, 1980), pp. 481–82; English translation by W. Weaver, *The Name of the Rose* (London, Secker and Warburg, 1983), pp. 477–78.

10 Salimbene de Adam, *Cronica*, edited by G. Scalia, 2 vols (Bari, Laterza, 1966), I, 117: "Hi [Florentini], quadam vice audientes quod frater Iohannes de Vincentia ex Ordine Predicatorum [...] Florentiam ire volebat, dixerunt: 'Pro Deo non veniat huc. Audivimus enim quod mortuos suscitat, et tot sumus, quod civitas nostra capere nos non potest.' Et valde bene sonant verba Florentinorum in ydiomate suo."

11 *Conv.*, II. 6, I. 9, I. 7. 3, IV. 23–28. Dante's discussion of ages is analysed by J. A. Burrow, *The Ages of Man: A Study in Medieval Writing and Thought* (Oxford, Clarendon Press, 1986), pp. 6–8, 32–36, and by E. Pears, *The Ages of Man: Medieval Interpretations of the Life Cycle* (Princeton, Princeton University Press, 1986), pp. 103–04.

12 *Conv.*, IV. 23; see J. A. Burrow, *The Ages of Man*, p. 6.

13 *Inf.*, V. 67, IX. 79, etc. For a fuller treatment of this subject, see J. Usher, "'Piú di mille': Crowd Control in the *Commedia*", in *Word and Drama in Dante: Essays on the "Divina commedia"*, edited by J. C. Barnes and J. Petrie (Dublin, Irish Academic Press, 1993), pp. 55–71.

14 *Par.*, XV. 106–08. This interpretation is followed in P. Biller, "Birth-control in the West in the Thirteenth and Early Fourteenth Centuries", *Past and Present*, 94 (Feb. 1982), 1–26 (pp. 5, 21–22). See n. 41 below on Sardanapalus in an Italian translation of Giles of Rome's *De Regimine Principum*.

15 See C. T. Davis, "Il buon tempo antico", reprinted in his *Dante's Italy and Other Essays* (Philadelphia, University of Pennsylvania Press, 1984), pp. 71–93.

16 Remigio is one example; see C. T. Davis, "An Early Florentine Political Theorist: Fra Remigio de' Girolami", reprinted in his *Dante's Italy*, pp. 198–223 (p. 206 and n. 30). See also J. K. Hyde, "The Social and Political Ideal of the *Comedy*", in *Dante Readings*, edited by E. Haywood (Dublin, Irish Academic Press, 1987), pp. 47–71.

17 See E. Fiumi, "La demografia fiorentina nelle pagine di Giovanni Villani", *Archivio storico italiano*, 108 (1958), 78–158; A. Sapori, "L'attendibilità di alcune testimonianze cronistiche dell'economia medievale", *Archivio storico italiano*, 12 (1929), 19–30; A. Frugoni, "G. Villani, *Cronica*, XI. 94", *Bullettino dell'Istituto storico italiano per il medio evo*, 77 (1965), 229–55.

18 *Chronica de Origine Civitatis*, edited by O. Hartwig, in his *Quellen und Forschungen zur ältesten Geschichte der Stadt Florenz*, 2 vols (Marburg, Elwert/Halle, Niemeyer, 1875–80), I, 35–65. Some aspects of Villani's free use and "completion" of the *Chronica* are studied by N. Rubinstein, "The Beginnings of Political Thought in Florence", *Journal of the Warburg and Courtauld Institutes*, 5 (1942), 198–227 (pp. 214–24).

19 *Nuova cronica*, I. 2. 33–36: "le genti viveano in que' tempi lungamente. E nota che in lunga vita, avendo piú mogli, aveano molti figliuoli e discendenti, e multiplicaro in molto popolo"; XII. 2.191–93. Patriarchal longevity had been noted by Brunetto Latini; see below.

20 *Nuova cronica*, I. 32. 46–47: "per lo buono sito e grasso luogo multiplicando i detti abitanti"; II. 13. 12–29: "avea molte città e molti popoli, che oggi sono consumati e venuti a niente per corruzzione d'aria: [...] e dov' era abitata e sana è oggi disabitata e inferma, *et e converso*"; IV. 3. 25–27: "e in piccolo tempo per lo buono sito e agiato luogo, per lo fiume, e per lo piano, la detta piccola Firenze fu bene popolata." It is also implicit in I. 7. 18–34.

21 *Nuova cronica*, II. 11. 12–16: "genti vi s'acolsono ad abitare, e crebbono e edificaro la città di Pisa."

22 *Nuova cronica*, VIII. 31. 76–78 (on mortality in battle): "Siena, a comparazione del suo popolo, ricevette maggiore danno de' suoi cittadini in questa sconfitta, che non fece Firenze a quella di Monte Aperti."

23 *Nuova cronica*, X. 80. 6–7: "piú che 'l terzo de la gente morirono."

24 *Nuova cronica*, I. 5. 45–46: [Europe] "è del tanto la piú popolata parte del mondo."

25 Villani's emphasis is on large numbers and their military significance. See *Nuova cronica*, III. 17. 7–9: "i quali Saracini passarono con grande navilio in Italia, e fu sí grande moltitudine che copria la terra come i grilli"; VIII. 37. 72–75: "con tutto che·ll'oste de' Saracini fosse cresciuta d'innumerabile gente, che di tutte parti erano venuti gli Arabi a·lloro soccorso, e fossono troppi piú che ' Cristiani [...]".

26 *Nuova cronica*, VI. 29. 21–22: "erano multiplicati in innumerabile numero." See n. 50 below.

27 *Nuova cronica*, XIII. 84. 8: "albitrando al grosso".

28 *Nuova cronica*, V. 7. 28: (in Florence) "non v'avea abitanti il quarto ch'è oggi"; XII. 114. 10–11: "morinne piú che il sesto di cittadini."

29 *Nuova cronica*, XII. 114. 12–13: "non rimase famiglia ch'alcuno non ne morisse, e dove due o·ttre o piú."

30 *Nuova cronica*, III. 8. 135: (Mahomet) "fece legge ch'a ciascuno fosse lecito d'avere e usare tante mogli e concubine quante ne potesse fornire, per generare figliuoli e crescere il suo popolo."

31 *Nuova cronica*, VI. 16. 42–44: (conception by Queen Constance) "in età di lei di piú di LII anni, ch'è quasi impossibile a natura di femmina a portare figliuolo"; XII. 2. 152–56: (conception by Sarah) "ch'avea anni LXXX ed era sterile; [...] questo fu sopra natura, e per grazia di Dio." This point had appeared in Brunetto Latini; see below.

32 *Nuova cronica*, II. 13. 18–29, IV. 1. 67–77, X. 80. 17–20, XII. 2, XII. 33. 5–8, XII. 68. 17–26, XIII. 84. 16–26. See the discussions of Ristoro of Arezzo and Bartholomew of Parma below and n. 48. Giordano of Pisa preached in Florence against astral determinism; see *Prediche del beato f. Giordano da Rivalto dell'Ordine de' Predicatori*, edited by D. M. Manni (Florence, Viviani, 1739), pp. 99–105. On

Giordano, see C. Delcorno, *Giordano da Pisa e l'antica predicazione volgare* (Florence, Olschki, 1975). Cormac Ó Cuilleanáin has kindly reminded me of Boccaccio's mention of possible astral influence on the 1348 plague (*Decameron*, Introduction to Day I).

33 Giordano of Pisa, *Prediche*, ed. Manni, p. 237. On the Florentine *sensale* see C. Klapisch-Zuber, *Women, Family and Ritual in Renaissance Florence* (Chicago–London, University of Chicago Press, 1985), p. 183.

34 Giordano of Pisa, *Prediche*, ed. Manni, p. 38; Giordano of Pisa, *Quaresimale fiorentino 1305–1306*, edited by C. Delcorno (Florence, Sansoni, 1974), p. 328.

35 Giordano of Pisa, *Quaresimale*, pp. 84, 222; *Prediche del beato fra Giordano da Rivalto dell'Ordine dei Predicatori recitate in Firenze dal MCCCIII al MCCCVI*, edited by D. Moreni, 2 vols (Florence, Magheri, 1831), II, 220.

36 G. Holmes, "The Emergence of an Urban Ideology in Florence, *c*.1250–1450", *Transactions of the Royal Historical Society*, fifth series, 23 (1973), 111–34; G. Holmes, *Florence, Rome and the Origins of the Renaissance* (Oxford, Clarendon Press, 1986), Ch. 4.

37 *Li Livres dou tresor de Brunetto Latini*, edited by F. J. Carmody (Berkeley–Los Angeles, University of California Press, 1948). This edition underestimates the amount of Aristotle transmitted by Brunetto. For example, I. 120. 3 (p. 108, line 15) comes from Aristotle's *Physics*, B1, 192b 20–23; see *Les Auctoritates Aristotelis*, edited by J. Hamesse (Louvain, Publications Universitaires; Paris, Béatrice-Nauwelaerts, 1974), p. 144, no. 50.

38 *La composizione del mondo di Ristoro d'Arezzo: testo italiano del 1282*, edited by E. Narducci (Rome, Tipografia delle Scienze Matematiche e Fisiche, 1859).

39 *Del reggimento de' principi di Egidio Romano: volgarizzamento trascritto nel MCCLXXXVIII*, edited by F. Corazzini (Florence, Le Monnier, 1858); *Li Livres du gouvernement des rois: A Thirteenth-century French Version of Egidio Colonna's Treatise "De Regimine Principum"*, edited by S. P. Molenaer (New York–London, Macmillan, 1899); on the translator see p. xxvi.

40 E. Moore, "Appendix on Dante and Ristoro d'Arezzo", in his *Studies in Dante: Second Series* (Oxford, Clarendon Press, 1899), pp. 358–72; L. Minio-Paluello, "Dante's Reading of Aristotle", in *The World of Dante*, edited by C. Grayson (Oxford, Clarendon Press, 1980), pp. 61–80: "Some remarkable coincidences point to Giles of Rome's *De Regimine Principum* as Dante's source of knowledge for the *Politics*" (p. 69).

41 Giles of Rome, *Del reggimento de' principi*, I. 2. 16: "Sardanapalo [...] tutte le sue parole, et tutto il suo intendimento era ne la camera in seguire le sue malvagie volontà di lussuria." When one compares the Latin and French versions— "omnes collocutiones eius erant in cameris ad mulieres" with "toutes ses paroles estoient en chambres as dames"—one detects special emphasis in the added "tutto il suo intendimento [...] malvagie volontà di lussuria". See n. 14 above.

42 G. Holmes, *Florence, Rome and the Origins of the Renaissance*, p. 86.

43 N. G. Siraisi, *Taddeo Alderotti and His Pupils: Two Generations of Italian Medical Learning* (Princeton, Princeton University Press, 1981). Further material on Aristotelian moral philosophy in Bologna is provided by J. Dunbabin, "Guido Vernani of Rimini's Commentary on Aristotle's *Politics*", *Traditio*, 44 (1988), 373–88.

44 On this, see the summary in N. G. Siraisi, *Medieval and Early Renaissance Medicine* (Chicago–London, University of Chicago Press, 1990), pp. 70–76.

45 *Aetates* schemes are encountered quickly in the *Articella*, the standard collection of texts used in medical education; e.g. in the *Isagoge* of Johannitius and the Hippocratic *Aphorisms*.

46 Avicenna, *Liber Canonis Medicine*, edited by A. di Belluno (Venice, Giunta, 1527), I. 2, 11, "De His Quae Proveniunt ex Habitacionum Locis" (fol. 27rb–vb).

47 T. Alderotti, *Expositiones in Arduum Aphorismorum Ipocratis Volumen* (Venice, Giunta, 1527), fols 368v–69r, 375r.

48 E. Narducci, "Intorno al *Tractatus Sphaerae* di Bartolomeo da Parma astronomo del secolo XIII e ad altri scritti del medesimo autore", *Bullettino di bibliografia e di storia delle scienze matematiche e fisiche*, 17 (1884), i, 220–22. An illuminating introduction to astrology in Italy around 1300 is given by M-T. d'Alverny, "Pietro d'Abano et les 'naturalistes' à l'époque de Dante", in *Dante e la cultura veneta*, edited by V. Branca and G. Padoan (Florence, Olschki, 1966), pp. 207–19.

49 G. B. Fowler, *Intellectual Interests of Engelbert of Admont* (New York, Columbia University Press, 1947), pp. 21–25 (Engelbert in Padua, 1278–87), 59, 73–85 (pp. 74–76 on Peter d'Abano's ideas about life-span); N. G. Siraisi, *Arts and Sciences at Padua: The Studium of Padua before 1350* (Toronto, Pontifical Institute of Medieval Studies, 1973), Ch. 4.

50 *Nuova cronica*, VI. 29. 57–59: "il libro detto Milione, che fece messere Marco Polo di Vinegia, il quale conta molto di loro [the Tartars'] podere e signoria".

51 *Liber Sententiarum Inquisitionis Tholosanae*, edited by P. van Limborch (in his *Historia Inquisitionis* [Amsterdam, Wetstenius, 1692]), p. 81: "Item vidit pluries Philippum hereticum & in pluribus locis, & stetit cum eodem in Florencia in eadem domo multis diebus & septimanis cum quibusdam aliis credentibus, & cum Raymundo Fabri qui tunc faciebat abstinencias hereticorum." On Catharism in Florence, see J. N. Stephens, "Heresy in Medieval and Renaissance Florence", *Past and Present*, 54 (Feb. 1972), 25–60, and on Catharism in Italy as a whole see L. Paolini, "Italian Catharism and Written Culture", in *Heresy and Literacy, 1000–1530*, edited by P. Biller and A. Hudson (Cambridge, Cambridge University Press, 1994), pp. 83–103.

52 Salimbene, *Cronica*, I, 302, 305–06.

53 Ricoldo of Monte Croce, *Itinerarius*, edited by J. C. M. Laurent, (in *Peregrinatores Medii Aevi Quatuor* [Leipzig, Hinrichs, 1864], pp. 105–41), XIX (p. 127): "In hac itaque civitate creduntur esse plus quam ducenta milia Saracenorum." U. Monneret de Villard discusses Ricoldo's description of Baghdad in his *Il libro della peregrinazione nelle parti d'Oriente di frate Ricoldo da Montecroce* (Rome, Institutum Historicum Fratrum Praedicatorum, 1948), pp. 76–89.

54 L. Minio-Paluello, "Remigio Girolami's *De Bono Communi*: Florence at the Time of Dante's Banishment and the Philosopher's Answer to the Crisis", *Italian Studies*, 11 (1956), 56–71 (see the references to Grabmann's work on p. 70), and "Dante's Reading of Aristotle", pp. 66–67, 71–72; C. T. Davis, "Education in Dante's Florence", reprinted in his *Dante's Italy*, pp. 137–65, and "An Early Florentine Political Theorist"; see also n. 73 below. For Holmes see n. 36 above and n. 73 below.

55 D. L. d'Avray, *The Preaching of the Friars: Sermons Diffused from Paris before 1300* (Oxford, Clarendon Press, 1985), pp. 156–60. D. R. Lesnick, *Preaching in Medieval Florence: The Social World of Franciscan and Dominican Spirituality* (Athens, Georgia–London, University of Georgia Press, 1989) should be used

with caution. Lesnick's contrast between "Scholastic" Dominicans and affective, "experiential" Franciscans is based on a comparison of different genres— Dominican sermons (pp. 96–133) set against Franciscan devotional writings (pp. 142–71)—, and (probably) the most important preacher at S. Croce, Servasanto of Faenza, whose sermons are as "Scholastic" (in Lesnick's sense) as those of a "Scholastic" Dominican, is completely ignored. David d'Avray has confirmed in conversation that one could not distinguish between Franciscan and Dominican sermons of around 1300 on this point.

56 C. T. Davis, "The Early Collection of Books of S. Croce in Florence", *Proceedings of the American Philosophical Society*, 107 (1963), 399–414. A useful term of comparison is the reconstruction of books—from a slightly earlier date (mainly 1278) and in a Dominican convent—by F. Pelster, "Die Bibliothek von Santa Caterina zu Pisa, eine Büchersammlung aus den Zeiten des Hl. Thomas von Aquin", in *Xenia Thomistica*, edited by S. Szabó, 3 vols (Rome, Tipografia Poliglotta Vaticana, 1925), III, 249–80. S. Caterina, as the convent where Giordano of Pisa first studied, is also important in the study of the sources of ideas flowing into Florence through the (at least) 700 vernacular sermons delivered in Florence by Giordano. On Giordano's life, see C. Delcorno, *Giordano da Pisa*, pp. 3–28; see pp. 13 and 17 for the duration of his preaching in Florence (by January 1303 and up to spring 1307).

57 L. Minio-Paluello, "Dante's Reading of Aristotle", pp. 66–67.

58 D. L. d'Avray, *The Preaching of the Friars*, p. 157.

59 In what follows, where a work is unprinted, the most conveniently available manuscript—not the S. Croce manuscript—has been consulted.

60 E. L. Eisenstein, *The Printing Press as an Agent of Change*, 2 vols (Cambridge– New York, Cambridge University Press, 1979), I, 76–77.

61 Gratian, *Decretum*, II. 30. 2; Gregory IX, *Decretales*, IV. 2; both texts are edited by E. Friedberg, *Corpus Iuris Canonici*, 2 vols (Leipzig, Tauchnitz, 1879), respectively occupying the whole of vol. I, and cols 1–928 of vol. II; the references are to I, cols 1099–1100 and II, cols 672–79. Huguccio on Gratian, *Decretum*, II. 30. 2 (Paris, Bibliothèque Nationale, fonds latin, 3891, fol. 247b) begins thus: "Tunc enim primo possunt consentire in matrimonium quando uterque incipit esse aptus ad officium carnis, et sit in anno XIIII° quoad masculos, in XII° quoad feminas. Ad hoc enim officium maturiora sunt vota femine quam viri ut in lege continetur, ut causam reddere quare hoc sit phisicorum est."

62 Peter of Auvergne's commentary on *Politics*, VII. 12 is to be found in St Thomas Aquinas, *In Libros Politicorum Aristotelis Expositio*, edited by R. M. Spiazzi (Turin–Rome, Marietti, 1951), p. 402, no. 1234. Later study of medieval commentaries on the *Politics* is indebted to the brilliant, fundamental, and unpublished dissertation of the late Fr Conor Martin, *The Commentaries on the "Politics" of Aristotle in the Late Thirteenth and Fourteenth Centuries, with Reference to the Thought and Political Life of the Time*, Oxford D. Phil (1949), Ch. 4 of which is devoted to Peter. On Peter's commentary, see now the admirable short discussion by J. Dunbabin, "The Reception and Interpretation of Aristotle's *Politics*", in *The Cambridge History of Later Medieval Philosophy*, edited by N. Kretzmann et al. (Cambridge, Cambridge University Press, 1982), pp. 725–28.

63 See Gregory IX, *Decretales*, IV. 19. 8 (cols 723–24).

64 *Il Breviloquium super Libros Sententiarum di Gherardo da Prato*, edited by M. da Civezza (Prato, Giachetti, 1882), p. 147.

65 William of Auxerre, *Summa Aurea*, edited by J. Ribaillier, 5 vols (= *Spicilegium Bonaventurianum*, vols XVI-XX [Paris, Centre National de la Recherche Scientifique; Rome, Collegium S. Bonaventurae, 1980-87]), II. 9. 2. 4 (XVII, 253): "modo populus Dei augmentatus est per totum mundum, et innumerabiles nuptie ubique modo generant filios Dei ad sufficientiam."
66 Until the second (complete) Moerbeke translation appears in the *Aristoteles Latinus* series, it is most conveniently cited as it appears in modern editions of commentaries on it; here, Bekker 1326a, in St Thomas Aquinas, *In Libros Politicorum Aristotelis Expositio*, p. 351, no. 943. On Moerbeke as a translator, see now *Guillaume de Moerbeke*, edited by J. Brams and W. Vanhamel (Louvain, Louvain University Press, 1989). For the point about vocabulary, see L. Minio-Paluello, "La Tradition aristotélicienne dans l'histoire des idées", reprinted in his *Opuscula: The Latin Aristotle* (Amsterdam, Hakkert, 1972), pp. 405-24 (pp. 421-24).
67 Giordano of Pisa, *Prediche*, ed. Manni, p. 240.
68 Discussed by J. T. Noonan, Jr, *Contraception: A History of Its Treatment by the Catholic Theologians and Canonists* (Cambridge, Massachusetts, Harvard University Press, 1965), pp. 214-15.
69 Paris, BN, f. lat., 3891, fol. 256va: "*Aliquando*: tres casus ponuntur in hoc capitulo. Quidam enim coniuges faciunt ut non concipiunt [r concipiant]. Si hoc non possunt vitare, faciunt ut partus conceptus non ageretur [r animetur?]. Si in hoc non habent effectum, faciunt ut non exeat [ad] lucem."
70 P. Biller, "Birth-control in the West", p. 16 and n. 53.
71 St Bonaventure, *In Librum Secundum Sententiarum* (= vol. II of his *Opera Omnia*, 10 vols in 11 [Quaracchi, Collegium S. Bonaventurae, 1883-1902)], XX. 1. 6, (p. 485): "Utrum aequalis fieret multiplicatio virorum et mulierum, si homo stetisset."
72 William of Auxerre, *Summa Aurea*, IV. 17. 3. 2 (XIX, 394-97).
73 On Remigio, see the works cited in n. 54 above, the bibliography in Remigio de' Girolami, *Contra Falsos Ecclesie Professores*, edited by F. Tamburini with a preface by C. T. Davis (Rome, Pontificia Università Lateranense, 1981), and D. R. Lesnick, *Preaching in Medieval Florence*, pp. 108-11. Holmes has written of a danger of exaggerating Remigio's importance, suggesting that one should not think of him in relation to the intellectual quality of Florence's lay intelligentsia: "His historical personality is almost entirely a creation of modern research" (G. Holmes, *Florence, Rome and the Origins of the Renaissance*, pp. 82, 87).
74 D. L. d'Avray, *The Preaching of the Friars*, p. 76, quoting from Oliger. See further, in d'Avray's book, pp. 76 n. 5, 155 n. 2, 158 n. 60, and 160 (and n. 83 below); L. Oliger, "Servasanto da Faenza O. F. M. e il suo *Liber de Virtutibus et Vitiis*", in *Miscellanea Francesco Ehrle* (= *Studi e testi*, XXXVII), 6 vols (Rome, Biblioteca Apostolica Vaticana, 1924), I, 148-89.
75 On Olivi, see D. Burr, *Olivi and Franciscan Poverty* (Philadelphia, University of Pennsylvania Press, 1989).
76 On Tolomeo, see C. T. Davis, "Roman Patriotism and Republican Propaganda: Ptolemy of Lucca and Pope Nicholas III" and "Ptolemy of Lucca and the Roman Republic", reprinted in his *Dante's Italy*, pp. 224-53 and 254-89.
77 I am grateful to David d'Avray for lending me his microfilm copy of the Florence, Biblioteca Nazionale Centrale, Conventi Soppressi MS G. 4. 396 of Remigio's sermons.

78 See C. T. Davis's preface to *Contra Falsos Ecclesie Professores*, pp. viii–xi for a discussion of the treatise's purpose, and the hypothesis that it was intended to furnish material for sermons.

79 I have used Servasanto, *Antidotarium Animae* [= *Summa de Poenitentia*] (Louvain, John of Westphalia, 1484/87) (see L. Oliger, "Servasanto da Faenza", pp. 148, 153–56); London, British Library, Arundel MSS, 198 for the *Liber de Exemplis Naturalibus* (it contains extracts: see L. Oliger, "Servasanto da Faenza", pp. 156–62). For sermons I have used BL, Harleian MSS, 3221, and those printed (because of misattribution) in St Bonaventure, *Opera Omnia*, edited by A. C. Peltier, 15 vols (Paris, Vivès, 1864–71), XIII, 493–636 and XIV, 1–138 (on Servasanto's authorship, see L. Oliger, "Servasanto da Faenza", p. 167). I am grateful to David d'Avray for referring me to the British Library manuscripts.

80 The two *quaestiones* are in Rome, Biblioteca Apostolica Vaticana, Latin MSS, 4986; the first (*De Perfectione Evangelica*, VI: *An Virginitas Sit Simpliciter Melior Matrimonio*) has been edited by A. Emmen in his "Verginità e matrimonio nella valutazione dell'Olivi", *Studi francescani*, 64 (1967), 11–57 (pp. 21–57); see pp. 12–13 on the date of its composition, and D. Burr, *Olivi and Franciscan Poverty*, pp. 43–47, 53–54, n. 26 on the collection from which it comes. I am grateful to Christopher Tyerman for obtaining a copy of Emmen's edition.

81 Tolomeo of Lucca, *Exaemeron*, edited by P-T. Masetti (Siena, Bernardini, 1880); *De Regimine Principum Continuatio*, in St Thomas Aquinas, *Opera Omnia*, edited by R. Busa, 7 vols (Stuttgart–Bad Cannstatt, Frommann-Holzboog, 1980), VII, 550–70.

82 In Giordano of Pisa's sermons one may find the idea that heresy is a spent force, though one should note the context of praise of St Dominic's or Dominican efforts against heresy, and therefore possible exaggeration of the success of those efforts; see Giordano of Pisa, *Prediche*, ed. Moreni, I, 44–45, 172–80. One may also find Giordano using the present tense when referring to heretics who do not wish to show themselves: see his *Quaresimale*, p. 18. On heretics in Florence see above and n. 51.

83 Remigio refers to "hereticos qui dampnant nuptias carnales" near the beginning of his *Nuptie facte sunt* sermon (Florence, BNC, Conv. Sopp. MSS, G. 4. 396, fol. 22vb). Servasanto's *Nupcie facte sunt* (BL, Harl. MSS, 3221, fols 72r–74r) defends marriage against those who condemn it, referring to heretics in language which might indicate contemporaneity: "In novissimis temporibus discedunt quidam a fide, attendentibus spiritibus erroris etc., et prohibentes nubere et abstinere a cibis quos Deus creavit. Manifestum ergo est quod omnes illi errant qui nupcias damnant, et cibos aliis comedere vetunt. Sed ista faciunt patarini" (fols 72v–73r). See also a reference on fol. 217r: "Sunt enim heretici qui olim dicti sunt manichei, nunc autem communi usu appellantur patareni, qui [...] duo ponunt esse principia"; and a mention of heretics who heed Mani, not Christ, and hide their doctrine, [speaking] with lowered voices, in St Bonaventure, *Opera Omnia*, ed. Peltier, XIV, 88. I am grateful to David d'Avray for making available to me before publication his "Some Franciscan Ideas about the Body", *Archivum Franciscanum Historicum*, 84 (1991), 343–63, which includes consideration of Servasanto, marriage, and heresy.

84 S. Burci, *Liber supra Stella*, edited by I. Da Milano, *Aevum*, 19 (1945), 218–341, IX (p. 316); Moneta of Cremona, *Adversus Catharos et Valdenses*, edited by T. A. Ricchini (Rome, Pallas, 1743), v. 1. 4 (p. 406a).

"Demographic Thought" and Dante's Florence   91

85 Remigio de' Girolami, *Contra Falsos Ecclesie Professores*, XXXVIII (pp. 80–83). For Sacconi see n. 4 above.
86 St Bonaventure, *Opera Omnia*, ed. Peltier, XIII, 556, 559, 623; XIV, 60; Servasanto, *Antidotarium Animae*, v. 22.
87 Servasanto, *Antidotarium Animae*, v. 23; BL, Arundel MSS, 198, fol. 78ra; St Bonaventure, *Opera Omnia*, ed. Peltier, XIII, 556. On the image and *humidum radicale*, see M. McVaugh, "The *Humidum Radicale* in Thirteenth-century Medicine", *Traditio*, 30 (1974), 259–83.
88 BL, Arundel MSS, 198, fol. 79vb: "Est autem gens libera, nulli omnino regi subiecta, imo omni morti se exponunt pro libertate tuenda, et primo mori eligunt quam iugo opprimi servitutis. [...] Populus igitur iste castitatem mirabiliter colet, et omnem inpudicitiam severius iudicant, filios suos et filias usque ad conpletum adolescencie terminum castas servant, et ideo cum nuptui tradunt eas prolem robustam genera[n]t."
89 Bartholomaeus Anglicus, *De Rerum Proprietatibus* (Nuremberg, Peypus, 1519), XV. 60, "De Frisia". Bartholomaeus's source for his material on Frisia, an obscure "Erodatus", is discussed by M. C. Seymour in M. C. Seymour et al., *Bartholomaeus Anglicus and His Encyclopaedia* (Aldershot–Vermont, Variorum, 1992), p. 167.
90 St Bonaventure, *Opera Omnia*, ed. Peltier, XIII, 519: "Sic [like St Agnes] nunquam virgines nostris temporibus sunt tales, quae ante sunt corruptae quam aptae. [...] Et oportet quod nuptui prius tradantur, quam ad tempus pubertatis attingant, ne prius forte stuprentur, quam maritis tradantur. [...] Non sunt tales apud Frisones christianae puellae. Nam gens illa Frisonum miro modo castitatem zelat, et gravissime punit, si quos, vel si quas transgressores inveniant [sic]. Filias ergo suas in domibus propriis diu servant, nec ante triginta quasi annos permittunt quod nubant: et ideo non, sicut nostrae, filios debiles et parvos generant, sed robustos et magnos, sicut experientia probat." The editors of the present volume have kindly drawn my attention to Dante's reference to the giant size of Frisians in *Inf.*, XXXI. 58–66.
91 St Bonaventure, *Opera Omnia*, ed. Peltier, XIII, 568, 598; XIV, 24; L. Oliger "Servasanto da Faenza", pp. 182–86.
92 St Bonaventure, *Opera Omnia*, ed. Peltier, XIV, 2: "Nam inter pisces continentia conjugalis servatur, et nullum inter pisces adulterium committitur, cum hoc inter homines non servetur; imo plures sunt coitus adulterini, et incestuosi, quam legitimi; plures contra naturam, quam opere naturali."
93 St Bonaventure, *Opera Omnia*, ed. Peltier, XIV, 92–93: "Bruta coeunt ad generationem, unde suam valeant conservare speciem; homo communiter ad solam delectationem carnis; unde nec cessat a muliere praegnante, cum multa sin[t] animalia, quae post conceptum foetum abstinen[t] a foemina. Bruta etiam in actu carnali modum naturae non mutant, sed servant, praeter pauca; sed homines naturae modum saepius mutant, et cum uxoribus non servant."
94 Giordano of Pisa, *Prediche*, ed. Moreni, I, 240.
95 J. T. Noonan, Jr, *Contraception*, pp. 226–27.
96 See the texts cited in P. Biller, "Birth-control in the West", pp. 8, 15, 16 n. 53, 22–23.
97 Biblioteca Vaticana, Lat. MSS, 4986, fol. 110r: "Queritur an exercens opus coniugale propter voluntatem solam aut principalius propter illam, sic

tamen quod nullo modo hoc faceret nisi cum leggitime sua, nec modo aliquo innaturali aut proli procurando impeditivo, peccet aut peccatum committat mortaliter." On birth-control see above and nn. 14, 41, 68–70, 92–96.

98 Peter of John Olivi, *De Perfectione Evangelica*, VI, pp. 38–42.
99 Giordano of Pisa, *Prediche*, ed. Moreni, II, 274. See Exodus 12. 37 and Numbers 2. 32 for figures for arms-bearing men of 600,000 and 603,550. Data about population in parts of Tuscany are discussed by D. Herlihy and C. Klapisch-Zuber, *Tuscans and their Families: A Study of the Florentine Catasto of 1427* (New Haven–London, Yale University Press, 1985), Ch. 3. Richard Smith informs me that Giordano's estimate accords with what one would project on the basis of that chapter.

THE TOPOGRAPHY OF THE OTHER WORLD AND THE INFLUENCE OF TWELFTH-CENTURY IRISH VISIONS ON DANTE

Yolande de Pontfarcy

The study of the topography of the other world immediately raises the question of the existence of Purgatory. This issue cannot be properly addressed without first of all discussing Jacques Le Goff's thesis in his book *La Naissance du Purgatoire*.[1] Le Goff argues that Purgatory did not exist before the late twelfth century because the noun *purgatorium* was not used. Only its adjectival form was found (in expressions such as *ignis purgatorius, loca purgatoria, poenae purgatoriae* etc.), and this referred to a particular type of punishment in some part of Hell. Although Le Goff does not of course deny the existence before the twelfth century of the belief in some sort of purgatorial process, he nevertheless places the birth of Purgatory in the 1170s (attested by a sermon of Petrus Comestor), when the word began to be used as a noun in theological-spiritual literature at the prompting of Parisian masters and Cistercian monks, referring to an autonomous place situated between Hell and Paradise. As a nominalist, Le Goff believes that "a place that is not named does not quite exist in the full sense of the word."[2] He maintains that this linguistic and spatial development is parallel to a socio-structural evolution. He explains that in the early Middle Ages thought naturally organized itself in binary patterns: for example in religion there was the opposition of God and Satan and of virtue and vice; in society the opposition of powerful and poor, clergy and laity.[3] But from the turn of the millennium pluralistic and above all ternary models began to overtake dualistic ones. This is evident for Le Goff in the way society was divided into three orders: *oratores* (those who pray), *bellatores* (those who fight) and *laboratores* (those who work). In the new context of much-enlarged cities, this model is visible in the shape of *maiores, mediocres* and *minores*. Between the great (lay and ecclesiastic) and the small (rural and urban workers) an intermediate category, namely the "bourgeois", had been born. Le Goff sees a reflection of this in the appearance of the adverb *mediocriter* to replace the old adverbial expression *non valde*, which used to refer to the not quite good (*non valde boni*) and the not quite bad (*non valde mali*). The appearance of Purgatory is therefore understood by Le Goff as an element in the evolution of a socio-economic structure:

> Let me be clear about my meaning. It would be absurd to argue that the bourgeoisie created Purgatory, or that Purgatory in one way or another derived from the bourgeoisie, assuming a bourgeoisie even existed at the time. What I am proposing as a hypothetical interpretation of Purgatory is this: that Purgatory was one of a group of phenomena associated with the transformation of feudal Christendom, of which one key expression was the creation of ternary logical models through the introduction of an intermediate category.[4]

Le Goff's book is all the more fascinating and stimulating because somehow one does not fully agree with his nominalist and socio-structural approach. Alternatives have been suggested. Richard Southern, for example, thinks it would be more appropriate to speak of a process of enlargement than of birth, since the idea of Purgatory was deeply rooted in theological tradition. He also believes that this process of enlargement started a century earlier, in the period after about 1050. His hypothesis is that, from the seventh to the eleventh century, the Church was dependent for its existence and prosperity on great military and political families who relied for their hopes of salvation, and success in this life, on large benefactions to monastic communities engaged in permanent prayer. With the growth of productivity and population in the eleventh century the Church acquired new sources of income (tithes) and became "increasingly dependent on, and concerned with, the goodwill and co-operation of the whole population". As the body of parish clergy increased, a new effort towards theological definition and practical discipline to fulfil the new needs appeared. It was at this point, in Southern's view, that the idea of Purgatory found its new role.[5]

Two other critics, A. H. Bredero and A. J. Gurevich, are of the opinion that Purgatory was the creation of a monastic culture rather than of Scholasticism. They have discovered that "purgatory" had been used as a noun earlier than Petrus Comestor. Bredero has shown that a sermon attributed by Le Goff to Nicholas of Clairvaux (who died some time after 1176 and was St Bernard's secretary), in which "purgatory" is used as a noun, is in fact by St Bernard (who died in 1153); and, situating the appearance of Purgatory between the ninth and the twelfth century, Bredero suggests that *purgatorium* is a neologism born in the context of the flowering of Latin literature in the twelfth century.[6] Gurevich has noticed the use of "purgatory" as a noun in an eleventh-century text: Othlo, a monk of St Emmeram, used it in the title of a chapter about the penalties to which sinners were subjected "in purgatorio".[7]

A text which would appear to demonstrate the monastic creation of Purgatory, as the result of an evolution in the structural topography of the other world, is the *Tractatus de Purgatorio Sancti Patricii* ("Treatise on St Patrick's Purgatory"), which I shall refer to simply as the *Tractatus*.[8] Its author, an Anglo-Norman monk of the Cistercian abbey of Saltrey, in Huntingdonshire (England), who identifies himself only by the initial H., wrote a first version in 1184 and a longer version before 1189. The story centres on a journey in the other world undertaken by a knight named Owein. The entrance to the other world is a cave or pit known as St Patrick's Purgatory, to be found on an island in a lake in north-western Ireland, Lough Derg in County Donegal.

For Le Goff the *Tractatus* has a crucial role in the birth of Purgatory, partly because he believes that here "Purgatory is named as one of three regions of the other world."[9] This text did play an important part but not, I suggest, for the reasons given by Le Goff. Robert Easting writes, in relation to the sixteen occurrences of the noun *purgatorium* in the longer version of the *Tractatus*, that "the majority of these uses refer not to Purgatory in general but to St Patrick's Purgatory proper, that is, to the 'cave' entrance to the other world."[10] One may go further than Easting by stating that not once does it refer to Purgatory as one of the three regions or states of the afterlife, not even in two debatable cases,[11] because when Owein arrives in the Earthly Paradise and is met by two archbishops who explain the meaning of what he has seen, they never call the place of torments he has traversed Purgatory. They use expressions such as "in locis que vidisti penalibus" ["in the places of punishment which you have seen"] or "illa loca" ["those places"].[12] The Terrestrial Paradise, on the other hand, is unambiguously named: "Patria igitur ista terrestris est paradisus" ["Now, this land is the Earthly Paradise"].[13] Thus "Purgatory" in the *Tractatus* refers principally to a precise place in this world, namely the cave on Station Island in Lough Derg, and secondarily to the suffering endured during a stay there. This leads to an interesting question. Who created the name St Patrick's Purgatory? Was it invented in 1140 by the Augustinian Canons when they transformed the old anchoretic tradition of the island into a short-term pilgrimage?[14] Or was it H. of Saltrey's literary creation in 1184?

Two other contemporary works mention St Patrick's Purgatory or Lough Derg. One is the *Vita Sancti Patricii* written in 1185/86 by Jocelin of Furness at the request of John de Courcy, while the other is the first version of the *Topographia Hibernica* by Giraldus Cambrensis (1186–87). None of the three authors (including H. of Saltrey) would appear to have any knowledge of the works of the other two. Jocelin and the monk of Saltrey mention a place called St Patrick's Purgatory: Jocelin identifies it as Croagh Patrick, a mountain in County Mayo in the west of Ireland, while H. of Saltrey speaks of a "deserted place" where the Lord showed St Patrick "a round pit, dark inside".[15] Giraldus describes a lake in Ulster which contains an island with nine pits, where malignant spirits torment anyone rash enough to spend the night there. It is in the second version of the *Topographia*, written before July 1189, that Giraldus adds that the place is called St Patrick's Purgatory. One may leave aside Giraldus's testimony, because his second version may have been influenced by the *Tractatus*.[16] Jocelin's testimony is more interesting. It reveals that the name St Patrick's Purgatory is not a creation of the monk of Saltrey. In the *Tripartite Life of St Patrick*, which was written in the tenth century and based on oral sources, an account is given of what St Patrick endured on Croagh Patrick to obtain from God the salvation of the greatest number of Irish souls. It is related that when the Saint climbed Croagh Patrick, an angel came to tell him that God would not give him what he asked because he asked too much. The Saint answered that he would not move until he died or obtained what he was seeking, and he remained there without food or drink. At the end of forty days the mountain was so full of black birds that he could see neither the sky nor the earth. He chased them away by throwing his bell at them. Then he wept until his face and chasuble were wet. (After that no demons came to the land of Erin for seven years and seven months and seven days and seven nights.) Then an angel came to console him with white birds, by whose melodies he was comforted. Thereafter the Saint negotiated with God, through the angel, regarding the number of souls he wanted to save.[17] There is no doubt that by the tenth century the old pagan site at the top of Croagh Patrick was understood as an intermediate place from where, through pains and torments, God's will and human destiny in the other world could be influenced. Thus it is not surprising that Jocelin wrote:

> On the summit of this mountain many have the custom of watching and fasting, thinking that after this they will never enter the gates of Hell. They consider that they have obtained this from God through the merits and prayers of Patrick. Some who have spent the night there relate that they have suffered the most grievous torments, which they think have purified them from all their sins. For this reason many call this place the Purgatory of St Patrick.[18]

One should note that in Jocelin's mind the idea of torment is associated with Purgatory as a place in this world, namely the top of Croagh Patrick. And the fact that the name St Patrick's Purgatory was attributed to different places suggests that in the second half of the twelfth century it was a recent invention. It would seem that it was adopted by the Augustinian Canons at Lough Derg to give a second intermediate place—the cave on their island—and the new pilgrimage to it the same importance as attached to the very ancient pilgrimage to Croagh Patrick.[19]

One may speculate that if St Bernard used the word "purgatory" as a noun in one of his sermons, it must have been used thus in the Cistercian milieu; and the Cistercian Order had been introduced into Ireland in the 1140s, together with the Canons Regular of St Augustine, by Bernard's friend St Malachy. However this may be, St Patrick's Purgatory is a place in this world, where people undergo torments likened to the sufferings of the other world in order to gain for themselves or for others a desirable place in the beyond. Without doubt, the success of the *Tractatus* had an important role in defining Purgatory as the hellish part of the intermediate place between Hell and the Celestial Paradise, but the association is not made in H. of Saltrey's text. In the *Espurgatoire Seint Patriz*, however—the French verse translation of the *Tractatus* made by Marie de France in the 1190s—, one finds (line 113) the first example in a vernacular language of the use of "purgatory" as a noun referring to a place of purification in the beyond.[20]

Parallel to the birth of "purgatory" as a noun, Le Goff sees a dramatic shift from a binary topography of the other world (in reality a binary model of two pairs) to a ternary model. In fact it is not a dramatic shift, partly because ternary and quaternary groupings of souls coexisted (very often within the same work), and partly because the ternary division of the other world emerges not as a sudden change but as an evolution of the fourfold division, answering the need to define an intermediate place for the intermediate time between the transitory time of this world on the one hand and eternity on the other.

Ternary and quaternary alternatives are found in St Augustine's *Enchiridion*, XXIX. 110. At the beginning of the chapter Augustine refers to a fourfold division when he speaks of the differing modes of living which determine the degree of relief received—thanks to masses and almsgiving—by souls after death:

> There is a manner of life which is neither so good (*nec tam bonus*) as not to require these services after death, nor so bad (*nec tam malus*) that such services are of no avail after death; there is, on the other hand, a kind of life so good (*talis in bono*) as not to require them; and again, one so bad (*talis in malo*) that when life is over they render no help.[21]

But at the end of the same chapter he writes of only three categories of souls in relation to good and evil:

> When, then, sacrifices either of the altar or of alms are offered on behalf of all the baptized dead, they are thank-offerings for the very good (*pro valde bonis*), they are propitiatory offerings for the not very bad (*pro non valde malis*), and in the case of the very bad (*pro valde malis*), even though they do not assist the dead, they are a species of consolation to the living. And where they are profitable, their benefit consists either in obtaining a full remission of sins, or at least in making the condemnation more tolerable.

The last sentence is interesting because for the not quite bad Augustine mentions two kinds of treatment—either a total absence of suffering or a more bearable form of damnation. There are three kinds of souls but four types of treatment. This is how Le Goff explains St Augustine's attitude:

> I believe that Augustine was torn between two alternatives. On the one hand, despite his subtlety, he was forced to accept the binary schemes whose grip on men's minds was tightening in late antiquity, as men fell back for the sake of survival on simplified intellectual tools. [...] He basically favoured an other world consisting of three parts: Heaven, fire (Purgatory) and Hell, and it was by remaining faithful to the spirit rather than the letter of his writings that twelfth-century thinkers, much imbued with Augustinism, eventually came to propose a ternary model.[22]

Bede's *Vision of Drycthelm* (written in 696) played an important part in the evolution from a quaternary to a ternary division of the other world.[23] Drycthelm is guided in a north-easterly direction by a person in a shining robe. They come to a broad valley. On the left there are flames and on the right there is terrible cold. Souls are hurried from one side to the other. Drycthelm thinks it is Hell but the guide says it is not. The guide leads him to the further end. Darkness falls and an indescribable stench grows; he sees flames rising from a great pit and falling back into the chasm, and in the flames he sees souls. The guide, who has disappeared, comes back and leads Drycthelm towards the south-east. They arrive in a place surrounded by a huge wall, and, not knowing how, they find themselves on the other side in a pleasant meadow full of brightness, fragrance and happy people. Drycthelm wonders if he is in the Kingdom of Heaven, but the guide, responding to his thought, says: "No, this is not the Kingdom of Heaven as you imagine."[24] As they progress further, the light, the sound of music and the perfumes surpass what Drycthelm has experienced previously. As he is hoping to enter this delightful place, his guide brings him back to this world.

Then follows the guide's commentary. The valley with its horrible flames and icy cold is the place of punishment of souls who were slow to confess and amend their wicked ways but had recourse to penitence at the hour of their death. Because of this, they will be admitted into the Kingdom of Heaven on the Day of

Judgement, though many are helped by prayer and therefore set free before the Day of Judgement. The fiery, noisy pit is the mouth of Hell, and whoever falls into it will never be delivered throughout eternity. The flowery place is for souls who die having done good but are not so perfect as to merit immediate entry into the Kingdom of Heaven. They will enter Heaven on the Day of Judgement. Finally, all those who are perfect enter the Kingdom of Heaven as soon as their souls leave their bodies. The structure of the afterlife in the *Vision of Drycthelm* may be presented as in Figure 1.

Le Goff believes that this text would be of capital importance but for certain serious *lacunae*: the word "purgation" and other related words are lacking, these antechambers are given no name, and the structure is bipartite.[25] On the other hand, the *Vision of Drycthelm* does attempt to assign a spatial dimension in the other world to an intermediate time between the limited time of this world and eternity. Each half of the bipartite other world has been extended to accommodate the equivalent of St Augustine's *non valde mali* and *non valde boni* until the Day of Judgement. These two

Figure 1
STRUCTURE OF THE AFTERLIFE IN THE *VISION OF DRYCTHELM*

	Places visited (inhabited until the Day of Judgement)	Places not visited (inhabited after death and for eternity)
DARKNESS	North-easterly direction ANTECHAMBER OF HELL	HELL
LIGHT	South-easterly direction ANTECHAMBER OF HEAVEN for the imperfect	KINGDOM OF HEAVEN

appendages are linked, however, since through the effect of prayer souls may pass from the antechamber of Hell to the antechamber of Paradise. While Purgatory may not yet be fully born, a two-sided intermediate place (a place of torment and a place of happy waiting) has appeared without yet being textually placed between Hell and Paradise.

From the eighth century onwards in Anglo-Saxon and Irish eschatology one notices a tendency towards a tripartite differentiation of souls. Thus three kinds of souls appear in Alcuin's *De Fide Sanctae Trinitatis* (III. 21). Writing about the treatment of the different kinds of souls in the fire of Doomsday (which he assimilates to purgatorial fire), Alcuin mentions the following: *impii*, who will be cast from the torment of Doomsday fire into Hell; *sancti*, who will pass through the fire unscathed; and *justi*, who will be cleansed of minor sins by the heat of this fire and then admitted to Heaven. The Doomsday fire has a purgatorial function for the *justi*. But Le Goff does not recognize these three classes of souls; he finds Alcuin "vague and confusing" because the great Anglo-Saxon ecclesiastic adds that the *impii* will be more or less tormented depending on their degree of wickedness while the *sancti* will be more or less rewarded depending on their degree of sanctity.[26]

Father Gwynn mentions a similar ternary division of souls located in three places, to be found in an eighth-century Hiberno-Latin manuscript from Munich:

> Tres turmae in iudicio erunt: idest valde boni, idest angeli et sancti; valde mali, idest daemones et impii; nec valde boni nec valde mali. Et hii tales per ignem purgabuntur.
>
> [There will be three crowds in judgement: the wholly good, that is, angels and saints; the wholly wicked, that is, demons and the impious; and those who are neither wholly good nor wholly wicked. And these will be cleansed by fire.][27]

And St John Seymour gives other examples of such a division in Irish and Anglo-Saxon eschatology,[28] which confirm a tendency not to separate the intermediate state of the souls (the not quite bad and the not quite good) and a wish to find them a place to receive what they deserve within the context of a bipartite division of the other world.

In the *Tractatus* on St Patrick's Purgatory one may find a combination of three and four regions with elements from the Anglo-Saxon and Irish tradition. Here the afterlife is structured exactly as it is in the *Vision of Drycthelm*. It consists of four regions (not three as Le Goff says).[29] Sir Owein, however, visits only two of them: one is an unnamed hellish region while the other is the Terrestrial Paradise, which he enters after crossing a perilous bridge. Two other, unvisited, places are mentioned and their entrances pointed out. The first is Hell, situated beneath a very broad, fetid river covered in flames of burning sulphur and filled with a multitude of demons. (This is the river crossed by the perilous bridge.) The second is the Celestial Paradise, the gate of which is seen far away in the sky from the top of a mountain in the Earthly Paradise.

Figure 2
STRUCTURE OF THE AFTERLIFE IN OWEIN'S VISION (*TRACTATUS*)

	Places visited (inhabited temporarily)	Places not visited (inhabited for eternity)
DARKNESS	From the cave of St Patrick's Purgatory... PLACE OF TORMENTS *Bridge*	under the water HELL
LIGHT	TERRESTRIAL PARADISE ... to the top of a mountain	CELESTIAL PARADISE high in the sky

In his introduction, however, H. of Saltrey also mentions a ternary division of the other world:

> Creduntur tamen tormenta maxima, ad que culpa deorsum premit, in immo esse, maxima vero gaudia, ad que sursum per iusticiam ascenditur, in summo; in medio autem bona et mala media.

> [It is believed that the greater torments, towards which our faults weigh us down, are found at the bottom and inversely the greater joys, towards which we ascend through our virtue, are found at the top. As for the middle, things half way between good and evil are found there.][30]

Easting noticed that this statement is a quotation from Hugh of St Victor's *Summa de Sacramentis Christianae Fidei* (IV). Hugh also gives his own version of a quaternary division of souls: the *perfecti boni* go directly to Heaven; the *valde mali* go straight to Hell; the *imperfecti boni* undergo torments before reaching the joys to come; and the *imperfecti sive minus mali* (the less wicked) await the universal resurrection in an uncertain place and then will be sent below for ever.[31] H. of Saltrey, then, is following St Augustine and Hugh of St Victor when he mentions threefold and fourfold divisions.

Compared to Bede, however, the fourfold division has undergone a major change by the time it appears in the *Tractatus*. The intermediate places are no longer appendages of the lowest and the highest parts of the other world. Although opposite in nature they are not separated, since a bridge links them. As the two archbishops who welcome Owein in the Terrestrial Paradise explain, all must pass through the region of torments to be purified and stay there for a longer or shorter period according to their demerits. Then they go to the Earthly Paradise, where the length of time they must stay before proceeding to the Heavenly Paradise is likewise determined by the degree of their deserts.[32] This two-part intermediate place is situated between our world and the place where souls will remain for eternity, and is an obligatory stage in the itinerary of all souls, whether on their way to the depths of Hell or to the delights of the Celestial Paradise.

This new, unified topography of the other world in the *Tractatus* paves the way for Dante to combine the two intermediate places in a single structure—a mountain on an island—to which he gives the overall name Purgatory. St Patrick's Purgatory really is situated on an island, and although Sir Owein's journey is not physically an upward one it nevertheless terminates on the top of a mountain, from where he sees the gate of the Celestial Paradise. Thus the fundamental structure of Dante's Purgatory lies between the real and the fictional.

In the *Tractatus* this two-sided intermediate place has terrestrial features. Hell and the Celestial Paradise, which are not described, are beyond words. But a definite place in this world gives access to the place of torments and thence to the Terrestrial Paradise, so the places visited by Sir Owein are linked to earthly reality.[33] Directions are often given as if a precise road is followed. The sense of familiarity is underlined by the fact that the knight visits the other world with his body, not in spirit only like other visionaries, who usually left their bodies behind. The particular features of Dante's Purgatory, too, are its earthly aspects, such as the alternation of day and night.[34]

Sir Owein's journey is also a spiritual progression. In the company of the inhabitants of the Earthly Paradise and of the two archbishops who welcome him there and explain what he has seen, he receives celestial food, which takes the appearance of a pentecostal flame. From it the knight "felt such a delicious sweetness both in his heart and in his body that he was hardly able to make out whether he was alive or dead, so extreme was the sweetness".[35] On his way back Owein meets the fifteen messengers who welcomed him, and they say, "Hurrah, brother, now we know that you have been purified of all your sins through the torments which you have courageously endured and overcome".[36] Dante makes similar spiritual progress in Purgatory, since he emerges purified and able to understand what he has previously not understood.

Connections between the *Tractatus* and the *Commedia* have often been sensed; but they have never been explained, because they rest not on textual similarities but on matters of structure.

The most astounding vision and the most fully developed eschatology before Dante are found in the *Vision of Tnugdal*, a work written in 1149 in Regensburg, Germany by an Irish monk called Marcus. Tnugdal is a knight from Cashel, who goes to Cork to recover a debt from a friend. During dinner he falls into a sort of coma, which lasts three days, and his spirit visits the other world.[37] Brother Marcus divides his text into twenty-seven parts, of which the first is a prologue mentioning contemporary events, the second is an introduction characterizing Ireland and relating the circumstances of Tnugdal's vision, and the last is a conclusion telling of the return of Tnugdal's soul to his body. Of the twenty-four chapters between these extremities, the first two tell what happens when the knight's soul leaves his body and meets his guardian angel, while the remaining twenty-two describe the progress of his soul in the abode of the departed.

As in the case of the *Tractatus*, similarities to Dante's *Commedia* have been sensed. Many such details were enumerated by Boswell;[38] but here too the connection is deeper and at a structural level. Marcus's other world, though belonging to the tradition of St Augustine and Bede, has a cosmic quality which one will later find in Dante. This cosmic quality is expressed in the work's structure and through the symbolism of numbers.[39] The afterlife in the vision is divided into two parts: a World of Darkness named Hell (including an upper Hell—with eight torments—and a lower Hell) and a World of Light, never named Paradise. (The World of Light includes the *campus laetitiae* ["field of joy"]—which accommodates the *boni non valde*, the not quite good, while excluding the *mali non valde*, the not quite bad—and St Paul's three heavens, represented by three enclosures surrounded respectively by walls of silver, gold and precious stones.) These two worlds are of equal importance, since Marcus assigns eleven chapters to each. The total number of these chapters, twenty-two, might suggest completeness; for example, St Augustine's *De Civitate Dei*, which is numerologically proportioned, is also composed of twenty-two sections.[40]

This binary structure is again made up of four parts: in the World of Darkness there is upper Hell and lower Hell; in the World of Light one may distinguish between, on the one hand, the area of the *mali non valde* and the *boni non valde* and, on the other, the three heavens of St Paul. Altogether there are seven different places. Seven is also a symbol of totality (seven moving stars, seven days of the week, seven tones of the musical scale etc.). In Macrobius's *Commentary on the Dream of Scipio* (VI. 54–83) and Martianus Capella's *The Marriage of Philology and Mercury*, VII: *Arithmetic* (738–40), seven is associated with the universe and the human body;[41] and this number also corresponds to the sevenfold division of Heaven found in the Irish tradition.[42] There is, in addition, a symbolic relationship (as that of the microcosm to the macrocosm) between the inner structure and the outer structure of Tnugdal's vision. Upper Hell is composed of eight torments, and dealt with in eight chapters, while lower Hell is covered in three chapters. According to Macrobius, "The Pythagoreans [...] called the number eight Justice because it is the first number that may be divided into two equal even numbers and divided again into two more equal even numbers" (*Commentary*, v. 17). And the theme of justice is one which appears throughout the *Vision*.[43] According to Martianus Capella, "The number eight is the first cube and is a perfect number, assigned to Vulcan" (*Arithmetic*, 740). Now the eighth torment in the *Vision of Tnugdal* is that of the forges of Vulcan, who punishes those who have accumulated sins upon sins. In the World

Figure 3
STRUCTURE OF THE AFTERLIFE IN THE *VISION OF TNUGDAL*

	Places for those already called
	2nd Heaven 3rd Heaven 6 7
Places for those awaiting God's judgement	
1 Upper Hell 1st–7th torments 8th torment	1st Heaven 5 Mali ⊙ Boni non valde 3 4
Place for those already condemned Lower Hell 2	
WORLD OF DARKNESS	WORLD OF LIGHT

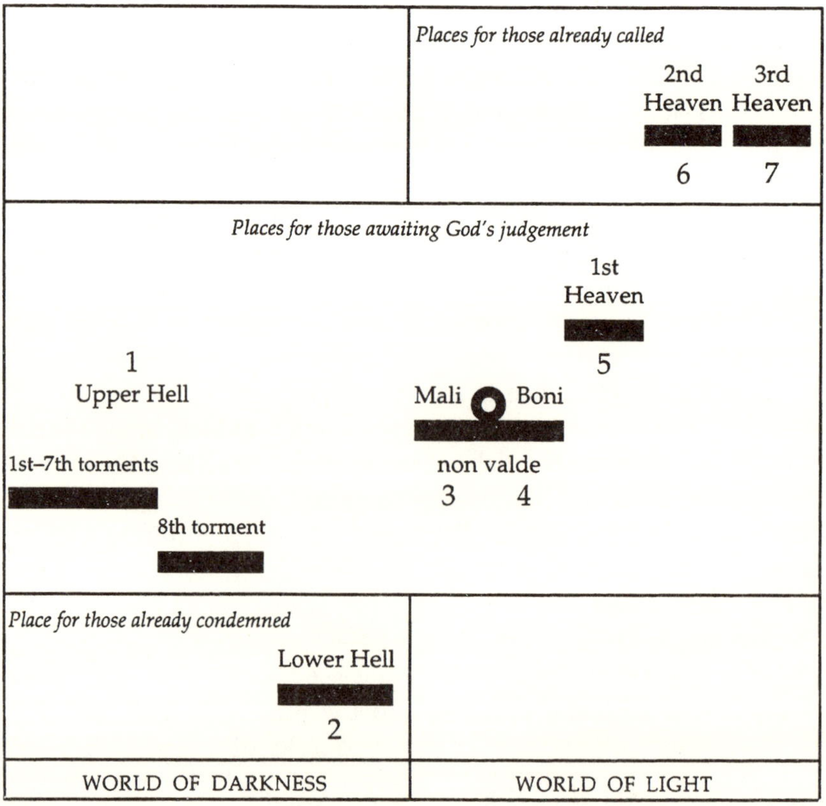

of Light, the three heavens of St Paul are covered in seven chapters, while four chapters are allotted to the *mali non valde* and the *boni non valde*.

This cosmic quality and idea of totality is also expressed through the twenty-four chapters which cover the vision from Tnugdal's entry into the other world to his departure from it; and it is further conveyed by the composition of the text in twenty-seven parts. Twenty-seven is the number of days in the sidereal period of the moon and seems to have had considerable significance in Ireland.[44] In the *Voyage of Bran*, for example, Bran sets out with three companies of nine. When they arrive at the house in the Land of the Women, they find three times nine couches, one for each couple.[45] Marcus may therefore be seen as the leader who guides the reader through his twenty-seven chapters as Bran led his three companies of nine. Macrobius in his *Commentary* (II. 8–19) explains the construction of the World-soul as the combination of the progression 1–2–4–8 (point, line, square, cube), which represents the tangible world, with the equivalent progression 1–3–9–27, representing the intangible.

In the *Vision of Tnugdal* there is a definite emphasis on the importance of transitional space and time, not only because Tnugdal has his vision while in a coma or because it occurs at the time of Samain,[46] but also because of the whole structure of the text. A binary other world was usually represented as a place for the bad and a place for the good, with a binary gradation inside each of these two divisions relating to evil or goodness, as is seen in the *Vision of Drycthelm*. The binary structure of the *Vision of Tnugdal* is created in relation to darkness versus light. This gives Marcus the opportunity to place a section of the wicked (the *mali non valde*) inside the World of Light, while the actual division between wicked and good is the wall with a gate in it surrounding the *campus laetitiae*. Indeed the place of the *mali non valde* is a "real" transitional space. These are souls who led a rigorous and virtuous life, "but they did not give worldly goods generously to the poor as was their duty." Not subject to darkness, or a horrible stench, or torturing devils, they suffer only from hunger, thirst, the wind and the rain. After some years, "they will be brought to a good resting place." Thus they will pass through the gate which leads into the *campus laetitiae*.[47]

Many critics have identified the place of the *mali non valde* as Purgatory, but there is no justification for this in the text. As in the

Vision of Drycthelm, however, the various places in Marcus's other world are associated either with eternity or with a transitional time which will last until the Day of Judgement. Thus the places fall into three groups: lower Hell accommodates those who are already judged and will remain there for ever; the enclosures of gold and of precious stones accommodate those who are already called by God and will remain there for ever; and an intermediate area includes upper Hell, the zones of the *mali non valde* and the *boni non valde*, and the enclosure of silver, which contains faithfully married people. (The occupants of all these places must wait for God's decision at Doomsday.) This intermediate state embraces eleven kinds of souls—eight types of sinners in upper Hell plus the *mali non valde*, the *boni non valde* and the faithfully married people. It is given a great deal of space in the text (twice as much as lower Hell and the two highest parts of Heaven). This enlargement of the state of those who must wait until Doomsday to go to their definitive abode seems to have come from a particular awareness of a proportion between sins committed and what, as seen in Irish Penitentials, must redeem them.[48]

Another interesting feature of the *Vision of Tnugdal* is the complexity of transitional space in the structure of Marcus's other world. In the World of Darkness there are two references to descending: one before the last torment of upper Hell (that is, the eighth torment) and one after. The eighth torment is thus isolated as the lowest of upper Hell and as almost pertaining to lower Hell. But in the eighth torment sinners are not definitively condemned to Hell. Conversely, the faithfully married people, in their place which is like Paradise—though there is a still better Paradise to graduate to at Doomsday—, are encountered between two references to ascending. The eighth torment and the enclosure of silver are the two extremes of the state of the souls who will move on to their definitive abode at Doomsday. The cosmic centre, the point of communication, is the gate in the wall of the *campus laetitiae* between the *mali non valde*, who stand outside, and the *boni non valde*, who are inside.

This type of structure reminds one of the mythic importance in early Irish literature of transitional space and time, and also of structures focusing on the cosmic centre. Ireland (which Marcus describes at the beginning of his introduction) was divided into two parts, a northern half and a southern half, besides which it was and still is divided into four provinces. But the Irish word for "province" (*coiced*) means "a fifth". According to one tradition the fifth province was Meath (Mide), "the Middle". Uisnech, the navel of Ireland, the cosmic centre, was also the cosmic boundary, since at that point the five provinces met. There is no doubt that Marcus tries to give a cosmic dimension to his other world in the manner of the Celtic tradition, in which transitional time and boundary areas were integral to the pattern of religious and social thinking.[49]

The cosmic quality of Dante's *Commedia* has long been recognized as being achieved partly through number symbolism. It is well known that the *Commedia* consists of 100 *canti* grouped into three *cantiche*. If, according to Pythagorean tradition, ten (1 + 2 + 3 + 4) is the perfect number, then ten squared is the height of perfection. Besides, numbers also have a geometric form. Ten in the Pythagorean tradition is a triangular number, and for Hugh of St Victor (who died in 1142) one hundred represents the square.[50] Thus Dante symbolically combines a quaternary and a ternary structure in his *Commedia*.

After the introductory canto, each part consists of thirty-three *canti* (that is, three times eleven, a number which reminds us of the number of chapters devoted to each part of Marcus's other world). Thirty-three also symbolizes totality because it is associated with the age at which Christ died.

A comparison between the *Commedia* and the *Vision of Tnugdal* proves to be a worthwhile exercise. The most striking feature of the *Vision* is its very precise references to either descending or ascending movements. These references, as has been pointed out, articulate a transitional space and underlie the sense of Tnugdal's progress, as well as giving an architectural quality to the structure. The same is noticeable in Dante. In accordance with the binary tradition, Dante's Hell is divided into two parts—an upper Hell accommodating sinners who sinned through thoughtlessness and a lower Hell for sinners who practised evil deliberately. This is marked in *Inferno* xi by a long description of the deep abyss which opens at Dante's feet and the horrible stench which comes out of it. Traditionally the number of Hell's torments was eleven or nine.[51] Both numbers, according to Hugh of St Victor,[52] can signify sin and lack of perfection: "Nine within ten, signifies defect within perfection (a 'falling short'), eleven beyond ten, transgression of the measure (of the ten commandments)."[53] In eleven chapters the *Vision of Tnugdal* combines nine torments, that is, the eight torments of upper Hell plus lower Hell as a whole. Dante's Hell has nine circles, and the structure of Hell is described in *Inferno* XI. Moreover the description of the Prince of Darkness at the bottom of Dante's Hell may well be inspired by the beast on the frozen lake in the *Vision of Tnugdal*.[54]

Strictly speaking, it is not legitimate to speak of Purgatory in the *Vision of Tnugdal*, since the word is never used. The intermediate function of Purgatory, however, as at worst a place of torment and at best a happy place of waiting until Doomsday, is expressed by four places (upper Hell, the places of the *mali non valde* and the *boni non valde*, and the enclosure of silver), which contain a total of eleven kinds of souls. Dante's Purgatory is divided into two parts: a place of expiation and the Earthly Paradise. Although these two places are now closely linked to each other, Dante nevertheless respects the tradition of an intermediate place having both hellish and paradisal features. *Purgatorio* also has four parts: the place of arrival at the foot of the mountain on the island shore; Ante-purgatory, on the lower part of the mountain, accommodating four groups of sinners; Purgatory proper, on the upper part of the mountain, with seven kinds of sinners; and the Terrestrial Paradise on the top of the mountain. Altogether there are eleven places for sinners awaiting or going through a process of purification. As in Marcus's scheme, the two middle places are linked by a gate.

In the *Vision of Tnugdal* the description of the places which are associated with good people, from the *boni non valde* upwards, is covered by ten chapters. But Paradise is associated with the three enclosures made of walls of different richness, though the first of these is more precisely an Earthly Paradise, since the souls of faithfully married people are waiting there to go to a higher place at Doomsday. The two other enclosures are quite separate from the first. Although of different kinds and degrees of richness, they are situated on the same horizontal level as each other. When Tnugdal enters the second of the three enclosures, that is, in the twenty-second chapter of the *Vision*, he sees the whole universe and the earth below. Dante's Paradise has ten spheres, though there is a binary division between, on the one hand, the nine finite spheres, which constitute a sort of Ante-paradise characterized by temporary arrangements, and, on the other, the infinite sphere or Empyrean, the true Paradise, which stands outside time as the eternal home of God and all the souls of the blessed. But Dante's Heaven also has three divisons, since the first nine heavens are customarily sub-divided into, firstly, the seven planetary spheres, associated with seven categories of blessed souls, and secondly, the two remaining finite spheres—the Heaven of the Fixed Stars and the Primum Mobile. As soon as Dante has ascended the ladder leading him to the second of these three divisons of Paradise, he too has a view of the earth, which occurs in the twenty-second canto of *Paradiso* (XXII. 124–53). He has another view of the earth in Canto XXVII (lines 76–87), where he is still in the second of the three divisions.

In the light of this comparison it does not seem unreasonable to suggest that the backbone or the tectonic structure of the *Commedia* could have been inspired by the *Vision of Tnugdal*, combined with the influence of the *Tractatus*. Dante took the structure of the other world already enlarged by Marcus a step further. To the ternary model more or less implied in the fourfold division of the other world he gave a life of its own. Both the *Tractatus* and the *Vision of Tnugdal* were circulating in continental Europe as early as the beginning of the thirteenth century. The *Vision of Tnugdal* radiated from Germany while the *Tractatus* was spread from England to the Continent by the French. Given the links which existed at that time between Germany, France and Italy, and also the established contacts between Italy and Ireland, these texts may have been known in Italy in the thirteenth century. Before 1264 Jacobus de Varagine had included an adaptation of the *Tractatus* in the chapter of his *Golden Legend* devoted to St Patrick.[55] And the representation of St Patrick's Purgatory in a fresco in Todi, painted in 1346, incorporates elements appropriated from the *Vision of Tnugdal*.[56]

One may speak neither of a "birth of Purgatory" nor of a sudden change in the topography of the other world. By and large, medieval thought and art were embedded in tradition and created from inside that tradition. Purgatory as such is thus the result of an evolution from which Celtic influence may not be excluded. This evolution is, on the one hand, a structural development which accompanies the great architecture of stones, words and thoughts of that time. On the other hand, although prompted by a growing importance of individualism—reflected by an emphasis on individual salvation—Purgatory also represents a limit to individualism, with a heavy price to be paid in the beyond for indulging in pleasure in this world.

NOTES

1. J. Le Goff, *La Naissance du Purgatoire* (Paris, Gallimard, 1981). In this essay quotations are drawn from the English translation by Arthur Goldhammer, *The Birth of Purgatory* (London, Scolar Press; Chicago, University of Chicago Press, 1984). The book is divided into three parts. The first, "The Hereafter before Purgatory", deals with the period between the remote origins and the end of the eleventh century. The second part is entitled "The Birth of Purgatory" and deals with the twelfth century. The last, "The Triumph of Purgatory", ends with Dante's *Commedia*.
2. J. Le Goff, *The Birth of Purgatory*, p. 115.
3. A. H. Bredero, in "Le Moyen Age et le Purgatoire", *Revue d'histoire ecclésiastique*, 78 (1983), 429–52, challenges this division, stressing that such oppositions are not absolute. He mentions the intermediate category between clergy and laity, "qui, déjà à l'époque carolingienne, jouait un rôle important, à savoir les religieux non clercs ou religieux laïcs" (p. 441).
4. J. Le Goff, *The Birth of Purgatory*, pp. 226–27.
5. R. W. Southern, "Between Heaven and Hell", *Times Literary Supplement*, 4133 (18 June 1982), 651–52. The quotation is from p. 652, col. 4.
6. See A. H. Bredero, "Le Moyen Age et le Purgatoire", pp. 432–45.
7. A. J. Gurevich, "Popular and Scholarly Medieval Cultural Traditions: Notes in the Margin of Jacques Le Goff's Book", *Journal of Medieval History*, 9 (1983), 71–90 (p. 79, col.1). See *Othloni Liber Visionum* (*Pat. Lat.*, CXLVI, cols 341–88), cols 359, 368, 372. See also E. Mégier, "Deux Exemples de 'prépurgatoire' chez les historiens: à propos de *La Naissance du Purgatoire* de Jacques Le Goff", *Cahiers de civilisation médiévale*, 28 (1985), 45–62. Mégier compares Otto of Freising's tripartite topography of the beyond and his tripartite differentiation of the dead with the other world (particularly the *familia Herlichini*) represented in the vision of Galchelin in Orderic Vitalis's ecclesiastical history. He suggests that the influence of popular tradition should be borne in mind when one studies the birth of Purgatory.
8. For the Latin text, see K. Warnke, *Das Buch vom "Espurgatoire S. Patrice" der Marie de France und seine Quelle* (Halle-Saale, Niemeyer, 1938; reprinted Geneva, Slatkine, 1976). An English translation of the longer version of the *Tractatus* may be found in *Saint Patrick's Purgatory: A Twelfth-century Tale of a Journey to the Other World*, translated by J-M. Picard with an introduction by Y. de Pontfarcy (Dublin, Four Courts, 1985), pp. 41–78.
9. J. Le Goff, *The Birth of Purgatory*, p. 193.
10. R. Easting, "Purgatory and the Earthly Paradise in the *Tractatus de Purgatorio Sancti Patricii*", *Cîteaux*, 37 (1986), 23–48 (p. 27 n. 16).
11. The first of these is contained in the opening sentence of the prologue: "Iussistis, pater venerande, ut scriptum vobis mitterem, quod de Purgatorio in vestra me retuli audisse presentia" (K. Warnke, *Das Buch vom "Espurgatoire S. Patrice"*, p. 2; *St Patrick's Purgatory*, p. 43). The second occurs when Owein is welcomed into the other world by fifteen messengers, one of whom says to him: "Et quoniam ad Purgatorium venisti ut a peccatis tuis purgeris [...]" (K. Warnke, *Das Buch vom "Espurgatoire S. Patrice"*, p. 52; *St Patrick's Purgatory*, p. 54).

12 See K. Warnke, *Das Buch vom "Espurgatoire S. Patrice"*, pp. 124, 126; *St Patrick's Purgatory*, pp. 68–69.
13 See K. Warnke, *Das Buch vom "Espurgatoire S. Patrice"*, p. 122; *St Patrick's Purgatory*, p. 68.
14 See Y. de Pontfarcy, "The Historical Background to the Pilgrimage to Lough Derg", in *The Medieval Pilgrimage to St Patrick's Purgatory: Lough Derg and the European Tradition*, edited by M. Haren and Y. de Pontfarcy (Enniskillen, Clogher Historical Society, 1988), pp. 7–34 (pp. 12–15).
15 *St Patrick's Purgatory*, p. 47.
16 On the dating of the *Tractatus* see Y. de Pontfarcy, "Le *Tractatus de Purgatorio Sancti Patricii* de H. de Saltrey, sa date et ses sources", *Peritia: Journal of the Medieval Academy of Ireland*, 3 (1984), 460–80 (pp. 461–63). The first recension of Giraldus's *Topographia* was translated into English (as *The First Version of the Topography of Ireland*) by J. J. O'Meara (Dundalk, Dundalgan, 1951; revised edition [*The History and Topography of Ireland*] published by the Dolmen Press, Mountrath, Portlaoise and the Humanities Press, Atlantic Heights, New Jersey, 1982); the description of the lake in Ulster is in Chapter 38.
17 See *The Tripartite Life of Patrick with Other Documents Relating to That Saint*, edited and translated by W. Stokes, 2 vols = *Rerum Britannicarum Medii Aevi Scriptores* (Rolls Series), LXXXIX (London, Eyre and Spottiswoode, 1887), I, 112–21.
18 See Jocelin of Furness, *The Life and Acts of Saint Patrick*, translated by E. L. Swift (Dublin, Hibernia, 1809), pp. 189–90. Translation revised.
19 See Y. de Pontfarcy, "The Historical Background", pp. 30–34.
20 See my edition and translation of this text in the Collection Ktêmata (Louvain–Paris, Peeters, 1995), p. 84.
21 See *Oeuvres de Saint Augustin, IX: Exposés généraux de la foi*, edited and translated by J. Rivière (Paris, Desclée and de Brouwer, 1947), pp. 302–05. For the English translation: *A Select Library of the Nicene and Post-Nicene Fathers of the Christian Church* [first series], edited by P. Schaff (Buffalo/New York, Christian Literature Company, 1886–90), III, 272–73.
22 J. Le Goff, *The Birth of Purgatory*, p. 221.
23 Bede, *A History of the English Church and People*, translated by L. Sherley-Price (Harmondsworth, Penguin, 1955), pp. 284–89.
24 Bede, *A History of the English Church and People*, p. 287.
25 J. Le Goff, *The Birth of Purgatory*, pp. 115–16.
26 J. Le Goff, *The Birth of Purgatory*, p. 103.
27 *The Writings of Bishop Patrick, 1074–1084*, edited and translated by A. Gwynn = *Scriptores Latini Hiberniae*, I (Dublin, Dublin Institute for Advanced Studies, 1955), p. 20.
28 St J. D. Seymour, "The Eschatology of the Early Irish Church", *Zeitschrift für celtische Philologie*, 14 (1923), 179–211 (pp. 193, 197).
29 See Robert Easting's *mise-au-point* in his "Purgatory and the Earthly Paradise", pp. 29–34.
30 See K. Warnke, *Das Buch vom "Espurgatoire S. Patrice"*, p. 10; *St Patrick's Purgatory*, pp. 44–45.
31 See R. Easting, "Purgatory and the Earthly Paradise", p. 31. Easting believes that the fate of the last group is unusual. But Hugh of St Victor is only trying to illustrate what St Augustine said about a moderate form of damnation for some of the *non valde mali*.

32 See *St Patrick's Purgatory*, p. 69.
33 One is reminded of the short treatise by Patrick, second bishop of Dublin (1074–84), entitled *Liber de Tribus Habitaculis Animae*, a work which was given "a very friendly reception in English monastic communities". (Bishop Patrick had previously been a Benedictine monk, trained in the school of St Wulfstan in Worcester: see *The Writings of Bishop Patrick*, pp. 6, 14). In this treatise the intermediate place has features of Heaven and Hell and is situated in this world: "Tria sunt sub omnipotentis Dei manu habitacula: primum, imum, medium. Quorum summum regnum Dei vel regnum celorum dicitur: imum vocatur infernus: medium mundus presens vel orbis terrarum appellatur. Quorum extrema omnino sibi invicem sunt contraria et nulla sibi societate coniuncta. [...] Medium autem nonnullam habet similitudinem ad extrema" (*The Writings of Bishop Patrick*, p. 106).
34 See also P. Cherchi, "Gervase of Tilbury and the Birth of Purgatory", *Medioevo romanzo*, 14 (1989), 97–110 (p. 108) for the alternation of day and night in Purgatory.
35 "Unde tantam delectationis dulcedinem in corde et corpore sensit ut pene pre nimietate dulcedinis non intellexerit utrum vivus an mortuus fuisset" (K. Warnke, *Das Buch vom "Espurgatoire S. Patrice"*, pp. 130–31; *St Patrick's Purgatory*, p. 70).
36 "Eya, frater, nunc scimus, quoniam per tormenta que sustinens viriliter vicisti, ab omnibus peccatis tuis purgatus es" (K. Warnke, *Das Buch vom "Espurgatoire S. Patrice"*, pp. 136–38; *St Patrick's Purgatory*, p. 71).
37 *Visio Tnugdali, lateinisch und altdeutsch*, edited by A. Wagner (Erlangen, Deichert, 1882); *The Vision of Tnugdal*, translated by J-M. Picard, with an introduction by Y. de Pontfarcy (Dublin, Four Courts, 1989).
38 C. S. Boswell, *An Irish Precursor of Dante: A Study on the Vision of Heaven and Hell Ascribed to the Eighth-century Irish Saint Adamnán, with Translation of the Irish Text* (London, Nutt, 1908), pp. 226–29. For example, Dante and Tnugdal both have frequent recourse to their guides; Dante and Marcus both mention incidents of contemporary history; Marcus, in giving the name Acheron to the beast in whose insides the misers are punished, introduces a classical element into Christian eschatology; Dante's Lucifer in the icy centre of Hell resembles Marcus's beast on the frozen lake; both Dante and Tnugdal in Paradise look downwards towards this world.
39 See also *The Vision of Tnugdal*, pp. 48–67.
40 See C. Butler, *Number Symbolism* (London, Routledge and Kegan Paul, 1970), pp. 27–28; J-C. Guy, *Unité et structure logique de la "Cité de Dieu" de saint Augustin* (Paris, Etudes Augustiniennes, 1961).
41 Macrobius, *Commentary on the Dream of Scipio*, translated by W. H. Stahl (New York, Columbia University Press, 1952), pp. 111–17; Martianus Capella, *The Marriage of Philology and Mercury*, translated by W. H. Stahl and R. Johnson = vol. II of *Martianus Capella and the Seven Liberal Arts*, 2 vols (New York, Columbia University Press, 1971–77), pp. 281–83.
42 St J. D. Seymour, "The Seven Heavens in Irish Literature", *Zeitschrift für celtische Philologie*, 14 (1923), 18–30.
43 See *The Vision of Tnugdal*, pp. 63–65.
44 See A. and B. Rees, *Celtic Heritage: Ancient Tradition in Ireland and Wales* (London, Thames and Hudson, 1961), pp. 192–95.

45 *Immram Brain: Bran's Journey to the Land of the Women*, edited by S. Mac Mathúna (Tübingen, Niemeyer, 1985), paragraphs 32 and 62 (pp. 38, 44, 51, 57).
46 Samain is the eve of 1 November (the beginning of the Celtic year), when the boundary between this world and the other world disappears. See my Introduction to *The Vision of Tnugdal*, pp. 22–24.
47 See *The Vision of Tnugdal*, p. 141.
48 See L. Bieler, *The Irish Penitentials*, with an appendix by D. A. Binchy = Scriptores Latini Hiberniae, v (Dublin, Institute for Advanced Studies, 1963).
49 See P. Ó Riain, "Boundary Association in Early Irish Society", *Studia Celtica*, 7 (1972), 12–29. Le Goff shows that he misunderstands this cultural background when he comments: "Tnugdal has made a clumsy attempt to organize a whole range of elements from literary and theological tradition into a vision that he is incapable of unifying. [...] The weakest point in Tnugdal's conception [...] is that Tnugdal does not establish any connection between the places of waiting (and expiation in one degree or another of severity) and the lower regions of Hell. If he had provided for passage first through the one and then through the other, he would have given a concrete solution to the issues raised by Augustine's categorization. He did not do so probably in part because his conception of space was still confused but, even more, because his conception of time did not allow a solution" (*The Birth of Purgatory*, p. 192). Le Goff is not assessing Marcus's work on its own terms.
50 Hugh of St Victor, *De Scripturis et Scriptoribus Sacris Prenotatiunculae* (Pat. Lat., CLXXV, cols 9–28), xv (col. 22). See also G. Beaujouan, "Le Symbolisme des nombres à l'époque romane", *Cahiers de civilisation médiévale*, 4 (1961), 159–69 (p. 162).
51 E. J. Becker, *A Contribution to the Comparative Study of the Medieval Visions of Heaven and Hell, with Special Reference to the Middle-English Versions* (Baltimore, Murphy, 1899), p. 30.
52 Hugh of St Victor, *De Scripturis et Scriptoribus Sacris*, xv (cols 22–23).
53 C. Butler, *Number Symbolism*, pp. 29–30.
54 See J-M. Picard, "*Inferno*, v. 73–142: The Irish Sequel", in this volume, pp. 271–86 (pp. 273–74).
55 *Jacobi a Voragine Legenda Aurea*, edited by T. Graesse [1845/1890] (Osnabrück, Zeller, 1969), pp. 213–16; Jacobus de Voragine, *The Golden Legend*, translated by W. Granger Ryan, 2 vols (Princeton, Princeton University Press, 1993), I, 193–96.
56 See J-M. Picard, "The Italian Pilgrims", in *The Medieval Pilgrimage to St Patrick's Purgatory*, pp. 169–89 (pp. 169–73) and the reproduction of the fresco at the end of that book; J-M. Picard, "*Inferno*, v. 73–142: The Irish Sequel", pp. 275–76 and n. 7 on p. 284.

PARADISO VII: MARKING THE DIFFERENCE BETWEEN DANTE AND ANSELM

Christopher Ryan

The distinguished Anselmian scholar F. S. Schmitt in his entry on Anselm in the *Enciclopedia dantesca*, after summarizing the account of the redemption given by Beatrice in *Paradiso*, VII. 19–120, comments: "Dante's exposition of the redemption is in its essential features a concise reproduction of Anselm's doctrine of satisfaction, as the latter had expounded it in *Cur Deus Homo*." He goes on to express the conviction that Dante based his exposition directly on Anselm's work; he holds this view not just because of verbal echoes he believes are present in *Paradiso* VII: "It is above all the affinity of content between the two expositions which banishes all doubt about the direct dependence of the one upon the other." To these assertions of identity in substance he adds a mild qualification: "In both Anselm and Dante the exposition of the doctrine of vicarious satisfaction starts from the doubt as to why God chose this particular means for the redemption. In the answer to this question—despite the identity of the content—a slight difference in mode of argumentation emerges. Anselm, with *a priori* argumentation, proves the necessity of the Incarnation; now Dante says 'convenia' ['it was fitting'] (line 103), whereas Anselm has 'oportet', 'necesse est' ['it is necessary']."[1] Schmitt's principal contention, that Dante's and Anselm's accounts are linked by substantial identity, is, I believe, seriously misleading; and to speak of what separates them as being "a slight difference" is quite inadequate.

What is of greater concern is that Schmitt's attribution of such a close degree of accord between Dante and Anselm is no isolated case. Quite the contrary: the settled view of Dante scholars who consider the relation between *Paradiso* VII and *Cur Deus Homo* seems to be much the same as that of Schmitt. Thus, for instance, the still influential commentary of Scartazzini–Vandelli, after its introductory summary of *Paradiso*, VII. 52–120, claims: "This doctrine conforms to that expounded by Anselm of Canterbury in the famous treatise *Cur Deus Homo*; and it is the doctrine of the Church."[2] Padoan, in an article published during the seventh centenary of Dante's birth, states that the substantial agreement between Dante and Anselm is a generally accepted fact among Dante scholars: "These days it is an established critical opinion that Dante substantially repeats here the arguments previously adduced by St Anselm in his treatise *Cur Deus Homo*, which is fundamental on this problem."[3] More recently, Giovanni Reggio in his commentary speaks in terms very similar to those of Scartazzini in an earlier era. Discussing Dante's treatment of the question of why God had chosen to redeem through the Incarnation, he declares: "It was a problem debated by the theologians and Church Fathers. The solution that Dante gives here is that expounded by St Anselm of Aosta in his famous treatise *Cur Deus Homo*, which was subsequently accepted by the Church."[4] And in one of the weightiest recent studies of Dante's theology and its sources Di Zenzo writes: "Anselm's doctrine underlies *Paradiso*, VI. 82–93 and is developed in *Paradiso*, VII. 49–120. In its essential features Dante's exposition is a concise reproduction of the doctrine expounded by Anselm in his *Cur Deus Homo*."[5] Even Torraca, who is sometimes cited as a lone voice with reservations about the affinity between *Paradiso* VII and *Cur Deus Homo*,[6] in fact accepted that "of course this dialogue by St Anselm [*Cur Deus Homo*] contains arguments similar to those used by Dante." His hesitation concerned rather the direct dependence of *Paradiso* VII on Anselm's work; the passage just quoted continues, with reference to *Paradiso* VII: "but it does not seem to me that [*Cur Deus Homo*] is the direct source of this canto."[7]

The consensus among many Dante scholars is perhaps the less surprising in that the only reasonably lengthy study of the relationship between Dante and Anselm remains that of Alberto Agresti, published in 1887.[8] There the author attempts principally to show that Dante's vocabulary in *Paradiso* VII is such that it shows that the poet had direct knowledge of Anselmian texts, especially *Cur Deus Homo*.[9] At no point does Agresti indicate that there was any disagreement in content between Dante and Anselm. It is particularly important to note that when arguing that Dante's use of *sodisfare* reflects familiarity with Anselm's use of *satisfacere* (and its cognates) in *Cur Deus Homo*, Agresti refers to passages where

Anselm claims that the Incarnation was absolutely necessary for the redemption of man, without suggesting that Dante's view might in any way differ from the views of Anselm.[10]

As several of the authors cited above rightly indicate, Anselm's *Cur Deus Homo* played a fundamental role in shaping the doctrine of the Western Church on the redemption. It is a curious fact that while the official church in the form of ecumenical councils in the patristic period pronounced on the nature of God and the nature (more precisely, natures) of the God-man, Christ, it made no comparable statement on the nature of redemption or salvation, even though it could be argued that this was the question which lay behind the other, more purely theological, disputes.[11] Be that as it may, at the dawn of the scholastic period there was no single accepted doctrine of soteriology (salvation); there were a number of competing theories, but no official doctrine, not even one dominant theory.[12] Anselm in part filled that notable lacuna with his work on the motive of the Incarnation, with its brilliantly direct title: *Cur Deus Homo*.[13]

The argument of that treatise, despite the complexity of its working-out in detail, can be fairly quickly summarized. In general, Book I describes an impasse brought about by the sinful condition of mankind; Book II indicates the only way in which that impasse can be broken, namely, through the initiative of God in bringing about the Incarnation.[14] Specifically, Book I describes the following impasse. On the one hand, the human race desires happiness from God, but, *as sinful*, cannot obtain that happiness unless two conditions be met: (*i*) that recompense be made to God for the infinitely horrendous fact of sin;[15] (*ii*) that the recompense in question be made by a human being, a member of the sinful race.[16] On the other hand, no human being can in fact make adequate recompense to God, since (*a*) recompense of its very nature involves offering something not already owed to the person offended, but every human being simply as a creature already owes everything to God;[17] and (*b*) adequate recompense must be comparable to the value of the person offended, but the human being as finite cannot in the nature of the case offer such recompense to the infinite God.[18] The result is, in purely human terms, an insoluble impasse: to attain happiness the human race must make a recompense it cannot in fact make.

Book II opens with the declaration that this impasse cannot remain unresolved, since God in creating the human race willed that its members should attain happiness with Him, and God's will cannot be frustrated.[19] But the impasse can be broken only if God brings it about that there is a being who has two natures: human (for the reasons given) and divine, so that he may offer to God some "thing" that is not already owed to Him as creator and that this offering be of infinite value, as coming from a being who is infinite.[20] It follows necessarily that someone who is both God and man must exist, to make adequate recompense to God and offer the possibility of happiness to mankind. The central claim of Christianity regarding Christ must, therefore, be true.

I cannot concern myself here with the details of Anselm's argument, and shall limit myself to two comments. First, Anselm's theory of salvation has the merit of great simplicity in its basic line of argument, and one imagines that the simplicity of his scheme was one of the main reasons for its subsequent widespread acceptance; second, this theory has come down in theological history as the theory of adequate satisfaction—a description which aptly catches the essential logic: enough must be done to balance, make up for, the infinite offence given to God; only Christ as God-man could offer such satisfaction; therefore... Anselm's concluding words in Chapter 6 of the second book may serve to indicate both the tenor and the essential logic of the work:

> If then, as is certain, that celestial city must be completed from among men, and this cannot happen unless the aforesaid satisfaction is made, while no one save God can make it and no one save man ought to make it, it is necessary for a God-man to make it.[21]

To those familiar with Beatrice's discourse in *Paradiso* VII (it is in fact her longest single speech in the *Commedia*) it will already be clear that there is considerable affinity between Anselm's position in *Cur Deus Homo* and the views espoused in that canto by Dante via Beatrice. Above all, the idea that adequate satisfaction can be rendered to God only by the God-man is stated with admirable clarity. Beatrice first resolves Dante the pilgrim's puzzlement at Justinian's statement that the destruction of Jerusalem involved punishment of the just vengeance of the Cross.[22] She does so by referring to human nature's sinning in Adam and then to the acceptance of that nature by the Word of God. She goes on to comment regarding the problem disturbing Dante:

> La pena dunque che la croce porse
> s'a la natura assunta si misura,
> nulla già mai sí giustamente morse;
>   e cosí nulla fu di tanta ingiura,
> guardando a la persona che sofferse,
> in che era contratta tal natura.
> (lines 40–45)

> [The penalty therefore which the Cross inflicted, if it be measured by the nature assumed—none ever so justly stung; also none was ever of such great wrong, if we regard the Person who suffered it, with whom that nature was bound up.]

Dante's curiosity is satisfied on one score only to be roused on another, a puzzlement which Beatrice articulates for him in these words:

> Ben discerno ciò ch'i' odo;
> ma perché Dio volesse, m'è occulto,
> a nostra redenzion pur questo modo.
> (lines 55–57)

> [I follow clearly what I hear, but why God willed this sole way for our redemption is hidden from me.]

The theory of adequate satisfaction is put forward by Beatrice in her reply to Dante's question, as, for example, when she states:

> Solo il peccato è quel che la disfranca
> e falla dissimíle al sommo bene,
> per che del lume suo poco s'imbianca;
>   e in sua dignità mai non rivene,
> se non rïempie, dove colpa vòta,
> contra mal dilettar con giuste pene.
> (lines 79–84)

> [Sin alone is that which disfranchises it and makes it unlike the Supreme Good, so that it is little illumined by Its light; and to its dignity it never returns unless, where fault has emptied, it fill up with just penalties against evil delight.]

Shortly thereafter she says in a similar vein:

> Non potea l'uomo ne' termini suoi
> mai sodisfar, per non potere ir giuso
> con umiltate obediendo poi,
> quanto disobediendo intese ir suso;
> e questa è la cagion per che l'uom fue
> da poter sodisfar per sé dischiuso.
>
> (lines 97–102)

[Man, within his own limits, could never make satisfaction, for not being able to descend in humility, by subsequent obedience, so far as in his disobedience he had intended to ascend; and this is the reason why man was shut off from power to make satisfaction by himself.]

However, what I wish particularly to draw attention to in this essay is that, despite the obvious similarity between Dante's view in *Paradiso* VII and that of Anselm in *Cur Deus Homo*, the perspectives from which the two writers present the Incarnation and redemption in fact significantly differ. The differences are so marked, I shall argue, as to make it incorrect to speak of *Paradiso* VII and Anselm's treatise as being identical in content, or to say that this canto is a concise representation of the doctrine found in Anselm's treatise. The position adopted here may be summarized as follows. Dante certainly incorporated the satisfaction theory of Anselm into his view of the motive of the Incarnation, but the framework within which that theory is accepted substantially modifies the role played by satisfaction. The nub of the difference is this: for Anselm adequate satisfaction to God was absolutely necessary for redemption, and hence the Incarnation was necessary for redemption; for Dante, by contrast, the rendering of adequate satisfaction was not necessary and neither, consequently, was the Incarnation. A second difference, connected with the first, is that for Anselm the main emphasis is on justice: the Incarnation was necessary because the demands of justice had to be fulfilled. For Dante, on the other hand, the principal emphasis is on love: God chose the Incarnation out of generous love, and *thereby* enabled the demands of justice to be fulfilled; but, in Dante's view, God was not compelled to fulfil the demands of justice, nor therefore compelled to bring about the Incarnation. Let us look again at the two works.

The first and major point to note about *Cur Deus Homo* is that the *necessity* of the Incarnation is integral to that work. Anselm makes this clear from the outset. He gives a summary of the work in the preface, which is worth quoting at some length:

> I have named [this work] *Why God Became Man,* from the theme on which it was written, and I have divided it into two short books. The first of these contains the objections of unbelievers who reject the Christian faith because they regard it as contrary to reason, along with the answers of believers. It ends by proving by necessary reasons (Christ being put out of sight, as if nothing had ever been known of him) that it is impossible for any man to be saved without him. In the same way, as if nothing were known of Christ, it is shown in the second book, by equally clear reasoning and truth, that human nature was created in order that hereafter the whole man, body and soul, should enjoy a blessed immortality. It is proved that it is necessary for this purpose for which man was made to be achieved, but only through a Man-God, and so that all the things we believe concerning Christ must necessarily take place.[23]

In Book I, Chapter 4, Anselm's interlocutor Boso goes out of his way to draw attention to the fact that Anselm must prove as a matter of necessity the existence of the God-man, otherwise unbelievers, to whom the work is in part directed, will regard his arguments as simply "beautiful things", mere "pictures":

> Now when we [Christians] present unbelievers with these harmonies you speak of, as so many pictures of a real event, they think that this belief of ours is a fiction, and not a real happening, and so they judge that we are, as it were, painting on a cloud. Thus the rational soundness of the truth—that is, the necessity which proves that it was fitting and possible for God to condescend to the things which we proclaim—must first be shown.[24]

The theme of necessity runs like a leitmotiv through the work.

The further point that justice is central to Anselm's argument also makes its appearance throughout the work. The centrality of justice is perhaps most clearly apparent in a chapter which also deals directly with the necessity of the Incarnation, Chapter 13 of Book I. The theme of the chapter is stated at its outset:

> ANSELM Nothing is less tolerable in the order of things, than for the creature to take away the honour due to the Creator and not repay what he takes away.

BOSO   Nothing is clearer than this.

ANSELM   But nothing is more unjustly tolerated than that which is most intolerable.[25]

Anselm goes on to argue (to Boso's entire satisfaction) that what is most important to God is that His honour be served:

ANSELM   Again, if nothing is greater or better than God, then the highest justice, which is none other than God himself, maintains nothing more justly than his honour, in the ordering of things.
BOSO   Nothing can be plainer than this.
ANSELM   Then God maintains nothing more justly than the honour of his dignity.
BOSO   I must grant this.[26]

Anselm concludes that it is absolutely necessary either that God's honour should be restored or that man should be punished: "Therefore, either the honour that was taken away must be repaid or punishment must follow. Otherwise, God will be either unjust to himself or powerless to accomplish either; but it is impious even to imagine this."[27]

Before going on to look again at the *Commedia*, we should recall that Anselm expressly rejected the idea that God could have restored man to righteousness simply by mercy, merely by His *fiat*. This point is implied throughout Anselm's argument, but it is significant that he should have thought it important enough to merit direct consideration on several occasions. Indeed he does this at the beginning of the treatise. In Book I, Chapter 1 Anselm contrasts his view with views mooted by unbelievers and debated even by believers. He must answer the question "For what reason or necessity did God become man and, as we believe and confess, by his death restore life to the world?",[28] a view opposed to that which holds that God "could have done this through another person (angelic or human), or even by a sheer act of will".[29] The whole of Anselm's work is designed to show the contrary, that salvation could be achieved *only* by the God-man. The rejection of the final alternative just mentioned, that God might have restored man to life "by a sheer act of the will" is expressly made in Book I, Chapter 12. That chapter begins: "Let us go back and see whether it is fitting for God to remit sins by mercy alone, without any payment for the honour taken away from him."[30] Anselm goes on to deny that God could thus simply forgive sin. He does so first on the general ground that to do so would be to act unjustly, for the just treatment of sin is punishment:

> To remit sin in this way is the same thing as not to punish it. And since to deal rightly with sin without satisfaction is the same thing as to punish it, if it is not punished it is remitted irregularly.[31]

Later in the same chapter he argues in the same vein:

> Then injustice is more free than justice, if it is remitted by mercy alone, and this seems very incongruous. This incongruity reaches the point of making injustice resemble God, since injustice will be no more subject to anyone's law than God is.[32]

He then corroborates this point by comparing and linking to this punishment the punishment meted out on earth by rulers whose dignity has been offended: "For when earthly authorities do this rightly, God himself, who appointed them for this purpose, really does it."[33] Anselm concludes the chapter: "Therefore, if it is not fitting for God to do anything unjustly or without due order, it does not belong to his freedom or kindness or will to forgive unpunished the sinner who does not repay to God what he took away."[34]

We have already noted how Dante responds to Beatrice's reference to the Incarnation in the first part of her discourse, her explanation of why Titus's destruction of Jerusalem was a just vengeance:

> ma perché Dio volesse, m'è occulto,
> a nostra redenzion pur questo modo.
> (lines 56–57)

> [but why God willed this sole way for our redemption is hidden from me.]

His manner of posing this question appears to echo that of Anselm, who in Book I, Chapter 3 declares to Boso:

> Si enim diligenter considerarent quam convenienter hoc modo procurata sit humana restauratio, non deriderent nostram simplicitatem, sed Dei nobiscum laudarent sapientem benignitatem.[35]

[And if they would earnestly consider how fittingly the restoration of mankind was secured in this way, instead of laughing at our simplicity they would join us in praising the wise loving-kindness of God.]

I say *appears* to echo, because whereas Anselm immediately continues with "Oportebat namque..." ["For it was fitting..."], Dante's *volesse* immediately alerts us to the possibility that God could have willed the redemption in some way other than through the Incarnation.

The accuracy of that signal is fully confirmed by the opening words of Beatrice's reply to Dante's question. She at once takes us into a very different thought-world, a very different logic, from that which governs the unfolding of *Cur Deus Homo*. In one of the justly most famous tercets of the *Commedia*, she addresses Dante in tones of friendship, indicating that the reason behind God's decision to redeem mankind "in this way" (that is, through the Incarnation) can be understood only by those sufficiently adult to know what it means to act out of love:

> Questo decreto, frate, sta sepulto
> a li occhi di ciascuno il cui ingegno
> ne la fiamma d'amor non è adulto.
> (lines 58–60)

[This decree, brother, is buried from the eyes of everyone whose understanding is not matured within love's flame.]

It is, I think, fairly clear that there is an edge of challenge to these lines: Beatrice is implying that not everyone will understand because not everyone has been made adult by the flame of love. And the challenge is that this view of adulthood is the reverse of that commonly found in the world: to act out of love is often thought to be juvenile rather than adult. Dante is claiming that to have one's life and mind (*ingegno*, note, not *cuore*) not just touched but shaped by love, is to grow up. Dante is in fact now bringing to bear the meaning of love on the relationship of *God* to human beings, as he had, in the first two *cantiche*, spoken principally of human beings' love for each other (or lack thereof) and *their* love for God.

The element of option in God's bringing about the Incarnation, hinted at in the *volesse* of line 56, is referred to more explicitly in line

63, where Beatrice launches into her explanation proper, with the words: "Dirò perché tal modo fu piú degno" ["I shall tell why that way was the most fitting"]. She then returns, as we have seen, to the themes of man's creation and the fall. It is in summarizing the situation after the fall that Beatrice expressly declares (in fact *contra* Anselm) that God could simply have forgiven man's sin. Speaking of the gifts (*dignitadi*) which man had lost at the fall, she says of human nature:

> Né ricovrar potiensi, se tu badi
> ben sottilmente, per alcuna via,
> sanza passar per un di questi guadi:
>   o che Dio solo per sua cortesia
> dimesso avesse, o che l'uom per sé isso
> avesse sodisfatto a sua follia.
> (lines 88–93)

[Nor could it recover them, if you consider carefully, by any way except the passing of one of these fords: either that God alone, solely by His clemency, had pardoned; or that man should of himself have given satisfaction for his folly.]

She goes on to make the point, in true Anselmian fashion, that man could not of himself make the required satisfaction, since he could not abase himself to the extent to which he had tried to rise. It devolved, then, on God to reverse the effects of sin. The element of choice on God's part is patent:

> Dunque a Dio convenia con le vie sue
> riparar l'omo a sua intera vita,
> dico con l'una, o ver con amendue.
> (lines 103–05)

[Therefore it was needful for God, with His own ways, to restore man to his full life—I mean with one way, or else with both.]

This, then, is the first major point of difference between Anselm and Dante: where to the former the Incarnation was a matter of necessity for God, in the latter's account it resulted from God's free choice.

The second difference, implicit in the first, is that for Dante God's motive in bringing about the Incarnation was not, as it was for Anselm, exclusively justice, nor even primarily justice, but generosity. For Dante the demands of justice were fulfilled not because they absolutely had to be but because God in decreeing salvation through the Incarnation acted out of pure generosity, *and so* enabled man to fulfil the demands of justice. Let me quote in full the final section of Beatrice's discourse on the mode of redemption, before elaborating on one or two points:

> Ma perché l'ovra tanto è piú gradita
> da l'operante, quanto piú appresenta
> de la bontà del core ond' ell' è uscita,
>   la divina bontà che 'l mondo imprenta,
> di proceder per tutte le sue vie,
> a rilevarvi suso, fu contenta.
>   Né tra l'ultima notte e 'l primo die
> sí alto o sí magnifico processo,
> o per l'una o per l'altra, fu o fie:
>   ché piú largo fu Dio a dar sé stesso
> per far l'uom sufficiente a rilevarsi,
> che s'elli avesse sol da sé dimesso;
>   e tutti li altri modi erano scarsi
> a la giustizia, se 'l Figliuol di Dio
> non fosse umilïato ad incarnarsi.
> (lines 106–20)

[But because the deed is so much the more prized by the doer, the more it displays of the goodness of the heart whence it issued, the divine Goodness which puts its imprint on the world, was pleased to proceed by all Its ways to raise you up again; nor between the last night and the first day has there been or will there be so exalted and so magnificent a procedure, either by one or by the other; for God was more bounteous in giving Himself to make man sufficient to uplift himself again, than if He solely of Himself had remitted; and all other modes were scanty in respect to justice, if the Son of God had not humbled himself to become incarnate.]

A linguistic point may first be noted. The concluding word of line 117 picks up a use of *dimesso* earlier in the canto, where Beatrice speaks of the two ways open to God of restoring man after sin:

> o che Dio solo per sua cortesia
> dimesso avesse, o che l'uom per sé isso
> avesse sodisfatto a sua follia.
> (lines 91–93)

[either that God alone, solely by His clemency, had pardoned; or that man should of himself have given satisfaction for his folly.]

This word seems to point up the contrast between Dante and Anselm on the matter of choice, for the Latin root word, *dimittere*, is used several times by Anselm in Chapter 12 of Book I, where, as we have seen, he is intent on rejecting the idea that God could have restored man to righteousness simply by forgiveness: Anselm there denies what Dante will later assert. The chapter opens with Anselm putting the following question to Boso:

> Redeamus et videamus utrum sola misericordia, sine omni solutione ablati sibi honoris deceat Deum peccatum dimittere.

> [Let us go back and see whether it is fitting for God to remit sins by mercy alone, without any payment for the honour taken away from him.]

It is Boso's laconic response to that question (that he does not see why not)[36] which occasions the reply from Anselm quoted above:

> Sic dimittere peccatum non est aliud quam non punire. Et quoniam recte ordinare peccatum sine satisfactione non est nisi punire: si non punitur, inordinatum dimittitur.

> [To remit sin in this way is the same thing as not to punish it. And since to deal rightly with sin without satisfaction is the same thing as to punish it, if it is not punished it is remitted irregularly.]

Dimittere recurs several times in this chapter:

> Liberior igitur est injustitia, si sola misericordia dimittitur, quam justitia; [...]. Quapropter si non decet Deum aliquid injuste aut inordinate facere, non pertinet ad ejus libertatem aut benignitatem aut voluntatem, peccantem qui non solvit Deo quod abstulit impunitum dimittere.

> [Then injustice is more free than justice, if it is remitted by mercy alone, (...). Therefore, if it is not fitting for God to do anything unjustly or without due order, it does not belong to his freedom or kindness or will to forgive unpunished the sinner who does not repay to God what he took away.]

Secondly, and concentrating more directly on a substantive point, lines 106–20 of Canto VII bring out that what primarily moved God to bring about salvation through the Incarnation was not justice but goodness. Certainly the desire to see justice fulfilled was present, as the final lines expressly indicate:

> e tutti li altri modi erano scarsi
> a la giustizia, se 'l Figliuol di Dio
> non fosse umiliato ad incarnarsi.
> (lines 118–20)

[and all other modes were scanty in respect to justice, if the Son of God had not humbled himself to become incarnate.]

But what moved God to see justice fulfilled was not that justice compelled Him to act, nor even that considerations of justice were, so to speak, uppermost in His mind. What moved Him to bring about the Incarnation was, rather, that by ensuring that justice would be fulfilled He was acting *even more generously* than if He had simply forgiven sin, which clearly (for Dante) He could have done.

This is stated most succinctly in lines 115–17:

> ché piú largo fu Dio a dar sé stesso
> per far l'uom sufficiente a rilevarsi,
> che s'elli avesse sol da sé dimesso.

[for God was more bounteous in giving Himself to make man sufficient to uplift himself again, than if He solely of Himself had remitted.]

I would suggest, however, that the clearest, most interesting, and most characteristically Dantean lines describing God's goodness as the motive in decreeing the Incarnation are those which open the climax to the discourse. I recall them here:

> Ma perché l'ovra tanto è piú gradita
> da l'operante, quanto piú appresenta
> de la bontà del core ond' ell' è uscita,
>   la divina bontà che 'l mondo imprenta,
> di proceder per tutte le sue vie,
> a rilevarvi suso, fu contenta.
> (lines 106–11)

Goodness as the key motive is most obviously indicated in the repeated *bontà*: "la bontà del cuore [...], la divina bontà." But the characteristically Dantean touch is to be seen in his explanation of how goodness operates. The language is an interesting mixture of the courtly and the philosophical. The philosophical we see in the word *operante* (the agent, the one who acts), equivalent to the Latin *operans* or *agens*. The courtly is seen linguistically above all in *gradita* ("l'ovra tanto è piú gradita"), but also I think in *appresenta* ("quanto piú appresenta/de la bontà del core ond' ell' è uscita"). *Appresenta* I would translate here not just as "manifests" (Sinclair)[37] or "displays" (Singleton) but as "presents". Dante uses it in this sense in *Paradiso*, XXII. 131 (one of the three other *loci* in the *Commedia* where the word is used),[38] when Beatrice invites Dante to glance back at how far he has travelled,

> sí che 'l tuo cor, quantunque può, giocondo
> s'appresenti a la turba triünfante.
> 		(*Paradiso*, XXII. 130–31)

[in order that your heart may present itself, joyous to its utmost, to the triumphant throng.]

And *appresentare* as used in our text, with this meaning of "present", carries also, I believe, the connotation of "to make a present of": a work pleases the doer the more it makes a present of the goodness of his heart, that is, makes a present to the person for whom the good act is done—in this case the human race. The noun *presente*, meaning "a present", is found in its only occurrence in the *Commedia* earlier in our canto, where Beatrice prefaces her first response to Dante's troubled mind with the words: "di gran sentenza ti faran presente" ["(my words) will make you the gift of a great doctrine": line 24]. *Appresenta* (line 127) picks up this notion of "making a present".

The personal connotation of *appresentare* as thus interpreted is entirely suitable to the passage as a whole, and to this tercet in particular, for what ultimately is most distinctively Dantean in these lines is the emphasis given to pleasure as the criterion for good action:

> Ma perché l'ovra tanto e piú gradita
> da l'operante, quanto piú appresenta
> de la bontà del core ond' ell' è uscita [...].

Lines 106–11 may be reconstructed as follows: God was happy ("la divina bontà fu *contenta*") to proceed both by kindness (*cortesia*, line 91) and justice (*giustizia*, line 119) ("di proceder per tutte le sue vie [...] fu contenta") because of the general "law" that a work is the more pleasing to the doer the more it presents of the goodness of his heart. The logic governing this general law of action is that it is the fact that something is truly or graciously pleasing in the first place to the doer (agent) that it is good: true or gracious pleasure is the criterion of good action. It is because presenting a greater degree of goodness of the heart is more pleasing to the doer that the divine goodness saw fit to decree the Incarnation.

I believe that this emphasis on pleasure or joy as the criterion of action is characteristically Dantean because Dante at key moments recurs to this idea in describing how good action takes place. This is a large theme which I shall only touch on here. I shall cite two examples from descriptions of both divine and human action. Statius, in his account of the creation of the human soul in *Purgatorio* xxv, talks first of the embryo's growth through the plant and animal stages. When, he says, the embryo is matured to the point where it can receive the soul, God creates the specifically human soul which gathers the lower powers into it. With the details of Dante's embryology I am not concerned; I would simply draw attention to the lines which introduce the description of God at the moment of action upon the embryo:

> lo motor primo a lui si volge lieto
> sovra tant' arte di natura.
> (*Purgatorio*, xxv. 70–71)

[the First Mover turns to it with joy over such art of nature.]

The same adjective, *lieto*, had occurred earlier in another passage dealing with the same subject, where God's delight in creating the human soul is particularly emphasized by Marco Lombardo:

> Esce di mano a lui che la vagheggia
> prima che sia, a guisa di fanciulla
> che piangendo e ridendo pargoleggia,
>   l'anima semplicetta che sa nulla,
> salvo che, mossa da lieto fattore,
> volontier torna a ciò che la trastulla.
> (*Purgatorio*, xvi. 85–90)

[From His hands, who fondly loves it before it exists, comes forth after the fashion of a child that sports, now weeping, now laughing, the simple little soul, which knows nothing, save that, proceeding from a glad Maker, it turns eagerly to what delights it.]

As for human beings, Dante in the *Convivio* (in words which also clarify his comments on divine joy in action in the *Commedia*) expressly calls attention to the fact that every operation of virtue must be joyful. On the ground that "li morali ragionamenti sogliono dare desiderio di vedere l'origine loro" ["adducing moral arguments usually prompts a desire to grasp the principles on which they are based": *Convivio*, I. 8. 6], he proposes to expand on his statement that usefulness must be part of a generous gift, by giving four reasons why this must be so. He begins:

Primamente: però che la vertú dee essere lieta, e non trista in alcuna sua operazione; onde se 'l dono non è lieto nel dare e nel ricevere, non è in esso perfetta vertú, non è pronta. Questa letizia non può dare altro che utilitade, che rimane nel datore per lo dare, e che viene nel ricevitore per ricevere.
(*Convivio*, I. 8. 7)

[The first reason is that in all of its acts a virtue must be joyful, not sad; so if a gift lacks joy in being given and received, it does not manifest perfect or whole-hearted virtue. This joy derives entirely from the quality termed usefulness, which remains with the giver in making the gift, and passes to the recipient in his receiving the gift.]

But joy is characteristic not only of human action on earth, for Heaven, where man is supremely active, is characterized by Dante simply as "esto viver lieto" ["this happy life": *Paradiso*, XXVII. 43].[39]

In this regard as in others, the divine and the human are brought together in the figure of Christ when Forese Donati adds a courteous self-correction to his reference to his own and his companions' suffering in Purgatory:

> Io dico pena, e dovria dir sollazzo,
>   ché quella voglia a li alberi ci mena
>   che menò Cristo lieto a dire "*Elì*",
>   quando ne liberò con la sua vena.
> (*Purgatorio*, XXIII. 72–75)

[I say pain and ought to say solace: for that will leads us to the trees which led glad Christ to say *"Elì"*, when He delivered us with His blood.]

The *lieto* here strikes home the more forcefully in that it is clearly a Dantean addition to a Biblical passage that would have been well known to the poet's intended audience.[40]

Dante, in common with late medieval theology generally,[41] undoubtedly drew on the rationale for the Incarnation and redemption elaborated by Anselm in *Cur Deus Homo*. Whether the verbal similarities between *Paradiso* VII and that work are sufficiently strong to indicate direct dependence must remain a moot point, though I have to say that I remain to be persuaded. What is undoubtedly the case is that the Dantean account significantly differs from the bold project of his fellow-countryman two centuries previously to show "ex necessitate omnia quae de Christo credimus fieri oportere".[42]

NOTES

1 *Enc. dant.*, I, 293–94.
2 *La "Divina commedia", col commento scartazziniano*, revised by G. Vandelli, nineteenth edition (Milan, Hoepli, 1965), p. 666.
3 G. Padoan, *Il canto VII del "Paradiso"* (Turin, Società Editrice Internazionale, 1965), p. 13. In a *lectura* published in the previous year, W. T. Elwert wrote in a similar vein: "Di fatti Dante riprende gli argomenti di S. Anselmo come traspare da allusioni verbali [...]. Col v. 64 inizia la dimostrazione della necessità del modo scelto da Dio per la redenzione dell'umanità" (*Letture dantesche*, edited by G. Getto [Florence, Sansoni, 1964], pp. 1463–86 [p. 1479]).
4 *La Divina commedia*, edited by U. Bosco and G. Reggio, 3 vols (Florence, Le Monnier, 1979), III, 107.
5 S. F. Di Zenzo, *Da Sofia a Beatrice: presupposti culturali e fonti teologiche nella "Divina commedia"* (Naples, Laurenziana, 1984), p. 314 (see also pp. 474–75 and 511–12).
6 See, for example, W. T. Elwert in *Letture dantesche*, edited by G. Getto, p. 1479.
7 *La Divina commedia*, edited by F. Torraca, sixth edition (Milan–Rome–Naples, Albrighi and Segati, 1926), at *Par.*, VII. 145–48 (p. 699).
8 A. Agresti, *Dante e S. Anselmo* (Naples, de Bonis, 1887).
9 Among modern commentators H. Gmelin, *Dante Alighieri, Die göttliche Komödie: Kommentar*, second edition, 3 vols (Stuttgart, Klett, 1966–70), vol. III, following Agresti, is particularly forthright in championing the view that *Paradiso* VII directly reflects the vocabulary of Anselm. See, for example, his

"Paradiso" VII: Dante and Anselm 135

comment at line 92: "Wie eingehend Dante den Text des Anselmus studiert hat, zeigt die einprägsame Wiederholung der scholastischen Begriffe. Vgl. *dimesso*."

10 A. Agresti, *Dante e S. Anselmo*, pp. 29–32, where the author also discusses the key words *dimesso* and *modo*.

11 An excellent, relatively short account of doctrinal and theological development in the early centuries of the Church is G. W. H. Lampe, "Christian Theology in the Patristic Period", pp. 21–180 of *A History of Christian Doctrine*, edited by H. Cunliffe-Jones (Edinburgh, Clark, 1978); on soteriology see especially pp. 149–69.

12 On medieval soteriology, and Anselm's role in its development, see, for example, J. Pelikan, *The Christian Tradition: A History of the Development of Doctrine*, 5 vols (Chicago–London, University of Chicago Press, 1971–89), III (*The Growth of Medieval Theology, 600–1300*), 106–57.

13 For a recent, magisterial account of Anselm, see R. W. Southern, *St Anselm: A Portrait in a Landscape* (Cambridge, Cambridge University Press, 1991). On *Cur Deus Homo* in particular, see the lengthy introduction (pp. 47–192) by René Roques to his edition and translation, *Anselme de Cantorbéry: Pourquoi Dieu s'est fait homme* [Sources chrétiennes, 91] (Paris, Editions du Cerf, 1963).

14 Anselm explains in his preface that the turbulent circumstances of his life as Archbishop of Canterbury did not allow him to give his work the final form he would have liked. In fact, themes are treated, dropped and taken up again. I give below what I regard as the main discussions of the topics I mention.

15 *Cur Deus Homo*, edited by R. Roques (see note 13 above), I. 11–13, 21.

16 *Cur Deus Homo*, I. 19, 22–23.

17 *Cur Deus Homo*, I. 20.

18 *Cur Deus Homo*, I. 21, 24–25.

19 *Cur Deus Homo*, II. 1, 4.

20 *Cur Deus Homo*, II. 6–7, 9–10, 14, 16, 18.

21 "Si ergo, sicut constat, necesse est ut de hominibus perficiatur illa superna civitas, nec hoc esse valet, nisi fiat praedicta satisfactio, quam nec potest facere nisi Deus nec debet nisi homo: necesse est ut eam faciat Deus-homo." The translations of Anselm's work are taken from *A Scholastic Miscellany: Anselm to Ockham*, edited and translated by E. R. Fairweather [Library of Christian Classics, 10] (London, SCM Press; Philadelphia, Westminster Press, 1956), pp. 100–83.

22 See *Par.*, VI. 88–93.

23 "Quod secundum materiam de qua editum est, *Cur Deus Homo* nominavi et in duos libellos distinxi. Quorum prior quidem infidelium Christianam fidem, quia rationi putant illam repugnare, respuentium continet objectiones et fidelium responsiones. Ac tandem remoto Christo, quasi numquam aliquid fuerit de illo, probat rationibus necessariis esse impossibile ullum hominem salvari sine illo. In secundo autem libro similiter quasi nihil sciatur de Christo, monstratur non minus aperta ratione et veritate naturam humanam ad hoc institutam esse, ut aliquando immortalitate beata totus homo, id est in corpore et anima, frueretur; ac necesse esse ut hoc fiat de homine propter quod factus est, sed non nisi per hominem-deum; atque ex necessitate omnia quae de Christo credimus fieri oportere."

24 "Quapropter cum has convenientias quas dicis infidelibus quasi quasdam picturas rei gestae obtendimus, quoniam non rem gestam, sed figmentum

arbitrantur esse quod credimus, quasi super nubem pingere nos existimant. Monstranda ergo prius est veritatis soliditas rationabilis, id est necessitas quae probet Deum ad ea quae praedicamus debuisse aut potuisse humiliari."

25 "ANSELMUS Nihil minus tolerandum in rerum ordine, quam ut creatura Creatori debitum honorem auferat et non solvat quod aufert. / BOSO Hoc nihil clarius. / ANSELMUS Nihil autem injustius toleratur, quam quo nihil est minus tolerandum."

26 "ANSELMUS Item. Si Deo nihil majus aut melius, nihil justius quam quae honorem illius servat in rerum dispositione summa justitia, quae non est aliud quam ipse Deus. / BOSO Hoc quoque nihil apertius. / ANSELMUS Nihil ergo servat Deus justius quam suae dignitatis honorem. / BOSO Concedere me oportet."

27 "Necesse est ergo, ut aut ablatus honor solvatur aut poena sequatur. Alioquin aut sibi Deus ipsi justus non erit aut ad utrumque impotens erit; quod nefas est vel cogitare."

28 "[...] qua scilicet ratione vel necessitate Deus homo factus sit, et morte sua, sicut credimus et confitemur, mundo vitam reddiderit."

29 "[...] cum hoc aut per aliam personam, sive angelicam sive humanam, aut sola voluntate facere potuerit."

30 "Redeamus et videamus utrum sola misericordia, sine omni solutione ablati sibi honoris deceat Deum peccatum dimittere."

31 "Sic dimittere peccatum non est aliud quam non punire. Et quoniam recte ordinare peccatum sine satisfactione non est nisi punire: si non punitur, inordinatum dimittitur."

32 "Liberior igitur est injustitia, si sola misericordia dimittitur, quam justitia; quod valde inconveniens videtur. Ad hoc etiam extenditur haec inconvenientia, ut injustitiam Deo similem faciat; quia sicut Deus nullius legi subjacet, ita et injustitia."

33 "Nam cum terrenae potestates hoc recte faciunt, ipse facit, a quo ad hoc ipsum sunt ordinatae."

34 "Quapropter si non decet Deum aliquid injuste aut inordinate facere, non pertinet ad ejus libertatem aut benignitatem aut voluntatem, peccantem qui non solvit Deo quod abstulit impunitum dimittere."

35 See also the concluding words of the same chapter: "Sunt quoque multa alia quae studiose considerata inenarrabilem quandam nostrae redemptionis hoc modo procuratae pulchritudinem ostendunt."

36 "Non video cur non deceat."

37 *The Divine Comedy*, with translation and commentary by J. D. Sinclair, 3 vols (London, Bodley Head, 1939–46), vol. III.

38 See also *Purg.*, XXXI. 49 and *Par.*, X. 33.

39 Compare the souls' address to Dante in *Purg.*, V. 46: "O anima che vai per esser lieta [...]." "Viver lieto" is also used of harmonious life on earth: *Par.*, XVI. 138.

40 Matthew 27. 46: "Et circa horam nonam clamavit Jesus voce magna, dicens: 'Eli, Eli, lamma sabacthani?', id est: 'Deus meus, Deus meus, ut quid dereliquisti me?'"

41 Reference is also often made by commentators on *Paradiso* VII to Aquinas's *Summa Theologiae*. It would exceed the scope of the present essay to comment in detail on the degree of similarity between Dante and Aquinas on the Incarnation and redemption. But I ought perhaps to state my view that, as in the case of Anselm, unqualified references to Aquinas's work in the context

of commenting on *Paradiso* VII are misleading when they give the impression that on these topics Dante's views were in complete accord with those of Aquinas. One instance of how they differed must suffice here. Dante and Aquinas were in agreement (contrary to Anselm) that the Incarnation was not the only way in which God could have redeemed the human race. However, where Dante draws a tight line, declaring that there were only two ways for God to redeem mankind, either by pure forgiveness or through the Incarnation (see especially *Par.*, VII. 115–20), Aquinas writes more expansively that it was not absolutely necessary for God to become incarnate for the human race to be redeemed, "for God by his almighty power could have restored human nature by many other ways" ("Deus enim per suam omnipotentem virtutem poterat humanam naturam multis aliis modis reparare": Thomas Aquinas, *Summa Theologiae*, edited by T. Gilby et al., 61 vols [London, Blackfriars, 1963–80], Part III. Q. 1, a. 2).

42 *Cur Deus Homo*, preface.

DANTE'S SIGNS: AN INTRODUCTION TO MEDIEVAL SEMIOTICS AND DANTE[1]

Zygmunt G. Barański

It is well known that at the end of *Purgatorio* (XXXIII. 31–78) Beatrice addresses the newly repentant pilgrim in a dense and original metaphorical language. What has been less widely recognized, however, is that she also speaks to him in clichés. In commenting on the effects of the waters of the Lethe on her lover's memory, she informs him that his inability to remember his "estrangement" from her (*Purgatorio*, XXXIII. 91–93) is a clear sign of his former guilt (lines 94–99), in the same way as "dal fummo foco s'argomenta" ["from smoke fire is inferred": line 97]. The few scholars who have lingered on this line have tended to conclude, somewhat generically, that it has all the air of a proverb.[2] That it is a commonplace is not in doubt; it is, however, a commonplace with a very precise and significant pedigree. "Et fumo viso, ignem subesse cognoscimus" ["If we see smoke, we know that there is a fire which causes it"],[3] we find at the beginning of the second Book of *De Doctrina Christiana* to illustrate Augustine's definition of *signum* as "res, praeter speciem quam ingerit sensibus, aliud aliquid ex se faciens in cogitationem venire" ["a thing which makes us think of something beyond the impression the thing itself makes upon the senses": II. 1. 1].[4] The Saint then quickly repeats the same example not once, but twice, as he distinguishes between natural signs—of which smoke is obviously one—and conventional signs (II. 1. 2). For centuries, the authority of Augustine on matters "symbolic" was paramount. Thus, given the expert manner in which his treatise synthesizes the "scientific" analysis of *signa* with a detailed and pragmatic discussion of the conventions of Biblical exegesis, and given, too, the enduring Christian fascination with all forms of semiosis, it comes as no surprise that the smoky sign, and much else from *De Doctrina Christiana*, should have exerted a wide-ranging and deep influence right up to Dante's time.[5]

That Beatrice speaks to the pilgrim in such elementary terms is also not surprising. As she herself recognizes, he has failed dismally to understand, or, more precisely, to interpret, her "narrazion buia" ["dark narrative": line 46], and so she must ensure that

> Veramente oramai saranno nude
> le mie parole, quanto converrassi
> quelle scovrire a la tua vista rude.
> (*Purgatorio*, XXXIII. 100–02)

[Truly from now on my words will be as plain as will be necessary to uncover these to your rude sight.]

Indeed, as far as the narrative economy of this episode is concerned, that she should have recourse to a topos drawn from contemporary discussions *de signis* enhances the psychological "realism" of their dialogue. Beatrice, at last sensitive to Dante-character's intellectual limitations, answers like with like, since a little earlier the increasingly bewildered pilgrim has assured his lady, using another semiotic commonplace, that

> Sí come cera da suggello,
> che la figura impressa non trasmuta,
> segnato è or da voi lo mio cervello.
> (*Purgatorio*, XXXIII. 79–81)

[Just as wax, once signed by a seal, does not change the impressed figure, so my brain is now marked with signs by you.][6]

The poet, too, seems to be stricken by the same conceptual bug. In bringing the second *cantica* to a close, he employs a further pair of similes which revolve around traditional elements belonging to the literature on signs. First, Dante explains that the manner in which the "sette donne" ["seven women": line 109] came to a halt was

> sí come s'affigge
> chi va dinanzi a gente per iscorta
> se trova novitate o sue vestigge.
> (*Purgatorio*, XXXIII. 106–08)

[just as someone stops, who goes ahead of people as an escort, if he finds a novelty or its traces.]

Vestigia are everywhere in medieval symbolic writing, ranging from the tracks made by animals to the traces which God leaves of Himself in Creation.[7] Secondly, in order to underline Matelda's keen desire to fulfil Beatrice's request that she should lead the pilgrim to the Eunoè, the poet somewhat prosaically describes her as having been

> come anima gentil, che non fa scusa,
> ma fa sua voglia de la voglia altrui
> tosto che è per segno fuor dischiusa.
> (*Purgatorio*, XXXIII. 130–32)

[like a gentle spirit, which makes no excuse, but makes its will of the will of another as soon as it is disclosed by a sign.]

The *terzina*'s prosaicness stems largely from the fact that its second half is closely modelled on the standard definition of the basic function of and reason for conventional signs:

> Data vero signa sunt, quae sibi quaeque viventia invicem dant ad demonstrandos [...] motus animi sui, vel sensa, aut intellecta quaelibet. Nec ulla causa est nobis significandi, id est signi dandi, nisi ad depromendum et trajiciendum in alterius animum id quod animo gerit is qui signum dat

[Conventional signs are those which living creatures show to one another for the purpose of revealing the motion of their spirits, or something which they have sensed or understood. Nor is there any other reason for us to signify, namely, to give signs, except to bring forth and to transfer to another mind what the giver of the sign has in his own mind]

—to borrow Augustine's terms once again (*De Doctrina Christiana*, II. 2. 3).[8]

It is—I believe—at the very least intriguing that, in one of the structurally most significant sections of the *Commedia*, at the very point where "piene son tutte le carte/ordite a questa cantica seconda" ["all the sheets pre-assigned to this second *cantica* are full": *Purgatorio*, XXXIII. 139–40], Dante should have considered it more important to recall the most banal contemporary ideas on signs than dedicate the brief remaining space to the "dolce ber che mai non m'avría sazio" ["sweet drink which would never have satiated me": line 138], or to some other matter which, at first glance, might appear of greater weight. The poet's choice, by its very unexpectedness, not to say "inappropriateness", cannot but stimulate reflection. What are these four references to the function of signs and to the semiotic status of smoke, vestiges, and imprints in wax doing at such a crucial juncture of the poem? Are they, in fact, anything more than instances of Dante's customary taste for concrete, realistic expression? If they are, what connections can they possibly have with the rest of the canto (not to mention the rest of the *cantica* and the *Commedia* as a whole)? And questions do have to be posed in such wide-ranging terms, since it is a Dantean commonplace to present key matters which affect the development of his whole poem, as well as its interpretation, in those sections of the *Commedia* which structurally are most foregrounded.[9]

The beginning of an answer resides in the four images' nature as topoi. I should like to suggest that, beyond the particular local illustrative values which, as similes, they have in their respective corners of the text, they were not really chosen for the specific semiological information which they could provide (like all clichés they were largely desemanticized, and so to achieve an effect Dante needed to pile one on top of the other). Rather, I believe (and, in particular, the first half of this study will be dedicated to demonstrating this point and its implications), they were chosen as metonymic signals for the centuries of pagan and Christian preoccupation with signs, with processes of signification and with the the means to interpret them—a Neoplatonist tradition which in the poet's day had been thrown into turmoil by the rationalist and abstract ambitions of Aristotelianism.[10] My proposed reading of the exemplary connotations of Dante's four allusions to semiosis would seem to be immediately confirmed by their uncontroversial character. Whatever positions were taken in the fourteenth century regarding the efficacy of symbolic procedures or regarding individual aspects of the debate on signs,[11] there would have been almost certainly no disagreement as regards the basic ideas associated with the poet's choices.

If the content of Dante's four explicit references to contemporary sign theory in *Purgatorio* XXXIII is straightforward, the same may not be asserted of his customary attitude to the symbolism of his day. This study is a first, not to say preliminary, attempt to point out some of the principal features and critical problems which emerge when the poet's art and thought are considered in the light of this tradition, a tradition which enjoyed a highly privileged position in medieval culture. Yet, despite the importance of its standing, Dante has rarely been assessed in terms of the semiotic reflection of his time.

"STATE CONTENTI, UMANA GENTE, AL *QUIA*"

Recognizing a function for Dante's semiological imagery does not, however, cast light on the possible relationship between medieval symbolism and *Purgatorio* XXXIII. What is striking about this canto is its deep concern with modes of intellection and acquisition of knowledge. Beatrice forcefully establishes her ability to see things, including future events, "certamente" ["as certain": line 40], since, like all the blessed and the angels, she is able to look into the mind of God. At the same time, she makes much of the pilgrim's—and by extension humanity's—intellectual limitations. In contrast to the clarity and directness of her vision (line 40), his mind becomes "obscured" (line 48): instead of "discerning" it sleeps (line 64) and it is full of "pensier vani" ["vain thoughts": line 68], so that as a consequence it is "fatto di pietra e, impetrato, tinto" ["turned to stone and, having become petrified, turns dark": line 74]. Furthermore, Beatrice emphasizes that our ability to retain knowledge, and hence to know, is largely dependent on something as precarious as memory (lines 55–57, 76–78), which, as the pilgrim himself acknowledges when he talks about imprints in wax, at best simply retains a "figura" of the original experience (lines 79–81). To make matters worse, if we wish to communicate with our fellows, we can only express what is "segnato" in our minds (line 81) by means of yet a further system of signs; as Beatrice tells Dante-*personaggio*:

> Tu nota; e sí come da me son porte,
> cosí queste parole segna a' vivi.
> (*Purgatorio*, XXXIII. 52–53)

[Take note; and as these words are said by me, so mark them down as signs for the living.]

With the poet's customary skill, the contrast between the unmediated intellectual certainties of the blessed and the poor cognitive sign-bound approximations of the living are sharply brought into relief. More notably, as far as my present discussion is concerned, the problems linked to this contrast, in keeping with traditional discussions of such matters (it is enough to recall the opening chapters of *De Vulgari Eloquentia*),[12] reveal that the canto has anything but a superficial interest in issues of symbolism. As I mentioned earlier, the four semiotic similes are only markers for a much more sophisticated and wide-ranging set of concerns on the subject, concerns which Dante also appears to have embedded in *Purgatorio* xxxiii. Indeed, we are moving close to the very ideological core of medieval reflection on signs.

As well as highlighting the gulf between the intellectual potentialities of the denizens of Paradise and those of the inhabitants of earth, Beatrice also evokes the chasm which separates divine from human wisdom:

> e veggi vostra via da la divina
> distar cotanto, quanto si discorda
> da terra il ciel che piú alto festina.
> (*Purgatorio*, xxxiii. 88–90)

[and you see that your way is as far from the divine one as the heaven that hurries highest is distant from the earth.]

Yet, despite this unfathomable distance, communication between God and humans is not only necessary, it is also a reality, as Beatrice's own divinely inspired prophesying reveals (lines 37–45, 49–51). Nevertheless, as was widely recognized, prophecy was a highly unusual and privileged method of divine revelation.[13] More accessible ways of making sense of God's will, and thereby of ensuring salvation, were available, ways which could help humanity both achieve an understanding of its Maker and avoid offending Him. To put it in Beatrice's terms, human beings had to learn to appreciate and respect the "uses" of what God had fashioned:

> Qualunque ruba quella o quella schianta,
> con bestemmia di fatto offende a Dio,
> che solo a l'uso suo la creò santa.
> (*Purgatorio*, xxxiii. 58–60)

[Whoever steals that (tree) or tears it, with blasphemy of act offends against God, Who created it holy solely for His own use.]

Immediately after this admonition, Beatrice proceeds, in the next tercet, to explain the most important means by which knowledge of God is made possible, namely, spiritual revelation through Christ (lines 61–63). What this notion meant in practice was the ability to interpret, in keeping with the dictates of faith, God's two great semiotic creations—His two "books", the universe and the Bible, beneath the surface of which He had left "vestiges" of Himself.[14] As a result of this conceptualization of the workings of God's will, issues of salvation and divine justice became tightly enmeshed with discussions of symbolism and human understanding. In part, this synthesis had its origins in and was legitimated by Solomon's celebration of *iustitia* in the Book of Wisdom:

> Et si iustitiam quis diligit,
> Labores huius magnas habent virtutes:
> Sobrietatem enim et prudentiam docet,
> Et iustitiam, et virtutem,
> Quibus utilius nihil est in vita hominibus.
> Et si multitudinem scientiae desiderat quis,
> Scit praeterita, et de futuris aestimat;
> Scit versutias sermonum, et dissolutiones argumentorum;
> Signa et monstra scit antequam fiant,
> Et eventus temporum at saeculorum.
> (Wisdom 8. 7–8)

[And if you love justice, the virtues are the result of her great labours: for she teaches temperance and prudence, and justice and virtue, and nothing is more useful in life to human beings than these. And if you desire a breadth of knowledge, she knows the things that have passed, and she assesses the future; she knows the subtleties of speech and how to solve riddles; she has foreknowledge of signs and prodigies, and of the events of the times and ages.][15]

It is thus appropriate that Dante's fullest analysis of signs in the *Commedia*, which ranges from *Deus artifex* to *mirabilia*, from augury to contemporary methods of alphabetization, from the sacraments to language, and from literature to forgery, should be found in the Heaven of Jove, the heaven which, tellingly, has "painted" on it (*Paradiso*, XVIII. 92) the opening verse of no other *auctoritas* than the

Book of Wisdom. As always, Dante gets his cultural bearings just right:

> "*DILIGITE IUSTITIAM*", primai
> fur verbo e nome di tutto 'l dipinto;
> "*QUI IUDICATIS TERRAM*", fur sezzai.
> (*Paradiso*, XVIII. 91–93)

["*LOVE JUSTICE*", were the first verb and noun of the whole painting, "*WHO JUDGE THE EARTH*", were the last.]

Within the particular framework of *Purgatorio* XXXIII's semiotic preoccupations Dante recalls, in a highly appropriate manner, the great universal questions connected with the symbolic character of the contacts between God and humanity. In line with his dramatization of history in the symbolic action of the Terrestrial Paradise (*Purgatorio* XXIX and XXXII), the poet similarly fashions a dramatic analogy of the divine creative act and its consequences (and it is worth remembering here that it was a commonplace of medieval semiological thought that, in life, God could be known only *per analogiam*).[16] Beatrice's richly metaphorical and highly allusive language, her "enigma forte" ["hard enigma": *Purgatorio*, XXXIII. 50], which stems directly from God, is a microcosm—and I intentionally use the term with all its Neoplatonic nuances—of the work of the *digitus Dei*.[17] Yet, while she effectively plays her part as the "Word of God",[18] the pilgrim fails disastrously in his part. In order for the exemplary drama of the relationship between God and humanity which is enacted at the top of the mountain to be played out successfully according to the dictates of the divine will, Dante-character has to offer a cogent exegesis of his lady's speech. He has to go beyond its "literal" sense. Because his intellect is still "obscured" by error, however, he reveals himself quite incapable of this task (*Purgatorio*, XXXIII. 46–48, 73–75, 82–84). Just as the vicissitudes of the symbolic figures in *Purgatorio* XXXII represent sin's perversion of the ideal order of providential history, so the pilgrim's sinful failure to interpret what he hears is shown to pervert the proper process of communication between God and humanity. That Dante should bring together providential history, earthly politics, semiotics, exegesis and the workings of the human intellect is not surprising. To appreciate God's will as it is expressed in time, human beings have to interpret his *vestigia* in a manner consonant with His designs. If they choose to exploit the divine *signa* for their own ends, however, then, as the events with which Canto XXXII closes reveal, they horrifically misuse and transform the very things which God fashioned for their salvation. I do not have the space here to pursue this absorbing question. I should simply like to note that history and signs, exegesis and politics also lie at the core of *Monarchia*. As a result, throughout the treatise, we discover some of Dante's most sophisticated and sustained analyses of semiotic matters.

The pilgrim is not confused by Beatrice's divine speech alone. He is equally unable to decipher that other microcosm of divine artistry which confronts him in the Earthly Paradise. Beatrice is quick to reproach him for his failure to tease out the true meaning of the symbolic drama which he has just witnessed:

> E se stati non fossero acqua d'Elsa
> li pensier vani intorno a la tua mente,
> e 'l piacer loro un Piramo a la gelsa,
> per tante circostanze solamente
> la giustizia di Dio, ne l'interdetto,
> conosceresti a l'arbor moralmente.
> (*Purgatorio*, XXXIII. 67–72)

[And if your vain thoughts had not been the waters of the Elsa around your mind, and their pleasure a Pyramus to the mulberry, by such circumstances alone you would have known morally (that is, thanks to the insights which result from an interpretation based on the conventions of the "moral" allegorical sense) God's justice in the interdict on the tree.]

There is much in these words that is important for my present argument. They confirm *Purgatorio* XXXIII's fascination with signs and their interpretation. More particularly, in keeping with the specific concerns of the drama of divine symbolism which the pilgrim and his lady are performing, Beatrice's condemnation echoes Augustine's discussion in *De Doctrina Christiana* both of the spiritual dangers of taking figurative expressions literally, and of the intellectual sin which is the cause of such behaviour. In fact, the pilgrim's unreasoning and unreasonable behaviour conforms precisely to that sin:

> When that which is said figuratively is taken as though it were literal, it is understood carnally. Nor can anything more appropriately be called the death of the soul than that state in which the

thing which distinguishes us from the beasts, namely intelligence/understanding, is subjected to the flesh in the pursuit of the letter. The person who follows the letter takes figurative expressions as though they were literal, and does not refer the things signified to anything else/to any other meaning/to any other sense. There is a miserable servitude of the spirit in this habit of taking signs for things, so that one is unable to raise the eye of the mind above corporal creatures in order to drink in the eternal light.[19]

To speak of the pilgrim "sinning" at this point in his journey, however, is—I admit—inappropriate. Within the overall narrative structure of the *Commedia*, rather than a mark of sinfulness, his exegetical obtuseness is simply another instance of how much he still has to learn before he can reach God. Yet there is also no escaping the fact that Dante-*personaggio*'s behaviour is akin to that of someone whose "understanding is subjected to the flesh in the pursuit of the letter". This apparent tension has its reasons. It stems from the polysemous nature of the exchange between Beatrice and her lover. We have just noted its universal and spiritual dimensions. As I shall go on to show, the poet also linked it to a key issue in thirteenth- and early fourteenth-century intellectual history. Finally and most specifically, through the two characters' otherworldly meeting, Dante has the pilgrim re-enact the intellectual error he had committed on earth after his lady's death. As we shall see, this involved a shift from a semiotically based epistemology to a "rational-scientific" one. When the layered allusiveness of this episode is recognized, the ties which, in the Earthly Paradise, appear "improperly" to bind Dante-*personaggio* to the world of sin are attenuated. Fittingly, the poet cloaks the event of the pilgrim's failure to appreciate Beatrice's words in that same rich symbolism which characterizes both the Terrestrial Paradise in general and *Purgatorio* XXXIII in particular. By interpreting correctly the *signa* which Dante lays before us, we can achieve that depth of understanding which his protagonist still finds beyond his powers.

Unlike his former self and all those other human beings who on earth are unable to "remain content [...] with the *quia*" (*Purgatorio*, III. 37), the pilgrim, who, by this point in the journey, has repudiated his sinful reasoning, acknowledges his intellectual limitations and shows himself keen to overcome their constraints. In frustration, he enquires:

> Ma perché tanto sovra mia veduta
> vostra parola disïata vola,
> che piú la perde quanto piú s'aiuta?
> *(Purgatorio,* xxxiii. 82–84)

[But why does your longed-for word fly so far above my sight that the more it strives to follow the more it loses it?]

And Beatrice wastes no time in offering him an explanation:

> Perché conoschi [...] quella scuola
> c'hai seguitata, e veggi sua dottrina
> come può seguitar la mia parola.
> *(Purgatorio,* xxxiii. 85–87)

[So that you may know that school which you have followed, and may see to what extent its doctrine can follow my word.]

Even leaving aside the precise identity of this "school", one thing is clear: it stands in direct opposition to the exegetical tradition. As Beatrice noted, the pilgrim's inability to interpret the symbolic action of Canto xxxii was the result of his lack of familiarity with allegoresis—he was unable to "know" the tree "moralmente" (line 72), that is, according to the insights offered by the so-called "allegory of the theologians".[20] His was that "miserable servitude of the spirit" which "ta*kes* signs for things, so that *he was* unable to raise the eye of *his* mind above corporal creatures in order to drink in the eternal light". The ideological opposition which Dante here evokes cannot but be highly suggestive. It recalls that bitter epistemological argument which marked the latter part of the Duecento and the beginnings of the Trecento, and which, today, is commonly referred to as the conflict between, on the one side, the "philosophers" and "theologians" and, on the other, the "exegetes". (To complicate matters further, the "philosophers" and the "theologians", despite their common Aristotelian origins, were also at war with each other.) In very simple terms, the basic dispute was between a rationally and "scientifically" based epistemology riven with internal divisions and a rather more homogeneous Scripturally based symbolic theory of knowledge. To recognize that, when he came to write the *Commedia,* Dante was openly declaring his support for the "exegetes" is of considerable importance in helping us not only define his poem but also understand his intellectual development, preferences and allegiances. Thus, in the light of his presentation of the conversation between Beatrice and the pilgrim in *Purgatorio* XXXIII, and against one of the long-established truisms of Dante scholarship, it is difficult to escape the conclusion that the poet's assessment of the cognitive efficacy of the rationalist "school" is unhesitatingly negative.[21]

In the opening canto of *Paradiso*, the poet carries on where he left off at the end of the previous *cantica* and makes his sympathies for the symbolic-exegetical tradition even more apparent. He spends much of Canto I presenting both the Creator and His creation in easily recognizable Neoplatonic semiotic terms:

> Le cose tutte quante
> hanno ordine tra loro, e questo è forma
> che l'universo a Dio fa simigliante.
> Qui veggion l'alte creature l'orma
> de l'etterno valore, il qual è fine
> al quale è fatta la toccata norma.
> (*Paradiso*, I. 103–08)

[All things are ordered among themselves, and this is the form which makes the universe resemble God. Here the high creatures see the trace of the eternal value, which is the end for which the norm just mentioned is made.][22]

Nor is there anything especially unusual about the perspective offered by *Purgatorio* XXXIII and *Paradiso* I. Time and again during the course of the poem—I have already alluded to *Paradiso* XVIII–XX— Dante repeats and refines the same basic points he is making in the final canto of *Purgatorio* and the first of *Paradiso* (and the remainder of this study provides further supporting evidence for the profound impact which symbolism and exegesis made on his work).[23]

The conclusion which I draw from this state of affairs is obvious, though it is one which scholars, blinkered by Dante's supposedly all-enveloping Aristotelianism, have largely been loath to recognize. The poet owes important, probably fundamental, debts to that line of thinkers which stretches from Plato (with his *Timaeus* as the key text) through to a figure such as St Bonaventure, a line which on its way also unites St Paul (particularly the Paul of the Letters to the Romans and to the Corinthians), Augustine, Macrobius, the pseudo-Dionysius, Boethius, Gregory the Great,

Dante's Signs 151

John Scotus Eriugena, Bernardian mysticism, the Victorines, and the school of Chartres. If my conclusion is acceptable—and it is supported by the recent work of two leading Dantists, Giuseppe Mazzotta and Lino Pertile—then a major revision of the poet's ideological history is necessary.[24] In particular, such a re-examination (which lies beyond the scope of this essay) will need to assess the interplay between the "symbolic" and the "rationalizing" in Dante's career, rather than lay exaggerated emphasis solely on the Aristotelian aspects of his intellectual formation. Such a one-sided definition of Dante-*pensatore*, which furthermore invariably presents the relationship between the poet and Aristotelianism in positive terms, is especially inappropriate given that it is precisely Aristotelianism which Dante appears keen to criticize in the *Commedia*.[25] As an alternative perspective, I should like to suggest that it would not be difficult to demonstrate for Dante what Bonaventure had claimed for Augustine, namely, that Augustine, enlightened by the Holy Spirit, achieved a synthesis of Plato's *sapientia* and Aristotle's *scientia*. This was a tradition, furthermore, which the Seraphic Doctor himself believed he was upholding in his writings;[26] and given both Dante's interest in Bonaventure and his constant ambition to achieve and promote intellectual, artistic and social harmony through his work, it is extremely likely that the poet would have found Augustinian-Bonaventurean syncretism highly appealing.[27] Dante's apparent efforts to reconcile the two warring traditions do not mean, however, that he considered them to be equally effective ways to the Truth. As we have begun to see, his preferences were very much for one side. According to Dante, ultimately the *Verbum* could be glimpsed only by interpreting His *signa*.

"Modicum, et non videbitis me"

The hypothesis of *Purgatorio* xxxiii's and, by extension, Dante's deep and sympathetic involvement with semiotics and the necessary symbolic foundations of knowledge receives support from an unexpected direction (unexpected, to be precise, only to modern minds which have lost a sense of the wealth, complexity and ramifications of medieval Christian exegesis).[28] The first of several interpretative *cruces* which characterize this canto involves the significance of the dramatic outburst by Beatrice which repeats almost verbatim the words spoken by Jesus to the apostles when prophesying His death and resurrection:

> Ma poi che l'altre vergini dier loco
> a lei di dir, levata dritta in pè,
> rispuose, colorata come foco:
> "*Modicum, et non videbitis me;
> et iterum*, sorelle mie dilette,
> *modicum, et vos videbitis me.*"
> (*Purgatorio*, xxxiii. 7–12)

[But when the other virgins gave place to her to speak, having risen upright on her feet, she replied, the colour of fire: "*Soon, and you will not see me; and again*, my dear sisters, *after a short time, and you will see me.*"]

Scholars have been divided over how best to interpret lines 10–12. Basically, the problem is whether to take them as a precise allusion to the transfer of the Holy See to Avignon in 1305, or whether they are to be viewed as a general allusion to the Church's contemporary degeneracy, which will soon be rectified by the arrival of a "messo di Dio" ["divine messenger": line 44].[29] Given the vagueness of Beatrice's pronouncement, I personally favour the latter position, especially in the light of Bosco's critique of the former.[30]

What has all this to do, however, with the semiotic purview of my discussion? At the broadest level, prophecy, on account of its characteristic lack of precision, was traditionally bound tightly together with exegesis, which—as we have seen—is a question that *Purgatorio* xxxiii explores in some depth. Indeed, that issues connected with exegesis do constitute one of this canto's major concerns is also suggested by the fact that there are many interpretative *cruces* in its *terzine*. These range from the infamous "cinquecento diece e cinque" ["five hundred ten and five", the so-called DXV: line 43] to the "waters of the Elsa" (line 67), and from the identity of the error-ridden "school" (line 85) to the considerations which led Dante to substitute the designation "cantica" (line 140) for the earlier "canzon" (*Inferno*, xx. 3) as the term with which to label each of the three parts of his poem.[31] This interest in hermeneutics is further confirmed by the difficulty of parts of Beatrice's speech, veritable exercises in the conventions of *trobar clus* (lines 34–36, 43–51, 61–63, 67–69), whose meaning and range of reference require a major interpretative effort—an effort, in fact, which itself is compelled to rely on the achievements of other exegetes (in the same way as the poet drew on the work of commentators to fashion the *Commedia* and to give his poem that subtle depth of meaning which is one of its most notable and satisfying features). Thus, when, somewhat surprisingly, Beatrice associates herself with Themis (line 47), I do not believe, in contrast to other Dantists, that this is just a simple comparison which serves to underscore the obscurity of her oracular statements.[32] In *Ovide moralisé*, that monumental Christian allegoresis of the *Metamorphoses* written soon after Dante's death and serving as the *summa* of a major Ovidian exegetical tradition, Themis is associated with repentance, defined as "the divine word" and presented as the guide to God—all elements which help to fix Beatrice's role in the *Commedia* in general and this episode in particular.[33] According to Dante, it is not enough for us to know how to interpret if we are to achieve understanding, but, to be successful exegetes in our turn, we also have to be aware of the hermeneutic insights already reached by others. Such a perspective was in no way peculiar to Dante. It was entirely in keeping with long-held views regarding the cumulative nature of knowledge. According to this perspective, it was not just the great "authoritative" texts that demanded to be interpreted: the interpretations themselves were the source of new intuitions and intellectual creations.[34]

Structurally, the words from St John's Gospel placed in Beatrice's mouth function in a manner not dissimilar to the role I believe Dante assigned to the allusion to Themis (the main difference being their greater substance and cultural resonance):

> *Modicum, et non videbitis me;*
> *et iterum*, sorelle mie dilette,
> *modicum, et vos videbitis me.*

The tercet's importance is immediately obvious from its position near the beginning of the canto. It is further highlighted not just by its status as a quotation in Latin, but, more specifically, as a quotation from the Bible embodying one of Jesus's sayings. Like the reference to the prophetic deity, this *terzina*, too, beyond its possible historical associations, serves to embed in Dante's text a complex set of broader ideological preoccupations. As I shall go on to argue, it acts as a signpost to *Purgatorio* XXXIII's symbolic and epistemological interests; and, once again, it does this by relying heavily on the established acquisitions of the exegetical tradition—Dante is nothing if not consistent in trying to make his points as effectively and memorably as possible, and in terms which would be accessible to the reading habits of his audience.

When they come to gloss *Purgatorio*, XXXIII. 10–12, Dante commentators inevitably cite John 16. 16: "Modicum, et iam non videbitis me; et iterum modicum, et videbitis me."[35] I am not convinced, however, that this verse should be put forward as the source, or at least as the sole source, of Beatrice's words. Let us consider the whole passage from which this gnomic statement is taken:

> [16] Modicum, et iam non videbitis me; et iterum modicum, et videbitis me, quia vado ad Patrem. [17] Dixerunt ergo ex discipulis eius ad invicem: Quid est hoc quod dicit nobis: Modicum, et non videbitis me; et iterum modicum, et videbitis me, et quia vado ad Patrem? [18] Dicebant ergo: Quid est hoc quod dicit: Modicum? nescimus quid loquitur.
>
> [19] Cognovit autem Iesus, quia volebant eum interrogare, et dixit eis: De hoc quaeritis inter vos quia dixi: Modicum, et non videbitis me; et iterum modicum, et videbitis me [...].
>
> [25] Haec in proverbiis locutus sum vobis. Venit hora cum iam non in proverbiis loquar vobis, sed palam de Patre annuntiabo vobis [...].
>
> [29] Dicunt ei discipuli eius: Ecce nunc palam loqueris, et proverbium nullum dicis.
>
> (John 16. 16–19, 25, 29)

[Soon, and already you will not see me; and again, after a short time, and you will see me, because I go to the Father. Therefore some of his disciples said among themselves: What is this he is saying to us: Soon, and you will not see me; and again, after a short time, and you will see me, because I go to the Father? They were saying therefore: What is this that he is saying: Soon? we do not understand what he is saying. However Jesus realized that they wanted to question him, and he said to them: You are asking among yourselves why I said: Soon, and you will not see me; and again, after a short time, and you will see me (...). I have been saying these things to you in proverbs. The hour will come when I will no longer speak to you in proverbs, but will speak openly to you of the Father (...). His disciples say to him: Now you are speaking openly, and not using any proverbs.]

It is immediately obvious that by omitting the *iam* of verse 16, verses 17 and 19 are closer to Dante's version of Christ's phrase (though it is also true that the poet needed to remove the adverb to ensure that line 10 read something like a hendecasyllable).[36] What makes verses 17 and 19 much more likely sources for the poet's *terzina* than verse 16, however, is the fact that they touch on a matter which—I have suggested—is close to the ideological heart of *Purgatorio* xxxIII: the bewilderment of humans when confronted by the Word of God (verses 17–19). This issue is devolped further in Chapter 16, when it addresses the need for God to speak in indirect symbolic forms (*proverbia*) on account of human intellectual limitations (verse 25), and when, in contrast to this indirect form of address, it announces the promise of unmediated communication in Paradise (verse 25; and see also verse 29). In fact, the basic relationship that exists between Jesus and the apostles is similar to that which unites Beatrice and her bewildered lover. And it is fairly clear that Dante did indeed model his episode on John's when one appreciates that Beatrice encourages the pilgrim to question her using a formula and words which recall Christ's appeal to his disciples: "Frate, perché non t'attenti / a domandarmi omai venendo meco?" ["Brother, why do you not dare to question me now that you are coming with me?": lines 23–24], which echoes (albeit with modifications) "Et nunc vado ad eum qui misit me; et nemo ex vobis interrogat me: Quo vadis?" ["And now I go to Him who sent me; and none of you questions me: Where are you going?": John 16. 5; and compare verse 19].

The full extent of John 16's involvement with and fundamental position in Christian discussions of semiotics and processes of understanding emerges only when we follow the hermeneutic current which flowed from this chapter and, in particular, from the six verses quoted above. Probably the most important text in this tradition, echoes of which may be heard in the thirteenth century in both St Bonaventure and Thomas Aquinas,[37] and whose considerable influence certainly had much to do with its author's standing as the "authority" *par excellence* on questions of symbolism, was Augustine's commentary on John.[38] The Bishop of Hippo's analysis of Chapter 16 makes fascinating reading, not least in the context of my present discussion. We find in it most of the same semiotic-exegetical points as Dante raises in the final canto of *Purgatorio*, namely: the primary importance of spiritual illumination for acquiring knowledge of God, a claim which is combined with comments on the restrictions of *signa* and on the narrowness of earthly understanding in comparison to what is intellectually possible in Heaven (*In Johannis Evangelium Tractatus*, XCVI. 4; and compare XCVII. 1, XCVIII. 4, CII. 3-4); warnings against following false teachers (XCVI. 5; and compare XCVII. 2-4, XCVIII. 4, 7); the need to distinguish between different forms of human understanding, the best of which is the ability to appreciate the things of God "spiritually" (XCVIII, CII. 4); and the fact that God grants knowledge of Himself in ways which can be appreciated by our "bodily senses" (XCIX. 2-3; but see also CII. 4). In addition, and also in close harmony with *Purgatorio* XXXIII, the phrase beginning "Modicum [...]" was presented not just by Augustine but in the whole tradition as an archetypal example of "obscure" divine discourse, precisely that "dark" and "enigmatic" form in which Beatrice speaks at the top of the mountain.[39] It might be suggested that the whole of *Purgatorio* XXXIII is already in lines 10-12; or, more precisely, that the canto's symbolic problematic is all in the exegesis to John 16. In order to establish the concerns of this demanding canto (and applying the same technique as he had exploited in devising his four semiotic clichés), Dante metonymically recalled both this part of the Gospel and its interpretative tradition by quoting the thrice-repeated "Modicum, et non videbitis me; et iterum modicum, et videbitis me"—the Johannine chapter's most memorable and hermeneutically demanding statement.[40]

In order to draw attention to the implications of allegoresis, Dante accumulated interpretation on top of interpretation. In this way, he could highlight both the wealth of this epistemology and its considerable limitations as a means of knowing God. The unmediated vision enjoyed by the angels and the blessed is in direct antithesis to the discursive stratifications of the exegetical tradition, which, paradoxically, by piling words onto more words only ends up distancing us from the original text and its divinely embedded meanings.[41] Yet there is little doubt in my mind that, when he wrote the *Commedia* (and also at other points in his life), the poet believed that a sign-based hermeneutics, with its emphasis on knowledge as a God-given process of illumination *per creaturas ad Creatorem*, offered the best mode of understanding. In particular, to support my position, I would argue that, while Dante consistently presented himself as a great writer, he only ever introduced himself as "inter vere phylosophantes minimus" ["the least among those who truly pursue philosophy": *Questio de Aqua et Terra*, 1].[42] This was not a conventional humility topos but a precise self-description. He was drawn to the greater flexibility and imaginative freedom of exegesis in contrast to the rationalizing rigour, with its obsessive urge to subdivide, of contemporary neo-Aristotelian philosophy and theology. Augustine and the highly influential hermeneutic tradition which followed in his wake afforded considerable interpretative and creative latitude to the individual exegete; a latitude, which—as we have just seen—the poet flexibly and imaginatively exploited in constructing his own work. As a consequence of the complexity of the divine "utterance", the strong belief existed that an infinite number of "readings" of it was potentially possible, the validity of which depended on the proper application of reason in conformity to the truths of faith.[43] Most importantly, as far as Dante would have been concerned, both the symbolic view of God and His creation, and the artistic and interpretative practices which this perspective generated, were intimately congenial and richly stimulating to a mind and an aesthetic such as his, bent on composing the ultimate Christian poem. As is well known, Dante repeatedly maintained that in writing the *Commedia* he was primarily "imitating" God's two "books". It follows from this ambitious claim that the *Commedia* is the "vestige" of the two fundamental "images" of the Divinity. In the symbolic chain of being, this was the highest ontological status to which a human creation could aspire; and there is no doubt that this is the appropriate status for a *divina comedía* whose purpose is to help in the salvation of humanity. Conversely, neither the mechanistic structures and formalized language nor the scientific categorizations and rationalizing speculations of the Aristotelians were the stuff out of which "divine" poetry could be fashioned.[44] I believe that Dante made his preference for the ways of the "exegetes" (in opposition to those of the "philosophers" and the "theologians") abundantly and repeatedly clear during the whole course of the *Commedia*, and especially in the second and third *cantiche*.

A BONAVENTUREAN THOMAS

Given the introductory character of this study, I cannot go into the crucial question of Dante's ideological sympathies in any depth. I should simply like to offer one brief, though highly indicative example of how the poet showed where his intellectual and artistic allegiances lay. Not incorrectly, it has often been asserted that many structural and stylistic features unite Thomas Aquinas's celebration of St Francis in *Paradiso* XI and Bonaventure's encomium of St Dominic in the following canto.[45] It has also been noted that by means of these formal parallels Dante intended to suggest that it was the divinely willed duty of the Franciscans and the Dominicans to work together in close harmony, a state of affairs which in no way could be said to exist on earth in 1300, not least because of their deep ideological divisions. Yet, by trying to draw the two episodes together, what scholars have failed to recognize is that in *Paradiso* XI and XII things are not as unproblematically neat and tidy as has generally been assumed.[46] A major discrepancy in fact exists between Dante's presentation of Thomas and his treatment of Bonaventure. The latter speaks in a language whose allegorizing and imagistic character is in keeping with his own intellectual and formal practices as an author; the former, on the other hand, by using a similar register, not only fails to speak in a manner which is in keeping with his customary style of writing, but also "imitates" the forms of the Franciscans, since he draws heavily on the "legends" which they composed of their founder's life.[47] Dante, in fact, underlines the peculiarity of Thomas's speech in Heaven by reminding us of the well-established characteristics of his earthly rationalizing prose:

> Tu dubbi, e hai voler che si ricerna
> in sí aperta e 'n sí distesa lingua
> lo dicer mio, ch'al tuo sentir si sterna,
>   ove dinanzi dissi: "U' ben s'impingua",
> e là u' dissi: "Non nacque il secondo";
> e qui è uopo che ben si distingua.
>   (*Paradiso*, XI. 22–27)

[You are bewildered, and you would like my words to become clear in such an open and extended language that it reaches to your hearing, as regards what I said earlier, "Where there is good fattening", and there where I said, "The second one has not been born"; and here it is necessary to distinguish properly.]

Dante recalls the careful division of "philosophy" into clear "distinctions", its reliance on "clarity" and "literalness", and the "length" of its exposition—all elements which are the antithesis of that concision and complex metaphoricity which are the hallmarks of *signa*. Tellingly, *sub specie aeternitatis*, Thomas, too, comes to recognize the superiority of symbolic discourse.[48]

In saying this, I am not trying to devalue either Dante's interest in Aristotelianism or the *Commedia*'s rationalizing ambitions. Rather, I am trying to take the first tentative steps towards defining the nature and range of the poet's ideological formation with greater precision and nuance than has hitherto been customary. Like other "poet-philosophers" before him—most notably twelfth-century figures such as Bernardus Silvestris and Alan of Lille, who, inspired by *Timaeus* and in keeping with their Platonizing symbolic cosmologies, tried to employ *integumenta* as vehicles for abstract thought—Dante, too, was drawn both to the aesthetic and to the speculative potential of *signa*, those "building-blocks" of Creation and of every subsequent "artistic" act. In this context—and once again without being able to go into detail—it is worth noting the poet's extremely suggestive defence of *Timaeus* and of Plato's "figurative" language in *Paradiso* IV—a defence which is all the more significant in that it is preceded by Beatrice's explanation of the symbolic character both of the pilgrim's experience of Heaven (lines 28–42) and of Scripture (lines 43–48):

> Quel che Timeo de l'anime argomenta
> non è simile a ciò che qui si vede,
> però che, come dice, par che senta.
> [...] e forse sua sentenza è d'altra guisa
> che la voce non suona, ed esser puote
> con intenzion da non esser derisa.
> S'elli intende tornare a queste ruote
> l'onor de la influenza e 'l biasmo, forse
> in alcun vero suo arco percuote.
> (*Paradiso*, IV. 49–60)

[What Timaeus argues about souls is not similar to what one sees here, since he seems to believe what he says. (...) and perhaps his meaning is of a different guise than his voice sounds, and may be with an intention that is not to be derided. If he intends to return to these wheels the honour and blame of their influence, perhaps his bow strikes a certain truth.]

"Per Speculum in Aenigmate"

It is not primarily in the medieval Plato, however, that the bases of Dante's semiotics should be sought; they are to be found, as I hope my earlier discussion has made clear, in Biblical symbolism and in that vast array of exegesis which it inspired. While this tradition owed much to Augustine—and not only to *De Doctrina Christiana* but also to *De Magistro*, Books XII and XIII of the *Confessions*, *De Trinitate* and his many works of Scriptural hermeneutics—it had in fact received its first great stimulus from the writings of St Paul. This is evident, for instance, in the many explicit references to Paul's letters found in tractates XCVI–CII of Augustine's commentary on John's Gospel—precisely the tractates which lie behind so much of *Purgatorio* XXXIII.[49] Nor does it come as a surprise that, as Dante attempted to establish his commitment to symbolism, echoes from Paul's epistles should also be heard in the canto—in particular, echoes from the Epistle to the Romans and the First Epistle to the Corinthians—both texts which had a fundamental role in shaping Christian thinking on divine knowledge, human intellection, language and semiotics. It is worth recalling here that it is in the Epistle to the Romans and the First Epistle to the Corinthians that we find those almost proverbial phrases on which the whole edifice of Christian symbolic thinking may be said to stand: "Invisibilia enim ipsius, a creatura mundi, per ea quae facta sunt, intellecta, conspiciuntur: sempiterna quoque eius virtus, et divinitas" ["For, since the creation of the world, His invisible things are seen, being perceived through the things which are made: even His eternal virtue and divinity": Romans 1. 20]; "Videmus nunc per speculum in aenigmate [Beatrice's "enigma forte"?]: tunc autem facie ad faciem" ["We now see by means of a mirror in an enigma: then however we will see face to face"]—and, to appreciate the full import of Paul's declaration, it is also worth quoting the second half of the verse: "Nunc cognosco ex parte: tunc autem cognoscam sicut et cognitus sum" ["Now I know in part: then however I will know as I in my turn am known": I Corinthians 13. 12].

The links which I have been able to establish between *Purgatorio* XXXIII and Paul's two letters are all concentrated in the canto's central panel (lines 48–90)—precisely the part which deals primarily with human intellectual life and its immeasurable distance from God's wisdom, also the main topic being discussed by the

Dante's Signs 161

apostle. When Beatrice reproaches the pilgrim for failing to "interpret" the tree—

> per tante circostanze solamente
> la giustizia di Dio, ne l'interdetto,
> conosceresti a l'arbor moralmente
> (*Purgatorio*, xxxIII. 70–72)

[by such circumstances alone you would have known morally God's justice in the interdict on the tree]

—, she is calquing a phrase from the Epistle to the Romans: "qui cum iustitiam Dei cognovissent" ["those who although they knew the justice of God": Romans 1. 32; and see also 1. 18–19]. Although Paul's verse is part of a ferocious attack on human presumption, which continues to sin even when it "knows" God's "justice", and although Beatrice is criticizing her lover, the *rapprochement* between the Epistle and the *Commedia* ultimately works to Dante-character's advantage. Unlike Paul's sinners, who suffer divine punishment (Romans 1. 18–32), as soon as the pilgrim is able to "interpret" God's will he follows it and is saved. In general, however, the borrowings from the two epistles have a darker quality. They serve to underline and ideologically to legitimate the negative tenor of Beatrice's assessment of human intellectual capacities: "perch' a lor modo lo 'ntelletto attuia" ["because in their manner it obscures your intellect": line 48] and "ne lo 'ntelletto/ fatto di pietra e, impetrato, tinto" ["in the intellect turned to stone and, having become petrified, turns dark": lines 73–74] recall "sed evanuerunt in cogitationibus suis, et obscuratum est insipiens cor eorum" ["but they became vain in their reasonings, and their foolish hearts are darkened": Romans 1. 21]; while "Qualunque ruba [...]/con bestemmia di fatto offende a Dio" ["Whoever steals (...) with blasphemy of act offends against God": lines 58–59] echoes "qui praedicas non furandum, furaris: [...] Deum inhonoras. (Nomen enim Dei per vos blasphematur)" ["you who preach against stealing, steal: (...) you dishonour God. (For the name of God is blasphemed by you)": Romans 2. 21, 23–24]. In addition, *Purgatorio*, xxxIII. 60–64, like I Corinthians 1. 18–24 and 2. 5–16, bring together in a single discussion the matter of the crucifixion, of divine knowledge available through Christ, of the workings of God's mind, and of human intellectual possibilities. The most interesting contacts between Dante and Paul, however, are found in their respective bitter condemnations of those "doctrines" evolved by the *stulti* [foolish] which completely fail to account for the symbolic creations of *Deus artifex* (*Purgatorio*, XXXIII. 85–90; compare Romans 1. 19–25, I Corinthians 1. 17–3. 4; see also Wisdom 13. 6–9).

What I hope is beginning to emerge from my analysis is, on the one hand, the sophistication and range of Dante's knowledge of semiotics, and, on the other, the skilful and culturally adept manner in which he went about revealing his dependence on and allegiance to doctrines of symbolism. We can only appreciate this fundamental operation if we recognize both the technical precision of Dante's language and the contemporary ideological implications of his quotations and allusions (and it goes without saying that Dante utilized the passages from Paul in *Purgatorio* XXXIII in accordance with the principal meanings assigned to them by medieval Biblical exegesis).[50] Yet it has been made difficult to approach the poet in the terms I am suggesting by the fact that, at least since the nineteenth century, "Dante the thinker" has been too closely associated with that intellectual current which has been perceived as the most "modern", namely, Aristotelianism. One result of this monotony of focus, which needs to be coupled with an equally "modern" mistrust and dislike of allegory and its perceived "excesses", has been a quite overwhelming lack of attention to the possible impact of the symbolic tradition on the poet's ideological and artistic development. Since I concentrate on these critical-historical issues in considerably greater detail elsewhere,[51] here I should like to put forward just one last example in support of my semiotic reading of Dante.

A BONAVENTUREAN TRINITY

The recognition of the artistic difficulties which faced the poet as he attempted to render in verse the ineffabilities of Paradise is a scholarly commonplace, and, like all commonplaces, it has largely ceased to be felt as a critical issue. Yet how Dante overcame these difficulties remains a crucial matter for defining both the poetics of *Paradiso* and Dante's debts to medieval symbolism. As he begins to compose his final *cantica*, the poet immediately highlights his impasse and tries to overcome it by appealing to Apollo for help:

> O divina virtú, se mi ti presti
> tanto che l'ombra del beato regno
> segnata nel mio capo io manifesti [...].
> (*Paradiso*, I. 22–24)

[O divine virtue, if you lend me so much of yourself that I can manifest the shadow of the blessed kingdom marked as a sign in my head (...).]

Once again, Dante defines the interplay between memory and language in immediately recognizable and technically appropriate semiotic terms.[52] The really significant piece of jargon, however, is not line 24 but the word "ombra". Commentators have normally glossed it in a very bland manner; Bosco and Reggio's note is typical: "*the shadow*: what the memory can retain of so many ineffable beauties; a faded image".[53] But this kind of explanation seriously weakens the doctrinal toughness and precision of Dante's lexical choice. In Bonaventure's commentary on Peter Lombard's *Sentences*—the *Sentences* were one of the most widely read works of the later Middle Ages—we discover, during the course of a dense presentation of different types of divine analogy, that *umbrae* constitute the least specific kind of mark which God leaves of Himself.[54] A "shadow" offers a "distant and confused" representation of the Divinity (and Bonaventure proceeds by clarifying the nature of the relationship between God and an *umbra*, the type of knowledge a "shadow" provides, and its particular characteristics). Without entering into the theological niceties of the Seraphic Doctor's discussion, I feel that, by having recourse to the Bonaventurean "ombra", Dante offers an excellent shorthand definition of his *Commedia* in general and *Paradiso* in particular. Thanks to this term, he is able to highlight the divine "hand" (*Paradiso*, XXV. 2) behind both the journey and the poem, while at the same time acknowledging the *Commedia*'s limitations in comparison to other more sophisticated creations of the *digitus Dei*. Furthermore, by alluding to the "distance and confusion" of his account of Heaven, he is able to indicate that, unlike the other two *cantiche*, it is an extremely poor and inaccurate record of his experience—it is a text, in fact, whose words have no referents, whose only semanticity is metaphorical.[55] Not only is *Paradiso* faced with the standard problems of the failure of human language to "talk about God", but, as Beatrice makes manifest, until the pilgrim bathes his eyes in the river of light, what he experiences during his ascent through the heavens is a "sign", accessible to his senses, of the celestial hierarchy:[56]

> Qui si mostraron [the blessed], non perché sortita
> sia questa spera lor, ma per far segno
> de la spiritüal c'ha men salita.
>   Cosí parlar conviensi al vostro ingegno,
> però che solo da sensato apprende
> ciò che fa poscia d'intelletto degno.
> (*Paradiso*, IV. 37–42)

[The blessed have shown themselves here, not because this sphere is assigned to them, but to act as a sign of the spiritual one which is least high. One has to speak like this to your faculty, since it can only learn from sense perceptions what it then makes worthy of the intellect.]

Dante's is a brilliant *trovata*. By underscoring the layered semiotic mediations of his account of Paradise, on the one hand he registered the distance between God and any possible representation of the divine reality, while on the other he opened up a space in which his imagination and his poetry could flourish.[57] Both his "alta fantasia" (*Paradiso*, XXXIII. 142) and his art are largely sanctioned and explained in terms of contemporary symbolic thought. Indeed, as Dante makes clear, the *Commedia*—though he would not have put it quite in this way—is the "semiotic" poem *par excellence*. To return to his terminology, *Paradiso* is the linguistic expression (the "manifestation") of the memorial "semiotic mark" of the "shadow" (*Paradiso*, I. 23–24) of a "sign" of Heaven (*Paradiso*, IV. 38–39). And to ensure that the extreme metaphoricity of his celestial narrative would not be lost, he arranged for the most accessible formal feature of *Paradiso* to be its tropological style. Indeed, the symbolic character of Dante's Paradise is the formal correlative of that structure of "desire" which underpins the final *cantica*, so that, as a result, *Paradiso* is permanently just a "prelude" to the actual vision of the divine.[58]

That in *Paradiso* I the poet was in fact dependent on Bonaventurean symbolism is confirmed towards the end of the canto, where Beatrice explains the order of Creation:

> E cominciò: "Le cose tutte quante
> hanno ordine tra loro, e questo è forma
> che l'universo a Dio fa simigliante.
>   Qui veggion l'alte creature l'orma
> de l'etterno valore, il qual è fine
> al quale è fatta la toccata norma."
> (*Paradiso*, I. 103–08)

[And she began: "All things are ordered among themselves, and this is the form which makes the universe resemble God. Here the high creatures see the trace of the eternal value, which is the end for which the norm just mentioned is made."]

Beyond the obvious and generic Neoplatonizing character of this description, one term, *orma*—that is, *vestigium*—catches the eye by virtue of its technical precision. *Vestigia* are, in fact, the second type of analogy in Bonaventure's semiotic hierarchy, those material and spiritual creatures which provide a "distant but distinct" representation of the three persons of the Trinity on account of their character as creations which "reflect God by reason of his triple cause, efficient, formal [i.e. extrinsic or exemplary] and final"—which, to me, sounds like a good general definition of "l'universo" according to contemporary commonplaces.[59] And once the cultural value of these tercets is recovered, another long-standing interpretative knot is also loosened: it becomes obvious that the "alte creature" of line 106 cannot be the angels (who "look at" God directly and have no need of a semiotically mediated vision of their Maker) but are the great human exegetical "authorities".[60] Lastly, the opposition which *Paradiso* I establishes between *ombra* and *orma* helps further to define the symbolic specificity of the *Commedia*. There seems little doubt that in fashioning the last *cantica* Dante expressly drew on and adapted Bonaventure to his needs, since it is only in the Seraphic Doctor that we find the tripartite analogical distinction between *umbra*, *vestigium* and *imago*.[61] It thus comes as no surprise that, when the pilgrim is finally about to enjoy the direct vision of the Godhead, the last reference which Dante should make in the whole poem to a divine sign is to an *imago*. According to Bonaventure, the *imago* spiritually reveals God "in propinquitate et distinctione" ["closely and distinctly"], its properties "reflect Him not so much as cause, but as object", and it offers an insight into those attributes that, respectively and exclusively, characterize each of the three persons of the Trinity (in this instance, the Son):

> tal era io a quella vista nova:
> veder voleva come si convenne
> l'imago al cerchio e come vi s'indova.
> (*Paradiso*, XXXIII. 136–38)

[I was thus at that astonishing sight: I wanted to see how the image fitted the circle and how it has its place there.]

It seems to me that *imago* reflects exactly the situation which the poet describes as his character is about to reach the goal of his otherworldly journey. In imitation of *Deus artifex*, Dante, too, wants to be sought, recognized and interpreted in the "traces" which he has left in his great book.

Conclusion

It is obvious that this essay has only begun to scratch the surface of a topic—Dante and medieval symbolism—which has a considerable bearing upon the genesis, structure and ideological character of each of the poet's works. Much research still needs to be done on the subject; in particular, Dante's place within what is a highly complex tradition, with many ramifications and internal tensions, needs to be defined, so that we may properly follow the drift of his arguments and the forms of his writing. For the present I should like to do no more than conclude by returning one last time to *Purgatorio* XXXIII. As we might have expected him to do at a key moment in the *Commedia*, Dante displays one of the primary ideological foundations of his great poem: its dependence on symbolic traditions. More specifically, he also offers a first hint of, and establishes the ideological framework for, the problems associated with trying to talk about God, problems which will be a fundamental feature of *Paradiso* from its very first lines. As was his custom, he introduced such matters with considerable subtlety. He did not present them directly but constructed the "literal" level of his text in such a manner that these underlying ideas would emerge as a consequence of interpretation; in a similar manner, as I have noted, he also ensured that, formally, the canto was dependent on traditions, such as prophecy and *trobar clus*, which enjoyed close links with exegesis. Given the canto's support for symbolist positions, it is difficult to think how the poet might have made his points more appropriately; nor should it be forgotten that Dante was writing imaginative poetry rather than philosophical prose. On a more general level, such a "metaphoricizing" approach was also highly revealing in the light of Dante's claims that his poem imitated the artistic conventions of *Deus artifex*—a claim which receives one of its most overt expressions precisely in this semiotically involved canto, at the moment when Beatrice tells the pilgrim that on his return to earth he must "mark down as signs" her divinely inspired words for the benefit of the living (lines 52–53).

The *rapprochement* between God and Dante has all sorts of implications—into which I cannot delve here—for the poet's sense of the epistemological value of poetry.[62] Suffice it to say that, just as I believe that he favoured symbolic-exegetical epistemologies over other intellectual systems, so I believe that, within symbolism, he privileged poetry—his poetry—as the most effective way of catching a glimpse of the divine hidden in signs. Knowledge and the means to achieve understanding are key themes in all Dante's works. Both our human limitations and the debts we owe to God make it an absolute necessity—as *Purgatorio* XXXIII reveals—that we recognize and follow that epistemology which is most likely to yield a sense of creation and its Maker—the two key mysteries for any medieval intellectual—, while at the same time avoiding misleading and reductive "doctrines". As far as Dante was concerned, signs can both save us and damn us. It is imperative, therefore, that we learn to discriminate between different semiotic orders, between, say, *narrazion buie* and *vestigge*, between *ombre* and *orme*, and even between *figure impresse in cera* and *comedíe*.[63]

NOTES

1   I first began thinking about the relationship between Dante and medieval semiotics in 1987, when I was invited to give a lecture, "The Eagle's Speech: Bestial, Graphic and Other Signs in the Heaven of Jove", as part of the annual Dante Series in University College, Dublin, which between 1987 and 1988 was dedicated to "Word and Drama in the *Divine Comedy*". The lectures, minus my contribution, have now been collected in *Word and Drama in Dante*, edited by J. C. Barnes and J. Petrie (Dublin, Irish Academic Press, 1993). My lecture is missing because, when I came to prepare the version for publication, I quickly realized that the problem of symbolism in the Middle Ages was so complex that I needed to complete a large amount of further research before I could hope to begin to do justice to the range of Dante's semiotic thinking present in *Paradiso* XVIII–XX. John Barnes, kindly appreciating my difficulty, agreed that a sensible alternative would be for me to prepare an

introductory study of the poet's fascination with *signa* for the general volume he was planning on "Dante and the Middle Ages". This is that introductory study, in which—I should like to add—occasional *vestigia* of my original 1987 talk are still discernible. It is itself now part of a much larger project. I am currently engaged in writing a book on Dante's intellectual history and, in particular, on his contacts with medieval semiotics. In this I have been significantly aided by generous grants from the Leverhulme Trust and from the Research Board of the University of Reading. I am profoundly grateful to both these bodies for their help.

During the last few years, I have given a number of lectures and seminars on aspects of Dante and medieval semiotics at Harvard University, McGill University and Princeton University (1991), at Stanford University (1992), and at the University of Pennsylvania, the Italian Colloquium of the University of Wales in Gregynog, the Research Seminar of my own Department in Reading and the Biennial Conference of the Society for Italian Studies held—not inappropriately—in Dublin (1993). In April 1993 I also gave a short course on "Medieval Semiotics" at the University of Connecticut. I am very grateful for the valuable comments of friends, colleagues and students who attended my talks. I should especially like to thank Robert Dombroski, John Freccero, Bob Hollander, Franco Masciandaro and Steve McGrade. My deepest gratitude, as always, goes to my three sternest and most illuminating interlocutors and readers—Maggie Barański, Giulio Lepschy and Lino Pertile.

Next, a terminological caveat. During the course of this essay I use "symbolism" and "semiotics" in a loosely synonymous manner to stand for (i) medieval reflection on signs, (ii) medieval interpretation of signs, (iii) the practical uses to which signs were put in the Middle Ages, and, most frequently, (iv) the combination of these three activities. No one is more aware than I am of the shortcomings of my usage. However, not only did I require some portmanteau terms in order to proceed with my discussion, but also medieval technical vocabulary associated with *signa* was of such variety that I needed to discover terms which could encompass all this terminology in a relatively neutral manner. Conveniently, since neither "symbolism" nor "semiotics" was really current in the Middle Ages, they offered the ideal solution to my problem. My broad use of "symbolism" is, of course, different from the influential use made of the same term by scholars such as Salvatore Battaglia, D. W. Robertson Jr and Charles Singleton, who, both anachronistically and narrowly, employed it as if it were an integral part of medieval culture. It is, in fact, almost identical to the way in which M-D. Chenu applies "symbolism" in his magnificent collection of essays, *La Théologie au douzième siècle* (Paris, Vrin, 1957). Some sense of the range of semiotic terminology in the Middle Ages, and of the critical problems stemming from this, should emerge during the course of my study. In Dante alone, we find *atto, cenno, essemplo, figura, forma, idolo, imagine, imago, imprenta, impressione, indizio, insegna, isplendor, ombra, orma, segno, sembiante /-anza, signaculo, simigliante / -anza, stampa, testimone, velame, velo, vestig[g]lia, vestigio* etc. As if this confusing proliferation of terms were not enough in itself, the poet almost always used individual words with their own precise technical connotations, which cannot be understood unless, in each instance, we recognize the specific area of the semiotic tradition to which he is alluding. For discussions of the variety of symbolic terminology current in the Middle Ages, see, for example, R.

Javelet, *Image et ressemblance au douzième siècle*, 2 vols (Paris, Letouzey and Ané, 1967); R. W. Bernard, *In Figura: Terminology Pertaining to Figurative Exegesis in the Works of Augustine of Hippo*, unpublished PhD dissertation (Princeton University, 1984); *Medieval Literary Theory and Criticism, c.1100– c.1375*, edited by A. J. Minnis and A. B. Scott (Oxford, Clarendon Press, 1988), p. 168. See also G. B. Ladner, "Medieval and Modern Understanding of Symbolism: A Comparison", *Speculum*, 54 (1979), 223–56, now in his *Images and Ideas in the Middle Ages*, 2 vols (Rome, Storia e Letteratura, 1983), I, 239– 82. A convenient list of "Terms Relating to the Notion of *Integumentum*" may be found in *The Commentary on Martianus Capella's "De Nuptiis Philologiae et Mercurii" Attributed to Bernardus Silvestris*, edited by H. J. Westra (Toronto, Pontifical Institute of Mediaeval Studies, 1986), p. 280.

2   See, for instance, the commentaries on the *Commedia* by D. Mattalia [1960], 3 vols (Milan, Rizzoli, 1975), II, 616; and by U. Bosco and G. Reggio, 3 vols (Florence, Le Monnier, 1979), II, 97.

3   St Augustine, *De Doctrina Christiana*, in *Le Magistère chrétien* [= vol. XI of *Oeuvres de saint Augustin*], edited by G. Combès and J. Farges (Paris, Desclée de Brouwer, 1949), II. 1. 1. All translations into English from this work are modified versions of St Augustine, *On Christian Doctrine*, translated by D. W. Robertson Jr (New York, Macmillan; London, Collier Macmillan, 1987). For instances of the diffusion of the smoky sign, see Peter Lombard, *Sententiarum Libri Quatuor*, IV. 1. 4 (*Pat. Lat.*, CXCII, 839); Pseudo-Robert Kilwardby, *Commenti super Priscianum Maiorem Excerpta*, edited by K. M. Fredborg et al., *Cahiers de l'Institut du Moyen Age grec et latin*, 15 (1975), 1–143, I. 1. 1 (p. 3); Roger Bacon, *De Signis*, in K. M. Fredborg et al., "An Unedited Part of Roger Bacon's *Opus Maius: De Signis*", *Traditio*, 34 (1978), 75–136, § 6; Thomas Aquinas, *Summa Theologica*, 4 vols (Paris, Migne, 1864), I. Q. 45, a. 7.

4   For a useful anthology of definitions of *signum* current in the Middle Ages, see J. Chydenius, *The Theory of Medieval Symbolism* (Helsinki, n. n., 1960). See also nn. 11, 14, 16, 20 and 28 below.

5   On Augustine's contribution to semiotic thought, see H. M. Féret, "Res dans la langue théologique de saint Augustin", *Revue des sciences philosophiques et théologiques*, 29 (1940), 218–43; R. A. Markus, "St Augustine on Signs", *Phronesis*, 2 (1957), 60–83; J. Engels, "La Doctrine du signe chez saint Augustin", in *Studia Patristica*, VI [= *Papers Presented to the Third International Conference on Patristic Studies*, Part IV], edited by F. L. Cross (Berlin, Akademie, 1962), pp. 366–73; J. A. Mazzeo, "St Augustine's Rhetoric of Silence: Truth vs Eloquence and Things vs Signs" [1962], in his *Renaissance and Seventeenth-century Studies* (London, Routledge and Kegan Paul, 1964), pp. 1–28; B. D. Jackson, "The Theory of Signs in St Augustine's *De Doctrina Christiana*", *Revue des études augustiniennes*, 15 (1969), 9–49; R. Simone, "Semiologia agostiniana", *La cultura*, 7 (1969), 88–117; G-H. Allard, "L'Articulation du sens et du signe dans le *De Doctrina Christiana*", in *Studia Patristica*, XIV [= *Papers Presented to the Sixth International Conference on Patristic Studies*, Part III], edited by E. A. Livingstone (Berlin, Akademie, 1976), pp. 377–88; D. E. Daniels, "The Argument of the *De Trinitate* and Augustine's Theory of Signs", *Augustinian Studies*, 8 (1977), 33–54; M. Baratin, "Origines stoïciennes de la théorie augustinienne du signe", *Revue des études latines*, 59 (1981), 260–68; H. Ruef, *Augustin über Semiotik und Sprache* (Berne, Wyss Erben, 1981); M. Baratin and F. Desbordes, "Sémiologie et métalinguistique chez saint Augustin", *Langages*,

65 (1982), 75–89; M. Colish, *The Mirror of Language: A Study in the Medieval Theory of Knowledge*, second edition (Lincoln, Nebraska–London, University of Nebraska Press, 1983), pp. 7–54; G. Manetti, *Le teorie del segno nell'antichità classica* (Milan, Bompiani, 1987), pp. 226–41. For examples of *De Doctrina Christiana*'s *fortuna* in the Middle Ages, see Peter Lombard, *Sententiae*, I. 1. 1 (*Pat. Lat.*, CXCII, 521; there are echoes of *De Doctrina Christiana* and of several of Augustine's other works throughout the *Sentences*: see, for instance, cols 521–25); Pseudo-Robert Kilwardby, *Excerpta*, I. 1. 1 (pp. 2–3); Dante, *Mon.*, III. 4. 8. See also A. Maierú, "*Signum* dans la culture médiévale", in *Sprache und Erkenntnis im Mittelalter*, edited by J. P. Beckmann et al., 2 vols (Berlin–New York, De Gruyter, 1981), I, 51–72; F. Bottin, "Teoria dei segni e logica tardo-medievale", in *Sprache und Erkenntnis*, II, 498–503 (p. 503). See also nn. 18 and 40 below.

6 All translations from the *Commedia* are my own. For instances of *sigillum/signaculum*, see Alan of Lille, *De Planctu Naturae*, edited by N. M. Häring, *Studi medievali*, third series, 19 (1978), 797–879, VIII. 217–59; Pseudo-Robert Kilwardby, *Excerpta*, II. 1. 4a (pp. 54–55). See also A. Blaise, *Dictionnaire latin-français des auteurs chrétiens*, revised edition (Turnhout, Brepols, 1954), s.v. *signaculum*; A. Pézard, "Le Sceau d'or: Dante, Abélard, saint Augustin", *Studi danteschi*, 50 (1973), 1–96; P. Boyde, *Dante Philomythes and Philosopher* (Cambridge, Cambridge University Press, 1981), pp. 224–29, 354–55; W. Wetherbee, notes on his translation of Bernardus Silvestris, *The Cosmographia* (New York, Columbia University Press, 1990), pp. 146–47.

7 As the editors of St Bonaventure's commentary on Peter Lombard's *Sentences* note: "Quod vestigium Trinitatis in omni creatura inveniatur, est sententia communis" (*Opera Omnia*, 10 vols in 11 [Quaracchi, Collegium S. Bonaventurae, 1883–1902], I, 73), and the same may also be said of other kinds of "vestiges". As regards *Purg.*, XXXIII. 106–08, the following quotation from Aquinas is particularly noteworthy: "Vestigium autem demonstrat motum alicujus transeuntis, sed non qualis sit" (*Summa Theologica*, I. Q. 45, a. 7).

8 Similar definitions may be found, for instance, in Augustine, *De Dialectica*, edited by J. Pinborg (Dordrecht–Boston, Reidel, 1975), p. 5; Pseudo-Robert Kilwardby, *Excerpta*, I. 1. 1 (p. 2); Roger Bacon, *De Signis*, §§ 2, 7; Dante, *DVE*, I. 3. 1–2 (quoted in n. 11 below). See also Augustine, *De Magistro*, in *Dialogues philosophiques* [= vol. VI, iii of his *Oeuvres*], edited by F. J. Thonnard (Paris, Desclée de Brouwer, 1941), I. 2: "Qui enim loquitur, suae voluntatis signum foras dat per articulatum sonum."

9 See C. S. Singleton, "The Vistas in Retrospect", in *Atti del Congresso internazionale di studi danteschi*, 2 vols (Florence, Sansoni, 1965–66), I, 279–303; Z. G. Barański, "Structural Retrospection in Dante's *Comedy*: The Case of *Purgatorio* XXVII", *Italian Studies*, 41 (1986), 1–23.

10 See below for various brief asides on the ideological conflicts which took place during the second half of the thirteenth century and the early years of the fourteenth. See also the bibliography listed in n. 21 below.

11 On medieval semiotic thought, see A. Michel, "Signe", in *Dictionnaire de théologie catholique*, edited by A. Vacant and E. Mangenot, vol. XIV, ii (Paris, Letouzey and Ané, 1941), cols 2053–61; D. Van den Eynde, "Les Définitions des sacrements pendant la première période de la théologie scolastique (1050–1235)", *Antonianum*, 24 (1949), 185–226, 439–88 and 25 (1950), 3–78; M-D. Chenu, *La Théologie au douzième siècle*; J. Chydenius, *The Theory of Medieval*

Symbolism; U. Eco, *Trattato di semiotica*, third edition (Milan, Bompiani, 1975), Ch. 1; *Simboli e simbologia nell'alto medioevo*, by various authors, 2 vols (Spoleto, Centro Italiano di Studi sull'Alto Medioevo, 1976); T. Todorov, *Théories du symbole* (Paris, Seuil, 1977), pp. 13–83; J. B. Friedman, *Monstrous Races in Medieval Art and Thought* (Cambridge, Massachusetts–London, Harvard University Press, 1981), pp. 108–30; A. Maierú, "*Signum* dans la culture médiévale"; J. Deely, *Introducing Semiotic* (Bloomington, Indiana University Press, 1982); *Langages,* 65 (1982), special issue on "Signification et référence dans l'antiquité et au Moyen-Age", edited by M. Baratin and F. Desbordes; *Archéologie du signe*, edited by L. Briand' Amour and E. Vance (Toronto, Pontifical Institute of Mediaeval Studies, 1983); M. Colish, *The Mirror of Language;* J. Evans, "Medieval Studies and Semiotics: Perspectives on Research", in *Semiotics 1984*, edited by J. Deely (Lanham, Maryland, University Presses of America, 1985), pp. 511–21; *Semiotica,* 63, i–ii (1987), special issue on "Semiotica Mediaevalia", edited by J. Evans; *Versus,* 50–51 (1988), special issue on "Signs of Antiquity/Antiquity of Signs", edited by G. Manetti; U. Eco and C. Marmo, *On the Medieval Theory of Signs* (Amsterdam, Benjamins, 1989; this collection of essays is in part based on *Versus*, 38–39 [1984]). See also nn. 5, 14, 16, 17, 20 and 28.

12   *DVE*, I. 2–3. See especially: "Nec per spiritualem speculationem, ut angelum, alterum alterum introire contingit, cum grossitie atque opacitate mortalis corporis humanus spiritus sit obtectus. Oportuit ergo genus humanum ad comunicandas inter se conceptiones suas aliquod rationale signum et sensuale habere" (I. 3. 1–2).

13   See N. Mineo, *Profetismo e apocalittica in Dante* (Catania, Università di Catania, Facoltà di Filosofia e Lettere, 1968).

14   On *Deus artifex* and related ideas, see, at least, E. R. Curtius, *European Literature and the Latin Middle Ages* [1948] (London–Henley, Routledge and Kegan Paul, 1979), pp. 544–46; M. T. d'Alverny, "Le Cosmos symbolique du XIIe siècle", *Archive d'histoire doctrinale et littéraire du Moyen Age*, 20 (1953), 31–81; P. Artamendi, "El *liber creaturae* en san Augustin y san Buenaventura", *Augustinus,* 19 (1974), 25–29; K. Emery Jr, "Reading the World Rightly and Squarely: Bonaventure's Doctrine of the Cardinal Virtues", *Traditio,* 39 (1983), 183–218; F. Ohly, "*Deus geometra*: appunti per la storia di una rappresentazione di Dio", in his *Geometria e memoria*, edited by L. Ritter Santini (Bologna, Mulino, 1985), pp. 189–247. See also nn. 5, 11, 16, 17, 20 and 28.

15   All translations from the Vulgate are my own. See also Rom. 1. 18–23 and my discussion of this and other passages from the Epistles of St Paul in the section "Per Speculum in Aenigmate" below.

16   On the theological role of *analogia* and related concepts such as the *imago Dei*, see, at least, M-D. Chenu, "Grammaires et théologie aux XIIe et XIIIe siècles", *Archives d'histoire doctrinale et littéraire du Moyen Age*, 10 (1935–36), 5–28; H. Lyttkens, *The Analogy between God and the World: An Investigation of Its Background and Interpretation of Its Use by Thomas of Aquino* (Uppsala, Almqvist and Wiksells, 1953); P. T. Camelot, "La Théologie de l'image de Dieu", *Revue des sciences philosophiques et théologiques*, 40 (1956), 443–71; R. Javelet, *Image et ressemblance;* T. A. Fay, "The Problem of God-language in Thomas Aquinas: What Can and Cannot Be Said", *Rivista di filosofia neo-scolastica*, 69 (1977), 385–91; W. Beierwaltes, *Identität und Differenz* (Frankfurt am Main–Berne, Lang, 1980); G. B. Ladner, *Images and Ideas.* On the linguistic and logical implications

of analogy, see E. J. Ashworth, "Signification and Modes of Signifying in Thirteenth-century Logic", *Medieval Philosophy and Theology*, 1 (1991), 39–67. A basic introduction to the concept and history of analogy may be found in A. Chollet, "Analogie", in *Dictionnaire de théologie catholique*, vol. I (1903), cols 1142–54; N. W. Mtega, *Analogy and Theological Language in the "Summa contra Gentiles"* (Frankfurt am Main etc., Lang, 1984). See also nn. 5, 11, 14, 17 and 20.

17 On the notion of microcosm see W. Wetherbee, "Philosophy, Cosmology, and the Twelfth-century Renaissance", in *A History of Twelfth-century Western Philosophy*, edited by P. Dronke (Cambridge, Cambridge University Press, 1992), pp. 21–53. See also L. Barkan, *Nature's Work of Art: The Human Body as Image of the World* (New Haven, Yale University Press, 1975); J. A. Coulter, *The Literary Microcosm: Theories of Interpretation of the Later Neoplatonists* (Leiden, Brill, 1976).

18 In *Purgatorio* xxxIII, Beatrice is a very effective *signum* for the Word of God, since, as well as His prophetic and "figurative" voices, she also embodies the "openness" and "plainness" of Scriptural language. In the Bible, it was claimed, the Holy Spirit had coupled this style with the more effective "obscure and ambiguous" register, in order to ensure that the divine message would reach people with different needs and intellectual abilities. See Augustine, *De Doctrina Christiana*, II. 6. 7–8; and compare this passage with *Purg.*, XXXIII. 46–51, 100–02.

19 "Cum enim figurate dictum sic accipitur, tanquam proprie dictum sit, carnaliter sapitur. Neque ulla mors animae congruentius appellatur, quam cum id etiam quod in ea bestiis antecellit, hoc est, intelligentia carni subjicitur sequendo litteram. Qui enim sequitur litteram, translata verba sicut propria tenet, neque illud quod proprio verbo significatur, refert ad aliam significationem [...]. Ea demum est miserabilis animae servitus, signa pro rebus accipere; et supra creaturam corpoream, oculum mentis ad hauriendum aeternum lumen levare non posse" (Augustine, *De Doctrina Christiana*, III. 5. 9). This view has its origins, like so much else connected with Christian symbolism, in St Paul: "Sed sufficientia nostra ex Deo est: qui et idoneos nos fecit ministros novi testamenti: non littera, sed Spiritu: littera enim occidit, Spiritus autem vivificat" (II Cor. 3. 5–6). See also my discussion below in the section "Per Speculum in Aenigmate".

20 On the medieval allegorical tradition, see C. Spicq, *Esquisse d'une histoire de l'exégèse latine* (Paris, Vrin, 1944); B. Smalley, *The Study of the Bible in the Middle Ages* [1952], third edition (Oxford, Blackwell, 1983); M-D. Chenu, *La Théologie au douzième siècle*; H. de Lubac, *Exégèse médiévale*, 2 vols (Paris, Aubier, 1959–64); A. Strubel, "*Allegoria in factis et Allegoria in verbis*", *Poétique*, 23 (1975), 342–57; *Le Moyen Age et la Bible*, edited by P. Riché and G. Lobrichon (Paris, Beauchesne, 1984); J. Pépin, *La Tradition de l'allégorie de Philon d'Alexandrie à Dante* (Paris, Etudes Augustiniennes, 1987); J. Whitman, *Allegory: The Dynamics of an Ancient and Medieval Technique* (Oxford, Clarendon Press, 1987). See also nn. 11, 14, 16 and 28.

21 The bibliography on this dispute is vast. Important studies are M. Grabmann, "Il concetto di scienza secondo S. Tommaso d'Aquino e le relazioni della fede e della teologia con la filosofia e le scienze profane", *Rivista di filosofia neoscolastica*, 26 (1934), 127–55; C. Spicq, *Esquisse d'une histoire*; B. Smalley, *The*

Study of the Bible; E. Gilson, *History of Christian Philosophy in the Middle Ages* [1955] (London, Sheed and Ward, 1980), pp. 325–485; H. de Lubac, *Exégèse médiévale*; A. Ghisalberti, *Medioevo teologico* (Bari, Laterza, 1990), pp. 85–145. On Dante's reactions to this conflict, see G. Mazzotta, *Dante's Vision and the Circle of Knowledge* (Princeton, Princeton University Press, 1992); Z. G. Barański, "Dante fra 'sperimentalismo' e 'enciclopedismo'", in *L'enciclopedismo medievale*, edited by M. Picone (Ravenna, Longo, 1994), pp. 373–94; Z. G. Barański, "Dante commentatore e commentato: riflessioni sullo studio dell'*iter* ideologico di Dante", in *Letture classensi 23* (Ravenna, Longo, 1994), pp. 135–58.

22 On the Neoplatonic patina of *Paradiso* I, see P. Dronke, "L'amor che move il sole e l'altre stelle", *Studi medievali*, third series, 6 (1965), 389–422 (especially pp. 389–91); B. Nardi, *Saggi di filosofia dantesca*, second edition (Florence, La Nuova Italia, 1967), pp. 73–78; N. Sapegno's commentary on the *Commedia*, 3 vols, third edition (Florence, La Nuova Italia, 1985), III, 6, 12, 16. On Dante's Neoplatonism, see, first and foremost, B. Nardi, *Saggi di filosofia dantesca* [1930], second edition (Florence, La Nuova Italia, 1967); B. Nardi, *Dante e la cultura medievale* [1942], new edition edited by P. Mazzantini (Bari, Laterza, 1990). See also R. Palgen, "Scoto Eriugena, Bonaventura e Dante", *Convivium*, 25 (1957), 1–8; A. Mellone, "Emanatismo neoplatonico di Dante per le citazioni del *Liber de Causis*?", *Divus Thomas*, 54 (1951), 205–12; J. Mazzeo, *Structure and Thought in the "Paradiso"* (Ithaca, New York, Cornell University Press, 1958); J. Freccero, "Dante e la tradizione del *Timeo*", *Atti e memorie dell'Accademia nazionale di scienze, lettere e arti di Modena*, sixth series, 4 (1962), 107–23; L. Temperini, "*La Divina commedia* in relazione alla spiritualità e al misticismo francescani", *Analecta Tertii Ordinis Regularis Sancti Francisci de Poenitentia*, 33 (1964–65), 244–91; *Il "Paradiso" come universo di luce: la lezione platonico-bonaventuriana* = vol. II of *Dante europeo*, edited by E. Guidubaldi, 3 vols (Florence, Olschki, 1965–68); M. Cristiani, "Platonismo", in *Enc. dant.*, IV, 550–55; P. Dronke, *Dante and Medieval Latin Traditions* (Cambridge, Cambridge University Press, 1986), pp. 1–31; J. Freccero, *Dante: The Poetics of Conversion*, edited by R. Jacoff (Cambridge, Massachusetts–London, Harvard University Press, 1986); G. Mazzotta, "Order and Transgression in the *Divine Comedy*", *Acta: Ideas of Order in the Middle Ages*, 15 (1988), 1–21; C. Vasoli's commentary on *Convivio* (Milan–Naples, Ricciardi, 1988), pp. 341–43 and *passim*; M. De Bonfils Templer, "Le due *ineffabilitadi* del *Convivio*", *Dante Studies*, 108 (1990), 67–78; M. De Bonfils Templer, "La prima materia de li elementi", *Studi danteschi*, 58 (1986 [but published 1990]), 275–91; J. F. Took, *Dante: Lyric Poet and Philosopher* (Oxford, Clarendon Press, 1990), especially pp. 94–105. See also nn. 24, 27 and 28 below. On Dante and Plato, see A. Pézard, "Regards de Dante sur Platon et ses mythes", *Archives d'histoire doctrinale et littéraire du Moyen Age*, 21 (1954), 165–81; R. Palgen, "Die Spur des Timaios in Dantes *Paradiso*", *Anzeiger der Oesterreichischen Akademie der Wissenschaften: Philosophisch-historische Klasse*, 92 (1955), 272–84; M. Cristiani, "Platone", in *Enc. dant.*, IV, 547–50.

23 Other cantos which make important contributions to an understanding of Dante's symbolic thought are *Purgatorio* X–XII, XV, XXX–XXXI and *Paradiso* II, IV, VII, X–XIV, XXVIII–XXIX, XXXIII.

24 See G. Mazzotta, *Dante's Vision*; L. Pertile, "'La punta del disio': storia di una metafora dantesca", *Lectura Dantis*, 7 (1990), 3–28; L. Pertile, "L'antica fiamma:

la metamorfosi del fuoco nella *Commedia* di Dante", *The Italianist*, 11 (1991), 29–60; L. Pertile, "*Paradiso*: A Drama of Desire", in *Word and Drama*, pp. 143–80.

25 The best-known and critically most established studies of Dante's intellectual formation, all of which, with one notable exception, while recognizing other ideological influences on the poet, have placed much the major stress on his Aristotelianism, are those by Boyde, Corti, Foster, Gilson, Nardi and Vasoli. The exception is Nardi, who made a very strong case for a significant Neoplatonic influence on the poet (see n. 22; it is interesting to observe that in his commentary on the *Convivio* Vasoli accepts the majority of Nardi's non-Aristotelian proposals). My thinking in this study is deeply indebted to Nardi's exemplary scholarship. My main objection to his work is that, as a historian of ideas interested in establishing the poet's possible intellectual parameters, Nardi did not (i) examine the formal and structural implications of Dante's ideological eclecticism; (ii) assess the relationship between "Dante the poet" and "Dante the thinker"; or (iii) pay enough attention to the implications of the shifts in the poet's ideology and to the tensions which these generated in his works. The most recent narrowly Aristotelian-Thomist reading of the *Commedia* is A. Mastrobuono, *Dante's Journey of Sanctification* (Washington, Regnery Gateway, 1990). Important correctives to this general perspective (in addition to the studies cited in the previous note) are P. Dronke, *Dante and Medieval Latin Traditions*, pp. 1–31; J. Freccero, *Dante*; see also nn. 22, 27 and 28. For a fuller discussion of Dante's criticism of Aristotelianism and his championing of Scripturally based exegesis, see my "Dante commentatore e commentato", which also explores the reasons why Dante scholarship has favoured the image of the poet as an Aristotelian with as much vigour as it has.

26 See Bonaventure, *Sermones Selecti de Rebus Theologicis* (in his *Opera Omnia*, vol. v), III. 18–19. See also E. Gilson, *The Philosophy of St Bonaventure* (London, Sheed and Ward, 1938); E. Gilson, *History of Christian Philosophy*, pp. 336–37.

27 For Dante's interest in Bonaventure, see M. Sanarica, *Ancora su Dante e Bonaventura* (Bologna, S. A. B., 1952); R. Palgen, "Scoto Eriugena"; F. Sarri, "S. Bonaventura e l'ordinamento morale del *Purgatorio* dantesco", *L'Italia francescana*, 33 (1958), 103–16, 244–60; M. Schmaus, "Die Philosophie und die Theologie der Dantezeit", *Deutsches Dante-Jahrbuch*, 40 (1963), 18–42; L. Temperini, "*La Divina commedia*"; *Il "Paradiso" come universo di luce*; R. Vanni Rovighi, "Bonaventura da Bagnoregio, santo", in *Enc. dant.*, I, 669–73; E. Hagman, "Dante's Vision of God: The End of the *Itinerarium Mentis*", *Dante Studies*, 106 (1988), 1–20. See also the standard *lecturae* of *Paradiso* XII, and, below, my sections entitled "A Bonaventurean Thomas" and "A Bonaventurean Trinity". On Dante's syncretism, see the following by Z. G. Barański: "'Significar *per verba*': Notes on Dante and Plurilingualism", *The Italianist*, 6 (1986), 5–18; "Re-viewing Dante", *Romance Philology*, 42 (1988), 51–76 (pp. 59–60); "Dante's (Anti-)Rhetoric: Notes on the Poetics of the *Commedia*", in *Moving in Measure*, edited by J. Bryce and D. Thompson (n. p., Hull University Press, 1989), pp. 1–14 (pp. 9–11); "Dante Alighieri: Experimentation and (Self-)Exegesis", in *The Cambridge History of Literary Criticism*: II, *The Middle Ages*, edited by A. J. Minnis (Cambridge, Cambridge University Press, 1994). Peter Dronke provides an excellent example of how, in the *Commedia*, Dante

synthesizes in a single image the Neoplatonic and the Aristotelian view of cosmic love ("L'amor che move", pp. 389–90).

28 By and large, there have been few specific studies of Dante's semiotic ideas, and most of these, in my view, need to be approached with considerable caution, since they underestimate the complexity of the problem. With this warning in mind, see H. F. Dunbar, *Symbolism in Medieval Thought and Its Consummation in the "Divine Comedy"* (New Haven, Yale University Press, 1929); E. Lugarini, "Il segno in Dante: ipotesi sul primo libro del *De vulgari eloquentia*", in *Psicanalisi e strutturalismo di fronte a Dante*, edited by E. Guidubaldi, 3 vols (Florence, Olschki, 1972), III, 79–86; A. Lanci, "segnare", in *Enc. dant.*, V, 127; D. Consoli, "segno", in *Enc. dant.*, V, 127–30; M. Rak, "significanza–significare–significazione", in *Enc. dant.*, V, 242–45; M. Corti, "La teoria del segno nei logici modisti e in Dante", in *Per una storia della semiotica: teorie e metodi*, edited by P. Lendinara and M. C. Ruta = *Quaderni del circolo semiologico siciliano*, 15–16 (1981), pp. 69–86; M. Corti, *La felicità mentale* (Turin, Einaudi, 1983), pp. 139–41; M. Colish, *The Mirror of Language*, pp. 152–220; S. Noakes, "Dante and Orwell: The Antithetical Hypersign as Hallmark in Literature and Politics", *Semiotica*, 63, i–ii (1987), 149–61; G. Gorni, *Lettera nome numero: l'ordine delle cose in Dante* (Bologna, Mulino, 1990); M. Corti, *Percorsi dell'invenzione* (Turin, Einaudi, 1993), pp. 86–87. Considerable attention, however, has been paid to Dante's allegory: see, at least, R. Hollander, *Allegory in Dante's "Commedia"* (Princeton, Princeton University Press, 1969); J. Pépin, *Dante et la tradition de l'allégorie* (Paris, Vrin, 1970); P. Armour, "The Theme of Exodus in the First Two Cantos of the *Purgatorio*", in *Dante Soundings*, edited by D. Nolan (Dublin, Irish Academic Press, 1981), pp. 59–99; *Dante e le forme dell'allegoresi*, edited by M. Picone (Ravenna, Longo, 1987). For the poet's reworking of the notion of *Deus artifex* and for his contacts with the medieval commentary tradition, see my various studies cited in these Notes, and, in particular, "Dante Alighieri" (see n. 27); on the former, see also T. Barolini, *The Undivine Comedy: Detheologizing Dante* (Princeton, Princeton University Press, 1993), pp. 122–42. As regards Dante's debts to medieval symbolism, see also E. G. Gardner, *Dante and the Mystics* (London, Dent, 1913); A. Marigo, *Mistica e scienza nella "Vita nuova" di Dante* (Padua, Drucker, 1914); I. Brandeis, *The Ladder of Vision* (London, Chatto and Windus, 1960); F. Mazzoni, "Canto XXXI", in *Lectura Dantis scaligera*, 3 vols (Florence, Le Monnier, 1967–68), II, 1139–88; A. Mellone, "L'esemplarismo divino secondo Dante", *Divinitas*, 9 (1965), 215–43; V. Branca, "Poetica del rinnovamento e tradizione agiografica nella *Vita nuova*", in *Studi in onore di Italo Siciliano*, 2 vols (Florence, Olschki, 1966), I, 123–48; G. Farris, *Dante e "imago Dei"* (Savona, Sabatelli, 1985); A. Battistini, "L'universo che si squaderna: cosmo e simbologia del libro", in *Letture classensi 15* (Ravenna, Longo, 1986), pp. 61–78; M. Colombo, *Dai mistici a Dante: il linguaggio dell'ineffabilità* (Florence, La Nuova Italia, 1987); J. G. Demaray, *Dante and the Book of the Cosmos* (Philadelphia, American Philosophical Society, 1987); J. Ahern, "Dante's Last Word: The *Comedy* as a *Liber Coelestis*", *Dante Studies*, 102 (1984 [but published 1988]), 1–14; M. Corti, *Percorsi dell'invenzione*, especially pp. 51–74. See also notes 22, 24 and 27 above.

29 For useful summaries of this debate, see the commentaries by Bosco and Reggio, II, 557–58 and Sapegno, II, 368.

30 See U. Bosco, "Canto XXXIII", in his and Reggio's commentary, II, 554–56 (pp. 554–55).
31 On *cantica*, see L. Pertile, "*Canto-cantica-Comedía* e l'Epistola a Cangrande", *Lectura Dantis*, 9 (1991), 105–23; L. Pertile, "*Cantica* nella tradizione medievale e in Dante", *Rivista di storia e di letteratura religiosa*, 27 (1992), 389–412.
32 See, for instance, Sapegno's commentary, II, 370–71.
33 "Je di que bien se rapareille,/Ensi con Themys le conseille,/Homs ou feme, qui vit au monde,/De pechié, qui noie et afonde/Les pecheors et met a mort,/Quand il le delesse, et s'amort/A fere loial penitance,/S'il vient a vraie repentance/Et is de voie male et fole./Themys c'est devine parole,/Qui nous amonneste et avoie/D'aler a Dieu la droite voie,/Et qu'a Dieu nous acopaignons,/Si dist que nous desceignons" (*Ovide moralisé: poème du commencement du quatorzième siècle*, edited by C. De Boer et al., 5 vols [Amsterdam, Muller, 1915–38], I. 2317–30).
34 See M-D. Chenu, *La Théologie au douzième siècle*, pp. 351–65; M. Irvine, "Interpretation and the Semiotics of Allegory in Clement of Alexandria, Origen, and Augustine", *Semiotica*, 63, i–ii (1987), 33–71 (pp. 34, 61–63).
35 See, for instance, the commentaries of Mattalia, II, 605, Bosco and Reggio, II, 557 and Sapegno, II, 368.
36 See the commentary of Bosco and Reggio, II, 558.
37 See Bonaventure, *Commentarius in Evangelium S. Ioannis* (in his *Opera Omnia*, vol. VI), XVI. 37, 48; Thomas Aquinas, *Catena Aurea in Quatuor Evangelia*, 2 vols, edited by A. Guarienti (Turin–Rome, Marietti, 1953), II, 541–45; Thomas Aquinas, *Super Evangelium S. Ioannis Lectura*, edited by R. Cai (Turin–Rome, Marietti, 1952), XVI. v. 2. 2124, XVI. vi. 4. 2146, XVI. viii. 1. 2165.
38 See Augustine, *In Iohannis Evangelium Tractatus* CXXIV, edited by R. Willems (Turnhout, Brepols, 1954).
39 See, for instance, Augustine, *Tractatus*, CI. 1. 1–3; Bonaventure, *Commentarius*, XVI. 49; Thomas Aquinas, *Catena Aurea*, II, 541–44 (with references to John Chrysostom, *Homiliae in Iohannem*, LXXVIII. 1; Augustine, *Tractatus*, CI. 1). All these passages apply the same epithet, *obscura*, to Jesus's prophecy; as a result, it is tempting to conjecture that this technical Biblical usage of the term is the likely source behind Dante's decision to describe Beatrice's divine speech as "narrazion buia". Other commentaries also stress the unintelligibility of Christ's words but without mentioning its "obscurity"; see *Glossa Ordinaria* (*Pat. Lat.*, CXIII, 414).
40 The texts from John, Paul, Augustine and the various commentators which I suggest constitute the ideological and formal background to *Purgatorio* XXXIII belong to a single culturally determined network. This is apparent from the fact that they are linked by an internal economy of cross-referencing; hence both the force of their impact on the poet's memory and the appropriateness of their status as "signposts" for the problems which Dante raises in the canto. Thus, when Bonaventure discusses John 16. 25, he quotes *De Doctrina Christiana*, II. 6. 7–8 (XVI. 49), which also lies behind *Purg.*, XXXIII. 46–51, 100–02 (see n. 18 above), while at XVI. 39 he alludes to I Corinthians, which also plays an important part in the canto (see the section "Per Speculum in Aenigmate" below). For other instances of this fascinating system of allusion, see nn. 18, 49 and 50.
41 See M. Irvine, "Interpretation and the Semiotics of Allegory", pp. 61–63.

42 On Dante's "self-construction", see G. Contini, "Dante come personaggio-poeta della *Commedia*" [1958], in his *Un'idea di Dante* (Turin, Einaudi, 1976), pp. 33–62; R. Hollander, *Allegory in Dante's "Commedia"*; Z. G. Barański, "'Primo tra cotanto senno': Dante and the Latin Comic Tradition", *Italian Studies*, 46 (1991), 1–36, and my other articles cited in these Notes.

43 On Augustine's belief in exegetical freedom, see his *De Genesi ad Litteram*, edited by P. Agaesse and A. Solignac, 2 vols (Bruges, Desclée de Brouwer, 1972), I. 18. 37–I. 21. 41, his *Tractatus*, LXIV. 2 and his *Confessions*, XII. See also M. Irvine, "Interpretation and the Semiotics of Allegory", pp. 63–66; Z. G. Barański, "Dante's Biblical Linguistics", *Lectura Dantis*, 5 (1989), 105–43 (p. 127).

44 With his customary insight, M-D. Chenu excellently summarizes the fundamental formal difference between the two "schools": "le style, extérieur et intérieur, du scolastique [in contrast to "symbolists"] sacrifie tout à une technicité dont l'austérité le dépouille des ressources de l'art. Ou plutôt il se crée une rhétorique speciale où les images, les comparaisons, les métaphores, les symboles sont immédiatement conceptualisés, hors toute complaisance sensible. D'où ce style abstrait, fait de classement, de divisions, de distinctions, d'oppositions formelles, favorables à la précision de la pensée et à l'art de la discussion" (*Introduction à l'étude de saint Thomas d'Aquin* [Montreal, Institut d'études médiévales; Paris, Vrin, 1950], p. 52). To Chenu's observations should be added K. Emery's aside that "by the time of the *Collationes in Hexaëmeron* Bonaventure had fully developed an extravagantly symbolic mode of expression, wholly alien to the language of the schools" ("Reading the World Rightly" [see n. 14 above], p. 187). For a discussion of the *Commedia*'s relationship to the "two books" of Creation and Scripture, see Z. G. Barański, "La lezione esegetica di *Inferno* I: allegoria, storia e letteratura nella *Commedia*", in *Dante e le forme dell'allegoresi*, pp. 79–97.

45 See, for instance, U. Cosmo, *L'ultima ascesa*, revised edition by B. Maier (Florence, La Nuova Italia, 1965), pp. 123, 142, 148; Sapegno's commentary, III, 145.

46 Two important recent studies have, however, preferred to focus on the differences between, and the tensions in, Dante's presentations of the two saints; see K. Foster, "Gli elogi danteschi di S. Francesco e di S. Domenico", in *Dante e il francescanesimo* (Cava dei Tirreni, Avagliano, 1987), pp. 231–49; T. Barolini, "Dante's Heaven of the Sun as a Meditation on Narrative", *Lettere italiane*, 40 (1988), 3–36 (which includes good bibliographies on various aspects of these cantos), now in revised form in her *The Undivine Comedy*, pp. 194–217.

47 See Sapegno's commentary, III, 148, 150–52; T. Barolini, "Dante's Heaven of the Sun", p. 6.

48 T. Barolini, "Dante's Heaven of the Sun" is a sustained and original meta-narrative reading of *Paradiso* XI and XII with which my brief aside has some potential points of contact (as well as of difference). Unfortunately, I do not have the space here to pursue these matters in any detail. It is, however, noteworthy within the context of my present discussion that Barolini believes that, in these cantos, Dante is involved in "a bold attempt to deny the Aristotelian precept that 'to be diverse necessarily means to be unequal [*Summa Theologica*, I. Q. 47, a. 2]'" (p. 7).

49 See the notes to Augustine, *Tractatus*, pp. 571–97.
50 See, for example, Thomas Aquinas, *Super Epistolam ad Romanos Lectura*, I. 7. 116–45 (on Rom. 1. 20–25); *Super Primam Epistolam ad Corinthios Lectura*, I. 3. 44–61 (on I Cor. 1. 17–24); XIII. 4. 800–04 (on I Cor. 13. 12); both *lecturae* are in *Super Epistolas S. Pauli Lectura*, edited by R. Cai, 2 vols (Turin–Rome, Marietti, 1953). As further evidence of the ideological and structural interconnections which had grown up between the Scriptural, patristic and exegetical texts which I am utilizing here to illustrate my analysis of *Purgatorio* XXXIII, it is noteworthy that Thomas cites Rom. 1. 20 at I. 3. 55 and XIII. 4. 800 of his commentary on I Corinthians, while at I. 7. 122 of his "reading" of Romans he quotes I Cor. 1. 24. In addition, at I. 3. 40–41 of the former *lectura*, he introduces references to *De Doctrina Christiana*; see nn. 18, 40 and 49 above.
51 See Z. G. Barański, "Dante commentatore e commentato".
52 See n. 8 above.
53 "*L'ombra*: ciò che può rimanere nella memoria di tante ineffabili bellezze: un'immagine sbiadita" (Bosco and Reggio's commentary, III, 23). Two studies which do examine Dante's "shadow" from a sophisticated point of view are R. Hollander, *Allegory in Dante's "Commedia"*, pp. 201–02 and J. Pépin, *Dante et la tradition de l'allégorie*, pp. 39–40; Pépin's discussion is in fact dependent on Hollander's, and, in her turn, M. Corti (*Percorsi dell'invenzione*, p. 63) follows the work of both scholars. All three critics acknowledge that Dante derives *ombra* from the Biblical exegetical tradition, but without recognizing a precise source for his borrowing. Dante uses the same word with very different resonances in *Par.*, III. 114 ("l'ombra de le sacre bende") and *Par.*, XXXIII. 96 ("l'ombra d'Argo").
54 "Et ideo intelligendum, quod cum creatura ducat in cognitionem Dei per modum *umbrae*, per modum *vestigii* et per modum *imaginis*, differentia eorum *notior*, a qua etiam denominatur, accipitur penes *modum repraesentandi*. Nam *umbra* dicitur, in quantum repraesentat in quadam elongatione et confusione; *vestigium*, in quantum in elongatione, sed distinctione; *imago* vero, in quantum in propinquitate et distinctione./Ex hac differentia colligitur *secunda*, quae est penes conditiones, in quibus attenduntur haec. Nam creaturae dicuntur *umbra* quantum ad proprietates, quae respiciunt Deum in aliquo genere causae secundum rationem indeterminatam; *vestigium* quantum ad proprietatem, quae respicit Deum sub ratione triplicis causae, efficientis, formalis et finalis, sicut sunt unum, verum et bonum; *imago* quantum ad conditiones, quae respiciunt Deum non tantum in ratione causae, sed et obiecti, quae sunt memoria, intelligentia et voluntas./Ex his concluduntur *aliae duae* differentiae: quantum ad ea ad quae *ducunt*; nam creatura ut umbra ducit ad cognitionem *communium*, ut *communia*: vestigium in cognitionem *communium*, ut *appropriata*; imago ad cognitionem *propriorum*, ut *propria*./Alia differentia est penes ea in quibus *reperiuntur*. Quoniam enim omnis creatura comparatur ad Deum et in ratione causae et in ratione triplicis causae, ideo omnis creatura est umbra vel vestigium. Sed quoniam sola rationalis creatura comparatur ad Deum ut obiectum, quia sola est capax Dei per cognitionem et amorem: ideo sola est imago" (Bonaventure, *Commentaria in Quatuor Libros Sententiarum* [in his *Opera Omnia*, vols I–IV], I. Dist. 3, Pars 1, Q. 2, Concl.; italics in the critical edition). As well as Bonaventure's work on the *Sentences*, important commentaries on Peter Lombard's text were written by Albertus Magnus and Thomas Aquinas; and see M-D. Chenu, *La Théologie au douzième*

siècle, p. 329. On the influence of the *Sentences* in Florence during the period of Dante's residence there, see C. T. Davis, *Dante's Italy and Other Essays* (Philadelphia, University of Pennsylvania Press, 1984), pp. 149, 152, 156. On Dante and Peter Lombard, see A. Ciotti, "Dante e Pietro Lombardo nell'esegesi trecentesca della *Commedia*", *L'Alighieri*, 7, i (1966), 74–97; S. Vanni Rovighi, "Pietro Lombardo", in *Enc. dant.*, IV, 508–10.

55 See R. Hollander, *Allegory in Dante's "Commedia"*, pp. 192–202; J. Freccero, *Dante*, pp. 209–44; L. Pertile, "*Paradiso*: A Drama of Desire", pp. 145–46. See also T. Barolini's discussion of the poetics of *Paradiso*, which includes a suggestive critique of the position adopted by Freccero (*The Undivine Comedy*, pp. 166–256).

56 Given the traditional and the Dantean emphasis (see nn. 8 and 12 above) on the indivisible relationship between the human body and the human need for signs, it is obvious that the question of whether the pilgrim travels through the heavens bodily or in spirit is not actually a problem at all. It is self-evident from what Beatrice tells him in *Paradiso* IV that the pilgrim is travelling "con quel d'Adamo" (*Purg.*, IX. 10). The doubt is first raised in *Paradiso* I ("S'i' era sol di me quel che creasti/novellamente, amor che 'l ciel governi,/tu 'l sai, che col tuo lume mi levasti", lines 73–75) soon after the poet's admission of the difficulties facing him as he tries to write about his celestial journey. He is so bewildered at this point that he cannot even recall what he will be able to remember in a few cantos' time. More significantly, lines 73–75 function in a manner similar to the now proverbial "Io non Enëa, io non Paulo sono" (*Inf.*, II. 32). Rather than delimit the pilgrim, both passages, by drawing attention to the significant differences between his otherworldly experiences and those of Paul (as recorded in II Cor. 12. 3 and the *Visio Pauli*), underscore the superiority and uniqueness of Dante-character's divine journey. In addition, they highlight the complexity of the *Commedia* in comparison to both Paul's Epistle and the apocryphal, though extremely popular, vision.

57 In strictly literary terms, Dante may be said to have located the *Commedia* in a similar intermediary position between God's "books" and human writing; see Z. G. Barański, "La lezione esegetica di *Inferno* I", pp. 96–97.

58 "Ciò che caratterizza ideologicamente il discorso dantesco sul piano semantico è proprio l'assenza di una siffatta distinzione, e cioè il fatto che l'approssimazione a Dio viene sentita dal personaggio e narrata dal poeta come esperienza di una tensione e di un fervore in cui amore e conoscenza fanno tutt' uno. Ciò non toglie che la vertigine del *Paradiso*, inteso appunto come preludio e approssimazione all'ultima visione e non come visione in atto, sia costantemente di natura duplice, e affettiva (spesso anzi erotica) e intellettuale" (L. Pertile, "L'antica fiamma", pp. 33–34). I believe that the poet's notion of desire should now be considered against the broader canvas of medieval (and Dantean) symbolic thinking.

59 On Dante's view of the universe and creation, see A. Mellone, *La dottrina di Dante Alighieri sulla prima creazione* (Nocera Superiore, Convento S. Maria degli Angeli, 1950); J. A. Mazzeo, "The Analogy of Creation in Dante", *Speculum*, 32 (1957), 706–21; A. Mellone, "Creazione: dottrina della creazione", in *Enc. dant.*, II, 251–53.

60 For a summary of this debate, see Sapegno's commentary, III, 14–15.

61 See the notes of the editors of the *Commentaria*, I. 73; E. Gilson, *The Philosophy of St Bonaventure*, p. 515.

62 On this question, see G. Mazzotta, *Dante's Vision*; Z. G. Barański, "Dante fra 'sperimentalismo' e 'enciclopedismo'".
63 It is intriguing how, despite the breadth and complexity of his preoccupations in the *Commedia*, Dante, by an uncanny inevitability, almost always ended up returning to matters related to the writing of his poem and to its status as literature.

DANTE AND THE HOHENSTAUFEN: FROM CHRONICLE TO POETRY

Clotilde Soave-Bowe

Since the Hohenstaufen were one of the most important ruling families of the twelfth and thirteenth centuries, it was to be expected that members of the dynasty should appear in Dante's *Commedia*. But they are not present in some of the places where we might perhaps have expected to find them. For example, Dante includes no medieval German emperor among the ideal emperors mentioned by Justinian in Canto VI of *Paradiso*, and none of them appears among the champions of the faith in the Heaven of Mars (*Paradiso* XVIII) or among the six righteous rulers in the Heaven of Jupiter (*Paradiso* XX).

In *Paradiso*, XV. 139-44 Dante's ancestor Cacciaguida speaks of his service under Conrad III in the Second Crusade. This, the only reference to Conrad, might be interpreted as an indirect homage to the house of Swabia, since it shows Dante's most illustrious ancestor as being proud to have served under a Swabian ruler and to have been ennobled by him. But it is doubtful whether Dante regarded Conrad III as the first of the Hohenstaufen emperors: in view of the complexity of the political and dynastic situation after the death of Henry V in 1125, with proclamations of kings and anti-kings, popes and anti-popes, Conrad's final victory had an aura of dubious legality. Nonetheless, the house of Hohenstaufen did achieve royal dignity when in a solemn ceremony on 29 June 1138 Archbishop Pusterla placed the iron crown of Lombardy on Conrad's head. He was, however, under a sentence of excommunication issued by Pope Honorius II, the first of a series of excommunications of members of the house of Swabia extending over a century and a half. Later, on his return from the Second Crusade (1147-49), the King of the Romans was invited by the Senate to receive the imperial crown in Rome.[1] Thus the final step—the coronation of the first Duke of Swabia as Holy Roman Emperor—seemed close at hand. But Conrad never received imperial coronation because the expedition to Italy never took place. He died, after a brief illness, at Bamberg in 1152.

Dante does not seem to have had a very high opinion of Conrad III precisely because, like the three rulers who came immediately after the last of the Hohenstaufen—Rudolph of Habsburg, Adolf of Nassau and Albert of Habsburg—, he neglected Italy. Besides, although all four were elected kings of the Romans Dante does not regard them as lawful emperors because they never received imperial coronation in Rome.[2] That is perhaps why Cacciaguida's mention of Conrad is more in praise of himself, and of the other Florentine nobles who were the Emperor's devoted subjects, than of the Emperor. Dante regards the great Swabian emperor Frederick I (Barbarossa) as the real founder of the line, the first "vento di Soave" ["blast of Swabia": *Paradiso*, III. 119].

The *Commedia* contains one passing reference to Frederick I, who is mentioned by name. One of the penitents on the *cornice* of sloth in Purgatory introduces himself as an abbot of San Zeno in the time of the good Barbarossa (who was Emperor between 1152 and 1190):

> Io fui abate in San Zeno a Verona
> sotto lo 'mperio del buon Barbarossa,
> di cui dolente ancor Milan ragiona.
> (*Purgatorio*, XVIII. 118–20)

[I was Abbot of San Zeno at Verona under the rule of the good Barbarossa, of whom Milan still talks with sorrow.]

The word "buon" repeats the adjective used of "'l buono Augusto" ["the good Augustus"] in line 71 of *Inferno* I, and is intended to denote not moral virtue but ability as a warrior and ruler. In the words "di cui dolente ancor Milan ragiona" the Abbot recalls an important episode in Frederick I's reign, the siege, conquest, sack and destruction of Milan in 1162. Villani writes about this in his *Nuova cronica* (VI. 1), but as a good Guelf he is far from praising Barbarossa's action; indeed, he interprets the resistance of the Milanese as a measure of assistance and solidarity towards the embattled Pope, Alexander III. In Dante's lines, however, we hear a note of defiance and triumph over the Emperor's opponents, who got what they deserved. Dante sees the destruction of Milan, regrettable in itself, as a legitimate act of justice: Barbarossa was the emperor, the supreme legitimate power, while the Lombard League had perpetrated an illegal and factious revolt, and the actions of the Papacy represented an impious and unwarranted interference, an example of "officio non commesso" ["an office not given in charge", that is, exceeding one's powers: *Purgatorio*, x. 57].

We find confirmation of this attitude in Dante's letter of 31 May 1311 "to the most iniquitous Florentines", where he warns his fellow citizens that they will incur the same punishment as Milan if they persist in their wicked resistance to Emperor Henry VII, the guardian of the Roman Empire and the elect of God: "Bethink you of the thunderbolts of the first Frederick; consider the fate of Milan."[3]

Frederick's contemporaries, including his opponents, admired his sense of duty and his faith. Just when the Swabian eagle was soaring over Europe after decades of defeats and victories, there came the news of the fall of Jerusalem (1187). Frederick put himself at the head of the Third Crusade and met an accidental death, without sacraments, crossing the River Salef in Cilicia.[4] It is perhaps surprising that Dante does not include him among the crusaders and defenders of the faith, such as Godefroy de Bouillon and Robert Guiscard, the conqueror of Sicily, listed by Cacciaguida (*Paradiso*, XVIII. 47–48). Instead, he characterizes Barbarossa as the upholder of universal empire against the divisiveness—internal as well as external—of the Italian city-states (though it is in a way paradoxical that in his passing reference to Barbarossa he should pick out an occasion when those city-states showed that power of collaboration and common action which Dante so longed for). Like his Swabian predecessor Conrad III, Frederick I is presented not as an individual but as a representative of the idea of empire.

The picture of the crusader Barbarossa and of other Swabians has been clouded by the Florentine Guelf historiographical tradition, because of their long and bitter struggle against the Papacy. For example, the belief that the Crusade had been imposed on Barbarossa by the Pope as a penance for his schismatic tendencies is traceable in Dante's time in the historical compilation which Thomas of Tuscany, writing in about 1279, based on the chronicle of Martin of Troppau, and which records every bit of slander ever propagated against the Hohenstaufen, as well as in Brunetto Latini's *Tresor* (I. 92. 8), the historical sections of which reflect Florentine Guelf views.[5]

On the reign of Henry VI, the son of Frederick I, Geoffrey Barraclough has remarked, "Few reigns have given rise to such diverse judgement."[6] Dante solves the problem by mentioning him only as the "secondo vento di Soave". But in *Paradiso*, III. 118–20 we have a detached and regal presentation of his queen, "la gran Costanza" ["the great Constance"], the only one of the Swabians located in Paradise. She is pointed out to Dante in the Heaven of the Moon among the spirits of those nuns who were forced to break their vows but remained faithful to them in their hearts. Dante picked up an improbable myth which had found acceptance in the gullible Guelf historiography of the thirteenth century. According to this story, the elderly Constance had been taken forcibly from her convent to become Henry's bride and secure for him the inheritance of the Norman kingdom of Sicily. Villani has a different version, that "she unwillingly lived in the guise of a nun in a certain convent of nuns; [...] already perhaps fifty years old, she was a nun in body but not in mind in the city of Palermo" (*Nuova cronica*, V. 20). These legends had been propagated in order to discredit the Hohenstaufen, especially Frederick II. There was even a prophecy, attributed to Joachim of Fiore, according to which Constance had become pregnant by a devil and her son (Frederick II) would die excommunicate.[7] Villani uses this legend to explain why Frederick II turned out to be such a persecutor of the Church: "born of a nun, and at an age of more than fifty-two years, when it is almost impossible for woman's nature to give birth to a son; so that he was born of two contraventions, the one spiritual and the other—almost contrary to the laws of nature—temporal" (*Nuova cronica*, VI. 16). Dante, who accepts the legend of the elderly nun, sees

> la luce de la gran Costanza
> che del secondo vento di Soave
> generò 'l terzo e l'ultima possanza.
> (*Paradiso*, III. 118–20)

[the great Constance, who bore to the second blast of Swabia the third and final power.]

The "winds" of Swabia derive from a myth of violence and political intrigue, and the image suggests a whirlwind on earth which vanishes as rapidly as it has appeared, leaving behind a trail of devastation.

Dante's attitude to Frederick II (Emperor between 1215 and 1250) is quite different from his attitude to the earlier Frederick. Chronologically and ideologically Frederick II is much closer, and Dante mentions him a number of times in his works. In a passage in the *Convivio* (IV. 3. 6) he refers to a supposed theory of Frederick II's about the basis of nobility, which in fact, as Dante notes in *Monarchia* (II. 3. 3), goes back to Aristotle (*Politics*, IV. 8. 1294a. 21): "Domandato che fosse gentilezza, rispuose ch'era antica ricchezza e belli costumi" ["When asked how he would define nobility (he) replied that it consisted in age-old wealth and pleasing manners"]. While Dante accepts the authority of the Emperor's definition he declares himself "non reverente" ["not (...) respectful": IV. 8. 11–14] towards it and concludes that "messere lo Imperadore in questa parte non errò pur ne le parti de la diffinizione, ma eziandio nel modo di diffinire" ["his lordship the emperor erred in this matter not only regarding the components he posits in his definition, but in the very way he constructed his definition": IV. 10. 6]. Dante maintains that "le divizie [...] non possono causare nobilitade, perché sono vili" ["riches cannot cause nobility, because they are base": IV. 10. 7] and that virtue is derived from nobility (IV. 20. 2); he concludes by affirming that "nobilitade umana non sia altro che 'seme di felicitade', 'messo da Dio ne l'anima ben posta'" ["human nobility is nothing less than 'the seed of happiness' 'infused by God into the soul that is well placed'": IV. 20. 9]. For Dante Frederick is a "loico e clerico grande" ["great thinker and scholar": IV. 10. 6]; in Book I of *De Vulgari Eloquentia* he celebrates him and his son Manfred for their patronage of writers and scholars, and for their nobility and rectitude: "Those great heroes the Emperor Frederick and his nobly born son Manfred made manifest the fine loftiness of their souls while fortune allowed, and lived like men, by reason, scorning to live like beasts."[8] Dante felt that they, like him, had pushed to the very limits of their own times and aspired to something new and better. The interest in and admiration for Frederick expressed by Dante have been well attributed by Aldo Vallone to Frederick's "wisdom, the power of his position and his courage in war, to the nobility and candour of his character, to his use of reason, which is cognition and virtue [...], to his generosity and erudition, to his cultivation of knowledge and art, to his boundless love of freely pursued learning."[9]

But Frederick II, "ultimo imperadore de li Romani" ["the last emperor of the Romans": *Convivio*, IV. 3. 6], while being a "clerico grande", was at the same time tainted by vice. The poet's sympathy and admiration for him do not cloud his moral judgement. In *Inferno*, XXIII. 66 he compares the leaden copes weighing down the hypocrites with the hoods which Frederick is supposed to have used in executing prisoners: an image of ruthless justice.

But it is not for his cruelty that Dante condemns Frederick to Hell. Instead he is perfunctorily placed in a flaming tomb among the Epicureans, that is, those who denied the immortality of the soul: "Qua dentro è 'l secondo Federico" ["Here within is the second Frederick": *Inferno*, x. 119]. In placing him there, Dante follows the propaganda of the Emperor's Guelf enemies. When in 1247 the struggle between Pope and Emperor reached its most acrimonious phase, Frederick was described by the Pope as "the limb of the devil, the servant of Satan, the miserable precursor of Antichrist".[10] Suspected of heresy, he had been excommunicated—not for the first time—at the Council of Lyons in 1245 and "deposed" both for his alleged contempt of the Church's supreme authority and for his well-known favour towards the Moslem inhabitants of his kingdom.[11] Scholars have long ceased to doubt that he received the last sacraments and died reconciled to the Church. His son Manfred was present at his death and wrote to his half-brother Conrad, "Professing the orthodox faith, he humbly and with a contrite heart recognized the Holy Roman Church as his mother."[12] Despite this, Guelf writers did not hesitate to assert that he died excommunicate, without penitence or sacraments.[13] Dante, who was not in a position to obtain an impartial account, accepted the Guelf version of events. But, one might ask, why not invent an imaginary last-minute repentance and thus issue the Emperor with a passport to Purgatory? What must have put Frederick beyond pardon was the fact that he and his Florentine partisans were adherents of a sect "che l'anima col corpo morta fanno" ["who make the soul die with the body": *Inferno*, x. 15].[14] In the *Commedia* therefore Dante's judgement on Frederick—a man so rich in virtues and kingly qualities, a personality which to our eyes is so interesting and so complex—, inspired by quite different criteria, is simple and decisive, and with no hesitation or qualification the poet condemns the monarch who had been "d'onor sí degno" ["so worthy of honour": *Inferno*, XIII. 75] to the everlasting fire among those who had denied God.

The phrase "d'onor sí degno" is pronounced by Pier della Vigna, protonotary and chancellor at Frederick's court. Piero still defends his emperor and proclaims his own innocence. After serving the Emperor for more than twenty years, he was arrested at Cremona in 1249 and subsequently tried and found guilty of peculation, but committed suicide rather than suffer undeserved torture and imprisonment. Dante condemns him for having taken his own life, but seems to regard him as innocent of any offence against the Emperor. Rather than censuring Frederick, however, he diverts the blame onto envious courtiers, who had traduced Piero and brought him to ruin, allowing Piero to say:

> Fede portai al glorïoso offizio,
> tanto ch'i' ne perde' li sonni e ' polsi.
> La meretrice che mai da l'ospizio
> di Cesare non torse li occhi putti,
> morte comune e de le corti vizio,
> infiammò contra me li animi tutti.
> (*Inferno*, XIII. 62–67)

[So faithful was I to the glorious office that for it I lost both sleep and life. The harlot that never turned her whorish eyes from Caesar's household—the common death and vice of courts—inflamed all minds against me.]

Salimbene, never prepared to put a favourable interpretation on Frederick's actions, is in agreement with Dante about Piero's innocence: "Although the Emperor had exalted him [...], afterward [...] he found occasion of word and slander against him and these brought death upon him." The same chronicler goes further, suggesting that the Emperor planned to "despoil him of the honour and riches and take them for himself."[15] However this may be, it is interesting to note that in the course of a recent restoration of the triumphal gateway in Capua the figures of Pier della Vigna and his colleague Thaddeus of Suessa have been identified in two niches under the statue of Frederick. It was their duty as imperial ministers and judges to put into effect the maxims expressed round the edges of the niches. Piero's caption states prophetically (the Capua gate was begun in 1234): "Let the faithless fear to be shut out or to die in prison."[16]

Conrad IV, Frederick II's legitimate heir and potentially the fourth wind of Swabia, who died only four years after his father, is non-existent for Dante, while Conradin, Conrad IV's son, cruelly put to death in 1268 before he had reached the age of eighteen, is named only in order to criticize the cruelty of Charles of Anjou, not to comment on Conradin:

> Carlo venne in Italia e, per ammenda,
> vittima fé di Curradino.
> (*Purgatorio*, xx. 67–68)

[Charles came into Italy and, for amends, made a victim of Conradin.]

Following the death of Frederick II in 1250, and in Conrad's absence (he was detained in Germany), Conrad's half-brother Manfred assumed the regency of the Regnum, which extended from Sicily to Naples and bordered on the territories of the Church. After Conrad's death, and in the name of his nephew Conradin, Manfred, already excommunicated by the Pope, who challenged the validity of his position, was proclaimed king of the Regnum on 10 August 1258. Leader of the Italian Ghibellines and an opponent of papal intervention, he struggled against successive popes, Innocent IV, Alexander IV and Urban IV. The last of these, who was French by birth, induced King Louis IX of France to permit his brother Charles of Anjou to intervene in Italy. Manfred fell near Benevento in 1266, aged only 35, in a battle that crowned the victorious expedition of Charles of Anjou, who had already been invested with the Regnum by Clement IV. These, briefly, are the events that led up to Manfred's death.

Since the conquest of the Regnum by the Angevins was an enterprise linked to the long-standing disputes between Empire and Papacy, and especially to the struggle between the Hohenstaufen and the Papacy, it is not surprising that it had repercussions throughout Europe. Apart from the documents issued by the various chanceries, these events are recorded largely by chroniclers who were ecclesiastics and therefore likely to defend the interests of the Holy See. There were relatively few lay writers, whom we might expect to have upheld the interests of lay or Ghibelline society, and even those few were also influenced by the popes' widespread and persuasive propaganda. A campaign against Manfred was launched as early as 1255. The projected conquest of the Regnum by Charles of Anjou was always designated a crusade, and both Charles and his followers were to enjoy the same indulgences as were granted to those who took part in the holy war against the infidel.[17] In the summer of 1264 Urban IV lamented that he was unable to stem the rising tide of heresy because Manfred had cut the Curia's communications with the outside world: "Heretics are spreading their errors [...] while ecclesiastical liberty is trampled underfoot with impunity."[18] The crusade was preached in France, Lombardy, Tuscany, other parts of Italy and even England at the end of 1255.[19] It comes as no surprise therefore that the poet Rutebeuf, who appears to have followed Charles of Anjou to Italy, describing Charles as a good king, comparable in both name and deeds to Charlemagne, fighting for France, for the Church and for God, should stress that the enterprise is a means offered by God for the achievement of Paradise.[20] Adam of Clermont writes: "Manfred, son of Frederick, born they say of a concubine, usurped Sicily, Apulia, Calabria and part of Italy from the Church. [...] Charles [...], at the instance of the Pope and cardinals, [...] takes the cross against him with a large army and defeats him in the field at Benevento."[21] The chroniclers mention Manfred's last moments, alone except for a few faithful followers, facing the ranks of Charles's army; but the fullest picture is that offered by Dante in lines 55–145 of *Purgatorio* III.

Dante and Virgil reach the foot of the mountain and pause there doubtfully. While Virgil, who is unfamiliar with the place, applies his intelligence to identifying the best path ("essaminava del cammin la mente"; line 56), Dante scrutinizes the sheer face, more unclimbable than the stretch of Tyrrhenian coastline between Lerici and Turbia. Suddenly he sees

> una gente
> d'anime, che movieno i piè ver' noi
> e non pareva, sí venïan lente.
> (*Purgatorio*, III. 58–60)

[a company of souls who were moving their feet towards us and yet seemed not to approach, they came on so slowly.]

The two poets move towards them, but when they are still a thousand paces away the penitents stop and

> si strinser tutti ai duri massi
> de l'alta ripa, e stetter fermi e stretti
> com' a guardar, chi va dubbiando, stassi.
> (*Purgatorio*, III. 70–72)

[they all pressed close to the hard rocks of the steep cliff and stood still and close together, as men stop to look who are in doubt.]

Virgil addresses them courteously, calling them "O ben finiti, o già spiriti eletti" ["O you who have made a good end, spirits already elect": line 73]—a most welcome form of address to souls who lived their lives badly but made a good end. "Spiriti eletti" is a far cry from the words "mal nati" ["ill-born souls"] used in *Inferno*, XVIII. 76 and XXX. 48. Having reassured them, Virgil begs them to indicate the path to "andare in suso" ["go up"], in the name of that peace which everyone desires (lines 74–77). Virgil's words are brief though courteous, as befits a man with no time to delay: "ché perder tempo a chi piú sa piú spiace" ["for time lost irks him most who knows most": line 78]. Here Virgil not only makes amends for his "picciol fallo" ["little fault": line 9] in allowing Dante to linger and listen to Casella (*Purgatorio*, II. 76–133); he also expresses that thirst for knowledge and treasuring of time that Dante speaks of in the *Convivio* (IV. 2) in connection with troubles, misfortunes, complaints and lamentations, which he says would be much reduced if individuals, communities and peoples would take proper account of time.

As a result of Virgil's courteous request some of the souls approach, only to stop once more in wonder when they see Dante's shadow on the ground, while the others press against them from behind:

> Come le pecorelle escon del chiuso
> a una, a due, a tre, e l'altre stanno
> timidette atterrando l'occhio e 'l muso;
> e ciò che fa la prima, e l'altre fanno,
> addossandosi a lei, s'ella s'arresta,
> semplici e quete, e lo 'mperché non sanno;
> sí vid' io muovere a venir la testa
> di quella mandra fortunata allotta,
> pudica in faccia e ne l'andare onesta.
> (*Purgatorio*, III. 79–87)

[As sheep come forth from the fold by one and two and three, and the rest stand timid, bending eyes and muzzle to the ground; and what the first does the others also do, huddling themselves to it if it stops, simple and quiet, and know not why; so saw I then the head of that happy flock move to come on, modest in countenance, in movement dignified.]

Apart from its echoes of Virgil's eclogues and the Bible,[22] the simile reminds us that in *Convivio*, I. 11. 9 Dante uses such an image, but with the emphasis on sheep's stupidity, likened to the foolishness of those who blindly follow the opinions of others, true or false, without thought or reflection. In *Purgatorio* the simile carries no overtones of condemnation; on the contrary, its application to this flock of penitents anticipates one of the central themes of Purgatory, the communion of souls. Two characteristics stand out in this group of souls' behaviour: timidity and lack of individuality. Virgil's reassuring words induce them to resume their approach, but the sight of Dante's shadow brings renewed hesitation and drawing back. This excessive timidity is accompanied by a lack of individual will. What is the significance of these characteristics? With this first group of souls in Purgatory the poet initiates the practice of attributing to each category of shades a disposition which is the diametric opposite of the sin or condition which caused them to end up where they are. These "pecorelle" are, as we shall shortly discover, the souls of those who died excommunicated by the Church. Excommunicates are persons excluded from the Christian community, individuals in sinful opposition to the collective spirit of the faithful. In death, they have reached Purgatory thanks to their repentance. Once bold, they have become timid, once rebellious, they have become obedient, submerging their individuality in the collectivity.

Our interest in this flock would soon be exhausted, however, were it not that Manfred, one of the most striking figures in the poem, emerges from it and stands out as the hero of this canto:

> E un di loro incominciò: "Chiunque
> tu se', cosí andando, volgi 'l viso:
> pon mente se di là mi vedesti unque."
> (*Purgatorio*, III. 103–05)

[And one of them began, "Whoever you are, turn your face as you thus go: consider if ever you saw me yonder."]

The shade obviously expects to be recognized. In his speech he forgets or suppresses the fact that he was a king; but he retains a sovereign air. With a lordly carelessness he does not seek to know to whom he is speaking, despite the fact that he has just learned from Virgil's words that this pilgrim is still alive and has been chosen by God for a lofty mission. Dante is so affected by his courteous but regal tone that when he has to admit that he has never seen him before he comes close to apologizing:

> Io mi volsi ver' lui e guardail fiso:
> biondo era e bello e di gentile aspetto,
> ma l'un de' cigli un colpo avea diviso.
> Quand' io mi fui umilmente disdetto
> d'averlo visto mai, el disse: "Or vedi";
> e mostrommi una piaga a sommo 'l petto.
> (*Purgatorio*, III. 106–12)

[I turned to him, and looked at him fixedly: blond he was, and handsome, and of noble mien, but a blow had cloven one of his eyebrows. When I had humbly disclaimed ever to have seen him, he said, "Look now," and showed me a wound high on his breast.]

Dante never knew Manfred in his lifetime but his portrayal corresponds to descriptions furnished by contemporaries. Saba Malaspina records Manfred as being of fair colouring, with a charming face and pleasing aspect;[23] and Niccolo de Jamsilla goes further: "Nature formed him as a repository for all the graces and composed all parts of his body with similar beauty, so that there was no part that could have been improved upon."[24] Previous commentators on *Purgatorio* III have remarked on echoes of a portrait in the *Chanson de Roland* and of the Biblical description of King David ("He was handsome, with ruddy cheeks and bright eyes") in this description of Manfred.[25] When Dante fails to recognize him, the penitent insists and draws attention to another wound "a sommo 'l petto". His handsome appearance is marred by the wounds to his face and breast, but it is a disfigurement that does him honour because it indicates his valour, the courage of having fought with his face uncovered.[26] When this second distinguishing mark also fails to win him recognition, he announces, smiling:

> Io son Manfredi,
> nepote di Costanza imperadrice;
> ond' io ti priego che, quando tu riedi,
> vadi a mia bella figlia, genitrice
> de l'onor di Cicilia e d'Aragona,
> e dichi 'l vero a lei, s'altro si dice.
> (*Purgatorio*, III. 112–17)

[I am Manfred, grandson of the Empress Constance. Therefore I beg of you that when you return you go to my fair daughter, mother of the pride of Sicily and of Aragon, and tell her the truth, if aught else be told.]

Why does Manfred smile as he reveals his name? His smile suggests many things, such as the joy of salvation and an awareness of the wonder that the unknown visitor will feel, since although he has never seen Manfred before he will certainly have heard of him and will now realize that despite everything he too—the well-known excommunicate cursed by the Church—is among the saved. But why, many commentators have asked, does he refer to himself as the grandson of Constance and avoid naming his father, the great Frederick, and his mother, Marchioness Bianca Lancia? It has been suggested that Manfred is probably moved to pass over his father's name in silence by that feeling of *verecundia* (shame), which Dante defines in *Convivio*, IV. 25. 10 as "una paura di disonoranza per fallo commesso" ["a fear of being held in disgrace for a fault one has committed"],[27] illustrating the concept with the case of Polynices, who when questioned by Adrastus did not declare himself to be the son of Oedipus, "per li falli d'Edippo suo padre, ché paiono rimanere in vergogna del figlio; e non nominò suo padre, ma li antichi suoi" ["because of the wrongs done by his father Oedipus (...), a father's faults being regarded as an enduring source of shame for the son. Accordingly, he did not mention the name of his father, only those of his ancestors"]. If his reticence indeed stems from *verecundia*, it is a quality that belongs to Manfred's penitential state, because in his lifetime he was thoroughly proud to be the son of such a father. We need only quote a phrase from the prologue to his translation of the *Liber de Pomo*, where he has no hesitation in calling himself "Manfred, son of the divine Augustus, Emperor Frederick", and refers again to "the divine Augustus, the most serene Emperor, our lord and father".[28] Or perhaps he remains silent about the name of his father because he was born out of wedlock—"ex concubina natus", according to Adam of Clermont—;[29] but above all he is now aware that Frederick, in worldly terms the highest-placed man on earth, is a reprobate as far as the eternal life is concerned, while Constance is one of the elect. (As we have seen, she has a place in Paradise.)

The fair king, urged on by solicitude for his daughter and by a desire shared with other characters in the *Commedia* to refurbish his earthly fame, begs Dante when he returns to the world to inform his "bella figlia" of the truth, that is, that his soul is saved, since quite different reports of his fate are current. One may detect a polemical note in the words "s'altro si dice", since in fact two versions of his ultimate fate were current: one considered him to be damned in Hell, while the other had him repenting at the moment of death.

The reference to Constance, Manfred's daughter and the wife of Peter III of Aragon, as "genitrice / de l'onor di Cicilia e d'Aragona" (lines 115–16) has been much discussed. Elsewhere in the *Commedia* (*Purgatorio*, VII. 119–20; *Paradiso*, XIX. 130–38) James II, King of Aragon, and Frederick II, King of Sicily, are castigated, which might suggest that the word "onor" is here to be understood as something which kings must receive passively, not that these kings themselves do honour to Sicily and Aragon. But here the speaker is a father, proud of his daughter and grandchildren, a king who sees his kingdom reclaimed by his descendants.

Manfred proceeds to recount "the truth", and for him the truth is that he finds himself in a place of salvation. The history of the battle, of his defeat and death, are well known, but Manfred starts his personal story from the few minutes when he was mortally wounded and his earthly course was coming to an end:

> Poscia ch'io ebbi rotta la persona
> di due punte mortali, io mi rendei,
> piangendo, a quei che volontier perdona.
> (*Purgatorio*, III. 118–20)

[After I had my body pierced by two mortal stabs I gave myself weeping to Him who pardons willingly.]

How did Dante know of this repentance? Was he here again making use of that "prerogative of pardon" that he granted himself in order to save certain other noted sinners, or was he following information that was well known at the time in showing Manfred this favour? These questions arose in the minds of two early commentators on the *Commedia*, Francesco da Buti and Benvenuto da Imola, but the terms they use are very vague and may derive from Dante himself. "The author," writes Buti, "claims that Manfred showed this repentance on the point of death [...]; but no one knows whether Manfred was indeed contrite at the last moment, except God Himself."[30] Benvenuto says much the same, prefacing it with the words "aliqui dicunt".[31] But this "some say" suggests that there was a tradition regarding Manfred's penitence. In any case it is perfectly possible that Manfred, fatally wounded, turned to God on the point of death, and unless there was a public confession, which is not the case for Manfred, it is impossible to find authentic documentation of an act so intensely private as this "turning to God". Failing genuine evidence, already by Dante's time recourse was being had to the supernatural. This is what Novati suggests, referring both to the fourteenth-century commentary of the Anonimo Fiorentino and to a passage in the *Imago Mundi* of Fra Jacopo da Acqui.[32] In the commentary of the Anonimo we read that Manfred's "bella figlia" Constance, "a most upright and virtuous woman, preoccupied about her father's fate, since he had lived a sinful life and been an enemy of the Church, consulted a saintly hermit, who, having made prayers and petitions to God, told her that God had revealed to him that Manfred was among the elect in Purgatory." Fra Jacopo relates that some unnamed person questioned a devil as to whether King Manfred was saved and received the reply that five words pronounced on the point of death had saved him: "Deus propitius esto mihi peccatori" ["God be merciful to me, a sinner"]. We shall never know whether Dante heard these rumours before he wrote *Purgatorio* III or whether the canto itself was their source. If we wish to believe in this last-minute repentance, we must base that belief on Manfred's personality and note a phrase that he wrote after a serious illness and included in the prologue that he added to the *Liber de Pomo*: "We do not have any regret for our end, possessing the prize of our perfection, not relying on justice for our deserts but only on the mercy of the Creator."[33] Are these the words that inspired Dante's lines, or is the resemblance purely coincidental? We do not know, but they certainly supply a precedent, a testimony of faith, which renders credible the words "io mi rendei,/ piangendo, a quei che volontier perdona." Manfred, who had not surrendered to the enemy, "surrenders" to God. This is the trusting surrender of an obstinately contumacious soul, both a surrender and a homecoming.

Manfred continues his story and his confession:

> Orribil furon li peccati miei;
> ma la bontà infinita ha sí gran braccia,
> che prende ciò che si rivolge a lei.
> (*Purgatorio*, III. 121–23)

[Horrible were my sins, but the Infinite Goodness has such wide arms that It receives all who turn to It.]

Dante chooses not to detail Manfred's sins, but the use of the plural, if it does not specify them, allows one to imagine what is not stated. Papal propaganda described Manfred as a "son of iniquity, foster-child of perdition". By 1264 his wickednesses were "suffocating the Church, so that because of these oppressions the Church can hardly breathe."[34] The Curia attributed these oppressions to the fact that Manfred was the son of Antichrist, and since everything is possible for the son of the devil, his enemies' accusations were pushed to the extreme limits of calumny. Giovanni Villani even accuses him of having smothered his father with a pillow (*Nuova cronica*, VII. 41), of having killed his brother Conrad in order to obtain power (VII. 44), and of having plotted against the life of his youthful nephew Conradin (VII. 45). Villani concludes his account of this last crime as follows:

> They [Manfred's ambassadors], believing that they had succeeded in poisoning Conradin, departed from Germany; [...] and they dressed themselves in black, and when they reached Apulia they put on a great show of grief, as Manfred had instructed them. And when it was reported to Manfred and the German barons and the Regnum that Conradin was dead, and Manfred had put on an appearance of great affliction, he was elected King of Sicily and Apulia on the acclamation of his friends and the whole people, as he had ordered.

It is not surprising, then, that the same accusations should make their appearance in the works of Brunetto Latini and Thomas of Tuscany,[35] and they presumably reached the people through the preaching of crusade sermons.[36] It is doubtful whether Dante gave credence to this avalanche of accusations, because if he did it would mean he regarded a parricide and fratricide as worthy of salvation, which is not very likely. What is certain is that Dante must have heard echoes of these accusations, since they had formed part of a massive propaganda campaign in preparation for the crusade against the Swabian king. Dante was aware of the degeneration of the original idea of crusading in the Christian West, and criticized the increasingly frequent use of the crusade in pursuit of purely political and economic objectives. His views on the matter are revealed when he accuses Boniface VIII of making war "non con Saracin né con Giudei,/ché ciascun suo nimico era cristiano" ["not with Saracens or with Jews, for his every enemy was Christian": *Inferno*, XXVII. 87–88; and compare *Paradiso*, XXVII. 46–51]. Thus we should not suppose that the words "orribil [...] peccati" necessarily correspond to an objective judgement on Dante's part. It is Manfred himself who in retrospect regards his sins, whatever they may have been, as "orribil" and uses words of harsh condemnation against himself—as is fitting for a sincere penitent who has become aware that God's "bontà infinita" extends to everyone.

Manfred, almost as if to contrast the amplitude of divine mercy with human pettiness, pauses to consider the wretched fate that befell his mortal remains:

> Se 'l pastor di Cosenza, che a la caccia
> di me fu messo per Clemente allora,
> avesse in Dio ben letta questa faccia,
>   l'ossa del corpo mio sarieno ancora
> in co del ponte presso a Benevento,
> sotto la guardia de la grave mora.
>   Or le bagna la pioggia e move il vento
> di fuor dal regno, quasi lungo 'l Verde,
> dov' e' le trasmutò a lume spento.
>   (*Purgatorio*, III. 124–32)

[If Cosenza's pastor, who was then sent by Clement to hunt me down, had well read that page in God, the bones of my body would yet be at the bridge-head near Benevento, under the guard of the heavy cairn. Now the rain washes them and the wind stirs them, beyond the Kingdom, hard by the Verde, whither he transported them with tapers quenched.]

Once again we wonder whether these lines were inspired by a precise knowledge of events. Charles of Anjou, Manfred's victor, who on the eve of the decisive battle had used harsh words against the "Sultan of Lucera", declaring that the bitter contest would be settled by the death in battle of one or the other of them ("Either I will send him to Hell or he will send me to Paradise"),[37] seems, once the victory was his, to have put aside these feelings of personal hatred, and after a first letter to the Pope announcing his victory, sent a second on 1 March 1266 to inform him that Manfred's body had been found and taken for burial: "And so, moved by natural piety, I had his body taken for burial with certain honours, though not ecclesiastical burial."[38] We cannot tell whether Charles of Anjou gave him an honourable burial on his own initiative or in answer to the pleas of Provençal knights who had been moved by the tears of Manfred's surviving vassals, as both Villani and Malispini relate.[39] In any case, although the burial was honourable, it was not performed according to the rites of the Church. Charles allegedly said he would have been happy to observe those rites had Manfred not been excommunicate, and Villani continues: "Since he was excommunicate, King Charles would not allow him to be taken into a holy place; but he was buried at the end of the bridge at Benevento, and over his grave a stone was placed by each member of the army, so as to create a great cairn."[40] Exactly what took place we do not know, because contemporary chroniclers are sparing with details, but in the *Annals of Genoa* we read: "King Charles commanded that the body should be washed, since it was encrusted with blood. Once washed he ordered that it be dressed in garments with gold thread, and having made a new monument he had the said lord Manfred buried with the greatest honour and as was fitting for so great a man."[41]

All sources are agreed on this first burial of Manfred near the bridge at Benevento, and it seems to be an indisputable historical fact. As Dante's Manfred explains, however, Rome's hatred pursued him and the pastor of Cosenza hunted him down like a wild animal on the orders of Pope Clement. According to the *Commedia*'s earliest commentators, this pastor, who persecuted Manfred instead of looking for lost sheep, was Bartolomeo Pignatelli, Archbishop of Cosenza from 1254 to 1266, although it has more recently been suggested that it was another archbishop. Bartolomeo Pignatelli was Archbishop of Cosenza for almost the whole of the period during which Manfred ruled Sicily. It has been amply demonstrated that he was a bitter opponent of Manfred; in fact in 1258 he had the worst of it in an armed encounter with Manfred's forces and returned defeated to the papal court.[42] This military defeat increased his hatred for Manfred, and he did everything he could to bring about Manfred's downfall. He also engaged in vigorous diplomacy, encouraging Charles of Anjou to undertake the expedition against Manfred. In a bull of 25 May 1263, Pope Urban IV sent him as his nuncio to both Louis IX of France and Henry III of England, for negotiations about the future of the Kingdom of Sicily.[43] In September 1265 he was in Lombardy recruiting forces for the crusade against Manfred. After the victory he made a triumphal entry into Naples at Charles of Anjou's side.

Pignatelli seems to have everything it takes to be the villain of the piece, but in fact no one except Dante attests to the sad ceremony of the "translation" of the cursed bones from the bridge at Benevento to the banks of the River Verde (now identified as the Liri or Garigliano, which separated the Regnum from the Papal States). Pietro di Dante echoes his father's words: "Hence with tapers extinguished and tolling of bells, after the custom of the Church, the Archbishop had the bones, as those of an anathematized heretic, cast down by the River Verde."[44] Landino states that the Archbishop had sworn to drive Manfred out of the Kingdom, and, as he could not do so while he was alive, cast out his body when he was dead.[45] Contemporary chroniclers such as Saba Malaspina and Niccolo de Jamsilla say nothing about all this with regard to either the Pope or the Archbishop. Villani does mention it, but cautiously adds, "This, however, we cannot affirm" (*Nuova cronica*, VIII. 9). To date no trace of any mandate by the Pope has been found in any of the papal registers; but if we recall the words of execration Innocent IV pronounced against Manfred ("May this name of Babylon be wiped out, may his remains, his progeny, his seed be scattered") and the contents of a letter from Urban IV to his legate to England, the Cardinal of Sant' Adriano, in which he rejoices that Charles of Anjou is now in possession of the whole territory and of "the stinking body of that pestilential man, his wife, children and treasure",[46] I do not think we can exclude the possibility that such a request reached the Archbishop of Cosenza, or that the latter took action on his own initiative.

All the uncertainties arising from the accounts in medieval chronicles, and the suppositions and interpretations of Dante commentators, ought to have been settled once and for all by the discovery in April 1614, in the stonework of the old Roman bridge at Ceprano over the Liri—the river that marks the boundary between Campania and Lazio—, of a sarcophagus with a marble cover carrying this Latin inscription:

> Hic jaceo Caroli Manfredus Marte subactus
> Caesaris heredi (?) non fuit urbe locus
> Sum patris ex odiis ausus confligere Petro
> Mars dedit hic mortem, mors mihi cuncta tulit.

The gist of these confused lines is that Manfred lies here and that he died fighting Peter, losing everything by his death. Information about this discovery is contained in a detailed study published in 1924 by Giovanni Colasanti,[47] who believed that the coffin, measuring 0.90 x 1.10 metres, must have contained Manfred's bones, and suggested reasons for the change of location. The area around Ceprano had seen the most notable diplomatic and military events in the struggle to establish papal supremacy over the Kingdom of Apulia, beginning with the meeting of Gregory VII and Robert Guiscard in 1080, when "Duke Robert, with his hands between the Pope's, swore the solemn oath of vassallage for that Kingdom which Manfred would later hold in rebellion against the Church."[48] Later, in 1230, the peace of San Germano between Frederick II and Gregory IX was ratified at Ceprano, and the Emperor was released from sentence of excommunication. Most importantly of all, twelve years before his death Manfred, accompanied by his nobles, had prostrated himself before the Pope on this very bridge at Ceprano. According to Colasanti, it was "at this spot, where the Church had seen its hegemony over the Regnum originate and where Manfred had suffered such total humiliation, that the Church decided he should be buried in perpetual expiation". Nothing is known of the present whereabouts of the sarcophagus and its inscription.

Returning to Canto III of *Purgatorio*, ought we perhaps to give something other than a literal interpretation to the line "Or le bagna la pioggia e move il vento", which echoes Virgil's "Nunc me fluctus habet versantque in litore venti" ["Now the wave holds me, and the winds toss me on the beach": *Aeneid*, VI. 362]? King Manfred laments the fact that his bones, which first rested on the field where he had honourably fallen, have been transferred elsewhere and lie exposed to the wind and rain. But whatever may have happened,

> Per lor maladizion sí non si perde,
> che non possa tornar, l'etterno amore,
> mentre che la speranza ha fior del verde.
> (*Purgatorio*, III. 133–35)

[By curse of theirs none is so lost that the Eternal Love cannot return, so long as hope keeps aught of green.]

In other words, while there is life there is hope of achieving salvation. An interesting article by Louis La Favia shows how Manfred's affirmation has been interpreted, first by Foscolo in his *Discorso sul testo della "Divina commedia"*, as an open polemic against ecclesiastical authority, with Manfred in the role of both victim and accuser of the Church.[49] But this *terzina* was not understood thus by its earliest interpreters, who were closest to the mentality and culture of the society in which Dante lived. In fact, according to the doctrine of the Church itself, the sentence of anathema or greater excommunication, which was visited on Manfred, although *per se* involving the penalty of "damnation of eternal death", did not irrevocably condemn the individual to damnation, but rather abandoned him to his own devices, so that the possibility of repentance *in articulo mortis* in the absence of a priest was not excluded.[50] But obstinate contumacy, the arrogant disobedience which led Manfred to wait until the very last moment, has to be "paid for" here in Purgatory, and Manfred declares as much:

> Vero è che quale in contumacia more
> di Santa Chiesa, ancor ch'al fin si penta,
> star li convien da questa ripa in fore,
> per ognun tempo ch'elli è stato, trenta,
> in sua presunzïon, se tal decreto
> piú corto per buon prieghi non diventa.
> (*Purgatorio*, III. 136–41)

[True it is that whoso dies in contumacy of Holy Church, even though he repent at the last, must stay outside upon this bank thirtyfold for all the time that he has lived in his presumption, if such decree is not made shorter by holy prayers.]

We can hardly fail to ask what custom or law led Dante to fix this penalty of waiting in Ante-Purgatory at thirty times the duration of Manfred's contumacy. Why not forty or ninety? The figure thirty might have its origin simply in the "trichotomous structure" of Dante's mind, as is suggested by Philip McNair.[51] Or perhaps the poet was inspired by the punishment of the Hebrews when, rebellious against God and unwilling to believe His promises, they were condemned to forty years of wandering in the wilderness instead of forty days, *annus pro diem* [a year for a day].[52] Or again, we may consider that the sins of Christians are infringements of God's Ten Commandments, and that God is triune. The learned Bishop Durandus (1230–96) argues: "Three times ten are thirty. By three we understand the Trinity, by ten the Ten Commandments. Which is why we perform trentals for the dead, so that the mercy of God will pardon them for their failings in the observation of the Ten Commandments."[53] The punishment Dante designed for Manfred is a remarkably good fit: the excommunicate King wanders in Ante-Purgatory, like the Hebrews in the wilderness, tormented by a constant thought and a constant anxiety to enter the place where souls are purged in order to expiate his "orribil [...] peccati". Manfred was declared a rebel by Alexander IV on 23 January 1255 and died on 26 February 1266, so that he was contumacious for eleven years and thirty-four days; on the basis of the penalty inflicted on him by Dante, he will therefore have to remain where he is for 332 years and 290 days, so that he will cross the threshold of Purgatory in December 1598,

> se tal decreto
> piú corto per buon prieghi non diventa.

His wait can be shortened by the sincere and devoted prayers of good people, including his daughter, "my good Constance":[54]

> Vedi oggimai se tu mi puoi far lieto,
> revelando a la mia buona Costanza
> come m'hai visto, e anco esto divieto;
> ché qui per quei di là molto s'avanza.
> (*Purgatorio*, III. 142–45)

[See now if you can make me glad by revealing to my good Constance how you have seen me, as well as this ban: for much is gained here through those who are yonder.]

Manfred desires that Dante, besides telling Constance the truth about his salvation—the truth concealed by the common belief that he was damned—should also impress on her his need for suffrages. The reference to prayers for the dead and the remission of penalties brings the canto to a close, and this theme will be developed further throughout *Purgatorio*. Bearing in mind that the doctrine of indulgences and suffrages for the dead was already a matter for debate in Dante's day, it is interesting to note that Dante includes it with a clear personal affirmation, but he also seems to believe that the efficacy of prayers depends on goodness and sincere love. These are the only prayers that are effective.

I said at the outset that it was to be expected that the Hohenstaufen should figure in the *Commedia*. This is, however, far from Bruno Lucrezi's assertion that "none of the ruling houses of the twelfth and thirteenth centuries has the same prominence in Dante's works as the house of Swabia", or Aldo Vallone's view that "the presence of the house of Swabia in Dante is strong, deep, witnessed in numerous direct and indirect references, and sanctioned both instinctively and reflectively."[55] It seems to me that the Capetians of France occupy a more prominent place in Dante's work (and life). We do not meet the first "wind", Frederick I, face to face; there is only a brief reference to him by an abbot of San Zeno, who is himself not clearly identified (*Purgatorio*, XVIII. 119–20). And yet Frederick Barbarossa had dominated the European political scene for forty years and transformed the empire of the German nation, which was Roman only in name, into the Sacratissimum Imperium (Holy Roman Empire), a term chosen to match the description of the Roman Church as Sancta Romana Ecclesia. The meagre attention Dante gives him is hardly in keeping with his historical importance. Henry VI and Conrad IV are ignored altogether, while Conradin remains a figure of no intrinsic interest in the *Commedia*. To the third wind and "ultima possanza" Dante devotes a single line of *Inferno* X and a few words in *Inferno* XIII, telling us no more than his name and his place of punishment, together with a damned soul's statement that he was worthy of honour. The *stupor mundi* perhaps deserved a little better. Even if we also bear in mind what Dante says about Frederick in the *Convivio* and *De Vulgari Eloquentia*, I must admit to a certain sympathy with Barlow,[56] who was convinced that the Guelf writers who blackened Frederick's name acted in bad faith, and almost reproached Dante for having given them credence when he ought to have assigned Frederick a glorious place in the sixth heaven among the wise and the just.

Clearly Dante considers the "possanza" of the house of Swabia to have in effect finished with the death of Frederick II, "ultimo imperadore de li Romani" ["the last emperor of the Romans": *Convivio*, IV. 3. 6] in 1250. It is true that he takes an interest in another member of the house of Swabia, but Manfred is not a legitimate heir. Manfred places himself, so to speak, at the centre of the Swabian family tree, referring to his ancestors in the person of his paternal grandmother, Empress Constance, last of the Norman line, and mentioning his descendants through his daughter, Constance of Aragon, the last of the royal line of Swabia and mother of the man who in 1297 was crowned King of Sicily not as Frederick III (a style which would have seemed to continue the Swabian line) but as Frederick II of Aragon, King of Trinacria.

Dante sees a fundamental contrast between the idealized perfection of the past and the decadence of the present. It is a contrast about which he felt deeply: the corrupt Church's worst fault is that of having overstepped the limits of its spiritual authority and aimed at the exercise of earthly power, thus setting itself up against the designs of divine justice. On the imperial side the flight of the eagle (*Paradiso* VI) stopped with Charlemagne, because the emperors who followed him were unworthy of praise. In recent times there had been no sign of an ideal ruler—valiant, wise, magnanimous—; not even the Hohenstaufen qualified for this description. The Empire was no longer a guarantor of peace, justice and wellbeing for Christendom. "Antiquity," Vico suggests, "is the more venerable the more obscure it is." Leopardi concurs: "Mankind is in the habit of criticizing the present and praising the past."[57] Manfred is a figure on his own; a stupendous example of a repentant excommunicate, who bewails the loss of a few spadefuls of earth, not that of a whole kingdom. On his head there is no imperial crown but the "guardia de la grave mora"; and Dante places him among the saved above all for reasons of religion and faith, not politics, even if—given the importance of the person involved and his notoriety—there is an inevitable hint of antipapal polemic.

Any work of art is bound to its own historical period. Can we then regard the *Commedia* as a historical source? The answer must be a cautious "no", because if we did, we would consider Boniface VIII solely as a simoniac pope, Barbarossa only as the destroyer of the bastions of Milan, and so on. Dante accepted the Christian view of history as subordinate to an other-worldly end; one need only look at his providential interpretation of the flight of the eagle in Canto VI of *Paradiso*, stopping at Charlemagne. Dante also saw history as a preserver and dispenser of fame to those who, according to his extremely personal criteria, deserve it. We are well informed about the ancient and medieval texts that were available to him. His sources of information were extremely heterogeneous, including mythology, philosophy, Scripture, chronicles and legends. Taken cumulatively, they presented Dante with an inexhaustible repertory of characters and events, from which to select those he wanted to present to his readers as examples to support his opinions and designs. It is undeniably his privilege to choose what to show and how to show it. His poem is not a historical source; if we regard it as history, we shall be led into a mistaken interpretation of situations, events and individuals. Dante's art—his very great art—bears the stamp of truth on the artistic plane, but is arbitrary on the historical plane. Nevertheless, although its aim is a spiritual one, his poetry is steeped in history, and that is why for centuries we have striven to understand and to isolate, with the aid of history, the motives which governed choices and exclusions in Dante's poem. This is often an arduous task, since when a historical character is chosen by Dante that character begins a new life in the world of poetry, which may have no connection with historical truth but enjoys full poetic reality. Thus we may leave Empress Constance to enjoy the splendours of Paradise, Barbarossa to destroy the bastions of Milan, Frederick II to suffer in his flaming tomb, hoping he may occasionally remember the splendours of the Great Court; and above all we remember our smiling Manfred. He has no tomb, but he is immune to old age and death because (as Foscolo says of great poetry) the harmony of Dante's lines has overcome "di mille secoli il silenzio" ["the silence of a thousand centuries"].[58]

NOTES

1   "The title 'King of the Romans' did not denote simply a power to command which was straightway conceded to the person who wielded it; it implied also an idea of candidature or future expectations. The king who had been elected by the German princes was the future Emperor. He was the only one amongst

them all who could receive the imperial dignity [...]. But though a candidate for the Empire, the King of the Romans was not for all that already Emperor. What more was required for him to become so? A new consecration, under very strict conditions as to persons and place [...]. Only the Pope could [...] have the king anointed in his presence and then personally crown him Emperor; and this ceremony could only take place in [...] Rome—[...] capital—*caput*—both of the Roman Empire and of Christianity" (M. Bloch, "The Empire and the Idea of Empire under the Hohenstaufen", in his *Land and Work in Mediaeval Europe: Selected Papers*, translated by J. E. Anderson (London, Routledge and Kegan Paul, 1967), pp. 1–43 (pp. 14–15).

2   The poet-chronicler Godfrey of Viterbo has a different opinion, comparing Conrad III to the ancient personifications of virtues: "A Seneca in council, a Paris in appearance, a Hector in battle" (*Pantheon* [in *MGH: SS*, XXII, 107–307], XXIII. 51 [p. 263]).

3   "Scelestissimis Florentinis"; "Recensete fulmina Federici prioris, et Mediolanum consulite" (*Epist.*, VI. 1, 20; *Epistolae*, ed. Toynbee, pp. 77, 80).

4   In the *Annales Stadenses* (*MGH: SS*, XVI, 271–379) Albert of Stade offers his own reassuring version of the Emperor's death, in which Barbarossa sank beneath the waters of the river exclaiming, "Benedictus crucifixus Dei filius, quod aqua me suscipit, quae me regeneravit, et me martirem faciat, quae me fecit christianum!" (p. 351). Villani, on the other hand, considered his death in Asia Minor a punishment he had deserved by his hostility to the Church: "Federigo [...] disaventuratamente affogò; e ciò si crede che fosse per giudicio di Dio per le molte persecuzioni che fece a santa Chiesa" (*Nuova cronica*, VI. 3).

5   Thomas Tuscus, *Gesta Imperatorum et Pontificum*, in *MGH: SS*, XXII, 483–528 (p. 507); Brunetto Latini, *The Book of the Treasure (Li Livres dou tresor)*, translated by P. Barrette and S. Baldwin (New York–London, Garland, 1993), p. 53.

6   Quoted in D. Abulafia, *Frederick II: A Medieval Emperor* (London, Lane, 1988), p. 79.

7   Anonymus Vaticanus, *Historia Sicula*, in *RIS*, VIII, 741–80 (cols 778–79).

8   "Illustres heroes, Fredericus Cesar et benegenitus eius Manfredus, nobilitatem ac rectitudinem sue forme pandentes, donec fortuna permisit humana secuti sunt, brutalia dedignantes" (*DVE*, I. 12. 4). P. V. Mengaldo, in his note on this sentence, comments: "La collocazione di Manfredi [...] allo stesso livello del padre, e soprattutto la definizione *benegenitus*, andranno intese come polemiche nei confronti della libellistica guelfa, che ne sfruttava la nascita illegittima."

9   A. Vallone, "La componente federiciana della cultura dantesca", in *Dante e Roma* (Florence, Le Monnier, 1965), pp. 347–69 (p. 350).

10 *MGH: Epist. Pont.*, II, no. 456. Matthew Paris, in his *Chronica Majora*, edited by H. R. Luard [*Rerum Britannicarum Medii Aevi Scriptores*], 7 vols (London, Longman, Trübner, 1872–83), V, 60, speaks of the evil fame of Frederick II throughout the world: "Pejor Herode, Juda, vel Nerone."

11 *MGH: Const.*, II, no. 400; G. Villani, *Nuova cronica*, VII. 24.

12 "Sacrosanctam romanam ecclesiam matrem suam in corde contrito, velut fidei orthodoxe zelatur, humiliter recognovit": *Historia Diplomatica Friderici Secundi*, edited by J-L-A. Huillard-Bréholles, 7 vols in 12 (Paris, Plon, 1852–61), VI, ii, 811. See also B. Capasso, *Historia Diplomatica Regni Siciliae* (Naples, Stamperia della R. Università, 1874), pp. 5, 7.

13 Martin of Troppau, *Chronicon Pontificum et Imperatorum*, in *MGH: SS*, XXII, 377–475 (pp. 471–72); Brunetto Latini, *The Book of the Treasure*, I. 97. 6; G.

Villani, *Nuova cronica*, VII. 41. Matthew Paris, however, recounting the events of 13 December 1250, wrote: "Obiit [...] principum mundi maximus Frethericus, stupor quoque mundi et immutator mirabilis, absoluta a sententia qua innodabatur, assumpto, ut dicitur, habitu Cisterciensium, et mirifice compunctus et humiliatus" (*Chronica Majora*, v, 190).

14 "Frederick was an Epicurean, and so he and the learned men of his court searched out whatever Biblical passage they could find to prove that there is no life after death": *The Chronicle of Salimbene de Adam*, translated by J. L. Baird, G. Baglivi and J. R. Kane (Binghamton, New York, Medieval and Renaissance Texts and Studies, 1986), p. 353.

15 *The Chronicle of Salimbene de Adam*, pp. 190 and 446. Matthew Paris, as usual better informed, links Piero's treason with a plot to assassinate the Emperor: "The Emperor was unwell; della Vigna and the Emperor's doctor, supposedly acting at Urban IV's behest, added poison to the medicine" (*Chronica Majora*, v, 68). David Abulafia in his *Frederick II* adds (p. 402): "It is no coincidence that the charges against della Vigna arose just when Frederick was most worried at the shortage of cash available to cover his war expenses."

16 T. C. van Cleve, *The Emperor Frederick II of Hohenstaufen, "Immutator Mundi"* (Oxford, Clarendon Press, 1972), pp. 339, 343.

17 *Les Registres d'Innocent IV publiés ou analysés d'après les manuscrits originaux du Vatican et de la Bibliothèque nationale*, edited by E. Berger, 4 vols in 6 (Paris, Thorin/Fontemoing, 1884–1920), no. 2945.

18 *Les Registres d'Urbain IV (1261–1264): recueil des bulles de ce pape publiées ou analysées d'après les manuscrits originaux du Vatican*, edited by J. Guiraud, 4 vols in 13 (Paris, Fontemoing/Boccard, 1899–1958), nos 633, 809.

19 For details of crusades against Christian lay powers see N. Housley, *The Italian Crusades: The Papal–Angevin Alliance and the Crusades against Lay Christian Powers, 1254–1343* (Oxford, Clarendon Press, 1982); J. R. Strayer, "The Political Crusades of the Thirteenth Century", in *A History of the Crusades*, edited by K. M. Setton, 6 vols (Philadelphia, University of Pennsylvania Press; Madison, University of Wisconsin Press, 1955–89), II (*The Later Crusades, 1189–1311*, edited by R. L. Wolff and H. W. Hazard), 343–75. For the crusade against Manfred see also E. Jordan, *L'Allemagne et l'Italie au XIIe et XIIIe siècles* (Paris, Presses Universitaires de France, 1939)—an excellent account of the thirteenth-century struggle between the Papacy and the Hohenstaufen rulers. The last part of the conflict is discussed in detail in E. Jordan, *Les Origines de la domination angevine en Italie* (Paris, Picard, 1909).

20 "Le Dit de Pouille", in *Oeuvres complètes de Rutebeuf*, edited by E. Faral and J. Bastin, 2 vols (Paris, Picard, reprinted 1969), I, 435–39.

21 Adam of Clermont, *Flores Historiarum* [excerpt], in *MGH: SS*, XXVI, 591–92 (p. 592).

22 These are suggested by G. Giacalone in his commentary on *Purgatorio* III: Dante Alighieri, *La Divina commedia*, edited by G. Giacalone (Rome, Signorelli, 1967). The Biblical passages he cites are Jeremiah 12. 17, Luke 12. 32, John 10. 1–16 and I Peter 5. 2–3.

23 "Homo flavus, amoena facie, aspectu placibilis": S. Malaspina, *Rerum Sicularum Historia* (in *RIS*, VIII, 781–874), col. 830.

24 "Formavit enim ipsum natura gratiarum omnium receptabilem, & sic omnes corporis sui partes conformi speciositate composuit, ut nihil in eo esset, quod melius esse possit": N. de Jamsilla, *Historia de Rebus Gestis Friderici II Imper.*

Ejus Filiorum Conradi, et Manfredi Apuliae et Siciliae Regum ab Anno MCCX *usque ad* MCCLVIII, in *RIS*, VIII, 489–616 (col. 497).

25 "Erat autem rufus, et pulcher aspectu, decoraque facie" (1 Samuel 16. 12). M. Balfour, "'Orribil furon li peccati miei': Manfred's Wounds in *Purgatorio* III", *Italian Studies*, 48 (1993), 4–17, points out that the hero so described is not Roland (as Walter Binni had stated) but a Saracen (p. 8).

26 For an alternative view of Manfred's wounds, see M. Balfour, "'Orribil furon li peccati miei'".

27 P. McNair, "*Purgatorio* III", in *Cambridge Readings in Dante's "Comedy"*, edited by K. Foster and P. Boyde (Cambridge, Cambridge University Press, 1981), pp. 90–113 (p. 108).

28 B. Nardi and P. Mazzantini, *Il canto di Manfredi e il "Liber de Pomo sive De Morte Aristotilis"* [Lectura Dantis Romana] (Turin, Società Editrice Internazionale, 1964), p. 39.

29 Adam of Clermont, *Flores Historiarum*, p. 592.

30 *Commento di Francesco da Buti sopra la "Divina comedia" di Dante Allighieri*, edited by C. Giannini, 3 vols (Pisa, Nistri, 1858–62), II, 71.

31 *Benevenuti de Rambaldis de Imola Comentum super Dantis Aldigherii Comoediam*, edited by J. P. Lacaita, 5 vols (Florence, Barbèra, 1887), III, 109.

32 F. Novati, "Come Manfredi s'è salvato", in his *Indagini e postille dantesche: serie prima* (Bologna, Zanichelli, 1899), pp. 117–36.

33 "De nostra dissolucione non tantum [...] dolebamus, quemvis de nostre perfeccionis premio possidendo non nostris innitemur iusticie meritis, sed soli misericordie creatoris." See G. Vallese, "Teologia e poesia nel canto III del *Purgatorio*", in *Dante e la cultura sveva*, edited by A. and P. Borraro (Florence, Olschki, 1970), pp. 251–67 (p. 262).

34 *Les Registres d'Urbain* IV, nos 633 and 809.

35 *The Book of the Treasure*, I. 97. 6, 8, 9; Thomas Tuscus, *Gesta Imperatorum*, p. 516.

36 N. Housley, *The Italian Crusades*, Chapter 4.

37 R. Malispini, *Istoria fiorentina* [excerpts], edited by M. Marti, in *La prosa del Duecento*, edited by C. Segre and M. Marti (Milan–Naples, Ricciardi, 1959), pp. 947–79 (p. 969). Dante places both of them in Purgatory.

38 G. Del Giudice, *Codice diplomatico del regno di Carlo I e II d'Angiò*, 3 vols (Naples, Stamperia della R. Università/d'Auria, 1863–1902), I, 114.

39 G. Villani, *Nuova cronica*, VIII. 9; R. Malispini, *Istoria fiorentina*, p. 974.

40 G. Villani, *Nuova cronica*, VIII. 9.

41 *Annales Ianuae*, in *MGH: SS*, XVIII, 1–356 (p. 256).

42 See P. F. Russo, "'Il pastor di Cosenza' (nota storico-critica a *Purgatorio*, III. 103–33", in *Dante e la cultura sveva*, pp. 169–79 (p. 172). Russo demonstrates that in fact Archbishop Pignatelli was not guilty of persecuting Manfred after his death. See also E. Pontieri, *Ricerche sulla crisi della monarchia siciliana nel secolo* XIII, third edition (Naples, Edizioni Scientifiche Italiane, 1958), pp. 115ff.

43 P. F. Russo, "'Il pastor di Cosenza'", p. 172. See also *Calendar of Papal Registers: Papal Letters* I *(1198–1304)*, edited by W. H. Bliss (Nendel/Liechtenstein, Kraus, reprinted 1971): for example, *Regesta* XXIX, letters of 8 August 1264.

44 "Unde candelis extinctis et campanis pulsatis more ecclesiae, dictus episcopus dicta ossa, tamquam haeretici anathematizati, fecit projici juxta flumen Verdi": *Petri Allegherii super Dantis Ipsius Genitoris Comoediam Commentarium*, edited by V. Nannucci (Florence, Garinei, 1845). The passage quoted is found on p. 311 and ends with the following words: "illo modo de quo Lucanus:

Libera fortuna mors est: capit omnia tellus/quae genuit: coelo tegitur, qui non habet urnam."

45 In *Dante con l'espositione di Christoforo Landino, et di Alessandro Vellutello*, edited by F. Sansovino (Venice, Giovambattista, Marchiò Sessa, 1564), p. 176, we read: "Il cardinale di Cosenza fu legato di Clemente Papa quarto nello esercito di Carlo quando il Re Manfredi fu morto. Et dopo la vittoria fé trar il corpo suo del gran sepolcro che era in co', cioè in capo del ponte di Benevento come d'huomo scomunicato [...]. Dicono alcuni che il legato havea giurato di cacciarlo del regno & non havendo potuto cacciarlo vivo, cacciò il corpo quasi lungo il Verde [...] a lume spento, senza honoranza di lumi & disse a lume spento per dinotare che il cardinale l'havea per iscomunicato, imperoche quando alcuni si scomunica, il sacerdote getta il lume in forma che si spegne."

46 Odoricus Raynaldus, *Annales Ecclesiastici ab Anno quo Desinit Card. C. Baronius, 1198 usque ad Annum 1534(–1565)*, vols 13–21 (Cologne, Hemmerden, 1694–1727), under 8.5.1266.

47 G. Colasanti, "La sepoltura di Manfredi lungo il Liri", *Archivio della R. società romana di storia patria*, 47 (1924), 45–115.

48 G. Colasanti, "La sepoltura di Manfredi", p. 105.

49 L. M. La Favia, "Per una reinterpretazione dell'episodio di Manfredi", *Dante Studies*, 91 (1973), 81–100.

50 L. M. La Favia, "Per una reinterpretazione dell'episodio di Manfredi". See also A. Murray, *Excommunication and Conscience in the Middle Ages* [The John Coffin Memorial Lecture] (London, University of London, 1991).

51 P. McNair, "*Purgatorio* III", p. 90.

52 In the previous canto (*Purgatorio* II) the penitents arrive on the shore of Purgatory singing "In exitu Israel de Aegypto", the first verse of Psalm 114 (Vulgate 113), sung by the Jews when they left Egypt at the time of Moses. The same psalm is mentioned in *Conv.*, II. 1. 7 and *Epist.*, XIII. 21.

53 "Ter decem triginta faciunt. Per ter intelligimus trinitatem, per decem decalogum [...]. Quare trigenarium mortuis ideo facimus, ut quod in observatione decem preceptorum delinquerunt, Dei misericordia eis condonetur": R. D. Guglielmo Durando, *Rationale Divinorum Officiorum* (Venice, 1568) C. 6, pp. 371–72.

54 In Steven Runciman's *The Sicilian Vespers* (Cambridge, Cambridge University Press, 1958), pp. 262–63, we read: "King James [Constance's son] was crowned at Palermo in February 1286 [...]. Immediately after his coronation he sent an embassy to Honorius to offer him homage and ask for his confirmation of the title. Honorius answered by excommunicating him, his mother Queen Constance, and all the people of Sicily." She was reconciled with Rome, however, on the occasion of the treaty signed in the presence of Boniface VIII at Anagni on 12 June 1295.

55 B. Lucrezi, "Gli Svevi nella poesia di Dante", in *Dante e la cultura sveva*, pp. 129–45 (p. 129); A. Vallone, "La componente federiciana", p. 347.

56 H. C. Barlow, *Critical, Historical, and Philosophical Contributions to the Study of the "Divina commedia"* (London–Edinburgh, Williams and Norgate, 1864), pp. 337–60.

57 In Vico's *Princípi di scienza nuova* (in G. Vico, *Opere filosofiche*, edited by N. Badaloni and P. Cristofolini [Florence, Sansoni, 1971], pp. 377–702), I. 2 ("Degli elementi") we read: "*Fama crescit eundo,* [...] *minuit praesentia famam*

[...], per tal propietà della mente umana avvertita da Tacito nella *Vita d'Agricola* con quel motto: 'Omne ignotum pro magnifico est.' È altra propietà della mente umana ch'ove gli uomini delle cose lontane e non conosciute non possono fare niuna idea, le stimano dalle cose loro conosciute e presenti" (p. 432). In Leopardi's *Pensieri* (in G. Leopardi, *Opere*, edited by S. and R. Solmi, 2 vols [Milan–Naples, Ricciardi, 1956–66], I, 693–752) xxx, we read: "Come suole il genere umano, biasimando le cose presenti lodare le passate [...]."

58 U. Foscolo, *Poesie*, edited by G. Bezzola (Milan, Rizzoli, 1976), p. 100 ("Dei sepolcri", l. 234).

THE CLEAR AND THE OBSCURE: DANTE, VIRGIL AND THE ROLE OF THE PROPHET

Teresa Hankey

Dante's *Commedia* sometimes seems like a skein of many-coloured silks, in which the eye will pick out one colour and temporarily see it as dominant. Thus, according to our own concerns, we may see justice, love, poetry, Florence or some other topic not merely as constantly recurring but as Dante's chief theme. Part of the explanation for this phenomenon lies in the poet's use of allegory—the diversity of the "allegorical senses" towards which he points us in general and at times also in particular.[1] A further recurring theme, which often becomes entangled with the others and especially with political questions, is that of the poet as prophet. Contemporaries indeed had no more doubt than Dante himself that poet and prophet are synonymous, not least because they were well aware of the double sense of the Latin noun *vates*. For Guido da Pisa, for example, "this poet, in the manner of poets, predicts the future; whence poet and prophet are the same thing."[2] It is some of the implications for the reader of this identity between the poet as allegorist and the poet as prophet that I want particularly to examine in this essay.

In its early stages the *Commedia* has much to offer to the relatively stupid in moral lessons as well as in beautiful verse, but as the poem progresses it makes stiffer demands on the reader, until in *Paradiso*, II. 1–15 the reader in a "piccioletta barca" ["little bark"]—that is, the mentally ill-equipped—is warned against following the poet further. Those better endowed are expected to use their powers of thought as well as their knowledge of history, morals, theology and the world around them to extract the poem's meaning or meanings.

"Life for a human being," says Dante in *Convivio*, IV. 7. 11–15, "is the use of reason"; and he goes on to put the corollary even more strongly: to fail to use one's reason is to die as a man and to live on as a beast.[3] In *Monarchia*, the initial argument for a single ruler is that only under such a sway could men, "sedendo et quiescendo" ["sitting in quietude"], get down to fulfilling the "possible intellect", the sum of the intellectual potential of each individual.[4] As regards the *Commedia*, while no one is in Hell for mere stupidity (since each sinner has broken a rule of whose existence he was well aware), Dante-the-character's own discussions with those he meets as he descends are to a conspicuous extent with those who are eloquent and often subtle in defence of their actions—in either case, thought-provoking.[5] During the subsequent ascent, the saved reveal more thought, and raise and answer more complicated questions, until in *Paradiso*, xv. 37–46 Cacciaguida must loosen his bow to hit the mark of Dante's understanding and in Cantos xxiv–xxvi Peter, James and John keep their own powers in check and question Dante to the limit of his. The power of reasoning is lifted to higher and higher levels up to the final Rose.

Dante can thus surely never have meant his more intelligent readers to rest on a mere mechanical application of allegory, let alone yield to a great temptation to mental laziness which afflicts the modern reader even more than the author's contemporaries. Commentaries, some new, some older, were available in Dante's day on all the great writers of antiquity accessible in the late Middle Ages, whether poets or philosophers. Some of these commentaries simply elucidated the text, while others, such as those of Aquinas and Albertus Magnus on Aristotle, were considerable works of scholarship in their own right. Dante's own *Vita nuova* may be seen as owing much to commentaries on the classical poets. His justified optimism about the status his *Commedia* would attain may well have led him to visualize his own work receiving such an honour. It is unlikely, however, that he imagined the extent to which the commentaries would proliferate to meet his readers' need for help as the names mentioned meant less and less to them. This dependence encourages us to look to the notes for identification and explanation rather than seek at least the latter for ourselves. We thus avoid that intellectual activity in which Dante believed so strongly. Dante meant the educated reader to use his mind to bring home to himself the different lessons to be learned as he "tries on for size" the varied forms of allegorical interpretation. In the *Commedia* the literal sense—what the words tell us—normally carries the anagogical sense also, since the whole poem is concerned with life after death; but occasionally Dante sends us away from the literal meaning altogether and recommends thought about the meaning hidden beneath the "velame" ["veil"].[6] For example, the great dialogues with Farinata and Cavalcante in *Inferno* x have clear anagogical and moral senses, in so far as both personages continue to reject all concern with the eternal life into which they are now locked and both still show the moral defects (arrogance and family pride in the one, timidity in the other) which fed and perhaps even led to their "Epicureanism". The Guelf/Ghibelline struggle adds a "sensus historialis", both as between Farinata and Dante and as between Farinata and Cavalcante, neighbours in the tomb but still ignoring each other. Another reader might regard the canto as illustrating either love misdirected exclusively to the family or the justice which imprisons in tombs those who thought the tomb their final destination (the *contrapasso*), or again Dante's conviction of the high place of poets in divine esteem: Cavalcante's suggestion (lines 58–60) that Dante is there for his "altezza d'ingegno" ["high genius"] is not rebutted.

The reader may reasonably conclude, as did the early commentators, that other episodes have fewer allegorical meanings, while Boccaccio wisely warns us against trying to apply allegorical "senses" to every word.[7] Such decisions themselves however imply intellectual activity.

In the case of *Inferno* x we know who the protagonists are, and the effort required of us is one of interpretation. What are we to make of those cases where the very identity of the protagonists is in doubt? We should surely at least try to avoid total reliance on the commentaries and arrive at some individual judgement such as the author was clearly demanding of us; we should take from the commentary only such hints towards recognizing late medieval characters and symbols as our distance in time justifies.

At one end of the scale of such problems of interpretation we have the three beasts of *Inferno* I. Contemporaries seem to have had little hesitation in identifying them as lust, pride and avarice. But is Dante accusing himself of avarice (about which he does not seem to feel premonitory pangs on Mount Purgatory) or suggesting that the avarice of others will nearly bring about his damnation— perhaps through his sinful response to it? Such a mixture of sins within him (lust and pride) and in the world about him (avarice) will not have troubled the numerous readers of his age who knew the *Roman de la rose*; Guillaume de Lorris causes the Lover to meet personifications both of the girl's own qualities, such as Fair Welcome and False Shame, and of other people's, such as Jealousy and Slander. Whether considered only as vices or also as the forces of Florence, France and the Papacy, the beasts require thought, but little is perhaps lost if we rely largely on a commentary.

Such reliance becomes more dangerous almost immediately after, in Cantos II and III; that is, where it blurs the distinction between identified and unidentified characters and between various forms of prophecy.

Leaving aside for the moment the forms of prophecy, later commentators have found it harder than earlier ones to agree on the identity of "colui/che fece per viltade il gran rifiuto" ["him who from cowardice made the great refusal": *Inferno*, III. 59–60]. Most early and many later commentators state firmly that this is Pope Celestine v.[8] What perhaps needs emphasizing is that Dante must have intended his readers to think about who it might be. If he had wanted them to consider a single case of failure, he would have named the guilty party or at least given a clearer hint. The author of the *Commedia* was certainly not restrained by any consideration of tact, let alone fear, from naming a pope or anyone else. His intention must have been that each of us should consider what great refusals have been made through cowardice, moral or physical, and, as a corollary, of which of them we also might be guilty. Thus if we take the case made for Esau, Benvenuto da Imola's preferred candidate, we find Benvenuto leading us through mental processes of the sort which Dante certainly thought appropriate. We are reminded that we cannot possibly foretell what fatal consequences a simple inability to say "no" to our greed may have: Esau could not have known that he was losing the privilege of becoming Christ's ancestor.[9] Pontius Pilate, the favourite (among modern commentators) of Sapegno, saw himself as forced to choose between the death of an innocent man and the Emperor's anger, and tried to wash his hands of the matter. If a decision is laid on you, however, a decision not to act is still a decision, and moral cowardice does not absolve you. Pope Celestine v resigned "onori et oneri", as contemporary chroniclers described his action,[10] and this refusal of the honour and the burden abandoned the papacy to its evil course.

A simple, practical consideration leads one towards Celestine: that in his case alone among the more prominent candidates Dante might well have recognized him, even stark naked and covered in blood, either through personal acquaintance or, more probably, through the reputed ability of total strangers to recognize him.[11] More important perhaps is that Celestine's failure, unlike Esau's, had as a direct consequence the election of Boniface VIII, considered by Dante to be so fraught with evil results. Lastly, and to my mind most significantly, one may reasonably bear in mind the elaborate structure of the *Commedia* and consider Dante's attitude to Henry VII and the balance between the two figures, Celestine in *Inferno* III and Henry at the opposite extremity of the *Commedia* in *Paradiso* XXX, where his "gran seggio" ["great chair": line 133] is pointed out awaiting his arrival. These two figures illustrate the strength of Dante's conviction that men must try to do their duty whatever the odds against success. Celestine gave up, where Henry died still trying, even though to him rather than to his distant successor Joseph II one might justly apply the dictum "Here lies a man who failed in all he undertook."[12] Celestine (if it is he) suffers far more than the virtuous pagans "below" him in Canto IV, whereas it seems likely that Henry will go more or less straight to Heaven like the many thirteenth-century figures met in Paradise—not to speak of Beatrice herself. Has the author indeed not prepared us for an attack on Celestine's form of "viltade" by Virgil's reproof to Dante in *Inferno* II? First he is told:

> L'anima tua è da viltade offesa;
>   la qual molte fiate l'omo ingombra
> sí che d'onrata impresa lo rivolve,
> come falso veder bestia quand' ombra.
>   (*Inferno*, II. 45–48)

[Your spirit is beset by cowardice, which oftentimes encumbers a man, turning him from honourable endeavour, as false seeing turns a beast that shies.]

And even after describing Beatrice's visit to him Virgil still finds it necessary to say:

> Perché, perché restai,
> perché tanta viltà nel core allette [...]?
>   (*Inferno*, II. 121–22)

[Why, why do you hold back? Why do you harbour such cowardice in your heart?]

Dante has been called, like Celestine a few years earlier, to an "onrata impresa", apparently the journey, really perhaps his prophetic mission; he is seeking excuses to abandon it and has to be sharply called to order.

Irrespective of whether Celestine is really the subject, however, the reader is expected to examine the possibilities and thus learn more about human frailty. Dante may well have regarded this process as far more important than the reaching of the "correct" solution.

The need to consider a diversity of allegorical approaches in such scenes as that among the tombs also applies to the main protagonists. Guido da Pisa says of Beatrice that she is the "type and *figura* of the spiritual life [...]: sometimes to be taken literally for a certain noble Florentine lady [...]; sometimes [...] allegorically for the sacred science of theology; sometimes [...] morally [...], that is, for the spiritual life; and sometimes [...] anagogically, that is, for divine grace, poured into man, and the blessed life reserved for man."[13] Like Dante, he expects the reader, with or without his help as commentator, to distinguish her various roles from one another. As the poem proceeds, she is sometimes one and sometimes another, but almost always the noble Florentine lady who was Dante's great love.

In the case of Virgil, we have an even more complicated set of roles to bear in mind. On the "literal" level of the allegory, he is Dante's guide, instructor and, increasingly, father-figure. He is also the allegorical "exemplar" of a poet and prophet, and in the "historical" sense of the allegory he clearly stands for the Roman Empire, which he prophesied and in whose historic role Dante so firmly believed. He has other allegorical roles too, but it is with these and their implications that we shall be chiefly concerned.

Where Beatrice, that saint in Paradise, can seem remote from Dante and from us, we see Virgil from the beginning as kindly, firm when Dante needs it, always supportive; and we tend to relax into contemplation of their increasingly warm relationship—to confine ourselves unconsciously to the "literal sense". As an "exemplary" allegory of the role of the poet-prophet, however, Virgil illustrates that role through his inspiration and illumination of Dante himself (as he tells us in Canto I) and of Statius—a point to which we shall return. Throughout *Inferno* and *Purgatorio*, the theme of poets and their high vocation will recur, until in *Paradiso* that vocation is uniquely exemplified in Dante himself, as he becomes progressively more capable of understanding and transmitting the supreme vision. That high vocation itself can be betrayed, as Dante himself has been betraying it when we first meet him in the dark wood, but he is still helped and directed to fulfil his original mission. Virgil is portrayed as he was in the *Convivio*, as having a mission as poet-prophet of the Empire and of Christ; in the *Commedia*, however, he is shown as ultimately having betrayed his vision and lost his salvation through lack of faith. We should thus see him in the *Commedia* as guide both "literally" and allegorically, but not as himself free from faults. Because, however, we no longer accept that Virgil had prophetic powers, whether to illuminate his account of the past or to enlighten him on the future, we tend to ignore both the occasions when he is presented as a prophet and the question of why he has not been saved with the other prophets. We treat Dante's agreement with Virgil on the historical mission of the Empire as an idiosyncracy rather than as an acceptance of his prophetic powers.

Virgil is treated by Dante as a prophet in both *Convivio* and *Monarchia*, and for his *Aeneid* rather than for the inevitable Fourth Eclogue.[14] Some authorities suggest that in these works he is treated purely as a historian of the Roman Empire,[15] but such an approach ignores the fact that Virgil could only have known the detail of what happened to Aeneas, particularly in the Underworld, by divine inspiration, and this must also have supplied Jove's/God's words about him and about the Empire. Dante-the-character's words in *Inferno*, II. 13–27 and his "Io non Enëa, io non Paulo sono" ["I am not Aeneas, I am not Paul": line 32] suggest a belief in the historicity of Aeneas's visit to the Underworld which no historical knowledge of Virgil's could have established. In Book IV of the *Convivio*, discussing the divine origins of the Roman Empire, Dante asserts:

Non da forza fu principalmente preso per la romana gente, ma da divina provedenza, che è sopra ogni ragione. E in ciò s'accorda Virgilio nel primo de lo Eneida, quando dice, in persona di Dio parlando: "A costoro—cioè a li Romani—né termine di cose né di tempo pongo; a loro ho dato imperio sanza fine."

(*Convivio*, IV. 4. 11)

[This office (...) was obtained by the Roman people not principally by means of force, but by divine providence, which is the ultimate ground of all reason. Such is Virgil's view in the *Aeneid*, when he portrays God as declaring: "To their rule (the Romans') I set no limit, whether of place or time; to them have I given empire without end" (*Aeneid*, I, 278–79).]

In *Monarchia* he draws on both Virgil and Livy to establish divine protection for early Rome, but only Virgil is referred to as "divinus" himself and quoted freely verbatim.[16]

In *Purgatorio*, XXII. 40–41 we even find Virgil's "Quid non mortalia pectora cogis,/auri sacra fames!" ["To what dost thou not drive the hearts of men, O accursed hunger for gold!": *Aeneid*, III. 56–57] treated as having a role in Statius's conversion, and it is of course in the same canto that that conversion is specifically attributed to the influence of the Fourth Eclogue. Statius addresses Virgil as the one who "prima appresso Dio m'alluminasti" ["first did light me on to God"], and continues:

> Facesti come quei che va di notte,
> che porta il lume dietro e sé non giova,
> ma dopo sé fa le persone dotte.
>   (*Purgatorio*, XXII. 66–69)

[You were like one who goes by night and carries the light behind him and profits not himself, but makes those wise who follow him.]

This is however more qualified praise than it seems at first reading. Statius's "sé non giova" sounds unselfish and noble, but if you do not know where you are going it is rash not to illuminate your own path: not a case of the blind leading the blind, since Statius at least saw the path, but surely a strong suggestion (to put it no higher) that Virgil himself was blind to his own prophecy. We must now turn to the evidence that Dante saw Virgil as having in some sense betrayed his vision by failing to recognize it.

In *Inferno* we find Virgil saying that he lived "nel tempo de li dèi falsi e bugiardi" ["in the time of the false and lying gods": *Inferno*, I. 72], and that those in Limbo were virtuous, but:

> S'e' furon dinanzi al cristianesmo,
> non adorar debitamente a Dio:
> e di questi cotai son io medesmo.

> Per tai difetti, non per altro rio,
> semo perduti, e sol di tanto offesi
> che sanza speme vivemo in disio.
> (*Inferno*, IV. 37–42)

[If they were before Christianity, they did not worship God aright, and I myself am one of these. Because of these shortcomings, and for no other fault, we are lost, and only so far afflicted that without hope we live in longing.]

In pondering these lines, we must bear in mind that the knowledge of the souls in Hell is inadequate. Even where they seem anxious to tell the truth, their vision is limited. Francesca's appeal to our sympathies does not blind us to the fact that she sees "amore" as properly directed to "la bella persona/che mi fu tolta" ["the fair form that was taken from me": *Inferno*, V. 101–02]; and as we read on through *Purgatorio* and *Paradiso* our understanding of love is stretched and transformed. But Virgil is also in *Inferno*, and must also therefore be unable fully to understand those truths which either in life he had rejected or before which he had withdrawn in unhappiness or lack of trust. So he speaks the truth as he sees it; but we, wiser, should notice and give their true (which for Dante means Christian) weight to his words. In Virgil's very presence, Christ harrowed Hell and removed from it those who deserved salvation; so why, after his prophecies, was he not among those who "credettero in Cristo venturo" ["believed in Christ yet to come": *Paradiso*, XXXII. 24] and whom Christ then exalted to Heaven?

Dante's decision not to allow Virgil a place among the blessed cannot have been an easy one. There were clearly poetic advantages to being able to show Virgil as increasingly superfluous as Hell was left behind, but Dante's affection is surely so genuine that leaving him in Limbo must be the result of conviction, not expediency. The first step to an answer may be to consider what impact the *Aeneid* might make on you if, like Dante, you believed that God had spoken to its author. Some of us see pessimism as underlying much of the *Aeneid*.[17] Does the *Commedia* suggest that Dante shares this impression and sees the *Aeneid* as proving that Virgil failed to recognize his own voice as prophetic?

If we follow the path already indicated through the *Commedia*, and assume that as with *amor* so with Virgil himself we are being led to greater understanding, we find a number of statements which ring oddly in the mouth of a prophet. The first of the lines quoted above sounds as if Virgil thought the "false and lying gods" actually existed: if they were a poetic fiction, how could they have told lies? "False", in Italian as in English, can mean either treacherous or non-existent. In the passage from Canto IV, the implication of "debitamente" is that they failed to do as they ought, not that they could not. It is not simply being born before Christ that has damned them. Virgil's use of "difetto" and "rio" leaves ambiguous whether he now recognizes the failure as wrong, or whether he means "not for anything actually wrong"; Dante has so phrased it that the reader may take it either way, or see Virgil as coming closer to the truth than he knows.

Significant too for our approach to Virgil as a prophet who failed his vision is his remark in the same passage that they live "without hope [...] in longing". In *Purgatorio*, VII. 7–8, when he is perhaps joining Dante in enlarging his knowledge, he omits "difetto" in explaining his position and uses "rio" in an almost identical phrase: "Per null' altro rio/lo ciel perdei che per non aver fé" ["For no other fault did I lose Heaven than for not having faith"]. Since he goes on to point out that:

> Quivi sto io con quei che le tre sante
> virtú non si vestiro, e sanza vizio
> conobber l'altre e seguir tutte quante,
> *(Purgatorio, VII. 34–36)*

[There I abide with those who were not clothed with the three holy virtues, and without sin knew the others and followed all of them],

we are tempted to see these poor pagans as all damned solely by their date of birth and ignorance of the three theological virtues of faith, hope and charity; but as we have already noted this is clearly not true. Paradise in fact contains not only those who believed in "Cristo venturo" but Emperor Trajan, who actually persecuted Christians, and Virgil's own invention, the virtuous Ripheus, of whom he had said:

> Cadit et Rhipeus, iustissimus unus
> qui fuit in Teucris et servantissimus aequi.
> *(Aeneid, II. 426–27)*

[Ripheus, too, falls, foremost in justice among the Trojans, and most zealous for the right.]

We find him in *Paradiso* xx, where Dante rightly remarks:

> Chi crederebbe giú nel mondo errante
> che Rifëo Troiano in questo tondo
> fosse la quinta de le luci sante?
>
> (*Paradiso*, xx. 67–69)

[Who would believe, down in the erring world, that Ripheus the Trojan was the fifth of the holy lights in this circle?]

But in any event, whatever share of blame the other inhabitants of Limbo may bear, Virgil cannot be blameless so far as Dante is concerned, because faith and hope are particularly required of him to whom God has granted a prophetic vision. This is what Statius is referring to when he says, "sé non giova." Virgil has prophesied to the benefit of others, but has stumbled himself and thus been guilty of a lack of faith and hope.

It should also be said that Virgil betrays a lack of charity both in the Filippo Argenti episode, to which we shall return, and in his reproof to Dante over the punishment of the soothsayers:

> Qui vive la pietà quand' è ben morta;
> chi è piú scellerato che colui
> che al giudicio divin passion comporta?
> (*Inferno*, xx. 28–30)

[Here pity lives when it is altogether dead. Who is more impious than he who sorrows at God's judgement?]

While prophecy and charity are not so indissolubly linked to each other as both are separately to faith and hope—so that one may reasonably discuss Virgil as prophet without touching on his lack of charity—, the point is relevant to the contention that we are not meant to see Virgil as invariably right in any absolute sense, but rather as sharing Dante's prejudices. He did not rebuke Dante for feeling compassion for Paolo and Francesca in Canto v, and in Canto xvi he emphatically urged him to show courtesy to the sodomites:

> A costor si vuole esser cortese.
> E se non fosse il foco che saetta

> la natura del loco, i' dicerei
> che meglio stesse a te che a lor la fretta.
> (*Inferno*, XVI. 15–18)

[To these one should show courtesy. And were it not for the fire which the nature of this place darts, I should say that haste befitted you more than them.]

It is surely only a personal opinion of Virgil's that pity for Paolo and Francesca or respect for the sodomites is proper, but that pity for the soothsayers, rebuked by him in Canto XX, is a questioning of divine judgement.[18]

It is in this context that we should approach the quotation from *Aeneid*, VI. 883 which greets the group of griffin, chariot and the still invisible Beatrice in *Purgatorio*, XXX. 21. When Anchises cried out, "Manibus date lilia plenis" ["Give me lilies with full hand"], it was part of the poignant lament for the young Marcellus, nephew and heir of Emperor Augustus; the whole passage has a despairing ring, and the choice of a suitable alternative heir was in fact not altogether easy. But as a prophet Virgil should have realized that the death of Marcellus could not seriously damage an empire willed by God/Jove, let alone invalidate the prophecy. To Dante, neither Marcellus nor the child heralded in the Fourth Eclogue was to save mankind but another not yet born. Augustus's reign was leading towards the birth of Christ, and the death of his most promising heir was irrelevant, however sad. So Dante juxtaposes the acclamation to Christ as he entered Jerusalem and Anchises's lament, itself turned into an acclamation, and by so doing implicitly rebukes Virgil for his want of faith:

> Tutti dicean: *"Benedictus qui venis!"*,
> e fior gittando e di sopra e dintorno,
> *"Manibus, oh, date lilïa plenis!"*[19]
> (*Purgatorio*, XXX. 19–21)

[All cried, *"Benedictus qui venis"* and, scattering flowers up and around, *"Manibus, oh, date lilia plenis."*]

Relevant also to the figure of Virgil as prophet are the reminiscences of the commissioning of prophets, as are also his teaching and denunciations. Virgil is clearly commissioned by Beatrice, and at his first meeting with Dante we already find him prophesying the Greyhound as well as fulfilling his duty of reproof, here for the "viltade" which has already been discussed. His relationship with Dante has a warmth which is far more reminiscent of that between Elijah and Elisha than of that between the Sibyl and Aeneas, to which it is often likened. The Sibyl has been assigned a task which she performs satisfactorily. Where Virgil is happy to do Beatrice's bidding and succour Dante:

> Tanto m'aggrada il tuo comandamento,
> che l'ubidir, se già fosse, m'è tardi,
> (*Inferno*, II. 79–80)

[Your command so pleases me, that had I obeyed already it would be late],

Apollo controls the Sibyl with reins and goad.[20] She tells Aeneas about his future, and agrees to take him to see his father Anchises, but she does not treat him as a friend, let alone as a son, and her descriptions of the suffering in Dis, of Salmoneus and Tityus in particular, lack almost all sense of involvement; she might be describing a picture-gallery.[21]

Virgil, on the other hand, is portrayed by Dante as like himself in many respects. Both are close to the Old Testament prophets, whose task was as much that of denouncing the evils of society and leading men to better ways as of foretelling the future. It was indeed their denunciations of their contemporaries, rather than their foretelling of the future, which brought unpopularity and—according to tradition—usually death on the prophets. It is this denunciatory role of the prophet which seems to explain and justify the violence of the language not infrequently employed by both poet-prophets as they descend through Hell. Dante associates Virgil with his own anger in such passages as *Inferno*, VIII. 31–60, where Virgil not only abuses Filippo Argenti—"Via costà con li altri cani!" ["Away there with the other dogs!": line 42]—but approves and perhaps even brings about the fulfilment of Dante's uncharitable wish to see him suffer. The poets show wrath with the wrathful, just as in *Inferno*, XXXIII. 115–50 Dante shows treachery to the treacherous. But the sins which the two are in agreement in condemning are those which are damaging to the very fabric of society, and in this they resemble the prophets of old, at least as they are recorded: in the Old Testament, most denunciations are of whole classes of society, above all of the rich and the hypocrites. It is only rulers who are often reprimanded and if necessary warned of their forthcoming punishment for private faults, and even then only as these have affected others. Virgil, like Dante and the prophets and unlike the Sibyl, is shown by Dante as intimately involved with human society and reacting with striking vigour to certain of its faults.[22]

The prophet as teacher does not however merely denounce. In the Old Testament as in the *Commedia*, he teaches right relations with God as the first necessity of life, and in the *Commedia* as in the Old Testament justice is exalted and avarice and prodigality are denounced as violations of right relations among men. All three *cantiche* return again and again to these themes, though with many fewer references to the sufferings of the poor than in the Old Testament.

As prophets and as travellers, Virgil and Dante become so closely involved, both with each other and with what they see, that one may be forgiven at times for forgetting which is speaking. Both are believable human beings, and, as often happens in life, the pupil ends by surpassing his master. By the time they part in the Earthly Paradise, Virgil has no longer anything to offer Dante except his paternal affection. In his final words to his disciple, he not merely offers him a choice but expresses his trust in his judgement:

> Seder ti puoi e puoi andar tra elli.
>   Non aspettar mio dir piú né mio cenno;
> libero, dritto e sano è tuo arbitrio,
> e fallo fora non fare a suo senno:
>   per ch'io te sovra te corono e mitrio.
>   (*Purgatorio*, XXVII. 138–42)

[You may sit or go among them. No longer expect word or sign from me. Free, upright and whole is your will, and it would be wrong not to act according to its pleasure; wherefore I crown and mitre you over yourself.]

When Dante, puzzled by the sight of the great candelabra in the wood, turns to him, we discover not only that Virgil is equally baffled—"Esso mi rispuose/con vista carca di stupor non meno" ["He answered me with a look no less charged with amazement": *Purgatorio*, XXIX. 56–57]—but also that Virgil is now behind him rather than leading. His mantle does not however pass to Dante/ Elisha; instead we find one on Beatrice as she takes over and amplifies Virgil's role. Prophecy remains present, as her prophecy of the DXV follows Virgil's of the Greyhound, and she assumes the task for which, as we were told in *Inferno* II, she was commissioned by the Virgin Mary and St Lucy. By the end of the poem, Dante himself is ready for his task as he seeks the words with which to fulfil those prophetic duties towards us which have been repeatedly referred to in *Paradiso*.[23] Reason and prophecy from his teachers have given way to sight, that is, direct knowledge.

If we turn to the strictly "prophetic" passages, we find that they fall in two groups: the past-as-future and the real future. Into the first category come all references to events which had in fact already come to pass when Dante was writing, such as his own exile: they require little input of intelligence or knowledge from the reader beyond what a commentary provides. The prophecies of the real future are concerned with the sending of remedies by God. If Dante took his own prophetic role seriously, as he seems to, then we should expect a certain obscurity in these passages. The Messianic prophecies of the Old Testament were not, then as now, thought of as having been written by men who knew how or when the Messiah would come, whether it would be in the near future or centuries later. Their ignorance of the how and when did not invalidate their vision; it laid on the hearer or reader the task of recognizing the Messiah when He did appear. In Dante's own day, there was still much dispute as to when and how the prophecies of Abbot Joachim of Fiore would be fulfilled.[24] Indeed the whole cult of Joachim must have reinforced in Dante the Old Testament rather than the Sibylline view of the prophet which we have been discussing. But the direct influence on his portrayal of himself and of Virgil as poet-prophets was surely that of the Old Testament prophets themselves—Amos, Isaiah and Ezechiel perhaps above all. It is in their spirit that Dante talks of the Greyhound and the DXV. He was certain that God would send another remedy after the failure of "alto Arrigo" ["lofty Henry": *Paradiso*, XVII. 82, XXX. 137]; he may have thought of two messengers of God rather than one, with slightly different functions, or felt that his vision was not sufficiently clear on this point for it to be appropriate for him to speak clearly to his readers. What was vital was that he should so convey that vision that when the Greyhound and the DXV appeared, whether as one and the same or not, men should recognize them (or him) as indeed "messo di Dio" ["sent by God": *Purgatorio*, XXXIII. 44]. It is indicative of the force which he wishes to give these prophecies that he puts them into the mouths of Virgil and Beatrice respectively: the one with an established reputation as a prophet (up to and after Dante's own day), the other, as we are constantly made aware in *Paradiso*, with direct knowledge of anything she needs to know from God Himself. It is remotely possible that he thought Can Grande might turn out to be the Greyhound, but surely very improbable that he believed himself certain of its identity. Even John the Baptist foretold Christ's coming first, and recognized Him only later.[25] Dante's task as prophet of the future was to help men recognize those sent by God, just as his task as prophet-teacher was to help them face their own faults—though fulfilling this task would certainly not secure his return to the "bello ovile ov' io dormi' agnello" ["fair sheepfold where I slept as a lamb": *Paradiso*, xxv. 5].

As Marjorie Reeves has reminded us in her admirable discussion of "Dante and the Prophetic View of History",[26] already in his 1311 letter to the Florentines Dante had said, "si presaga mens mea non fallitur" ["if my prophetic soul be not deceived": *Epist.*, VI. 17].[27] In the *Commedia* he uses the figure of Virgil, *vates* in every sense, to give authority to his own inspired view of present and future: to us, inspired in the generic sense of poetic inspiration, but to himself inspired as the prophets were inspired, to criticize, warn and—to quote Dr Reeves directly—to "attempt, by given clues, to read the signs set in history which point towards the fulfilment of the whole divine plan".[28]

NOTES

1   For example, *Inf.*, IX. 61–63, *Purg.*, VIII. 19–21, *Par.*, x. 22–27.
2   Guido da Pisa, *Expositiones et Glose super Comediam Dantis*, edited by V. Cioffari (Albany, New York, State University of New York Press, 1974), p. 33, on Virgil and the Veltro: "Iste poeta, more poetarum, futura vaticinatur; unde poeta idem est quod propheta." On Guido and his fellow commentators, see L. Jenaro-MacLennan, *The Trecento Commentaries on the "Divina Commedia" and the Epistle to Cangrande* (Oxford, Clarendon Press, 1974), pp. 22–58.
3   *Convivio*, pp. 601–03: "Vivere ne l'uomo è ragione usare [...], e cosí da quello uso partire è partire da essere, e cosí è essere morto. [...] Potrebbe alcuno dicere: Come? è morto e va? Rispondo che è morto uomo e rimaso bestia."

4 *Mon.*, I. 3. 6–4. 2.
5 "Dante-the-character" suits the scope of this essay better than the more usual "Dante-the-pilgrim", since I am here concerned with his and Virgil's roles as poet-prophets, not with his function as pilgrim.
6 See n. 1 above. The common medieval mnemonic on the fourfold senses of allegory reads: "Littera gesta docet; quid credas, allegoria;/moralis quid agas; quo tendas anagogia", which roughly translates as "The letter teaches the actions; what you should believe, the allegory; what you should do, the moral; whither you may (*or* should) be bound, the anagogia." This was formulated primarily for scriptural texts, where the "letter which teaches the actions" must be assumed to be "literally" true. In the context of poetry, as Dante reminds us in *Conv.*, II. 1. 2, the allegorical sense may be "una veritate ascosa sotto bella menzogna": the "literal" sense may be a lie. You thus might have a historical event as one of the "hidden truths", as was common in Dante's day in commentaries on Ovid's *Metamorphoses*, where gods and goddesses are explained as "historically" kings and queens. Other ages have called this "euhemerism" but to the fourteenth century it was the "historical sense", a form of allegory. Examples of behaviour could similarly be regarded as a use of allegory. Compare *Epist.*, XIII. 20–22, which most would agree is authentically Dante's, and which discusses the fourfold senses as applied to Psalm 114 (Vulgate 113). For short discussions of Dante's understanding of allegory see C. S. Singleton, "Allegory", in his *Dante Studies, 1: "Commedia": Elements of Structure* (Cambridge, Massachusetts, Harvard University Press, 1954), pp. 1–17; T. G. Bergin, *An Approach to Dante* (London, Bodley Head, 1965), Chapter 13; P. Armour, "The Theme of Exodus in the First Two Cantos of the *Purgatorio*", in *Dante Soundings: Eight Literary and Historical Essays*, edited by D. Nolan (Dublin, Irish Academic Press, 1981), pp. 59–99.
7 G. Boccaccio, *Esposizioni sopra la "Comedia" di Dante*, edited by G. Padoan, in *Tutte le opere di Giovanni Boccaccio*, vol. VI (Milan, Mondadori, 1965), p. 92, on *Inf.* I (ii): "Possono per avventura essere alcuni, li quali forse stimano [...] ogni parola aver sotto sé alcun sentimento diverso da quello che la lettera suona; [...] acciò che piú pienamente si creda non ogni parola avere allegorico senso, leggasi quello che ne scrive santo Agostino."
8 Guido da Pisa, Iacopo della Lana and Pietro di Dante are among the categorical, the Ottimo Commento, Buti and Boccaccio less certain, though Boccaccio, after saying, "non si sa assai certo", goes on to make an excellent case for Celestine followed by a brief one for Esau (*Esposizioni*, pp. 148–51). For Benvenuto's views see below.
9 *Benevenuti de Rambaldis de Imola Comentum super Dantis Aldigherii Comoediam*, edited by J. P. Lacaita, 5 vols (Florence, Barbèra, 1887), I, 117. Benvenuto makes so good a case for Celestine that one suspects he only promotes Esau's case from contrariness or to be original: "quantuncumque forte Celestinus fecerit hanc magnam renunciationem bono et puro animo, tamen reputatum fuit sibi generaliter ad maximam vilitatem; quod negari non potest." He also makes a slightly better case for Esau than Boccaccio by adding the reference to becoming Christ's ancestor.
10 For example, Paolino Minorita, *Historiarum Epitome*, second version (Florence, Biblioteca Riccardiana, MS 3034), f. 178^v; Bernardo Gui, *Chronicon* (Rome, Biblioteca Vallicelliana, MS B.29), f. 170^r.
11 See E. G. Gardner, *Dante and the Mystics* (London, Dent, 1913), pp. 325–28. While it is probable that Dante had not heard of Celestine's canonization (see

F. Tocco, *Quel che non c'è nella "Divina commedia", o Dante e l'eresia* [Bologna, Zanichelli, 1899], pp. 81–88; F. D'Ovidio, *Studii sulla "Divina Commedia"* [Milan–Palermo, Sandron, 1901], pp. 418–24), knowledge of it would not, I am sure, have restrained him from placing Celestine in Limbo.

12 On Henry VII see W. M. Bowsky, *Henry VII in Italy: The Conflict of Empire and City-state, 1310–1313* (Lincoln, Nebraska, University of Nebraska Press, 1960), for a somewhat harsh judgement.

13 See, for instance, Guido da Pisa's *Expositiones*, pp. 31–32, where he betrays the usual vagueness about the exact distinctions between the types of allegory: "Beatrix tenet typum et figuram vite spiritualis; ubi nota quod Beatrix in ista Comedia accipitur quatuor modis: interdum enim accipitur licteraliter pro quadam videlicet nobili domina florentina, que sua pulcritudine et morum honestate mirabiliter emicuit in hac vita; aliquando accipitur allegorice pro sacra scilicet scientia theologie; aliquando accipitur moraliter, sive typice, pro vita scilicet spirituali; aliquando vero accipitur anagogice pro gratia scilicet divina, homini infusa, et vita beata homini attributa."

14 On Virgil as prophet see D. Comparetti, *Vergil in the Middle Ages*, translated by E. F. M. Benecke, second edition (London, Swan Sonnenschein, 1908), Part I, Chapter 7 and Part II, Chapter 7; P. Courcelle, "Les Exégèses chrétiennes de la quatrième Eglogue", *Revue des études anciennes*, 59 (1957), 294–319.

15 For example Bruno Nardi, who sees a more abrupt development than is being suggested here between Dante's attitude to Virgil in *Convivio* and *Monarchia* and that expressed in the *Commedia*. He interprets entirely as a development in thought what I see as in large measure a change of emphasis: in *Monarchia* II Dante is alleging that the facts of history prove divine support for Rome. Nardi himself says, in apparent reference to the earlier works, that Aeneas's "discesa all'Averno e l'andata all'Elisio non sono favola ma storia vera, assai piú di quella narrata da Livio che non seppe spingere tant' alto lo sguardo", which seems to imply that Dante believed in a knowledge beyond historical fact. See B. Nardi, *Saggi e note di critica dantesca* (Milan–Naples, Ricciardi, 1966), p. 62.

16 Especially *Mon.*, II. 3. 8–6. 11; the reference to Virgil as "divinus poeta noster" is in II. 3. 6.

17 The case for and against Virgil's underlying pessimism has been very well made by W. R. Johnson, *Darkness Visible: A Study of Vergil's "Aeneid"* (Berkeley–London, University of California Press, 1976). I personally find the *Aeneid* a deeply pessimistic poem, but the point here is that belief in Virgil as inspired by God to prophesy would probably create and certainly strengthen such an interpretation.

18 In *Conv.*, II. 10. 6 Dante had said: "Pietade non è passione, anzi è una nobile disposizione d'animo, apparecchiata di ricevere amore, misericordia e altre caritative passioni." Is Dante rejecting his own earlier view through Virgil's mouth in *Inferno* XX, or presenting Virgil as holding an unchristian view?

19 This reversal of Virgil's meaning is promptly followed by another, less drastic, change. Dante turns to run to Virgil, like an unhappy child to his mother, and to say to him, "Conosco i segni de l'antica fiamma" (XXX. 48); but when Dido uses these words (*Aen.*, IV. 23), she is referring to her transfer of her love from her husband Sichaeus to Aeneas, wrong because she had sworn fidelity to Sichaeus's ashes. Her husband is found in fact sharing her suffering

among the betrayed lovers in the Mourning Fields: "Coniunx ubi pristinus illi/respondet curis aequatque Sychaeus amorem" (*Aen.*, VI. 473–74).
20 *Aen.*, VI. 100–02: "Ea frena furenti/concutit et stimulos sub pectore vertit Apollo./Ut primum cessit furor et rabida ora quierunt [...]."
21 *Aen.*, VI. 585–600. A. D. Nuttall, now of New College, Oxford but then a colleague at Sussex, first drew my attention to the Sibyl's frightening detachment in this passage.
22 R. Jacoff, "Dante, Geremia e la problematica profetica", in *Dante e la Bibbia*, edited by G. Barblan (Florence, Olschki, 1988), pp. 113–23, has an excellent discussion of the use of prophetic language, more particularly in *Purgatorio* and *Paradiso*. On pp. 120–23 she discusses the wrath of God and comments, "È proprio l'arrossire dei beati a farsi rappresentazione dell'ira divina, che, nel poema, giustifica e corrisponde all'ira del poeta" (p. 121).
23 For instance, *Par.*, XVII. 127–29, XXI. 97–99, XXVII. 64–66 and Dante's own prayer for aid to convey his new "knowledge", XXXIII. 70–72: "Fa la lingua mia tanto possente,/ch'una favilla sol de la tua gloria/possa lasciare a la futura gente."
24 On Joachim of Fiore see M. Reeves, *The Influence of Prophecy in the Later Middle Ages: A Study in Joachimism* (Oxford, Clarendon Press, 1969); M. Reeves and B. Hirsch-Reich, *The "Figurae" of Joachim of Fiore* (Oxford, Clarendon Press, 1972).
25 I take this to be the implication of John's not naming "the one who comes after me" (Matthew 3. 11–12; Mark 1. 7–8; Luke 3. 15–17; possibly John 1. 26–27). R. Jacoff, "Dante, Geremia e la problematica profetica", p. 122, says: "Appropriandosi della Scrittura, Dante non solo legittima la sua voce ma anche inevitabilmente ci ricorda dell'ambiguità implicita del ruolo profetico."
26 M. Reeves, "Dante and the Prophetic View of History", in *The World of Dante: Essays on Dante and His Times*, edited by C. Grayson (Oxford, Clarendon Press, 1980), pp. 44–60.
27 *Epistolae*, ed. Toynbee, p. 79.
28 M. Reeves, "Dante and the Prophetic View of History", p. 51.

VESTIGES OF THE LITURGY IN DANTE'S VERSE

John C. Barnes

> BOCCACCIO Now do tell me, before we say more of the *Paradiso*, what can I offer in defence of the Latin scraps from litanies and lauds, to the number of fifty or thereabout?
> PETRARCA Say nothing at all, unless you can obtain some Indulgences for repeating them.[1]

It has been stated hundreds of times that medieval life was overwhelmingly dominated by the Christian religion and the Church. Indeed, Jacques Le Goff has shown how this applied to time itself: "Above all, medieval time is religious and clerical time."[2] He was thinking primarily of the influence of the liturgical year, which provided markers not only in ecclesiastical life but also in secular life (rent-cropping dates, for instance); and he was thinking, too, of the fact that church bells, despite the specifically ecclesiastical nature of their primary function, were the sole public indication of the time of day. Even if Dante's *Commedia*, then, were not the work with the explicitly religious and ecclesiastical dimensions that we know it to be, we should not be surprised by its reflections of the pervasive presence of the Church in everyday life. One need think only of the famous moment in *Paradiso* XV when Cacciaguida alludes to the fact that the bell of Florence's Benedictine abbey, in the shadow of which Dante was born, still rings out its call to terce and to nones (services for monks only):

> Fiorenza dentro da la cerchia antica,
> ond' ella toglie ancora e terza e nona [...]
> (*Paradiso*, XV. 97–98)

[Florence, within her ancient circle from which she still takes tierce and nones (...)]

—which Jacopo della Lana expands as follows: "This church rings out terce and nones and the other hours, at which the workers of the guilds go to work and come home again."[3] One might also think of the equally famous lines which open the eighth canto of *Purgatorio* and refer to the emotional effect of a distant bell in the evening—presumably the compline bell—on a pilgrim who is not used to being away from home:

> Era già l'ora [...]
> [...] che lo novo peregrin d'amore
> punge, se ode squilla di lontano
> che paia il giorno pianger che si more.
> (*Purgatorio*, VIII. 1–6)

[It was now the hour (...) that pierces the new pilgrim with love if he hears from afar a bell that seems to mourn the dying day.]

Or again, one might think of the simile in *Inferno* XXIII based on the distinctive custom of the Franciscans of walking along the road in single file:[4]

> Taciti, soli, sanza compagnia
> n'andavam l'un dinanzi e l'altro dopo,
> come frati minor vanno per via.
> (*Inferno*, XXIII. 1–3)

[Silent, alone, without escort, we went on, one before and the other behind, as Friars Minor go their way.]

These and numerous other brief passages provide the local colour—one might be tempted to coin the phrase "temporal colour"—which, in one respect, binds the *Commedia* to its own age.

But there are other respects in which Dante's poem may be said to have ecclesiastical characteristics. Indeed, one of the more venerable clichés in Dante scholarship is that the *Commedia* is the literary analogue of a Gothic cathedral.[5] Not all readers of the poem are equally impressed by this analogy with ecclesiastical architecture, but there is another, paradoxically more solid, way in which the Church—as an edifice and an institution—is represented in the *Commedia*. The doctrine of the Communion of Saints articulates the whole of humanity, past present and future—the Mystical Body of Christ—, into three churches: the Church Militant, made up of those who are alive on earth at any given time; the Church Suffering, consisting of the souls of those who have died in a state of grace but have not yet performed all the satisfaction required for the sins of which they were guilty during their mortal lives; and the Church Triumphant, comprising the souls of those who have died in a state of grace *and* washed away all their sins.[6] The second and third of these Churches obviously correspond to Purgatory and Paradise, and hence to the second and third *cantiche* of Dante's poem. The first *cantica*, however, cannot be equated with one of the Churches of systematic theology. At least in ideal terms, which are the terms postulated by the *Commedia*, the progression is from the Church Militant (here on earth) to the Church Suffering (after death) and thence to the Church Triumphant; and within that scheme, Hell represents a wrong turning. Its inhabitants, however, suffer in ways as logical and organized—though not so purposeful—as the repentant sinners who are punished in the Church Suffering of *Purgatorio*. Read against the second *cantica*, Dante's *Inferno* could be said to depict an anti-church.

If Hell is an anti-church, then we would expect it either to make little or no use of the liturgy, or to use the liturgy in some sort of inverted way, such as parody. And in fact we find that both these expectations are justified. The singing of hymns is parodied in Canto VII, where the designation "hymn" is applied to the utterance of the second, submerged group of souls guilty of anger:

> "Tristi fummo
> ne l'aere dolce che dal sol s'allegra,
> portando dentro accidïoso fummo:
>   or ci attristiam ne la belletta negra."
> Quest' inno si gorgoglian ne la strozza,
> ché dir nol posson con parola integra.
>   (*Inferno*, VII. 121–26)

["We were sullen in the sweet air that is gladdened by the sun, bearing within us the sluggish fumes; now we are sullen in the black mire." This hymn they gurgle in their throats, for they cannot speak it in full words.]

Similarly, the senseless babbling of the giant Nimrod is referred to as his psalmody:

> "Raphèl maí amècche zabí almi,"
> cominciò a gridar la fiera bocca,
> cui non si convenia piú dolci salmi.
> (*Inferno*, XXXI. 67–69)

["Raphèl maý amecche zabí almi," the fierce mouth, to which sweeter psalms were not fitting, began to cry.]

Inferno also contains a handful of allusions to the real psalms—perhaps as many as a dozen, which is a relatively small total—and perhaps ten (but no more) references to other liturgical texts. The most striking of these, and apparently the only Latin quotation in the first *cantica*, occurs at the opening of the final canto, where Virgil says to Dante:

> *Vexilla regis prodeunt inferni*
> verso di noi; però dinanzi mira
> [...] se tu 'l discerni.
> (*Inferno*, XXXIV. 1–3)

[*Vexilla regis prodeunt inferni* (The banners of the king of Hell advance) towards us; look forward therefore, (...) see if you discern him.]

Dante here adds a fourth word, *inferni*,[7] to the first three words of *Vexilla Regis prodeunt*, a processional hymn by the sixth-century bishop of Poitiers Venantius Fortunatus, which has been described as "one of the grandest hymns of the Latin Church".[8] It celebrates the mystery of love accomplished on the Cross, and in Dante's day was sung at vespers during the last two weeks before Good Friday.[9] The quotation is used by Dante to heighten the solemnity of the approach to the lord of all evil. There is also, however, an element of irony in the way he uses it. The king of Hell is Lucifer, and presumably his banners are his monstrous, bat-like wings. But the only sense in which Lucifer's wings advance towards Dante and Virgil is that they wave to and fro, causing the River Cocytus to freeze over; Lucifer himself is fixed motionless at the centre of the earth. As Guido da Pisa perceived, the allusion to the glorious banners of the Cross, by which Lucifer was vanquished, is an effective way of putting Lucifer in his place—of ensuring that he is seen in due perspective.[10] To some extent, though, Dante is using short-hand: he quotes only three words, in which, although Christ and His banners are mentioned, the Cross is not. A full appreciation of Dante's technique, then—or so it could be argued—, requires a knowledge of the hymn as a whole, not just the portion quoted. (That Dante welcomes intertextual comparisons is confirmed, for example, in *Purgatorio*, XXIX. 100–05.)

Although the *Vexilla Regis* quotation is a good example of what I have termed "vestiges of the liturgy", where *Inferno* is concerned it is the exception that proves the rule. Hell is not a church, the liturgy is out of place there, and I propose to devote no further attention to the opening *cantica*.

Up to now I have omitted to establish exactly what we mean by the liturgy. According to the *Shorter Oxford Dictionary* the word itself properly refers to "a collection of formularies for the conduct of [...] public worship". For present purposes, then, it applies principally to the contents of the Missal and the Breviary—the order of service for the mass and for the constituent parts of the Divine Office, which were observed every day at the various hours. In both the mass and the Office, much of the verbal content is taken from the Bible: this applies to the psalms, the canticles, the lessons, and shorter components such as antiphons. The non-Biblical elements are the hymns, the prayers, the creeds and the confession.[11] One problem, therefore, in identifying vestiges of the liturgy is that of deciding between conflicting claims. When, in *Purgatorio* xxx, the angels say "*Benedictus qui venis!*" (line 19), do we take this as a quotation of the words with which Christ was greeted on His entry into Jerusalem ("Blessings on him who comes in the name of the Lord!", Matthew 21. 9, Mark 11. 10, Luke 19. 38), or as a quotation from the canon of the mass, where the same words are used immediately after the *Sanctus*? The solution adopted here is to regard all disputed matter as liturgical except the lessons—which means that most of the Bible, and most of the Biblical allusions in the *Commedia*, fall outside the scope of this essay. The justification I claim for this solution is that the lessons were read only once a year, so that Dante's familiarity with them is more likely to derive from private perusal of the Bible than from sustained church-going. The lessons accounted for all of the Bible except the Psalms, which formed the backbone of the Divine Office and were sung not annually but weekly—and some of them (those prescribed for compline) daily. If phrases from any part of the Bible stuck in

Dante's mind as a result of liturgical use, then, with a few exceptions it seems much more plausible that this should be the Psalms than anything else—though with the Psalms we are still in danger of labelling something a vestige of the liturgy when in reality it is not.

Having disposed of *Inferno*, we may move on to *Purgatorio*, which is the most fertile of the three *cantiche* in its cultivation of liturgical language. This is no doubt connected with the fact that Dante modelled his Purgatory much more obviously on an earthly church than he did in the case of either Heaven or Hell. Many critics have noticed this: for instance, as long ago as 1906 Francesco D'Ovidio wrote that Dante's second *cantica* is "simile a un colossale monastero salmeggiante" ["similar to a colossal psalm-singing monastery"].[12] There are numerous striking examples of this, from the second canto (lines 45–48), where the souls of more than a hundred recently dead people destined for Purgatory arrive in a boat singing Psalm 114 ("When Israel came out of Egypt"), to the beginning of Canto XXXIII, where the seven nymphs of the Terrestrial Paradise sing Psalm 79 antiphonally ("O God, the heathen have set foot in thy domain, defiled thy holy temple and laid Jerusalem in ruins"). This is most understandable of all in the central part of the *cantica*, from Canto X to Canto XXVII, which covers the seven circles of Purgatory proper. By the end of this section, the souls have cleansed themselves of all but the memory of sin, thereby ceasing to be comparable to members of the earthly Church, while the gate of Purgatory, which Dante passes through in Canto IX, has, as Peter Armour has most persuasively shown, much of the character of a church door: the souls outside it, in Ante-Purgatory, are analogous to those in this life who are excommunicated, that is, denied admittance to the church.[13]

The essential business of the souls in the seven *gironi* is penance. A central part of penance is prayer, and in each *girone* the souls use a prayer from the Roman liturgy which is appropriate to their sin—except the slothful, whose very zeal seems to function as a prayer. Not all these purgatorial prayers were prayers, in the narrow sense, in earthly usage. In fact, only one of them was: the souls of the proud recite the Lord's Prayer, with amplifications emphasizing the theme of human humility, the opposite of pride

(*Purgatorio*, XI. 1–21). Among the rest, the prayer of the lustful, for example, is a hymn, *Summae Deus clementiae* (*Purgatorio*, XXV. 121), which was sung at matins on Saturdays, and is a request to God for protection from impurity with especial reference to lust: "Burn our loins and our soft liver with appropriate flames," it says, "so that our limbs, preserved from appalling lust, may be vigilant and ready."[14] Even the detail of fire in this hymn corresponds to the punishment of the souls in the seventh circle, and may perhaps have suggested it. Two of the other purgatorial prayers, that of the gluttons and that of the misusers of riches (misers and prodigal) are taken from the Psalms, but consist of only one verse, somewhat in the manner of antiphons. The gluttons sing verse 15 of Psalm 51, "Open my lips, O Lord, that my mouth may proclaim thy praise" (rather than eat or drink; *Purgatorio*, XXIII. 11); while the misusers of riches, who were excessively attached to earthly things, sing verse 25 of Psalm 119, "I lie prone in the dust; grant me life according to thy word" (*Purgatorio*, XIX. 73; here again the liturgical passage may have suggested the punishment, since the souls do lie prone on the ground). The souls of the wrathful sing the *Agnus Dei* (*Purgatorio*, XVI. 19), which makes the petitions "have mercy upon us" and "grant us thy peace". And the souls of the envious recite—indeed they shout—the first part of the Lenten litany:

> E poi che fummo un poco piú avanti,
> udia gridar: "Maria, òra per noi":
> gridar "Michele" e "Pietro" e "Tutti santi".[15]
> (*Purgatorio*, XIII. 49–51)

[And when we were a little farther on, I heard cries of, "Mary, pray for us!" then "Michael" and "Peter" and "All Saints".]

The narrow, mean individualism and egoism of the envious are replaced by a choral sense of prayer, which, in a transport of *caritas*, renews the harmony between the Church Triumphant, the Church Suffering and the Church Militant.

Other liturgical elements in Purgatory proper include Marco Lombardo's greeting "Dio sia con voi" ["May God be with you"] in *Purgatorio*, XVI. 141, and the Greater Doxology, *Gloria in excelsis Deo*, which is sung by all the souls in Purgatory in response to the liberation of Statius from the *gironi* of the mountainside:[16]

> "*Gloria in excelsis*" tutti "*Deo*"
> dicean.
>
> (*Purgatorio*, xx. 136–37)

["*Gloria in exclesis, Deo*" all were saying.]

This text, of course, originates in the words of the multitude of the heavenly host after the angel has brought the good tidings of great joy to the shepherds abiding in the field, keeping watch over their flock by night. But Dante is using the liturgical version rather than the Biblical version where the two diverge: in fact the Vulgate has not "Gloria in excelsis Deo" but "Gloria in altissimis Deo" (Luke 2. 14).[17]

The liturgical content of *Purgatorio*, however, is by no means confined to the seven *gironi* of the mountainside. In the Terrestrial Paradise two of the thematic strands—that of Beatrice's solemn appearance and that of Dante's confession and purification—are treated liturgically, mainly by means of psalms. The sequence is introduced by Matelda singing Psalm 32 (or perhaps only the first verse of Psalm 32): "Happy the man whose disobedience is forgiven, whose sin is put away!" (*Purgatorio*, xxix. 3), this being highly relevant to Dante's situation at the time.[18] When Beatrice harshly rebukes Dante and asks him how he comes to be in that place of felicity, the angels take pity on him, and also answer Beatrice on his behalf, by singing the first eight verses of Psalm 31—"With thee, O Lord, I have sought shelter, let me never be put to shame. Deliver me in thy righteousness" (*Purgatorio*, xxx. 83–84)—, which explain that Dante's presence is justified by his complete confidence in God's mercy: "Thou art to me both rock and stronghold; [...] into thy keeping I commit my spirit. [...] I put my trust in the Lord." And his immersion in the Lethe is accompanied by the angelic singing of Psalm 51 (one of the seven penitential psalms), verse 7 ("Take hyssop and sprinkle me, that I may be clean; wash me, that I may become whiter than snow"; *Purgatorio*, xxxi. 98), which was used in the earthly church for the rite of asperging the confessed sinner with holy water.[19]

Meanwhile, Beatrice appears at the centre and the culmination of a solemn procession (and processions themselves were a conspicuous part of medieval Italian piety),[20] in which the human participants are dressed in white (the main colour of liturgical vestments). At the beginning of the procession she is heralded by the acclamation "Hosanna" (*Purgatorio*, XXIX. 51), which occurs, among other places, in the *Benedictus* (part of the canon of the mass). I choose this source because less than a canto later (*Purgatorio*, XXX. 19) Beatrice's actual appearance is immediately preceded by the other half of the *Benedictus*—"Blessed is he [or she] that cometh in the name of the Lord." The strongly liturgical character of the scene is completed by two chants of which the words are not revealed: "'l dolce suon per canti era già inteso" ["the sweet sound was now heard as a song": *Purgatorio*, XXIX. 36]; and:

> Io non lo 'ntesi, né qui non si canta
> l'inno che quella gente allor cantaro.
> (*Purgatorio*, XXXII. 61–62)

[I did not understand the hymn, and it is not sung here, which that company then sang.]

This has the quality of what we shall find in *Paradiso*, and may be said to prepare us for it.

Ante-Purgatory, too, has a strong liturgical colouring. One element in this is the use of the *Te Deum* (*Purgatorio*, IX. 140) as Dante passes through the gate of Purgatory proper after his testing encounter with the angel. The *Te Deum* was the Church's hymn of thanksgiving, sung on occasions of deliverance and victory.[21] It is thus appropriate here by virtue of its subject-matter; and, in addition, the festive character of its use here, embodying a release from more intense preoccupations, reflects its festive use at the end of the nocturnal psalmody sung by choirs in earthly monasteries.[22] (It is used again in the same way in *Paradiso*, XXIV. 113, after Dante has successfully passed his examinations on the three theological virtues.) The *Te Deum* was also used at the end of liturgical dramas in Dante's day,[23] and it may not be too fanciful to view the events of the second half of Canto IX as a liturgical drama. Furthermore, the *Te Deum* contains the words "Thou hast opened the Kingdom of Heaven to all believers"; and in Dante's scheme the Kingdom of Heaven begins right here, at the entrance to Purgatory proper. Again, the *Te Deum* was sung when a man entered religion,[24] and of this Dante's entry into Purgatory proper may be seen as a projection. Purgatory, unlike even Ante-Purgatory, is a truly spiritual world, with its own "religione", as Statius will suggest:

> Cosa non è che sanza
> ordine senta la religïone
> de la montagna, o che sia fuor d'usanza.
> (*Purgatorio*, XXI. 40–42)

[The religious community of the mountain experiences nothing that is without order or is outside its custom.][25]

Much has been said and written about Dante's use of Psalm 114 ("When Israel came out of Egypt") in *Purgatorio* II and elsewhere.[26] Suffice it for now to recall that the events narrated at the beginning of *Purgatorio* take place on Easter Day,[27] and that the Exodus forms the background to the Easter liturgy—indeed Psalm 114 itself was sung at vespers on Easter Day and throughout Easter Week.[28] The Exodus from Egypt and from slavery in fact foreshadows firstly Christ's resurrection and breaking of the bonds of sin, secondly Dante's moral exodus from sin to grace in this life, and thirdly the soul's anagogical exodus from sin to grace after death.[29] Similarly, Psalm 114 was also sung to accompany the carrying of the body of a dead person to a holy place—as if to indicate the mystical journey of the Christian (prefigured by the journey of the Jews) towards the heavenly Jerusalem.[30] It is hardly surprising, then, that Psalm 114 should figure in Dante's poem. In fact it may be used twice in this *cantica*. If we listen to it as far as verse 4, we hear, "The mountains skipped like rams, the hills like young sheep." This may be reflected in the quaking of the whole mountain of Purgatory towards the end of Canto XX, as Statius completes *his* anagogical exodus.

In *Purgatorio* V the souls of the late repentant sing Psalm 51:

> E 'ntanto per la costa di traverso
> venivan genti innanzi a noi un poco,
> cantando "*Miserere*" a verso a verso.
> (*Purgatorio*, v. 22–24)[31]

[And meanwhile across the mountain slope came people a little in front of us, singing the *Miserere* verse by verse.]

This penitential psalm is exactly appropriate to the souls in Ante-Purgatory and nowhere else—it expresses the sinner's repentance, calls for divine mercy, and asks for the washing away of sins: "Be gracious to me, O God, in thy true love; in the fulness of thy mercy blot out my misdeeds. [...] For well I know my misdeeds, and my sins confront me all the day long. [...] Take hyssop and sprinkle me, that I may be clean; wash me, that I may become whiter than snow." This last verse, of course, is one that we have already seen used in a different context. In fact Dante may have been particularly attached to the fifty-first psalm. The very first thing the pilgrim says in the whole *Commedia* is "*Miserere* di me" ["Have pity on me": *Inferno*, I. 65]; and at the other end of the poem King David is identified as the "cantor che per doglia/del fallo disse '*Miserere mei*'" ["singer who, through sorrow for his sin, cried '*Miserere mei*'": *Paradiso*, XXXII. 11–12].[32]

It may be argued that the souls in Ante-Purgatory are those, in the whole *Commedia*, who have most in common with members of the Church Militant—even though, of course, the parallel is still incomplete, in that the souls in Ante-Purgatory have made sure of their eventual place in Heaven by dying in their repentant state. This explains—and many critics have remarked on this—the peculiar intensity of earthly preoccupations in the first eight cantos of *Purgatorio*. It becomes particularly striking, from the liturgical point of view, as the pilgrim's first day in the second realm draws to its close: in Cantos VII and VIII the souls sing the antiphon *Salve, Regina* and the hymn *Te lucis ante terminum*, both of which formed part of the compline service. The setting is the Valley of the Princes, which accommodates those rulers whose involvement in the concerns of government distracted them from repentance until the end of their lives. *Salve, Regina*, composed in the eleventh century,[33] is an expression of trust in the Virgin Mary, begging for divine mercy in this world and the privilege of seeing God in the next.[34] Addressed to a queen, it makes an effective expression of penitence for souls who sinned by inadequate love for their own subjects, neglecting the basic duty of rulers of peoples.[35] What is more, it contains the evocative phrase "in hac lacrimarum valle" ["in this vale of tears"], which may have given Dante the idea of the *Valley of the Princes*.

Salve, Regina is another text that Dante seems to have found particularly suggestive for his purposes elsewhere in the *Commedia*. The phrase "lacrimarum valle" may underlie the phrase "valle dolorosa" (*Paradiso*, XVII. 137), meaning Hell, which is itself an echo of line 8 in *Inferno* IV ("valle d'abisso dolorosa"). And another phrase in the antiphon is "exsules filii Hevae" ["banished children of Eve"], which is echoed not only in line 71 of *Purgatorio* xii, where the human race is addressed as "figliuoli d'Eva", but perhaps also in *Paradiso* xxvi, where Eve's husband refers to mortal life outside the Garden of Eden as exile:

> Or, figliuol mio, non il gustar del legno
> fu per sé la cagion di tanto essilio,
> ma solamente il trapassar del segno.
> *(Paradiso,* xxvi. 115–17)

[Now know, my son, that the tasting of the tree was not in itself the cause of so long an exile, but solely the overpassing of the bound.]

Eve is mentioned, too, in the Ante-Purgatory evening scene itself:

> una biscia,
> forse qual diede ad Eva il cibo amaro.
> *(Purgatorio,* viii. 98–99)

[a snake, perhaps such as gave to Eve the bitter food.]

Te lucis ante terminum prays more specifically for God's protection against temptation during the dangerous hours of darkness—against the adverse influence of dreams and diabolical suggestions.[36] The hymn is peculiarly appropriate to the context of Ante-Purgatory because its second stanza prays the Creator, "Drive back our adversary, that our bodies be not contaminated" ("Hostemque nostrum comprime,/ne polluantur corpora"). In this way the hymn foreshadows, subtly enough for the reader who is familiar with its words, the coming of the serpent in the Valley of the Princes.

It seems likely that still more of this evening scene is derived from the compline service.[37] In Canto viii we have the drama of the two angels coming down to guard the souls of Ante-Purgatory against temptation and subsequently putting the snake to flight. This may well owe something to Psalm 91,[38] which was one of the compline psalms. Not only does this psalm contain, in verses 5–6, the assertions "You shall not fear the hunters' trap by night or [...] the pestilence that stalks in darkness"; verses 11–13 run as follows:

> For he has charged his angels
> to guard you wherever you go,

> to lift you on their hands
> for fear you should strike your foot against a stone.
> You shall step on asp and cobra,
> you shall tread safely on snake and serpent.

And if this is not the source of the scene, then the source is the prayer which comes almost at the end of the compline service: "Visit this habitation, we beseech thee, O Lord, and keep all snares of the enemy far from it; may thy holy angels abide in it and guard us in peace; and may thy holy blessing be always upon us."[39]

We seem to be moving onwards here to a different type—a non-verbal, more dramatic type—of vestige. The evening scene in Canto VIII contains no obvious verbal reminiscences of Psalm 91 or the prayer "Visit this habitation", but the action is suggested by them. It is tempting to broaden this perspective and consider whether the liturgy may be seen as some sort of shaping presence in Dante's poem. Several attempts have in fact been made to do this.[40] I do not think any of them is entirely satisfactory, yet there are, I think, elements of liturgical suggestion of this dramatic, non-verbal kind. We may observe its limits, though, in this evening scene in Ante-Purgatory. Is this a compline scene? It is and it is not. The compline bell, as we saw at the beginning of this essay, is alluded to at the outset; *Salve, Regina* and *Te lucis ante terminum* are sung; the souls are guarded by angels which chase away the devil in the shape of a snake. What is more, the compline service included a reading from the First Epistle of St Peter (Chapter 5, verses 8–9), containing the phrase "your enemy the devil" ("adversarius vester diabolus"), which is echoed by Sordello when he says of the snake's arrival, "Vedi là 'l nostro avversaro" ["See there our adversary!": *Purgatorio*, VIII. 95]. Again, another of the compline psalms was Psalm 134, of which verse 2 says, "Lift up your hands in the sanctuary."[41] And what does the cantor—one had almost said the precentor—do before intoning the first line of *Te lucis ante terminum*? "Ella giunse e levò ambo le palme" ["He joined and lifted both his palms": *Purgatorio*, VIII. 10]. These features suggest to me that the compline service is a model for the evening scene in Ante-Purgatory in a fuller sense than has been generally realized. And yet the constituent parts are in the wrong order: the psalms should precede *Te lucis ante terminum*, and, more decisively, *Salve, Regina* should come at the end of the service, whereas it comes in the previous canto.

I am pointing this out not to criticize Dante or to say he was in error, but as a warning against excessive rigidity and an illustration of Dante's method. He does draw freely on the liturgy, but he always makes it serve his own purposes; any attempt to show that Dante followed a rigid pre-existing scheme will in my view fail. But provided we are willing to be flexible, we may perceive other vestiges of liturgical *practice*, as distinct from liturgical wording, in his verse. The second half of *Purgatorio* IX is a good place to do this. There we are told that the robe of the angel-doorkeeper is the colour of ash, or dry earth:

> Cenere, o terra che secca si cavi,
> d'un color fora col suo vestimento.
> *(Purgatorio,* IX. 115–16)

[Ashes, or earth that is dug out dry, would be of one colour with his vesture.]

Ash, together with sackcloth, symbolizes penitence, and is marked on the foreheads of the faithful on Ash Wednesday, the first day of Lent, the season of penance; and references to ash are naturally frequent in the liturgy for Ash Wednesday.[42] The colour of the angel's robe thus has strong associations with Lent and penance—and this, of course, is deliberate. But is this not Easter Day, the very antithesis of all that? Have we not already heard Psalm 114, "When Israel came out of Egypt"—one of the Easter psalms?

The fact is that Dante's poetry is operating on several levels at once. It is a metaphorical Easter in one sense—in the sense that Dante has risen with Christ from the bondage of sin. But just as Israel did not go straight from Egypt to the Promised Land, spending forty years in the wilderness in between, so Dante's liberation is not immediate: in fact it is not until *Purgatorio*, XXVII. 140 that Virgil can say to him, "Libero, dritto e sano è tuo arbitrio" ["Free, upright and whole is your will"]. Until then, Dante is in the wilderness, a wilderness characterized by penance, as is indicated by the seven Ps placed on his forehead by the angel-doorkeeper and subsequently removed, one by one, by the experience of the seven circles of the mountainside.[43] But Easter is not the time for penance: Lent is. So for Dante the pilgrim the season is both Easter and Lent: and it is Lent both before and after he passes through the gate of Purgatory.

This is further shown by his apparent use of the ritual of public penance. Public penance has not been practiced for centuries, so it is very unfamiliar to us; but it was normal in Dante's day. A public penitent was someone who was given a special opportunity to reform his or her life and expiate his or her sins of a grievous or public nature. The first part of public penance was the expulsion ceremony, which took place on Ash Wednesday, when the public penitents appeared at the church door, dressed in rough garments, barefoot, and with their eyes cast to the ground; after certain other formalities they were admitted to the nave, from where they were expelled again by the bishop, who sat on a faldstool.[44] During Lent they were to engage in fasting, prayers, pilgrimages, almsgiving, and so on; they were to reside in a monastery or convent; they were to wear penitential garb only; and they were not allowed to bath, shave or cut their hair. Then on Maundy Thursday, in the reconciliation ceremony, they returned to the church porch begging to be accepted for penitential exercises prescribed by the bishop, who, again sitting on a faldstool, would admonish them, absolve them, and permit them to bath, lay aside their penitential garments, shave and have their hair cut; after this they rejoined the Christian community and received Communion at the mass which followed.[45]

The point of all this is that there seems to be a definite connection between public penance and Dante's encounter with the angel-doorkeeper, who, like the bishop, is sitting—this being a sign of authority and dignity.[46] The most obvious point of contact is the imposition of the seven Ps representing penitential exercises which Dante must perform. And Dante is admitted to the church to perform them. Thus the reconciliation takes place without the expulsion. This is another example of Dante's flexibility in his use of the liturgy—and of other sources—, showing that it would be dangerous to try and force the full logic of the model onto the poem.

I turn now to *Paradiso*, which, as we have said, accommodates the Church Triumphant. But what did that mean to Dante? Does it mean that he actually conceived of his third realm as a church in the everyday, physical sense? There is a limited body of evidence to suggest that he did, chiefly in the cantos devoted to the Empyrean, the tenth and final heaven, which extends to infinity beyond the nine finite heavens contained within it. Of course, we should remember that only the Empyrean is the true Heaven: just as we customarily speak of an Ante-Purgatory which precedes Purgatory itself, so one may also speak of an Ante-Paradise, which occupies all but the last four cantos of the final *cantica*.[47] Although Dante encounters some of the blessed souls in the nine spheres of this Ante-Paradise, they are there only temporarily, or only in appearance (as is explained in *Paradiso*, IV. 37–39), and they are present again in the Celestial Rose, where all the souls of the Church Triumphant have their seat. And it is the Empyrean, "l'alto trïunfo del regno verace" ["the high triumph of the true kingdom": *Paradiso*, XXX. 98], that we may, with some stretching of the imagination perhaps, see as a church. Rosario Assunto has suggested that Dante's Empyrean is shaped by the same aesthetic principles as contemporary church architecture.[48] And Dante himself guides us in the same direction by comparing himself to a pilgrim visiting a church:

> E quasi peregrin che si ricrea
> nel tempio del suo voto riguardando,
> [...] menava ïo li occhi [...],
> mo sú, mo giú e mo recirculando.
> (*Paradiso*, XXXI. 43–48)

[And as a pilgrim who is refreshed within the temple of his vow as he looks around (...), so (...) I led my eyes (...), now up, now down, and now circling about.]

The liturgical content of the Empyrean cantos, however, is fairly slim. And apart from two reminiscences of the Psalms, it all focuses on the Virgin Mary,

> la regina
> cui questo regno è suddito e devoto.
> (*Paradiso*, XXXI. 116–17)

[the Queen to whom this realm is subject and devoted.]

There is St Anne's acclamation, "Hosanna" (*Paradiso*, XXXII. 135); there is the archangel Gabriel's "*Ave, Maria, gratïa plena*" (*Paradiso*, XXXII. 95),[49] which, as we found to be the case with *Gloria in excelsis Deo*, uses the wording of the liturgy rather than that of the Bible ("Ave gratia pleta", Luke 1. 28); and there is Dante's own *Ave, Maria*, as it has been called—the prayer offered up on his behalf by

St Bernard in the first thirty-nine lines of Canto XXXIII.[50] Dante has already told us ten cantos earlier that in his earthly life he recited the *Ave, Maria* twice a day:

> Il nome del bel fior ch'io sempre invoco
> e mane e sera [...].
> *(Paradiso,* XXIII. 88–89)

[The name of the fair flower which I ever invoke, both morning and evening (...).]

And before that he used the prayer in the Heaven of the Moon for Piccarda, who, when she has finished speaking to Dante, "cominciò 'Ave,/Maria' cantando" ["began to sing *Ave Maria*": *Paradiso,* III. 121–22] before disappearing with the other souls.

Even though Bernard's prayer has been called Dante's *Ave, Maria,* however, it is not at all obvious that that is what it is. In any case, the second half of the prayer as we know it today ("Holy Mary, Mother of God, pray for us sinners, now and in the hour of our death. Amen") was not added until the fourteenth century,[51] though the reference to the need for help until the moment of death is common to almost all the Marian prayers, and is taken up by Dante later in Bernard's "orazione":

> Ancor ti prego [...]
> [...] che conservi sani,
> dopo tanto veder, li affetti suoi.
> Vinca tua guardia i movimenti umani.
> *(Paradiso,* XXXIII. 34–37)

[Further I pray thee (...) that thou preserve sound for him his affections, after so great a vision. Let thy protection vanquish human impulses.]

It also seems certain that the word "ventre" in line 7 of Dante's final canto ("Nel ventre tuo si raccese l'amore" ["In thy womb was rekindled the Love"]) is a conscious or unconscious echo of the *Ave, Maria,* because elsewhere in the *Commedia,* with only one exception, the word is always used pejoratively, whether in connection with monsters in Hell—Cerberus and the Harpies—, with souls who are deformed as a result of their sins—the soothsayers, the thieves and the alchemists—, or with the siren of the second dream in *Purgatorio.* The one exception is another case in which

Dante is referring to the fruitful womb of the Blessed Virgin, in *Paradiso* XXIII, where the archangel Gabriel sings:

> Io sono amore angelico, che giro
> l'alta letizia che spira del ventre
> che fu albergo del nostro disiro.
> *(Paradiso*, XXIII. 103–05)

[I am angelic love, who circle the supreme joy that breathes from out the womb which was the hostelry of our Desire.]

So *ventre* is a word with negative overtones for Dante, except when it refers to the Virgin's womb, and this exception may well be due to his familiarity with the *Ave, Maria*.

We ought not to leave Bernard's prayer without noticing a reminiscence that it contains of the Virgin Mary's own canticle, the *Magnificat*, which even in Dante's era had for centuries been the high point of the daily service of vespers.[52] The *Magnificat* makes much of the paradox of Mary's greatness and her humility: "Tell out, my soul, the greatness of the Lord [...]; so tenderly has he looked upon his servant, humble as she is. [...] all generations will count me blessed, so wonderfully has he dealt with me, the Lord, the Mighty One. [...] he has brought down monarchs from their thrones, but the humble have been lifted high" (Luke 1. 46–52). Dante summarizes these statements in the second line of his prayer: "umile e alta piú che creatura" ["humble and exalted more than any creature": *Paradiso*, XXXIII. 2]. But all this does not amount to a particularly substantial liturgical element in Bernard's discourse as a whole, so, although it is a magnificent prayer, we must leave a fuller examination of it for another occasion.

The use of the *Ave, Maria* by the souls of the Moon is the first of a regular series of liturgical utterances in the six lowest heavens. In the sphere of Venus, for instance, the souls sing "Hosanna":

> e dentro a quei che piú innanzi appariro
> sonava "*Osanna*" sí, che unque poi
> di rïudir non fui sanza disiro.
> *(Paradiso*, VIII. 28–30)

[and within those that appeared most in front *Hosanna* sounded in such wise that never since have I been without the desire to hear it again.]

With these two exceptions, however—that of the *Ave, Maria* and that of the *Hosanna*—, we are not given a recognizable choice of texts from the Roman liturgy: this is a celestial liturgy. And in any case, as with many other facets of the third part of his journey, the poet declares himself unable to report the experience in full. In the Heaven of Mercury, which, like those of the Moon and Venus, lies within the shadow of the earth, the words themselves can be grasped but the text is one that has never been heard in our world—Dante invents it by combining phrases from the *Sanctus* with Hebrew words representing the language of Scripture:

> *Osanna, sanctus Deus sabaòth,*
> *superillustrans claritate tua*
> *felices ignes horum malacòth!*[53]
> (*Paradiso*, VII. 1–3)

[Hosanna, holy God of Hosts, Who with Your superabundant light illumine the joyful splendours of these realms.][54]

Beyond the earth's shadow, the words themselves become unreportable. In the Heaven of the Sun, which particularly celebrates the Trinity,[55] we are told only that the focus of the song is the triunity and the dual nature of God:

> *Lí si cantò non Bacco, non Peana,*
> *ma tre persone in divina natura,*
> *e in una persona essa e l'umana.*
> (*Paradiso*, XIII. 25–27)

[There they sang not Bacchus, and not Paean, but Three Persons in the divine nature, and it and the human nature in one Person.]

In the Heaven of Mars Dante himself is unable to catch the words, except for two of them:

> *s'accogliea per la croce una melode*
> *che mi rapiva, sanza intender l'inno.*
> *Ben m'accors' io ch'elli era d'alte lode,*
> *però ch'a me venía "Resurgi" e "Vinci"*
> *come a colui che non intende e ode.*[56]
> (*Paradiso*, XIV. 122–26)

> [a melody gathered through the cross which held me rapt, though I followed not the hymn. Well I discerned it to be of lofty praise, for there came to me: "Rise" and "Conquer", as to one who understands not, but hears.]

These two words, however, while they do not permit the identification of an earthly text, are sufficient to show that the song focuses on the Resurrection and Christ's triumph over death—as is appropriate to the sphere of the warriors for the faith. And in the Heaven of Jupiter it is implied that the text cannot be known outside Heaven ("con canti quai si sa chi là sú gaude" ["with songs such as he knows who thereabove rejoices": *Paradiso*, XIX. 39]), though in the following canto Dante implies that he grasped the words at the time:

> cominciaron canti
> da mia memoria labili e caduci.
> (*Paradiso*, xx. 11–12)

> [began songs that have lapsed and fallen from my memory.]

In the Heaven of Saturn Dante hears no singing at all because, as Peter Damian explains to him, his mortal senses would not be able to bear it (*Paradiso*, XXI. 58–63).

The most interesting part of *Paradiso*, I think, liturgically speaking, is the Heaven of the Fixed Stars, beyond the seven spheres in which Dante encounters representative souls. Dante's entry into the eighth heaven is marked by two liturgical echoes, the Latin neuter plural *peccata* and the striking of the breast as a sign of penitence, when he describes the Church Triumphant as

> quel divoto
> trïunfo per lo quale io piango spesso
> le mie peccata e 'l petto mi percuoto.
> (*Paradiso*, XXII. 106–08)

> [that devout triumph for the sake of which I often bewail my sins and beat my breast.]

The *Agnus Dei*, where the word *peccata* perhaps most memorably occurs, is recalled again in Canto XXIV, when Christ is referred to as the "benedetto Agnello" ["blessed Lamb": *Paradiso*, XXIV. 2]. (One is also reminded here of line 33 in Canto XVII, "l'Agnel di Dio che le peccata tolle" ["the Lamb of God who takes away sins"].) There are, too, in the cantos of the eighth heaven, quite prominent allusions to the Psalms, such as "If I lift up my eyes to the hills" (Psalm 121. 1)—"io leväi li occhi a' monti" ["I lifted up my eyes unto the hills": *Paradiso*, XXV. 38]—and "Bestir thyself, Lord; why dost thou sleep?" (Psalm 44. 23)—"o difesa di Dio, perché pur giaci?" ["O defence of God, wherefore dost thou yet lie still": *Paradiso*, XXVII. 57].[57] But the eighth heaven also includes two particularly striking uses of the liturgy.

The first is for the triumph of the Virgin Mary in Canto XXIII, which twice quotes the Litany of Loreto: for the idea of Mary as "rosa mystica":

> Quivi è la rosa in che 'l verbo divino
> carne si fece;
> (*Paradiso*, XXIII. 73–74)

[Here is the Rose wherein the Divine Word became flesh];

and for the idea of Mary as the morning star ("stella matutina"):

> la viva stella
> che là sú vince come qua giú vinse.
> (*Paradiso*, XXIII. 92–93)

[the living star which conquers up there even as down here it conquered.]

And the scene is completed with the singing by the blessed souls of *Regina caeli*, the Marian antiphon which the Church Militant sang between Easter and the octave of Pentecost.[58]

The other particularly striking use of the liturgy in the eighth heaven accompanies Dante's examination in faith, hope and charity. In the first place, the candidate—as is eminently suitable—, in his examination on faith, quotes or paraphrases two Creeds, both the Nicene and the Athanasian:[59]

> Io credo in uno Dio
> solo ed etterno, che tutto 'l ciel move,
> non moto, con amore e con disio; [...]

> e credo in tre persone etterne, e queste
> credo una essenza sí una e sí trina,
> che soffera congiunto "sono" ed "este".
> *(Paradiso,* xxiv. 130–41)

[I believe in one God, sole and eternal, who, unmoved, moves all the heavens with love and with desire; (...). And I believe in three Eternal Persons, and these I believe to be one essence, so one and so threefold as to comport at once with *are* and *is*.]

And in the second place, the choir of the blessed sings a chant taken from the Roman liturgy at the end of each of the candidate's three successful examinations. After the first, on faith, the blessed sing the *Te Deum (Paradiso,* xxiv. 112–14), presumably for much the same reasons as I rehearsed in connection with its use on Dante's entry into Purgatory proper in *Purgatorio* ix. After Dante's second performance as examination candidate, on the subject of hope, the blessed sing verse 10 of Psalm 9, "that those who acknowledge thy name may trust in thee", which in the Latin is expressed with the verb *sperare* ["to hope"]: "*Sperent in te [qui noverunt nomen tuum]*" *(Paradiso,* xxv. 98), which Dante himself has quoted during his answer, and which (slightly adapted) was used in the earthly Church as an offertory chant on the Tuesday after Passion Sunday and on the third Sunday after Pentecost.[60] After his third test, on charity, or love, the blessed sing the Tersanctus, "Holy, holy, holy, Lord God of Hosts, heaven and earth are full of Thy glory. Glory be to Thee, o Lord most high" *(Paradiso,* xxvi. 69). There seems to be no obvious connection between this and Dante's declaration on charity, but Dante is also at the end of his whole tripartite examination, and it may be that, since the Tersanctus comes at the most solemn point in the mass, its function is to confer solemnity on the gratitude of the blessed at this point.

One further outpouring of this kind comes from the whole choir of Heaven at the beginning of Canto xxvii, after the speech of Adam and before St Peter's condemnation of the corrupt papacy:

> "Al Padre, al Figlio, a lo Spirito Santo,"
> cominciò, "gloria!", tutto 'l paradiso.[61]
> *(Paradiso,* xxvii. 1–2)

This is one of the Church's most solemn texts, the Lesser Doxology, "Glory be to the Father and to the Son and to the Holy Ghost, as it was in the beginning, is now, and ever shall be, world without end. Amen", which was customarily sung at the end of any psalm or portion of a psalm and thus, in effect, as a punctuation-mark between consecutive psalms.[62] It seems to be used here not with reference to any single strand in the fabric of Canto XXVI or Canto XXVII, but as a magnificent punctuation-mark between episodes.

One could go on exploring ways in which Dante's poem draws on the Roman liturgy, but it is perhaps time for some conclusions. I should like to propose two. To my mind, one of the most striking conclusions to be drawn has to do with the place of the liturgy within the poet's experience. He obviously had a remarkable familiarity with it, as he did with his Virgil and his Bible. Indeed, not only is it clear that he was a regular church-goer, he seems to have reached parts of the liturgy that other laymen would have missed. Compline, for instance, was a monastic service, and there is no obvious reason why Dante should ever have attended it. But he must have done, repeatedly, to come to know it and love it as the *Commedia* attests. We are reminded of the image in *Paradiso* x which depicts monks getting up and going into choir to sing matins:

> ne l'ora che la sposa di Dio surge
> a mattinar lo sposo perché l'ami.
> *(Paradiso,* x. 140–41)

[at the hour when the Bride of God rises to sing her matins to her Bridegroom, that he may love her.]

Is this based on first-hand experience? (It perhaps does not have to be.) Did Dante stay at a monastery and participate fully in the Divine Office with the monks? From the internal evidence it seems likely that he did, but we cannot say more than that on this point. What we can say is that he drew extensively on the liturgy for his poem—drew indeed on many different parts of the liturgy for many different purposes—, so that one cannot read far in the *Commedia*, at least in the second and third *cantiche*, which correspond to the domain of grace, without detecting a liturgical flavour.

My second conclusion concerns the use that Dante made of the liturgy in his poem, and involves, rather belatedly, the introduction of a third kind of vestige—not verbal and not dramatic, but structural. Dante was so impressed by the earthly liturgy that he created a liturgy of his own in his second and third *cantiche*. Much of it is made up of texts from the liturgy of this world, but some of it is not: particularly in *Purgatorio*, Dante draws on other sources for what I am calling *his* liturgy, in the same process of assimilation as once brought the liturgy of the Church into being. The seven Beatitudes from the Sermon on the Mount in Matthew 5, for instance, sung one by each of the angels in the seven *gironi* of the mountainside, have a stongly liturgical character about them:

> Fuor de la fiamma stava in su la riva,
> e cantava *"Beati mundo corde!"*
> in voce assai piú che la nostra viva.
> *(Purgatorio,* xxvii. 7–9)

[He stood outside the flames on the bank and sang *"Beati mundo corde"* ("How blest are those whose hearts are pure") in a voice far more living than ours.]

(That is the last of the seven.) And other Biblical phrases are worked into the scheme, such as the words of the other angel in *Purgatorio* xxvii, who encourages the poets to traverse the fire: *"Venite, benedicti Patris mei"* ["You have my Father's blessing; come": Matthew 25. 34 and *Purgatorio,* xxvii. 58]; or the words of the figure in *Purgatorio* xxx representing the Song of Songs: *"Veni, sponsa, de Libano"* ["Come from Lebanon, my bride": Songs of Songs 4. 8 and *Purgatorio,* xxx. 11].[63] Even secular texts are drawn on for this purpose, as with—in the same canto—the words from the *Aeneid* uttered by Anchises in praise of Marcellus: *"Manibus, oh, date lilïa plenis!"* ["Give me lilies with full hand": *Aeneid,* vi. 883 and *Purgatorio,* xxx. 21].[64] Nor is Dante averse to inventing pseudo-liturgical texts, as we have seen on two occasions in *Paradiso*, and as seems to happen again—or earlier, rather—with the angel of mercy in the second *girone* of Purgatory, who sings not only his Beatitude but evidently also an imaginary hymn beginning "Rejoice, you who conquer":

> Noi montavam, già partiti di linci,
> e *"Beati misericordes!"* fue
> cantato retro, e *"Godi tu che vinci!"*
> *(Purgatorio,* xv. 37–39)

[We were mounting, having already departed thence, and "*Beati misericordes*" ("How blest are those who show mercy") was sung behind, and "Rejoice, you that overcome".]

A particularly remarkable part of this invented liturgy involves the whips and bridles (the examples of virtue and vice) in some of the *gironi* of Purgatory—the second and the last four, to be precise. Here, striking phrases are picked out of exemplary tales for meditation, in the same way as antiphons, responsories and versicles in the liturgy were once extracted from significant Biblical texts. The liturgical quality is particularly clear in the two cases where these pseudo-antiphons are recited by the souls themselves, the circle of lust and the circle of misuse of riches. For example:

> Appresso il fine ch'a quell' inno fassi,
> gridavano alto: "*Virum non cognosco*";
> indi ricominciavan l'inno bassi
> (*Purgatorio*, xxv. 127–29)

[After the end which is made to that hymn (*Summae Deus clementiae*), they cried aloud, "*Virum non cognosco*" ("I am still a virgin"), then softly began the hymn again]

—or is this outburst, "*Virum non cognosco*", perhaps an acclamation rather than an antiphon? In fact, on one occasion a whip is referred to, by Hugues Capet, as a responsory:

> Ciò ch'io dicea [...]
> tanto è risposto a tutte nostre prece
> quanto 'l dí dura.
> (*Purgatorio*, xx. 97–101)

[What I was saying (...) is the responsory to all our prayers as long as the day lasts.][65]

Sometimes these texts are paraphrases rather than direct quotations, and here again the source is often secular. For instance:

> O buon Fabrizio,
> con povertà volesti anzi virtute
> che gran ricchezza posseder con vizio.[66]
> (*Purgatorio*, xx. 25–27)

[O good Fabricius, you chose to possess virtue with poverty rather than great riches with iniquity.]

I have by no means exhausted my theme. I have said virtually nothing about liturgical gesture, and I have omitted some of what might have been said about liturgical word, liturgical situation and liturgical structure. When one considers the total accumulation of all these elements, one realizes that *Purgatorio* as a whole has an intensely liturgical atmosphere. *Paradiso*, too, has liturgical characteristics, but Dante was sufficiently keen on variety not to play the same card twice, at least in this respect. In *Purgatorio*, the liturgical inspiration may be seen as one of a small number of central informing principles—one of the others, for instance, being the constant illustration of the doctrine that God is Love. In *Paradiso*, which is structured very much according to the principle that God is Light, in combination with the poetics of inexpressibility, the sense that the place is a church is less strong, and the liturgical component has less importance in the construction. Not only is there less liturgical matter; less importance is also attached to it, so that in several cases the liturgical text is not even identified.

NOTES

1 W. S. Landor, *The Pentameron*, in his *"The Pentameron" and Other Imaginary Conversations*, edited by H. Ellis (London, Scott, 1889), pp. 1–155 (p. 50).

2 J. Le Goff, *La Civilisation de l'occident médiéval* (Paris, Arthaud, 1964), pp. 229–36: "Surtout, le temps médiéval est un temps religieux et clérical" (p. 229).

3 "[...] la quale chiesa suona terza e nona e l'altre ore, alle quali li lavoranti delle arti entrano ed esceno dal lavorío." See *"Comedia" di Dante degli Allagherii col comento di Jacopo della Lana bolognese*, edited by L. Scarabelli, 3 vols (Bologna, Tipografia Regia, 1866), III, 245.

4 "Usanza è quando li frati minori vanno da una cittade ad un'altra o da uno luogo ad un altro, s'elli fossero ben cento, vanno in fila l'uno dietro all'altro, può essere forse perché vanno contemplando con Dio, e può essere forse che non hanno usanza di comunicare, di parlare insieme" (*"Comedia" col comento di Jacopo della Lana*, I, 375–76). "Fratres minores communiter vadunt bini per viam tacite et honeste, et venerabilior praecedit in passu" (*Benevenuti de Rambaldis de Imola Comentum super Dantis Aldigherii Comoediam*, edited by J. P. Lacaita, 5 vols [Florence, Barbèra, 1887], II, 156). The practice may be observed in an independent source, the *Actus Beati Francisci et Sociorum Ejus* (probably compiled between 1322 and 1328); see the edition of P. Sabatier [= *Collection*

d'études et de documents, IV] (Paris, Fischbacher, 1902), pp. 25, 41. Excerpts from the *Actus* were later translated into Italian as *I fioretti di San Francesco*; see the edition of B. Bughetti (Florence, Salani, 1926), pp. 48–49, 56.

5   This hoary conceit goes back at least as far as A. F. Ozanam, *Dante et la philosophie catholique au treizième siècle*, second edition (Paris, Lecoffre, 1845), pp. 335–36. It has been developed in some detail. Seen horizontally, the argument goes, the poem is tripartite like a basilica, and has three pinnacles of equal height, all bristling with animated detail. Seen vertically, it begins in a dark wood or labyrinth (the labyrinth being a device commonly found on the floors of cathedrals, at least in the Ile de France); it proceeds through a zone of penumbra, thronged with three-dimensional human materiality, rather like the areas between the piers of the cathedral; in both *Purgatorio* and the triforium the opaque material is attenuated, while, correspondingly, the immateriality of light increases; and in the highest and most pointed arches of the *Commedia* there is no longer anything but pure light. But that is only the framework; and it probably refers to a purer, more northern version of Gothic than Dante's eye would have been accustomed to. It was never the intention of the Italian church-builders to create the mysticism and exaltation of the inspiring upward sweep that humbles the worshipper in northern cathedrals. Windows were of comparatively modest proportions, though adequate for the bright southern sun; and flying buttresses, essential to the fully evolved Gothic system, were regarded by Italians as barbaric. In a word, Italian Gothic is really a blending of Gothic forms with Romanesque forms; and to this Dante's poem may be seen as corresponding more closely. If the *Commedia* has a Gothic, abstract, structural framework, it is also true that individual figures and events of peremptory humanity and three-dimensionality break out of that abstraction, rather as they do from the Gothic frames of the pulpits of Giovanni Pisano in Siena Cathedral and the Pisan Baptistery. As examples of such thinking, see P. P. Trompeo, "L'azzurro di Chartres (lettura del canto XXIII del *Paradiso*)", *Quaderni di Roma*, 3 (1948), 20–31, reprinted in Trompeo's *L'azzurro di Chartres e altri capricci* (Caltanissetta-Rome, Sciascia, 1958), pp. 35–53, and abbreviated (as "Il canto XXIII del *Paradiso*") in *Letture dantesche*, edited by G. Getto, 3 vols (Florence, Sansoni, 1964), pp. 1813–26 ("Il paragone tra la *Commedia* e le cattedrali gotiche, giusto in sé, [...]", p. 36 of the 1958 edition); G. Fiocco, "Il dominio di Giotto", in *Il Trecento*, edited by the Libera Cattedra di Storia della Civiltà Fiorentina (Florence, Sansoni, 1953), pp. 163–76 ("La *Divina commedia* serba ancora nelle sue cantiche lo slancio tricuspidato del Duomo di Siena e di quello di Orvieto", p. 166); P. Frankl, *Gothic Architecture* (Harmondsworth, Penguin, 1962), p. 174 ("Arnolfo's S. Maria del Fiore and Dante's *Divina commedia*, created at about the same time, are truly comparable, as two artistic symbols of the progress of the human spirit towards the absolute. The basic idea of both works is a Christian one, but, in this distinctive form, it is specifically Gothic"); S. Bettini, "Introduzione al tema: 'Le arti figurative in rapporto a Dante'", in *Dante e la cultura veneta*, edited by V. Branca and G. Padoan (Florence, Olschki, 1966), pp. 273–75 ("Non c'è dubbio che l'impalcato del poema sacro sia quello d'una cattedrale gotica", p. 274); G. Fiocco, "La visione artistica di Dante", in *Dante e la cultura veneta*, pp. 277–83 ("Direi che la sua [Dante's] opera stupenda è l'unica genuina cattedrale gotica d'Italia", p. 279). See also R. Montano, "Dante e l'estetica gotica", in his *Suggerimenti per una*

lettura di Dante (Naples, Conte, 1956), pp. 51–90, or his "Dante's Style and Gothic Aesthetic", in *A Dante Symposium*, edited by W. De Sua and G. Rizzo (Chapel Hill, University of North Carolina Press, 1965), pp. 11–33.

6   See F. X. Lawlor, "Communion of Saints", in *The New Catholic Encyclopaedia*, 15 vols (New York etc., McGraw–Hill, 1967), IV, 41–43.

7   Guglielmo Gorni remarks that Dante "sfigura l'inno 'de cruce' [...] con l'addizione scandalosa di quella parola rima"; see his "Parodia e scrittura in Dante", in *Dante e la Bibbia*, edited by G. Barblan (Florence, Olschki, 1988), pp. 323–40 (p. 324).

8   *A Dictionary of Hymnology*, edited by J. Julian, second edition [1907], 2 vols (New York, Dover, 1957), II, 1220, col. 1. The following is the text of *Vexilla Regis*: "Vexilla Regis prodeunt:/Fulget Crucis mysterium,/Qua vita mortem pertulit/Et morte vitam protulit.//Quae vulnerata lanceae/Mucrone diro, criminum/Ut nos lavaret sordibus,/Manavit unda et sanguine.//Impleta sunt quae concinit/David fideli carmine,/Dicendo nationibus:/Regnavit a ligno Deus.//Arbor decora et fulgida,/Ornata regis purpura,/Electa digno stipite/Tam sancta membra tangere.//Beata, cujus brachiis/Pretium pependit saeculi,/Statera facta corporis,/Tulitque praedam tartari.//O Crux ave, spes unica,/Hoc passionis tempore/Piis adauge gratiam/Reisque dele crimina.//Te, fons salutis Trinitas,/Collaudet omnis spiritus:/Quibus Crucis victoriam/Largiris, adde praemiam./Amen." See *Liber Usualis: Missae et Officii pro Dominicis et Festis Duplicibus, cum Cantu Gregoriano* (Tournai, Desclée and Lefebvre; London, Breitkopf and Härtel, 1904), pp. 273–74.

9   See *Sources of the Modern Roman Liturgy: The Ordinals by Haymo of Faversham and Related Documents (1243–1307)*, edited by S. J. P. van Dijk, 2 vols (Leiden, Brill, 1963), II, 77, 79, 81, 82.

10 According to Guido da Pisa, Virgil's use of these words serves to frighten Lucifer, reminding him of "illa gloriosa vexilla crucis a quibus ipse fuit a Christo triumphaliter debellatus, et in profundo inferni usque ad diem iudicii religatus": see Guido da Pisa, *Expositiones et Glose super Comediam Dantis*, edited by V. Cioffari (Albany, New York, State University of New York Press, 1974), p. 713.

11 Useful works on the liturgy include Dom Baudot, *The Breviary: Its History and Contents*, translated by the Benedictines of Stanbrook (London–Edinburgh, Sands; St Louis, Missouri, Herder, n. d. [c.1930]); J. W. Tyrer, *Historical Survey of Holy Week: Its Services and Ceremonial* (London, Oxford University Press, 1932); S. J. P. van Dijk and J. Hazelden Walker, *The Origins of the Modern Roman Liturgy: The Liturgy of the Papal Court and the Franciscan Order in the Thirteenth Century* (Westminster, Maryland, Newman; London, Darton, Longman and Todd, 1960); L. Eisenhofer and J. Lechner, *The Liturgy of the Roman Rite*, translated by A. J. and E. F. Peeler, edited by H. E. Winstone (Freiburg, Herder; Edinburgh–London, Nelson, 1961); *Missale Gothicum (Vat. Reg. Lat. 317)*, edited by L. C. Mohlberg (Rome, Herder, 1961); T. Klauser, *A Short History of the Western Liturgy: An Account and Some Reflections* [1965], translated by J. Halliburton (London, Oxford University Press, 1969); A-G. Martimort et al., *L'Eglise en prière: introduction à la liturgie*, third edition (Paris etc., Desclée, 1965), English translation of the first part of the first (1961) edition, *The Church at Prayer: Introduction to the Liturgy* (Shannon, Irish University Press, 1968); *Canon Missae Romanae: Pars Altera, Textus Propinqui*, edited by L. Eizenhöfer (Rome, Herder, 1966); P. Salmon, *L'Office divin au*

Moyen Age: histoire de la formation du bréviaire du ixe *au* xvie *siècle* (Paris, Cerf, 1967); R. E. Kaske, *Medieval Christian Literary Imagery: A Guide to Interpretation* (Toronto etc., University of Toronto Press, 1988), pp. 53–79. On Dante's use of the liturgy see D. R. Malaspina, *Il bello liturgico nel poema di Dante* (Florence, Fiorentina, n. d. [*c*.1921]); H. A. Hatzfeld, "Das Heilige im dichterischen Sprachausdruck des *Paradiso*", *Deutsches Dante-Jahrbuch*, 12 (1930), 41–70, Italian translation "Una onomasiologia stilistica: il motivo sacro nella lingua poetica del *Paradiso*", in his *Saggi di stilistica romanza* (Bari, Laterza, 1967), pp. 203–37; A. Vallone, "La preghiera" [1955], in his *Studi su Dante medievale* (Florence, Olschki, 1965), pp. 83–109; G. Fallani, "Liturgia e preghiera", in his *Poesia e teologia nella "Divina commedia"*, 3 vols (Milan, Marzorati, 1959–65), ii, 15–28; E. Raimondi, "[*Purgatorio*] Canto i", in *Lectura Dantis scaligera* (Florence, Le Monnier, 1967–68), ii, 1–41, also (as "Rito e storia nel i canto del *Purgatorio*") in his *Metafora e storia: studi su Dante e Petrarca* (Turin, Einaudi, 1970), pp. 65–94; O. Graf, *Die "Divina commedia" als Zeugnis des Glaubens: Dante und die Liturgie* (Freiburg etc., Herder, 1965); H. Rheinfelder, "Dante als Beter", in *Serta Romanica: Festschrift für Gerhard Rohlfs*, edited by R. Baehr and K. Wais (Tübingen, Niemeyer, 1968), pp. 219–36, also in Rheinfelder's *Dante-Studien*, edited by M. Roddewig (Cologne–Vienna, Böhlau, 1975), pp. 231–48; A. Lanci and R. Liver, "preghiera", in *Enc. dant.*, iv, 642–44; M. Braccini, "Paralipomeni al 'personaggio-poeta' (*Purgatorio*, xxvi. 140–7)", in *Testi e interpretazioni: studi del Seminario di filologia romanza dell'Università di Firenze* (Milan–Naples, Ricciardi, 1978), pp. 169–256; J. J. Fiatarone, *From "selva oscura" to "divina foresta": Liturgical Song as Path to Paradise in Dante's "Commedia"*, unpublished doctoral dissertation, University of California, Berkeley, 1986; L. M. La Favia, "'... Ché quivi per canti...' (*Purg.*, xii. 113): Dante's Programmatic Use of Psalms and Hymns in the *Purgatorio*", *Studies in Iconography*, 9 (1984–86), 53–65; G. Salvetti, "Dante Alighieri", in *Dizionario enciclopedico universale della musica e dei musicisti*, edited by A. Basso, *Le biografie*, 8 vols (Turin, UTET, 1985–88), ii, 400–01; E. Ardissino, "I canti liturgici nel *Purgatorio* dantesco", *Dante Studies*, 108 (1990), 39–65. See also various further articles in the *Enciclopedia dantesca* and other studies cited elsewhere in these Notes.

12 F. D'Ovidio, *Il "Purgatorio" e il suo preludio* = his *Nuovi studii danteschi*, vol. i (Milan, Hoepli, 1906), p. 158. See also G. Fallani, "Liturgia e preghiera", p. 16, where it is stated that *Purgatorio* has "una tonalità distesa, che rassomiglia all'immagine di una chiesa; naturalmente di una chiesa elaborata con mezzi terreni, come nell'arte romanica e gotica del Medioevo"; D. Alighieri, *La Divina commedia*, edited by U. Bosco and G. Reggio, fourth edition, 3 vols (Florence, Le Monnier, 1981), ii, 190 ("Tutto il Purgatorio è come una grande chiesa"). P. Armour, *The Door of Purgatory: A Study of Multiple Symbolism in Dante's "Purgatorio"* (Oxford, Clarendon Press, 1983), especially pp. 39–46, 53–58 and 76–89, makes an excellent case for seeing Dante's Purgatory (proper) as a church.

13 P. Armour, *The Door of Purgatory*, pp. 81–83.

14 See *Sources of the Modern Roman Liturgy*, ii, 59–61. The text reads: "Summae Deus clementiae;/Mundique factor machinae,/Unus potentialiter,/Trinusque personaliter,/Nostros piis cum canticis/Fructus benigne suspice,/Quo corde puro sordibus/Te perfruamur largius;/Lumbos iecurque morbidum,/Adure igni congruo,/Accincti ut sint perpetui/Luxu remoto pessimo,/Ut

quinque horas noctium./Nunc continendo rumpimus:/Donis beatae patriae/ Dictemur omnes affati." The text is given by Jacopo della Lana: see *"Comedia" col comento di Jacopo della Lana*, II, 298. Lana says (on the same page) that this hymn was recited at compline on Fridays, and comments that it is time for compline on the pilgrim's third day in the second realm.

15   The Holy Saturday litany is an excerpt from the Lenten litany. The fragments quoted in *Purg.*, XIII. 50–51 are common to both. For the text of the Holy Saturday litany, see *Liber Usualis*, pp. 396–99; for that of the Lenten litany, see S. J. P. van Dijk and J. Hazelden Walker, *The Origins of the Modern Roman Liturgy*, pp. 520–23.

16   The versicle *Dominus vobiscum* is ubiquitous in the liturgy. The text of the Greater Doxology may be found in the *Liber Usualis*, p. 2*.

17   Hans Rheinfelder, in "Dante als Beter" (pp. 223–24 [1968], 235–36 [1975]), has made a similar observation about "cotidiana manna" (*Purg.*, XI. 13), which translates "panem [...] quotidianum" in the liturgical version of the Lord's Prayer rather than "panem [...] supersubstantialem" in Matthew 6. 11. It is true that Luke's version of the prayer has "panem [...] quotidianum" (Luke 11. 3), but with the exception of this one word Matthew's version has always been the one universally used by Christians.

18   In the *Commento di Francesco da Buti sopra la "Divina comedia" di Dante Allighieri*, edited by C. Giannini, 3 vols (Pisa, Nistri, 1858–62), II, 698, we read: "Viene questo salmo a proposito de la materia: imperò che l'autore era per passare lo fiume che tollie la memoria del peccato."

19   See *Sources of the Modern Roman Liturgy*, II, 235, 387, 389.

20   On processions, see L. Eisenhofer and J. Lechner, *The Liturgy of the Roman Rite*, pp. 90–91, 186–87, 204–05, 267–69, 277–79, 290–92; A-G. Martimort, *L'Eglise en prière*, pp. 649–57.

21   On the *Te Deum* see P. Armour, *The Door of Purgatory*, pp. 109–10. The text of the hymn may be found in the *Liber Usualis*, pp. 67–69.

22   The *Te Deum* was sung at the end of matins on Sundays (except in Advent and between Septuagesima and Easter), and also on weekdays between Easter and the octave of Pentecost; see *Sources of the Modern Roman Liturgy*, II, 89, 120.

23   See A. D'Ancona, *Origini del teatro italiano*, second edition, 2 vols (Turin, Loescher, 1891), I, 34, 40; M. Apollonio, *Storia del teatro italiano*, 4 vols (Florence, Sansoni, 1943–51), I, 47, 55, 65.

24   See *Commento di Francesco da Buti*, II, 218.

25   I have here amended Singleton's translation, because it does not capture the nuance in this use of *religione* upon which my argument hinges. Among the meanings of *religione* given in the *Grande dizionario della lingua italiana*, edited by S. Battaglia et al. (Turin, UTET, 1961–) is "Ordine o congregazione religiosa". Dante uses the word to mean "community" or "brotherhood" in *Conv.*, IV. 4. 6, where he writes of "la universale religione de la umana spezie".

26   See, for example, C. S. Singleton, "In Exitu Israel de Aegypto" [1960], in *Dante: A Collection of Critical Essays*, edited by J. Freccero (Englewood Cliffs, New Jersey, Prentice–Hall, 1965), pp. 102–21; D. J. Tucker, "In Exitu Israel de Aegypto: The *Divine Comedy* in the Light of the Easter Liturgy", *American Benedictine Review*, 11 (1960), 43–61; J. F. Mahoney, "The Role of Statius and the Structure of *Purgatorio*", *Annual Report of the Dante Society of America*, 79 (1961), 11–38; P. Armour, "The Theme of Exodus in the First Two Cantos of

the *Purgatorio"*, in *Dante Soundings: Eight Literary and Historical Essays*, edited by D. Nolan (Dublin, Irish Academic Press, 1981), pp. 59–99.

27 Antonio Mastrobuono has argued that the day the pilgrim spends in Ante-Purgatory is Holy Saturday; see his "From Vespers to Dawn", in his *Essays on Dante's Philosophy of History* (Florence, Olschki, 1979), pp. 81–189 and his "This Is the Day the Lord Has Made", in his *Dante's Journey of Sanctification* (Washington, DC, Regnery Gateway, 1990), pp. 131–66. C. Cioffi, in a review of the first of these books published in *Medioevo romanzo*, 9 (1984), 462–67, and D. S. Cervigni, *Dante's Poetry of Dreams* (Florence, Olschki, 1986), pp. 77n and 96n, while seeing grave faults in Mastrobuono's arguments, are quite kindly disposed towards his findings, but the majority of scholars are not. For my own disagreement with Mastrobuono's thesis, see my "Liturgical Schemes in Dante's *Purgatorio*?", in *Renaissance and Other Studies: Essays Presented to Peter M. Brown*, edited by E. A. Millar (Glasgow, University of Glasgow, 1988), pp. 1–16 (pp. 1–6) and my review of *Dante's Journey of Sanctification*, *Medium Aevum*, 61 (1992), 348–49.

28 See *Sources of the Modern Roman Liturgy*, II, 89.

29 See P. Armour, "The Theme of Exodus", pp. 71–80.

30 See G. R. Sarolli, "In exitu Israel de Aegypto", in *Enc. dant.*, III, 429–30 (p. 429, col. 2).

31 The words "venivan genti" bear a striking resemblance to "venerunt gentes" in the opening verse of Psalm 79 ("Deus, venerunt gentes in haereditatem tuam"), quoted in *Purg.*, XXXIII. 1; but the qualitative distance between the "genti" (souls of recently deceased penitents) and the "gentes" ("the heathen") who have "defiled thy holy temple and laid Jerusalem in ruins") makes it unlikely that this is a meaningful intertextual connection.

32 On Dante's use of Psalm 51 (50 in the Vulgate), see R. Hollander, "Dante's Use of the Fiftieth Psalm (A Note on *Purg.*, xxx. 84)", *Dante Studies*, 91 (1973), 145–50, also in his *Studies in Dante* (Ravenna, Longo, 1980), pp. 107–13; R. Frattarolo, "Il lievito del salmo *Miserere*", in *Da Malebolge alla Senna: studi letterari in onore di Giorgio Santangelo* (Palermo, Palumbo, 1993), pp. 229–34.

33 See D. Balboni, "Salve, Regina", in *Enc. dant.*, IV, 1091–92 (p. 1091, col. 2).

34 The text of *Salve, Regina* runs as follows: "Salve Regina, mater misericordiae, / Vita, dulcedo, et spes nostra salve. / Ad te clamamus exsules, filii Hevae. / Ad te suspiramus gementes et flentes in hac lacrimarum valle. / Eia ergo advocata nostra, illos tuos misericordes oculos ad nos converte. / Et Jesum benedictum fructum ventris tui, nobis post hoc exsilium ostende. / O clemens, O pia, / O dulcis Virgo Maria" (*Liber Usualis*, pp. 92–93).

35 It has been suggested that herein lies the significance of the fact that Rudolph of Habsburg (presumably because, like Macbeth [II. 2. 26–33] or the Ancient Mariner [IV. 6–7], he cannot pray) does not join in the singing (*Purg.*, VII. 93)—he being the most guilty of pusillanimity and negligence in that he did not intervene when he "potea/sanar le piaghe c'hanno Italia morta" (lines 94–95). See D. Balboni, "Salve, Regina", pp. 1091–92.

36 Boccaccio made comic use of this hymn in *Decameron*, VII. 1. 20; see also C. Ó Cuilleanáin, *Religion and the Clergy in Boccaccio's "Decameron"* (Rome, Storia e Letteratura, 1984), pp. 117–18. The text of the hymn is: "Te lucis ante terminum, / Rerum Creator poscimus, / Ut pro tua clementia / Sis praesul et custodia. / / Procul recedant somnia, / Et noctium phantasmata; / Hostemque

nostrum comprime,/Ne polluantur corpora.//Praesta, Pater piissime,/Patrique compar Unice,/Cum Spiritu Paraclito/Regnans per omne saeculum./Amen" (*Liber Usualis*, pp. 84–85).

37 See my "Liturgical Schemes in Dante's *Purgatorio*?", pp. 11–13. For a more individual interpretation of Dante's compline scene, see A. McCracken, "'In Omnibus Viis Tuis': Compline in the Valley of the Rulers (*Purg.* VII–VIII)", *Dante Studies*, 111 (1993), 119–29. See also A. A. Iannucci, "The Nino Visconti Episode in *Purgatorio* VIII (vv. 43–84)", *La fusta*, 3, ii (Fall 1978), 1–8 (pp. 1–4).

38 This has been tentatively suggested by P. Rigo, "Tempo liturgico nell'epistola dantesca ai principi e ai popoli d'Italia", *Lettere italiane*, 22 (1980), 222–31 (p. 228, n. 20), though Rigo sees the psalm as belonging to the first Sunday in Lent (which it also does: see *Sources of the Modern Roman Liturgy*, II, 222).

39 "Visita, quaesumus Domine, habitationem istam, et omnes insidias inimici ab ea longe repelle: Angeli tui sancti habitent in ea, qui nos in pace custodiant; et benedictio tua sit super nos semper [...]" (*Liber Usualis*, p. 89).

40 See D. J. Tucker, "In Exitu Israel de Aegypto"; D. J. Tucker, "Dante's Reconciliation in the *Purgatorio*", *American Benedictine Review*, 20 (1969), 75–92; A. C. Mastrobuono, "From Vespers to Dawn" and "This Is the Day the Lord Has Made"; J. C. Barnes, "Liturgical Schemes in Dante's *Purgatorio*?"

41 For the order of compline, see *Sources of the Modern Roman Liturgy*, II, 48–49.

42 See the *Liber Usualis*, pp. 240–43. On the colour of the angel's robe see P. Armour, *The Door of Purgatory*, pp. 49–51.

43 On the seven Ps see P. Armour, *The Door of Purgatory*, pp. 63–76.

44 A faldstool was a portable substitute for the bishop's throne; see L. Eisenhofer and J. Lechner, *The Liturgy of the Roman Rite*, pp. 132–33.

45 See D. Tucker, "Dante's Reconciliation", pp. 76–78, 84–85, who cites the official *Pontificale Romanum*; see also *S. Thomae Aquinatis Summa Theologiae*, edited by P. Caramello, 3 vols (Turin, Marietti, 1962–63), III, Supplement, q. 28 (pp. 83–85).

46 See L. Eisenhofer and J. Lechner, *The Liturgy of the Roman Rite*, pp. 87–88.

47 For this idea see, for example, E. G. Parodi, "La costruzione e l'ordinamento del *Paradiso* dantesco" [1911], in his *Poesia e storia nella "Divina commedia": studi critici* (Naples, Perrella, 1920), pp. 567–607 (pp. 567–79).

48 See R. Assunto, "Concetto dell'arte e ideali estetici in Dante", in his *La critica d'arte nel pensiero medioevale* (Milan, Saggiatore, 1961), pp. 259–84 (pp. 274–77). The final cantos of the poem are presided over by St Bernard, who was a Cistercian, and partly for this reason Assunto argues that Dante's Empyrean is analogous to a Cistercian abbey. Cistercian abbeys were designed to be unadorned except for the single natural adornment of light, which would alter according to the time of day and, with the mediation of stained-glass windows, colour the internal masonry with various patterns according to its own nature. This bareness was intended to provide the most appropriate setting for the concentration of the *affectus* in contemplation. Dante's Empyrean, too, is bare—unlike, at the opposite extreme, the circle of the proud in *Purgatorio* with its carved reliefs—, and light, together with colour, is the sole visual expression of God's glory in *Paradiso* as a whole. What is more, the angels in the Empyrean are like figures in stained-glass windows: they are coloured (red faces, gold wings and white elsewhere) and transparent; they allow light to filter through them and in a sense give light their own form: "Né l'interporsi tra 'l disopra e 'l fiore/di tanta moltitudine volante/

impediva la vista e lo splendore" (*Par.*, xxxi. 19–21). Lastly, this church is occupied by two *milizie* or *corti*, one of which Beatrice refers to as "'l convento de le bianche stole" (*Par.*, xxx. 129), while the other "canta/la gloria di colui che la 'nnamora" (*Par.*, xxxi. 4–5). It could also be borne in mind that a Gothic cathedral was seen as a recreation of Heaven on earth; see C. McDannell and B. Lang, *Heaven: A History* (New Haven, Connecticut, Yale University Press, 1988), pp. 78–79.

49   "Ave, Maria, gratia plena, Dominus tecum: benedicta tu in mulieribus, et benedictus fructus ventris tui" (*Liber Usualis*, p. 710).

50   Hans Rheinfelder calls this prayer Dante's *Ave, Maria* ("Dante als Beter", p. 229 [1968], 241 [1975]) in the course of an excellent study of it. On these *terzine* see also E. Auerbach, "Dante's Prayer to the Virgin (*Par.* xxxiii) and Earlier Eulogies", *Romance Philology*, 3 (1949), 1–26, Italian translation by D. Della Terza, "La preghiera di Dante alla Vergine (*Par.* xxxiii) ed antecedenti elogi", in Auerbach's *Studi su Dante*, third edition (Milan, Feltrinelli, 1971), pp. 263–92; A. Vallone, "La preghiera", pp. 91–109; A. Vallone, "Ancora del Veltro e della preghiera di S. Bernardo", *Letterature moderne*, 7 (1957), 735–38, also in his *La critica dantesca nel Settecento ed altri saggi danteschi* (Florence, Olschki, 1961), pp. 85–89 (pp. 88–89).

51   See D. Balboni, "Ave Maria", in *Enc. dant.*, i, 465 (col. 1).

52   See L. Eisenhofer and J. Lechner, *The Liturgy of the Roman Rite*, p. 469.

53   Helmut Hatzfeld, "Una onomasiologia stilistica", p. 214 observes that this mixture of Latin and a non-Romance language is characteristic of the liturgy when it expresses the holiest of mysteries, as in the Good Friday Reproaches ("Agios o Theos. Sanctus Deus. Agios ischyros. Sanctus fortis. Agios athanatos, eleison imas. Sanctus immortalis, miserere nobis"; *Liber Usualis*, p. 357).

54   My translation (Singleton leaves these lines untranslated).

55   The fourth sphere does particularly celebrate the Trinity: Canto x begins with six lines which do so, by way of prologue to this heaven; and the content of the souls' song is specified again towards the end of the episode, complete with an echo of the liturgical formula "Who liveth and reigneth with Thee" (compare, for instance, the final part of the prayer *Visita, quaesumus* quoted above: "qui tecum vivit et regnat in unitate Spiritus Sancti Deus", *Liber Usualis*, p. 89): "Quell' uno e due e tre che sempre vive/e regna sempre in tre e 'n due e 'n uno,/non circunscritto, e tutto circunscrive,/tre volte era cantato [...]" (*Par.*, xiv. 28–31).

56   This is not dissimilar to the experience described in the last line of *Purgatorio* ix, where the pilgrim hears the *Te Deum* in such a way "ch'or sí or no s'intendon le parole".

57   For some far-reaching reflections on the significance of the allusion to Psalm 121, see A. Stäuble, "*Paradiso*, xxv. 38 e i salmi dei pellegrinaggi", *Versants*, 5 (1983), 3–21.

58   For the Litany of Loreto, see the *Liber Usualis*, pp. 1213–14. The text of *Regina caeli* is as follows: "Regina caeli laetare, alleluia: Quia quem meruisti portare, alleluia: Resurrexit sicut dixit, alleluia: Ora pro nobis Deum, alleluia" (*Liber Usualis*, pp. 91–92).

59   The Nicene Creed may be read in the *Liber Usualis*, pp. 43–44; for the Athanasian Creed, see any edition of the *Breviarium Romanum ex Decreto Sacrosancti Concilii Tridentini*, in the order of service for prime on Sunday.

60   See *Sources of the Modern Roman Liturgy*, ii, 232, 262; *Liber Usualis*, pp. 506–07.

61 On the question of why, in the eighth heaven, the liturgy is quoted in the vernacular, see K. Brownlee, "Why the Angels Speak Italian: Dante as Vernacular *Poeta* in *Paradiso* xxv", *Poetics Today*, 5 (1984), 597–610.
62 See *Sources of the Modern Roman Liturgy*, II, 120, rubric 26 and note.
63 Some of these sentences (*Beati pacifici*, *Beati mundo corde* and *Venite, benedicti Patris mei*) did in fact make occasional appearances in the earthly liturgy: see *Sources of the Modern Roman Liturgy*, II, 69, 174, 178, 252, 303, 312. On Dante's use of *Veni, sponsa, de Libano* and *Benedictus qui venis in nomine Domini*, see E. Auerbach, "Figurative Texts Illustrating Certain Passages of Dante's *Commedia*", *Speculum*, 21 (1946), 474–89 (pp. 477–82).
64 Anchises's words, as re-used by Dante's angels, are seen as an acclamation by Teresa Hankey in her "The Clear and the Obscure: Dante, Virgil and the Role of the Prophet", in this volume, pp. 211–29 (p. 222). In the general context of secular texts it may not be inappropriate to view "*Amor che ne la mente mi ragiona*" (*Purg.*, II. 112) as an *anti*-liturgical text—sweetly sung (compare the references elsewhere to wonderful musical settings of liturgical texts) but inappropriate to the moment.
65 My translation.
66 Dante's sources here are *Aen.*, VI. 843–44 and Valerius Maximus, *Factorum ac Dictorum Memorabilium Libri* IX, I. 8, II. 9, IV. 18.

APPENDIX

The following is a list of obvious or speculative liturgical allusions or other liturgical elements in the *Commedia*. It includes and extends the list of references to the Psalms which may be derived from the "Index to Quotations. No. 1" in E. Moore, *Studies in Dante, First Series: Scripture and Classical Authors in Dante* [1896], edited by C. Hardie (Oxford, Clarendon Press, 1969), pp. 321–58 (pp. 323–24); no doubt others will add to it in their turn. The definition of "liturgical" adopted in the body of the essay is again implicit here. The following abbreviations are used: BR, *Breviarium Romanum*; BVM, Blessed Virgin Mary; COSMO, U. Cosmo, *L'ultima ascesa: introduzione alla lettura del "Paradiso"* (Bari, Laterza, 1936); EISENHOFER–LECHNER, L. Eisenhofer and J. Lechner, *The Liturgy of the Roman Rite*; LANA, "*Comedia" di Dante degli Allaghierii col comento di Jacopo della Lana*; LU, *Liber Usualis*; MONE, *Lateinische Hymnen des Mittelalters*, edited by F. J. Mone [1853–55], 3 vols (Aalen, Scientia, 1964); O'BRIEN, W. J. O'Brien, "'The Bread of Angels' in *Paradiso* II: A Liturgical Note", *Dante Studies*, 97 (1979), 97–106; Ps., Psalm; SMRL, *Sources of the Modern Roman Liturgy*.

Inferno

I. 1   Nel mezzo del cammin di nostra vita: Ps. 90. 10, Dies annorum nostrorum in ipsis septuaginta anni; Ps. 102. 24, in dimidio

Vestiges of the Liturgy in Dante's Verse   265

	dierum meorum; Canticle of Hezekiah (*LU*, 379; *SMRL*, II, 87; from Isaiah 38. 10–20), In dimidio dierum meorum vadam ad portas inferi
I. 16	guardai in alto: Ps. 121. 1, Levavi oculos meos in montes
I. 65	*Miserere* di me: Ps. 51. 1, Miserere mei
I. 128	quivi è la sua città e l'alto seggio: Ps. 11. 4, Dominus in caelo sedes eius
I. 129	oh felice colui cu' ivi elegge!: Ps. 65. 4, Beatus quem elegisti et assumpsisti:/Inhabitabit in atriis tuis
III. 4	fattore [= God]: Nicene Creed (*LU*, 43), factorem caeli et terrae
III. 133	terra lagrimosa: *Salve, Regina* (*LU*, 92), lacrimarum valle
IV. 53–54	vidi venire un possente,/con segno di vittoria coronato: Apostles' Creed (*BR*, "Ante Singulas Horas"), descendit ad inferos [not in the Bible]
V. 9	le peccata: *Gloria* and *Agnus Dei* (*LU*, 2*, 6*), qui tollis peccata mundi
V. 60	la terra che 'l Soldan corregge: Ps. 96. 10, Etenim correxit orbem terrae; Ps. 97. 2, Iustitia et iudicium correctio sedis eius
VII. 74–75	fece li cieli [...] / sí, ch'ogne parte ad ogne parte splende, / distribuendo igualmente la luce: Ps. 104. 2, Amictus lumine sicut vestimento. / Extendens caelum sicut pellem
VII. 125	inno
VII. 125	porta [of Hell]: *Recessit pastor noster* (*LU*, 373), hodie portas mortis et seras pariter Salvator noster disrupit
XI. 47	col cor negando [God]: Pss 14. 1, 53. 1, Dixit insipiens in corde suo: Non est Deus
XII. 88	alleluia
XVI. 88	amen
XIX. 16–21	[Dante's presence at a baptism]
XIX. 49	come 'l frate che confessa
XX. 9	le letane
XXI. 131	non vedi tu ch'e' digrignan li denti: Ps. 35. 16, Frenduerunt super me dentibus suis
XXII. 45	avversari [= devils]: *Fratres: Sobri estote* (*LU*, 81), adversarius vester diabolus
XXIII. 58–72	[quasi-monastic procession, including "cappe"]
XXIII. 90	stola [liturgical vestment]
XXVII. 78	ch'al fine de la terra il suono uscie: Ps. 19. 4, In omnem terram exivit sonus eorum; also widely used as an antiphon, a gradual, an offertory, a versicle or a responsory (see *SMRL*, II, 47, 49, 50, 55, 146, 149, 173, 174, 272, 287, 302, 306, 307)
XXIX. 57	che qui registra: *Dies irae* (*LU*, 1099–1100), Liber scriptus proferetur, / in quo totum continetur, / unde mundus judicetur
XXXI. 69	salmi
XXXII. 127	manduca: Canon of the mass (*LU*, 5*), Accipite, et manducate ex hoc omnes
XXXIII. 122–35	Come 'l mio corpo stea / nel mondo sú, nulla scïenza porto [...]: Ps. 55. 15, Veniat mors super illos, / Et descendant in infernum viventes [...]
XXXIV. 1	*Vexilla regis prodeunt*: *LU*, 273–74

Purgatorio

I. 26	oh settentrïonal vedovo sito: Lamentations (*LU*, 298), Quomodo sedet sola civitas plena populo? facta est quasi vidua
II. 46–48	*In exitu Isräel de Aegypto*: Ps. 114
II. 49	Poi fece il segno lor di santa croce
V. 24	*Miserere*: Ps. 51
V. 135–36	'nnanellata pria/disposando m'avea [marriage ceremony]
VI. 78	donna di provincie [= Italy]: Lamentations (*LU*, 298), civitas [...] domina gentium
VI. 113	vedova e sola [= Rome]: Lamentations (*LU*, 298), sola civitas [...] quasi vidua
VI. 120	son li giusti occhi tuoi rivolti altrove?: Ps. 44. 24, Quare faciem tuam avertis?
VII. 32	dai denti morsi de la morte: *O mors* (*LU*, 378), O mors, ero mors tua, morsus tuus ero inferne
VII. 82	*Salve, Regina*: *LU*, 92–93
VIII. 11	ficcando li occhi verso l'orïente [customary for prayer]
VIII. 13	*Te lucis ante*: *LU*, 84–85
VIII. 95	avversaro [= devil]: *Fratres: Sobri estote* (*LU*, 81), adversarius vester diabolus
IX. 76	porta: Ps. 100. 4, Introite portas eius in confessione
IX. 111	tre volte nel petto [...] mi diedi [customary during recitation of the *Confiteor*]
IX. 115	Cenere: Ash Wednesday liturgy (*LU*, 240–43)
IX. 140	*Te Deum laudamus*: *LU*, 67–69
XI. 1–21	O Padre nostro [...]: *Pater noster*
XI. 11	osanna
XI. 18	non guardar lo nostro merto: *Unde et memores* (*LU*,5*), non aestimator meriti, sed veniae, quaesumus, largitor admitte
XI. 20	l'antico avversaro [= devil]: *Fratres: Sobri estote* (*LU*, 81), adversarius vester diabolus
XI. 115	color d'erba: Ps. 90. 5, sicut herba transeat
XIII. 50–51	Maria, òra per noi [...] Michele [...] Pietro [...] Tutti santi: Litany (*LU*, 396–99)
XIV. 46–47	Botoli [...] ringhiosi: Ps. 104. 21, Catuli leonum rugientes
XIV. 143–44	camo/che dovria l'uom tener dentro a sua meta: Ps. 32. 9, In camo et freno maxillas eorum constringe
XIV. 146	l'antico avversaro [= devil]: *Fratres: Sobri estote* (*LU*,81), adversarius vester diabolus
XV. 132	l'etterno fonte: Ps. 36. 9, Quoniam apud te est fons vitae; *Veni Creator Spiritus* (*LU*, 467; *SMRL*, II, 52, 101, 102, 343), Fons vivus [= the Holy Spirit]; *Dies irae* (*LU*, 1100), Salva me, fons pietatis
XVI. 17–19	pregar per pace e per misericordia/l'Agnel di Dio che le peccata leva./[...] *Agnus Dei*: *Gloria* and *Agnus Dei* (*LU*, 2*, 6*)
XVI. 141	Dio sia con voi: *Dominus vobiscum*
XVIII. 44	l'anima non va con altro piede: Ps. 73. 2, Mei autem pene moti sunt pedes

XIX. 73	*Adhaesit pavimento anima mea*: Ps. 119. 25; also an antiphon (see *SMRL*, II, 34, 155)
XX. 89	rinovellar l'aceto e 'l fiele: Ps. 69. 21, Et dederunt in escam meam fel,/Et in siti mea potaverunt me aceto
XX. 94–95	quando sarò io lieto/a veder la vendetta: Ps. 58. 10, Laetabitur iustus cum viderit vindictam
XX. 100	risposto [= responsory]
XX. 136	*Gloria in excelsis* [...] *Deo*: Greater Doxology (*LU*, 2*)
XXII. 67–69	Facesti come quei che va di notte,/che porta il lume dietro e sé non giova,/ma dopo sé fa le persone dotte: Ps. 119. 105, Lucerna pedibus meis verbum tuum,/Et lumen semitis meis
XXII. 128–29	ascoltava i lor sermoni,/ch'a poetar mi davano intelletto: Ps. 119. 130, Declaratio sermonum tuorum illuminat,/Et intellectum dat parvulis
XXIII. 11	*Labïa mëa, Domine*: Ps. 51. 15, Domine, labia mea aperies; also used several times a day as an antiphon or a versicle (see *SMRL*, II, 42, 71, 78, 186, 187)
XXV. 34–36	Se le parole mie/[...] la mente tua guarda e riceve,/lume ti fiero al come che tu die: Ps. 119. 105, Lucerna pedibus meis verbum tuum,/Et lumen semitis meis
XXV. 121	*Summae Deus clementïae*: see LANA, II, 298 and *SMRL*, II, 59
XXVI. 32	[kiss: see EISENHOFER-LECHNER, 89–90]
XXVI. 130	un paternostro
XXVIII. 33	raggiar non lascia sole ivi né luna: Ps. 121. 6, Per diem sol non uret te,/Neque luna per noctem
XXVIII. 80	*Delectasti*: Ps. 92. 4, Quia delectasti me, Domine, in factura tua
XXIX. 3	*Beati quorum tecta sunt peccata!*: Ps. 32. 1, Beati [...] quorum tecta sunt peccata
XXIX. 51	*Osanna*
XXIX. 52ff	[procession]
XXIX. 65	vestite di bianco [principal colour of liturgical vestments]
XXIX. 85–86	*Benedicta tue/ne le figlie d'Adamo*: *Ave, Maria* (*LU*, 710), benedicta tu in mulieribus; *Benedicta tu in mulieribus* (antiphon/versicle: see *SMRL*, II, 22, 32, 127, 156, 160, 188, 189)
XXX. 15	alleluiando
XXX. 19	*Benedictus qui venis!*: *Benedictus* (*LU*, 4*), Benedictus qui venit
XXX. 74–75	Come degnasti d'accedere al monte? [...]: Ps. 24. 3–4, Quis ascendet in montem Domini? [...]; also used as a versicle (see *SMRL*, II, 208, 319)
XXX. 83–84	*In te, Domine, speravi* [...] *pedes meos*: Ps. 31. 1–8, In te, Domine, speravi [...]
XXX. 85–99	Sí come neve [...]: Ps. 147. 16–18, Qui dat nivem sicut lanam [...]
XXXI. 46	il seme del piangere: Ps. 126. 5, Qui seminant in lacrymis,/In exsultatione metent; also used as a tract (see *SMRL*, II, 276)
XXXI. 98	*Asperges me*: Ps. 51. 7, Asperges me hyssopo, et mudabor; Lavabis me, et super nivem dealbabor; *Asperges me hyssopo* (antiphon: see *SMRL*, II, 235, 348, 387, 389)
XXXII. 44	legno dolce: *Crux fidelis* (*LU*, 361), Dulce lignum
XXXII. 62	inno

XXXII. 81	stola [liturgical vestment]
XXXIII. 1	*Deus, venerunt gentes*: Ps. 79. 1, Deus, venerunt gentes in haereditatem tuam

Paradiso

II. 11	pan de li angeli: Ps. 78. 25, Panem angelorum; *Portas caeli* (see O'BRIEN, 100 and *SMRL*, II, 252, 259), panem angelorum; *Lauda Sion salvatorem* (see MONE, I, 277 and *SMRL*, II, 262), panis angelorum
II. 35–36	com' acqua recepe/raggio di luce permanendo unita: anon. sequence (see COSMO, 410–11), sicut vitrum radio/solis penetratur;/ inde tamen lesio/nulla vitro datur
III. 114	l'ombra de le sacre bende: Ps. 17. 8, Sub umbra alarum tuarum; also used as a responsory (see *SMRL*, II, 48)
III. 121–22	*Ave,/Maria*: *LU*, 710
VI. 7	sotto l'ombra de le sacre penne: Ps. 17. 8, Sub umbra alarum tuarum; also used as a responsory (see *SMRL*, II, 48)
VII. 1	*Osanna, sanctus Deus sabaòth*: Sanctus (*LU*, 4*), Sanctus, Sanctus, Sanctus Dominus Deus Sabaoth
VII. 103–05	le vie sue [= God's] [...] amendue: Ps. 25. 10, Universae viae Domini, misericordia et veritas
VIII. 29	*Osanna*
X. 129	da essilio [= earthly life] venne a questa pace: *Salve, Regina* (*LU*, 93), post hoc exsilium [= earthly life]
XI. 96	meglio in gloria del ciel si canterebbe: Ps. 115. 1, Non nobis, Domine, non nobis;/Sed nomini tuo da gloriam
XIV. 28–29	Quell' uno e due e tre che sempre vive/e regna sempre in tre e 'n due e 'n uno: *Visita, quaesumus* (*LU*, 89) etc., qui tecum vivit et regnat in unitate Spiritus Sancti Deus, per omnia saecula saeculorum
XIV. 62	Amme
XV. 62–63	di questa vita miran ne lo speglio/in che, prima che pensi, il pensier pandi: Ps. 139. 2, Intellexisti cogitationes meas de longe
XVII. 33	l'Agnel di Dio che le peccata tolle: *Gloria* and *Agnus Dei* (*LU*, 2*, 6*), Agnus Dei, qui tollis peccata mundi
XVII. 63	in questa valle [= exile]: *Salve, Regina* (*LU*, 92), exsules [...] in hac lacrimarum valle
XVII. 137	valle dolorosa [= Hell]: *Salve, Regina* (*LU*, 92), lacrimarum valle
XIX. 75	sanza peccato in vita o in sermoni: *Confiteor* (LU, 1*), peccavi [...] verbo et opere
XIX. 113–14	quel volume aperto/nel qual si scrivon tutti suoi dispregi: *Dies irae* (*LU*, 1099–1100), Liber scriptus proferetur,/in quo totum continetur,/unde mundus judicetur
XXII. 94	Iordan vòlto retrorso/piú fu, e 'l mar fuggir: Ps. 114. 3, Mare vidit, et fugit;/Iordanis conversus est retrorsum
XXII. 108	le mie peccata: *Gloria* and *Agnus Dei* (*LU*, 2*, 6*), qui tollis peccata mundi
XXII. 108	'l petto mi percuoto [customary during recitation of *Confiteor*]
XXIII. 73	rosa [= BVM]: Litany of Loreto (*LU*, 1214), Rosa mystica
XXIII. 92	stella [= BVM]: Litany of Loreto (*LU*, 1214), Stella matutina

Vestiges of the Liturgy in Dante's Verse 269

xxiii. 104	ventre/che fu albergo del nostro disiro: *Salve, Regina* (*LU*, 93), fructum ventris tui; *Ave, Maria* (*LU*, 710), fructus ventris tui
xxiii. 128	*Regina celi: Regina caeli* (*LU*, 91–92)
xxiii. 134–35	piangendo ne lo essilio/di Babillòn: Ps. 137. 1, Super flumina Babylonis illic sedimus et flevimus; also used as an offertory or a versicle (see *SMRL*, ii, 96, 233, 269)
xxiv. 2	benedetto Agnello: *Gloria* and *Agnus Dei* (*LU*, 2*, 6*), Agnus Dei
xxiv. 113	Dio laudamo: *Te Deum laudamus* (*LU*, 67–69)
xxiv. 130–32	Io credo in uno Dio [...]: Nicene Creed (*LU*, 43–44), Credo in unum Deum [...]
xxiv. 139–41	e credo in tre persone etterne, e queste/credo una essenza sí una e sí trina,/che soffera congiunto "sono" ed "este": Athanasian Creed (*BR*, Sunday, prime), ut unum Deum in Trinitate, et Trinitatem in unitate veneremur. Neque confundentes personas, neque substantiam separantes
xxv. 38	io leväi li occhi a' monti: Ps. 121. 1, Levavi oculos meos in montes
xxv. 73–74	Sperino in te [...] color che sanno il nome tuo: Ps. 9. 10, Et sperent in te qui noverunt nomen tuum; also used as an offertory (see *SMRL*, ii, 232, 262); see also xxv. 98
xxv. 95	bianche stole: *Ad regias Agni dapes* (*LU*, 426), Stolis amicti candidis; see also xxv. 127
xxvi. 40	verace autore [= God]: *A solis ortus cardine* (*LU*, 156), Beatus Auctor saeculi
xxvi. 69	Santo, santo, santo!: *Sanctus* (*LU*, 4*), Sanctus, sanctus, sanctus
xxvii. 1–2	Al Padre, al Figlio, a lo Spirito Santo/[...] gloria!: Lesser Doxology (*LU*, 3), Gloria Patri, et Filio, et Spiritui Sancto
xxvii. 57	o difesa di Dio, perché pur giaci?: Ps. 44. 23, Exsurge; quare obdormis, Domine?
xxviii. 94	osannar
xxviii. 118	*Osanna*
xxix. 40–41	questo vero [that the angels and the material world were created simultaneously] è scritto in molti lati/da li scrittor de lo Spirito Santo: Ps. 102. 26, Initio tu, Domine, terram fundasti
xxx. 129	bianche stole: *Ad regias Agni dapes* (*LU*, 426), Stolis amicti candidis
xxxi. 93	etterna fontana [= God]: Ps. 36. 9, Quoniam apud te est fons vitae; *Veni Creator Spiritus* (*LU*, 467; *SMRL*, ii, 52, 101, 102, 343), Fons vivus [= the Holy Spirit]; *Dies irae* (*LU*, 1100), Salva me, fons pietatis
xxxi. 100	la regina del cielo: *Regina caeli* (*LU*, 91–92)
xxxii. 12	*Miserere mei:* Ps. 51. 1
xxxii. 95	*Ave, Maria, gratïa plena*: *LU*, 710
xxxii. 135	osanna
xxxiii. 2	umile e alta piú che creatura: *Magnificat* (*LU*, 77), respexit humilitatem ancillae suae [...] beatam me dicent omnes generationes [...] fecit mihi magna
xxxiii. 7	Nel ventre tuo si raccese l'amore: *Salve, Regina* (*LU*, 93), fructum ventris tui; *Ave, Maria* (*LU*, 710), fructus ventris tui

INFERNO, v. 73-142: THE IRISH SEQUEL

Jean-Michel Picard

Ever since Pasquale Villari published his *Antiche leggende e tradizioni che illustrano la "Divina commedia"* in 1865, scholars have been aware of the possible influence on Dante's poem of Irish visions of the other world. In the last 130 years, however, further research has been undertaken, and we are now in a position to answer some of the questions raised by Villari's work.

Villari included in his collection two Latin texts which had enjoyed wide circulation in medieval Europe: the *Vision of Tnugdal*, written in 1149, and the *Tractatus de Purgatorio Sancti Patricii* (which I shall refer to simply as the *Tractatus*), written in 1184. Both texts describe the journey of a knight (Tnugdal in the *Vision* and Owein in the *Tractatus*) into an underground world where vivid torments are inflicted on sinners and heavenly abodes reward the just. In the *Vision of Tnugdal* the geographical location of such a place is not revealed but in the *Tractatus* the entrance to Purgatory is clearly set in Ireland, on Lough Derg, County Donegal.[1]

It is well known that one of these Irish texts, the *Tractatus*, played a major part in shaping the concept of Purgatory as it was created in the twelfth century,[2] but it seems to have had little direct influence on the literary representation of Dante's Purgatory. There are several important differences between the *Tractatus* and the *Commedia* which reveal two separate concepts of Purgatory. While H. of Saltrey, the author of the *Tractatus*, pictures the sinner's progress into Purgatory as a descent, Dante presents it as an ascent. In spite of the common setting of an island, the two opposite views are reflected in the geographical location, a pit in one and a mountain in the other. In the *Commedia*, Purgatory is half-way between Heaven and Hell and is already part of the world of light. As such it is a place of hope, and the mountain itself shakes and resounds with shouts of joy every time a soul is released to Paradise (*Purgatorio*, xx. 124–41, xxi. 40–72). St Patrick's Purgatory, on the other hand, is a place of gloom and pain ending in a blazing pit. Only after crossing the river of Hell is the soul allowed to rest in a sunny meadow to await the day when it will be called to its eternal reward. In fact St Patrick's Purgatory is more akin to Dante's *Inferno* than to his *Purgatorio*.

Another major difference is that in the monk of Saltrey's text the torments are not associated with specific sins. This is not unique to the *Tractatus*: the *Elucidarium*, a manual for clerics written in England by Honorius of Autun at the beginning of the twelfth century,[3] is another work which describes the nine torments of Hell without relating them to particular sins. By the time Dante wrote the *Commedia* this vagueness had been set aside and most descriptions of the other world did link the various sins to specific torments.

The second text, Brother Marcus's *Vision of Tnugdal*, is more relevant to an understanding of the tradition leading to the *Commedia*. Not only does it associate torments with specific sins, it also has a human dimension which is lacking in the *Tractatus*. H. of Saltrey presents Owein's self-imposed journey to Purgatory as the quest of the perfect Christian knight who triumphs over the devils by the strength of his faith in Christ. Tnugdal, on the contrary, is presented as a man of the world, a knight from Cashel who is interested in horses, games, women and fighting. The temporary "death" which takes him to the other world comes about as a result of over-indulgence at the house of a friend in Cork. His salvation from the torments of Hell is due not to his courage but to God's mercy. Furthermore, Tnugdal is not a lone bold warrior in Hell, redeeming his sins by his fortitude in dire situations, but a guest there protected by a guardian angel. The angel in the *Vision of Tnugdal* has a role similar to that of Virgil in Dante's afterlife, being both a guide and a protector. In contrast, the figure of the guide is absent from the *Tractatus*.

As regards the general concept and structure of the other world, of the two Irish visions the *Vision of Tnugdal* is the more akin to the *Commedia*. The descent into Hell is followed by an ascent leading to a place of rest for the good and thence to Paradise. Brother Marcus's geography of Hell, with its high mountains and succession of abysses linked by a small descending track, prefigures the geography of *Inferno*.

It would be pointless to look for exact equivalents in the descriptions of torments in the two texts. The monster in Chapter IX of the *Vision of Tnugdal* has been compared to Gerione in *Inferno* XVII.[4] The two monsters have similarly pointed tails, borrowed from the locusts in the Revelation of St John, and both stand half immersed in water (though Gerione only figuratively: *Inferno*, XVII. 19–24); but their other characteristics are different. Gerione has a human face, the body of a snake with legs, hair from his paws to his armpits with coloured knots and circlets painted on his front and back. The monster seen by Tnugdal has a bird-like shape: it has two feet, two wings, a very long neck, an iron beak and iron claws, and spurts fire from its mouth. If at any stage Dante had the *Vision of Tnugdal* in mind when creating Gerione, there are too many differences between the creatures for there to have been direct borrowing.

Several other similarities, however, are striking. Illustrating the function of Virgil as protector as well as guide, Dante describes an encounter with the devils in *Inferno* XXI which is similar to that in Chapter XII of the *Vision of Tnugdal*. As Tnugdal and the angel reach lower Hell they are surrounded by a company of devils:

> They immediately came around him with implements used to drag the souls of the poor wretches to the torments. [...] And brandishing their weapons they threatened him with everlasting death. These spirits were as black as coals, their eyes were like burning torches, their teeth were whiter than snow; they had tails like scorpions and very sharp iron nails and wings like vultures. So, as they were boasting that they would drag him with them without delay and that they would sing the canticle of death for him while he cried, the spirit of life arrived and the spirits of darkness fled.

In *Inferno* XXI, Virgil has to intervene in similar circumstances to protect Dante from the attacks of the aggressive devils of Malebolge. Needless to say, none of the wonderful farcical element developed by Dante is present in the *Vision of Tnugdal*.

The descriptions of Satan at the bottom of Hell also contain several similarities: in both texts the Prince of Darkness is immobilized (by ice in *Inferno*, by chains in the *Vision of Tnugdal*); his size is astonishingly large and his shape is that of a human body with monstrous attributes (three heads and six bat-like wings in *Inferno*, a thousand hands with twenty fingers and a prickly tail in the

Vision of Tnugdal); the treatment of lost souls is described in a metaphor drawn from rural life (Marcus's Lucifer squeezes the souls like a peasant pressing grapes, while Dante's Satan mangles the sinners in his three mouths as in a hemp-crusher).[5] But beyond the details, the important feature is that both writers avoid a facile enumeration of more and worse malformations and horrors and present instead a figure which is still majestic, fighting a hopeless destiny in its anger and pain.

To these few comparisons could be added similarities of descriptive detail found not only in the *Vision of Tnugdal* but also in the *Tractatus*. None of them would be sufficient to justify a definite claim of a direct influence of the Irish visions on Dante's *Commedia*. Nonetheless, these visions were part of the vast medieval repertoire of images of the other world from which Dante could have drawn the elements of his fantastic descriptions.

Like most educated men of his age, Dante would have known of the existence of St Patrick's Purgatory through the *Golden Legend* (*Legenda Aurea*), a collection of saints' lives which was one of the best sellers of the later Middle Ages. The *Golden Legend* was written before 1264 by Jacobus de Varagine, who later became Bishop of Genoa. Jacobus devotes most of his chapter on St Patrick to the visit to the Purgatory of a nobleman called Nicholas. The story is in fact a replica of the tribulations of Sir Owein as told by H. of Saltrey in the *Tractatus*. The influence of the *Golden Legend* on later Italian traditions involving St Patrick's Purgatory was important. It is at the origin of the notion of Patrick's well as a large, deep and virtually bottomless pit, which is still found in several idiomatic expressions of the Italian language containing the phrase *pozzo di san Patrizio*. For example, an object lost for ever is said to be "gone to St Patrick's well" (*andato nel pozzo di san Patrizio*); or a spendthrift family is called a *pozzo di san Patrizio*. Jacobus de Varagine describes St Patrick's well in the following terms:

> The earth opened [...] and a very deep, wide pit appeared. Then it was revealed to blessed Patrick that this was the place of Purgatory; that anyone who wished to go down into it would have no other penance to do and would endure no other purgatory for his sins; but that most would not come back from there, and that those who did come back would have had to stay below from one morning to the next. There were indeed many who went down into the pit and did not come out.[6]

The *Golden Legend* uses the character of Nicholas instead of Sir Owein. As a result, Nicholas appears as the protagonist of the story of St Patrick's Purgatory in some of the later accounts. For the fourteenth century, we have an excellent example of this in the Todi fresco painted in 1346 by a Sienese artist: the figure dressed in red to whom St Patrick is showing the purgatorial pit is called not Owein but Dominus Nicolaus.[7]

The *Vision of Tnugdal* was also known in Italy before Dante wrote his *Commedia*. The Latin text is found in several thirteenth- and fourteenth-century manuscripts of Italian origin.[8] The Irish setting of the vision would have been obvious to foreign readers. St Malachy, Bishop of Down and papal legate to the Irish, is mentioned in the prologue, together with Nemias, Bishop of Cloyne. The introduction contains a laudatory description of Ireland: "Ireland is an island situated at the extremity of the western ocean and stretches out from south to north. It is outstanding for its lakes and rivers, planted with woods, most fertile in cereals, opulent in milk, honey and all kinds of fish and game, lacking in vines but rich in wine." The status of Tnugdal's native city is also made clear: "This island has thirty-four dioceses, the bishops of which are under two metropolitans. Armagh is the metropole of the northern Irish, but Cashel is the most eminent see in the south, and there a nobleman was born, called Tnugdal."[9]

The Irish element in the *Vision of Tnugdal* must have impressed Italian readers to the extent that by the mid-fourteenth century the legend of Tnugdal was already superimposed on that of St Patrick's Purgatory. For example, the depiction of the Purgatory in the Todi fresco deviates from the tradition in both the *Tractatus* and the *Golden Legend* by associating the torments with specific sins, as in the tradition of the *Vision of Tnugdal*. Moreover, the crossing of the bridge—a traditional motif in journeys into the other world— differs in some respects from the description found in the *Tractatus*. The only bridge in the monk of Saltrey's text, crossing the river of Hell, is described in these terms:

> There were three things on this bridge which were most frightening for those who crossed it: first, it was so slippery that, even if it had been very wide, one could scarcely, if at all, get a foothold on it; secondly, it was so narrow and thin that apparently one could barely, if at all, stand or walk on it; thirdly, it stretched so

high in the air that even to lift one's gaze to its height seemed horrible.[10]

The artist who painted the Todi fresco used not this description but the one in Chapter VII of the *Vision of Tnugdal*:

> There was a very long and narrow bridge which extended for about two miles in length [...] and was about the size of a hand in width. It was longer and narrower than the bridge we mentioned earlier on. But this plank was inset with very sharp iron nails which pierced the feet of all who crossed it.[11]

The fresco shows a similar bridge covered with nails in St Patrick's Purgatory.

Assimilation between the two legends is also found in the *Vision of Louis d'Auxerre*, a late fourteenth-century text of northern Italian origin recounting the visit of an otherwise unknown French knight to St Patrick's Purgatory.[12] The best example of such assimilation is the episode where Louis is led by his guide to a room where a king sits on a golden throne, surrounded by magnificent objects, and receives gifts from the pilgrims he welcomed during his lifetime. The guide informs Louis, however, that the king sits on this throne for only three hours a day, and that every night he has to spend three hours in a bed of fire as a punishment for his lust.[13] This account corresponds almost exactly to the description of King Cormac of Cashel in Chapter XVII of the *Vision of Tnugdal*. Cormac sits in a similar setting and is offered gifts for the same reason, but for three hours every night he has to stand up to his waist in fire, dressed in a hair shirt. When asked the reason for this, the angel guiding Tnugdal answers: "He suffers the fire up to his waist because he sullied the sacrament of lawful marriage, and he suffers the hair shirt from the waist up because he ordered one of his vassals to be killed near the altar of St Patrick, thus betraying his oath."[14] The setting, the procession of pilgrims, the mention of the king's generosity and the torment of fire for lust are common to the two texts and clearly indicate a borrowing by the Italian redactor from the *Vision of Tnugdal*.

The *Vision of Louis d'Auxerre*, however, goes beyond a mere amalgamation of two Irish legends. Written after the *Commedia*, it reflects a renewed interest in vision literature which followed the dissemination of Dante's poem. The second half of the fourteenth century saw a spate of translations into Italian of Irish visions written in Latin. The tale of St Brendan's voyage to the other world was translated under the title *Come san Brandano andoe al paradiso dilitiano*.[15] The vision of the seventh-century Irish monk Fursa was narrated in the *Storia di Furseo monaco*.[16] The legend of Tnugdal itself became more accessible in the *Visione di Tundale* or *Istoria di Tugdalo d'Ibernia*.[17] St Patrick's Purgatory and the vision of Sir Owein became famous through various adaptations of the monk of Saltrey's work under the title *Il Purgatorio di san Patrizio*.[18] But the *Vision of Louis d'Auxerre* departs from the literary genre of the original twelfth-century texts by introducing courtly elements into its narrative. For example, the customary vision of torments is preceded by a meeting with three beautiful ladies dressed like queens, who do their best to tempt Louis to renounce his purgatorial visit.

The theme of the temptress appealing to the knight's chivalry in order to distract him from his quest had already entered the literature on St Patrick's Purgatory through the prose of the Provençal writer who compiled an account of the visions of the Hungarian knight George Grissaphan.[19] The visit of George Grissaphan to St Patrick's Purgatory in 1353 is a historical event which is attested in a series of letters by Archbishop Richard FitzRalph of Armagh, Prior Paul of Lough Derg, Nicholas Mac Cathasaigh, Bishop of Clogher, and John de Frowick, prior of the Hospitallers at Kilmainham.[20] George's visions, however, seem to owe much to literary imagination. His third vision belongs to the world of romance: as he reaches the gates of a rich and powerful city, George is met by a most beautiful lady, dressed like a queen and surrounded by more than two hundred beautiful damsels. She offers him her kingdom and herself in marriage, explaining that she is an orphan and needs a valiant knight like him as her defender. But George discovers that she is a manifestation of the devil and she disappears, leaving a fetid smoke behind her.

The *Vision of Louis d'Auxerre* also features a member of a family prominently represented in Dante's *Inferno*: the Malatesta of Rimini. When Louis is finally released from his ordeal in Purgatory, the first people he meets are Malatesta Ungaro and the monks of Lough Derg, who take him in procession to the monastery.[21] The mention of Malatesta Ungaro has both historical and literary implications.

Malatesta's visit to Lough Derg is, like that of George Grissaphan, a historical event; it is attested in a letter patent of King Edward III dated 24 October 1358. This document states that the knight Malatesta Ungaro and a young gentleman from Lombardy, Nicholas Beccari of Ferrara, have been to St Patrick's Purgatory, have remained locked underground for one day and one night as custom requires, and have endured many sufferings in the body. The text also points out that the King's certificate is based on letters written by Amaury de Saint Amand, his justiciar in Ireland, and by the prior of St Patrick's Purgatory, both of whom have confirmed the truth of the Italians' account.[22]

Malatesta Ungaro was one of the sons of Malatesta "Guastafamiglia", who died in 1364; and his grandfather Pandolfo (who died in 1326) was a brother of Paolo "il Bello" Malatesta, sadly celebrated in Canto v of Dante's *Inferno*.[23] He had acquired the surname Ungaro after being knighted by Louis the Great, King of Hungary, in 1347. His visit to St Patrick's Purgatory was doubtless inspired by the adventures of George Grissaphan as related in the *Visiones Georgii*. He may have known George personally since both men had taken part in an Italian campaign of King Louis of Hungary. The latter was a descendant of the Angevin rulers of Naples and had retained an interest in Italy. Among his Italian campaigns he made two expeditions to the south, in 1347 and 1350. George Grissaphan took part in the 1347 expedition and remained behind in charge of the garrison in Trani, near Bari.[24] According to the *Visiones Georgii* his pilgrimage to Ireland was undertaken in order to expiate the sins of murder and robbery committed against the people of that area. Malatesta joined Louis's service during this period and would have at least heard of George Grissaphan then. In subsequent years he took part in the incessant wars between the cities of the Marches and Romagna at the side of his father and his famous uncle Galeotto (who died in 1385). But his military career was to suffer a serious setback at the hands of the Church. Like other *signori* in the region, the Malatesta also controlled papal territories. After a succession of weak or corrupt administrators appointed by the distant papacy in Avignon, the arrival in Italy of Cardinal Albornoz in 1353 changed the military and political balance in the papal provinces.[25] Having secured an alliance with the Visconti in Milan, Albornoz recovered Rome and the neighbouring Patrimony in 1354 and then moved on to Romagna and the Marches. He isolated the Malatesta from their neighbours by having them excommunicated on 12 December 1354. Rimini's resistance was broken after a long siege; Galeotto Malatesta, the leader of the rebellion, was taken prisoner; and he and his family had to swear allegiance to the Pope. Probably in the context of his family's submission, Malatesta Ungaro went to Avignon in 1358 to declare his allegiance to Pope Innocent VI. He then went on travelling—to Flanders, England and Ireland, where he decided to visit St Patrick's Purgatory.

Malatesta's stay at Lough Derg is also recorded by Domenico di Bandino in his unfinished *Fons Memorabilium Universi*, written between 1374 and 1418. One of the chapters of Domenico's encyclopaedic work deals with islands (*Liber de Insulis*), and mention is made of the island of St Patrick's Purgatory in Lough Derg.[26] Domenico seems slightly doubtful about the story of Malatesta's descent into and safe return from the bottom of the well. He confirms, however, that the event was widely known and talked about. His scepticism was not shared by all his contemporaries, and a letter written to Malatesta by Cecco Meletti of Forlí expresses warm feelings of admiration for the courage of the man who, having gone nearly to the end of the world, dared to enter the cave "where a night thick with darkness and tenebrous clouds surrounds the black opening of Hell".[27]

The mention of Malatesta in the *Vision of Louis d'Auxerre* refers to that event. It may have been introduced to add a historical dimension to the account of Louis's visit to Lough Derg, firmly setting it in 1358; but it may also reflect the importance of the event in literary circles at the end of the fourteenth century.

Malatesta's visit to Lough Derg is also mentioned in a context entirely different from vision literature—a context which, in an ironic way, evokes Canto V of *Inferno*. All students and lovers of the *Commedia* have been fascinated and moved by the tragic story of Paolo Malatesta and Francesca da Rimini in the second half of this canto. Countless studies have been made of this passage to assess its historical and literary value.[28] Leaving aside the fanciful details added by medieval and Renaissance commentators on Dante, the historical story is a simple one: Francesca, daughter of Guido Minore da Polenta (†1310) of Ravenna, was married in 1275 to Giovanni "Gianciotto" (†1304), the crippled son of Malatesta da Verrucchio (†1312), lord of Rimini. She bore him a daughter the following year, but subsequently fell in love with one of her brothers-in-law, Paolo "il Bello". Gianciotto became aware of the affair and killed the two lovers in 1285. Under Dante's pen this story takes on the aspect of a tale of love and tragic destiny like those found in medieval French romances. The mention of Lancelot and his friend Gallehault in the canto indicates that Dante was aware of the literary genre suitable for such stories:

> Noi leggiavamo un giorno per diletto
> di Lancialotto come amor lo strinse;
> soli eravamo e sanza alcun sospetto.
> [...] Galeotto fu 'l libro e chi lo scrisse:
> quel giorno piú non vi leggemmo avante.
> (*Inferno*, v. 127–38)

[One day, for pastime, we read of Lancelot, how love constrained him; we were alone, suspecting nothing. (...) A Gallehault was the book and he who wrote it; that day we read no farther in it.]

It is clear, however, that the poet's intention is not (or not only) to celebrate *amour courtois* but to show the dangers of passion and unlawful love.

Malatesta Ungaro appears to have become entangled in a similar story some seventy years later. In the corpus of anonymous Italian *ballate* there is one which laments the state of the city of Rimini after the death of a young woman called Viola Novella. The poem's *ripresa* runs as follows:[29]

> Cità d'Arimin bella,
> quanta sei fata scura!
> Tu mi meti in paura
> da poi ch'è morta la Viola Novella.

[O beautiful city of Rimini, how dark you have become! You frighten me since the death of Viola Novella.]

The five stanzas tell the story of a lady killed by her husband's dagger for an unspecified crime; it is likely that the reason for the husband's anger was a love affair. The poem belongs to the courtly tradition and subscribes to the view that such a transgression does not warrant the death penalty. Viola is portrayed kneeling naked in front of her husband and begging him to spare her:

> Se mai mi trovi in cutal falimento
> dami pena e tormento.
> De, fai la [grazia], e non guardar in quella.
> (*Ballata della Viola Novella*, lines 27–29)

[If you ever find me similarly at fault, give me punishment and torture. Alas, spare me and look not on this incident.]

As she lies wounded she cannot comprehend the violence of her husband's act:

> De, guarda la mia mamela,
> quanta era vaga e bela;
> or è tuta insanguenata.
> No·lo avería pensata
> tu m'alcidesse ben che ne sia degna.
> (*Ballata della Viola Novella*, lines 16–20)

[Alas, look at my breast, how charming and beautiful it was; now it is covered in blood. I would never have thought that you would kill me even though I deserve it.]

The lady's violent death is lamented not only by the faithful servant who brought her up but by the whole town of Rimini, so that all the shops are closed in her honour.

Invoking the *vox populi* is a well-known device used by medieval writers to enlist the audience's sympathy for a character. (It is used, for example, by Beroul when Tristran and Yseut, accused of adultery, are condemned to death by Yseut's husband: all the people of Tintaguel, old and young, weep and condemn the king's decision in sending such a noble and beautiful couple to their death.)[30] On the other hand, the people's reported reaction may genuinely reflect the fame of the beautiful Viola in Rimini. Tommaso Casini, who edited this *ballata* in 1889, could not tell whether it alluded to a historical event or whether it was fictional; but on linguistic and stylistic grounds he attributed it to the end of the fourteenth century.[31] Since then, Ferruccio Ferri and Aldo Francesco Massèra have shown that the *ballata* is based on a well-known episode in the eventful life of Malatesta Ungaro.[32] Several fifteenth-century writers connect the death of Viola Novella with Malatesta's journey to St Patrick's Purgatory. In the 1470s Gaspare

Broglio (†1483), a native of Siena and a *condottiere* who served many lords including Francesco Sforza and Sigismondo Pandolfo Malatesta, wrote a *Cronaca universale* which is also called *Cronaca malatestina* since it is essentially a chronicle of Rimini.[33] Broglio was a reader of Dante, and he included large excerpts from the *Commedia* in his manuscript.[34] He writes: "In 1358, the lord Malatesta Ungaro came back to Rimini, having gone to the well of St Patrick, which is situated in England beyond Flanders. And the reason for his journey was one of his mistresses called Viola Novella. He resolved to learn her fate and that is why he went there."[35] (The location of St Patrick's Purgatory in England is not an isolated error; it is also found in the Italian text of the *Vision of Louis d'Auxerre*.)

The incident reported by Broglio must have been common knowledge in Rimini, as it caught the imagination of several poets. Basinio da Parma (†1457), like Broglio, was both a historiographer and a court poet of Sigismondo Pandolfo Malatesta.[36] He joined Sigismondo's household in 1449 and proceeded to write a large epic poem in Latin entitled *Hesperis* or *Hesperidos Libri XIII*. Basinio set out to do for his patron what Virgil had done for Emperor Augustus in the *Aeneid*, so his poem is a celebration of the Malatesta family. In Book VIII the figure of Malatesta Ungaro is evoked, and Basinio tells how "the Pannonian [i.e. the Hungarian] who was called Malatesta came to these parts, looking for the kingdom of Hell, overcome by his love for a tragically beloved girl."[37] The name Viola Novella is not mentioned, but there is little doubt that Basinio's lines allude to the same incident.[38] A similar allusion is found in one of Gaspare Broglio's own poems in praise of the Malatesta, where Malatesta Ungaro is described as an adept of love, "a son of Cythera, who did not fear exploring the darker regions in order to find his splendid goddess".[39] Viola Novella is named by a third contemporary poet, Benedetto da Cesena (†1464) in his work *De Honore Mulierum* [*On the Honour of Women*], written in 1454. As Piccioni has shown, Benedetto tries to emulate Dante, and the whole of Book IV of *De Honore Mulierum* plagiarizes Dante's *Paradiso*.[40] Like his ancestor Paolo, Malatesta Ungaro is described as a victim of love, and his affair with Viola Novella is given as an example of the cruel consequences of this passion. *De Honore Mulierum* is important not only because it helps us assess the influence of the *Commedia* in literary circles of Romagna but also because, like the other poems, it contributes to our knowledge of the mentalities of medieval Europe.

The late twentieth century has publicized the concept of the global village, but in its own way medieval Europe was also a small world. Countries as far apart in terms of days' travel as Ireland and Italy were in fact relatively close in cultural terms. When Dante wrote the *Commedia* tales of Irish travellers to the other world were circulating widely in Europe. They probably did not influence Dante to a significant extent since the scope of the *Commedia* is far wider than that of the Irish stories; but they may have provided some of the images and ideas used by the poet. Like many other aspects of Dante's encyclopaedic undertaking, the element of courtly love found in *Inferno* v is absent from the visions set in Ireland, which were written before French romances became fashionable in Europe. By a strange twist of fate, however, Malatesta Ungaro's visit to Lough Derg underlines the link between the world of Irish visions and medieval Italy. Some seventy years after the tragic death of Francesca da Rimini and Paolo Malatesta celebrated by Dante, their kinsman Malatesta Ungaro appears to have been involved in a similar love story. But according to the poets who sang of his love for Viola Novella, the aristocrat from Rimini did not look for an Italian Virgil to guide him to the other world, where he hoped to find the beautiful girl killed, like Francesca, by the husband she betrayed. Instead, he went to the far edge of Europe and undertook the descent into St Patrick's Purgatory. This choice is significant and shows that the fusion of different European traditions could be a reality for a man of the fourteenth century.

NOTES

1   These two texts have recently been translated into English with an introduction, notes and up-to-date bibliography: see *St Patrick's Purgatory: A Twelfth-century Tale of a Journey to the Other World*, translated by J-M. Picard with an introduction by Y. de Pontfarcy (Dublin, Four Courts, 1985); *The Vision of Tnugdal*, translated by J-M. Picard with an introduction by Y. de Pontfarcy (Dublin, Four Courts, 1989).

2   See J. Le Goff, *La Naissance du Purgatoire* (Paris, Gallimard, 1981); English translation by A. Goldhammer, *The Birth of Purgatory* (London, Scolar Press; Chicago, University of Chicago Press, 1984); Y. de Pontfarcy, "The Topo-

graphy of the Other World and the Influence of Twelfth-century Irish Visions on Dante", in this volume, pp. 93–115 (pp. 95–104).

3   See Y. Lefèvre, *L'Elucidarium et les lucidaires* (Paris, Boccard, 1954).
4   P. Villari, *Antiche leggende e tradizioni che illustrano la "Divina commedia"* (Pisa, Nistri, 1865), p. 24.
5   *Inf.*, XXXIV. 28–60; *Vision of Tnugdal*, Ch. XIII.
6   *Jacobi a Voragine Legenda Aurea*, edited by T. Graesse [1845/1890] (Osnabrück, Zeller, 1969), pp. 213–16; Jacobus de Voragine, *The Golden Legend*, translated by W. Granger Ryan, 2 vols (Princeton, Princeton University Press, 1993), I, 193–96. The passage quoted is on p. 194.
7   On the Todi fresco, see N. Mac Tréinfhir, "The Todi Fresco and Saint Patrick's Purgatory, Lough Derg", *Clogher Record*, 12 (1986), 141–58.
8   Thirteenth century: Rome, Biblioteca Nazionale, Farfa MSS, 5 [270]: *Visio Tundali*. Fourteenth century: Genoa, Civica Biblioteca Berio, MS m.r., IX. 3. 25 [D bis II/7/32]: *Visio Tugdali*; Rome, Biblioteca Apostolica Vaticana, Palatine Latin MSS, 138: *Relatio Cuiusdam Tundali Hybernensis*; Rome, Biblioteca Vaticana, Pal. Lat. MSS,1431: *Visio Tundali*.
9   *The Vision of Tnugdal*, p. 111.
10 *St Patrick's Purgatory*, p. 64.
11 *The Vision of Tnugdal*, p. 123.
12 This text is known in two manuscripts. One of them comes from the region of Padua and is now in Austria: Vienna, Österreichischen Nationalbibliothek, MS 3160 (fifteenth century). The text, here entitled *Visio Lodoyci de Sur*, is found on fols 259r–261v. The greater part of the work is written in Latin with some Italian words inserted here and there, but the end is written wholly in Italian. The second manuscript is in Venice, Civico Museo Correr, Correr MSS, 1508 [I, 384] (fourteenth century), fols 1–24. It is written in Italian throughout and beautifully illustrated with coloured drawings. The Latin text (*Visio Ludovici de Francia*) has been edited by K. Strecker in M. Voigt, *Beiträge zur Geschichte der Visionenliteratur im Mittelalter*, 2 vols (Leipzig, Mayer and Müller, 1924), II, 226–45.
13 L. Frati edited this episode and compared the Latin and Italian versions in his "Tradizioni storiche del Purgatorio di San Patrizio", *Giornale storico della letteratura italiana*, 17 (1891), 46–79 (pp. 77–78).
14 *The Vision of Tnugdal*, p. 145.
15 Fourteenth/fifteenth century: Florence, Biblioteca Nazionale Centrale, Conventi Soppressi MSS, C. II. 1550. Fifteenth century: Florence, BNC, Magliabechi MSS, XXXVIII, 10; Bologna, Biblioteca Universitaria, Latin MSS, 997 [1513] (AD 1461).
16 Fifteenth century: Florence, BNC, fondo principale, II. II. 89 [Magliabechi XXI, 123]; Florence, Biblioteca Riccardiana, MS 1340; Venice, Biblioteca Nazionale Marciana, MS 5644 [It. V. 28]; Venice, Museo Correr, MS Cic. 2242.
17 Fourteenth century: Florence, BNC, Panciatichi Palatine MSS, 40 [75]; Florence, BNC, Magliabechi MSS, XXXV, 173. Fifteenth century: Florence, BNC, Magliabechi MSS, XXIV, 158; Florence, BNC, fondo principale, II. II. 71 [Magliabechi VII, 22]; Biblioteca Riccardiana, MS 1408 [P. III. 23]; Biblioteca Vaticana, Chigi Latin MSS, M. V. 118.
18 Fourteenth century: Biblioteca Riccardiana, MSS 1294 and 2760; Rome, Biblioteca Corsiniana, Rossi MSS, 30 [44. C. 5]. Fifteenth century: Florence, BNC, Magliabechi MSS, XXXV, 3; Florence, BNC, fondo principale, II. IV. 64

[Magliabechi XXIX, 68]; Florence, BNC, Conventi Soppressi MSS, G. III. 676; Florence, BNC, Palatine MSS, 93; Biblioteca Corsiniana, Rossi MSS, 298 [43. A. 23]; Biblioteca Vaticana, Latin MSS, 13072, fols 86v–104v in Italian; Biblioteca Marciana, MS 5023 [It. I. 30]; Biblioteca Marciana, MS 4947 [It. I. 66]. One of these texts, based on three manuscripts located in Florence, has been edited by L. Bertolini, "Per una delle leggende 'che illustrano la *Divina commedia*': una redazione del *Purgatorio di San Patrizio*", *Studi danteschi*, 53 (1981), 69–128.

19 This text has been edited by L. L. Hammerich in his *Visiones Georgii: Visiones Quas in Purgatorio Sancti Patricii Vidit Georgius Miles de Ungaria A. D.* MCCCLIII (Copenhagen, Høst, 1930).

20 See M. Haren, "Two Hungarian Pilgrims", in *The Medieval Pilgrimage to St Patrick's Purgatory: Lough Derg and the European Tradition*, edited by M. Haren and Y. de Pontfarcy (Enniskillen, Clogher Historical Society, 1988) pp. 120–68.

21 *Visio Ludovici de Francia*, p. 245: "Aperiens oculos, vidi dominum Malatestam Ungarum de Arimeno et monachos illos qui me [...] ad monasterium cum processione duxerunt."

22 The Latin text of the royal letters may be found in *Foedera, Conventiones, Literae et Cujuscunque Generis Acta Publica*, edited by T. Rymer et al., 4 vols in 7 (London, Commissioners on the Public Records, 1816–69), III, 274–75.

23 The genealogy of the Malatesta in the period here under review may be reconstructed as follows:

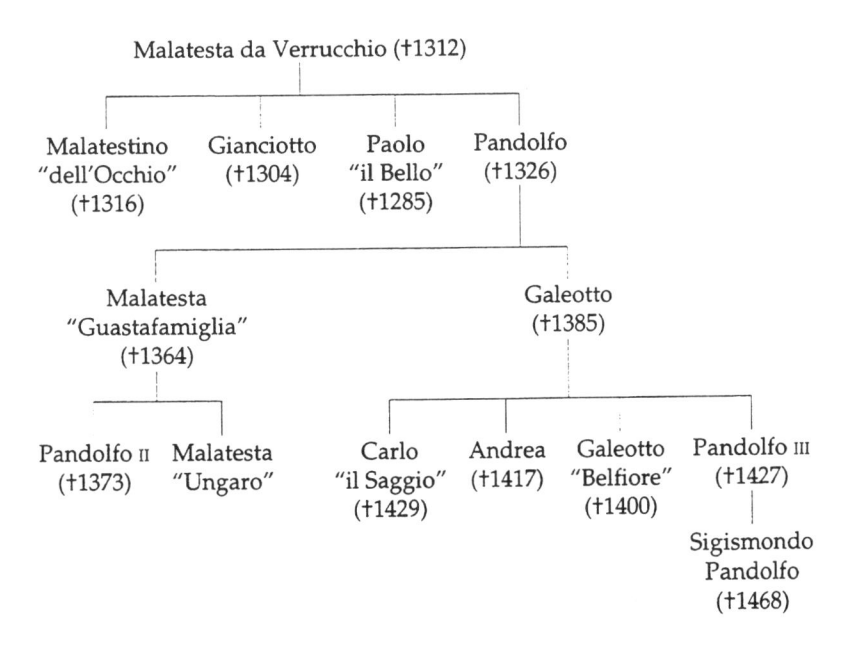

```
                    Malatesta da Verrucchio (†1312)
    ┌───────────────────┬───────────────┬──────────────┐
Malatestino       Gianciotto          Paolo         Pandolfo
"dell'Occhio"      (†1304)          "il Bello"       (†1326)
  (†1316)                            (†1285)            │
                                                        │
                    ┌───────────────────────────────────┤
                Malatesta                           Galeotto
             "Guastafamiglia"                        (†1385)
                 (†1364)                                │
           ┌─────────┴──────┐              ┌────────┬───────┬──────────┐
       Pandolfo II    Malatesta         Carlo    Andrea  Galeotto   Pandolfo III
         (†1373)      "Ungaro"        "il Saggio" (†1417) "Belfiore"   (†1427)
                                       (†1429)            (†1400)        │
                                                                    Sigismondo
                                                                     Pandolfo
                                                                     (†1468)
```

See P. Zama, *I Malatesti*, second edition (Faenza, Lega, 1965); J. Larner, *The Lords of Romagna* (London, Macmillan; New York, St Martin's Press, 1965); P. J. Jones, *The Malatesta of Rimini and the Papal State* (Cambridge, Cambridge University Press, 1974).

24 See L. L. Hammerich, "Eine Pilgerfahrt des XIV Jahrhunderts nach dem Fegfeuer des Hl. Patrizius", *Zeitschrift für deutsche Philologie*, 53 (1928), 25–40 (p. 36).

25 On Cardinal Egidio d'Albornoz see the large bibliography following the entry "Albornoz" in the *Dizionario biografico degli Italiani* (Rome, Istituto della Enciclopedia Italiana, 1960–), II, 45–53.

26 On Domenico di Bandino and his works see A. T. Hankey, "Domenico di Bandino of Arezzo", *Italian Studies*, 12 (1957), 110–28; A. T. Hankey, "The Successive Revisions and Surviving Codices of the *Fons Memorabilium Universi* of Domenico di Bandino", *Rinascimento*, 11 (1960), 3–49.

27 This letter is to be found in a manuscript of the Biblioteca Ambrosiana in Milan, MS P. 256 Sup., fol. 76r.

28 Among the more recent of these see F. Mazzoni, "Il canto v dell'*Inferno*", in *Inferno: letture degli anni 1973–'76*, edited for the Casa di Dante in Roma by S. Zennaro (Rome, Bonacci, 1977), pp. 97–143; P. Valesio, "'Regreter': genealogia della ripetizone nell'episodio di Paolo e Francesca", *Yearbook of Italian Studies*, 4 (1980), 87–104; D. Della Terza, "*Inferno* V: Tradition and Exegesis", *Dante Studies*, 99 (1981), 49–66.

29 The *Ballata della Viola Novella* has been edited by T. Casini in his "Due antichi repertori poetici", *Il propugnatore*, new series, 2, i (1889), 197–271 (pp. 260–61).

30 *The Romance of Tristran by Beroul*, edited by A. Ewert, 2 vols (Oxford, Blackwell, 1939–70), I, 25–26.

31 T. Casini, "Due antichi repertori poetici", pp. 261–65.

32 F. Ferri, "Il poeta Basinio e la leggenda di S. Patrizio", *Aurea Parma*, 2 (1913), 101–05; A. F. Massèra, "Malatesta Unghero e la Viola Novella", *Giornale storico della letteratura italiana*, 63 (1914), 174–75.

33 See the bibliography compiled by A. A. Strnad in the *Dizionario biografico degli Italiani*, XIV, 438–39.

34 The work of Gaspare Broglio is found in Rimini, Biblioteca Civica Gambalunga, MS 77 [69. D. III. 48]; see *Inventari dei manoscritti delle biblioteche d'Italia*, edited by G. Mazzatinti et al. (Florence, Olschki, 1890–), II, 148–49.

35 Biblioteca Gambalunga, MS 77, fol. 18v: "Nel 1358 ritornò inn Arimine miser Malatesta Ongaro, il quale era andato al Pozzo di san Patritio, el quale sta in Inghilterra apresso di Fiandra. E ll'andata sua per cagione d'una sua amorosa chiamata la Viola Novella; dove se dispose volerne sapere novella, e per dicta cagione andò."

36 See the biographical details and bibliography compiled by A. Campana in the *Dizionario biografico degli Italiani*, VII, 89–98.

37 *Hesperidos* (in *Basinii Parmensis Poetae Opera Praestantiora*, edited by L. Drudi, 2 vols in 3 [Rimini, Albertini, 1794]), VIII. 176–79 (I, 172): "Pannonio cui nomen erat Malatesta, recordor / venit ad has sedes, infernaque regna petivit / victis amore quidem dilectae, triste! puellae."

38 See F. Ferri, "Il poeta Basinio", p. 105.

39 Biblioteca Gambalunga, MS 77, fol. 20r: "L'altro fo quel figliol di Citerea / che non temé ciercar li luochi bui / per ritrovar la sua splendida dea. / Malatesta Ongar fo decto custui."

40 L. Piccioni, "A proposito di un plagiaro del *Paradiso* dantesco: Benedetto da Cesena", in his *Appunti e saggi di storia letteraria* (Livorno, Giusti, 1913), pp. 1–12.

DANTE'S MEDIEVAL AND RENAISSANCE COMMENTATORS: NINETEENTH- AND TWENTIETH-CENTURY CONSTRUCTIONS

Deborah Parker

Criticism of Dante's medieval and Renaissance commentators in the last fifteen years encompasses a wide range of philological activity: detailed investigations into the earliest commentators' use of sources; new attempts to settle questions concerning dating, dependences and attribution; and in-depth studies of one commentator or the commentaries of one period.[1] These studies testify eloquently to the recent resurgence of interest in Dante commentaries.[2] There is also, however, an uncanny sense of repetition. Resurgences of interest in commentary are periodic. The diverse interests of the last fifteen years have been in part conditioned by the kinds of studies of commentary that predominated in the nineteenth century, the period in which commentary first emerged as an object of criticism. The legacies of nineteenth-century studies still criss-cross the surface of recent work, largely unexamined yet exerting a considerable influence on later critical activity.

While no brief narrative can account for all the particulars, it is nonetheless possible to identify the influences which were significant in the move from commentary to criticism of the commentaries. That reorientation was largely due to the effects of positivism, nationalism and antiquarianism. These three impulses, each of which produced a different thread of the critical legacy, underwrote the renewed interest in Dante in the nineteenth century.

The work of scholars like Alessandro D'Ancona, Adolfo Bartoli, Giuseppe Vandelli and Isidoro Del Lungo is associated with the historical school of criticism which flourished in Italy in the late nineteenth and early twentieth centuries. The locus of most of this work was Florence, which had a long tradition of Dante studies and was the centre of other philological-historical research. Positivist research on Dante tended to focus on the state of the text of the *Commedia*, on the reconstruction of the poet's historical moment, and on the identification of Dante's literary precursors. We may best understand the spirit and practice of this positivist research by considering its contribution to one of the most prominent critical issues of the latter half of the nineteenth century: the question of whether Beatrice was strictly a symbol or a historical person. D'Ancona contended that she was a real woman; Bartoli, on the other hand, argued that Beatrice was based on a feminine ideal inspired by a number of women admired by Dante. This issue was resolved, in part, through recourse to an early commentary on the poem. Bartoli, after being informed by one of his students, Luigi Rocca, that Pietro Alighieri refers to Beatrice Portinari as the woman whom his father loved, published a letter to D'Ancona in the Florentine newspaper *La nazione*.[3] This letter, writes Rodolfo Renier, was widely regarded as "una mezza ritrattazione" on Bartoli's part.[4] What is significant in this debate is the particular use made of commentary at that time: as a means of adjudicating a dispute, as a kind of critical referee. Such a use was by no means unprecedented or unusual: in the previous century professional scholars and aristocratic connoisseurs had often consulted the medieval and Renaissance commentaries to determine the meaning of obscure points in the poem.[5] Bartoli, like other scholars, consulted the commentaries as one might other early documents in order to cast light on critical issues of the day. This unreflexive use of commentary is typical: Pietro Alighieri's remarks immediately acquired an authoritative status thanks to his vicinity to the poet— as a contemporary and as Dante's son. His comments settled, prematurely, a hotly contested interpretative point, with a serene innocence as to the historical status of this commentary in general.

D'Ancona's study of the figure of Beatrice was published in 1865. The date is significant: it coincides with the height of nationalist sentiment in Italy and with the sixth centenary of Dante's birth. Hence also the complexity of the legacy I am tracing: positivist scholarship was taken up into a system of purposes provided by partisan sentiment. The Risorgimento fuelled tremendous interest in the Middle Ages in general, but particularly in authors who, like Dante and Machiavelli, were perceived as patriotic. Dante incarnated nationalism: he was the first important author to write a significant work in Italian; he had eloquently defended the *volgare illustre* as a literary language; and in *De Vulgari Eloquentia* he had argued for the necessity of a national language. Even the hardships of exile had not diminished Dante's love for his homeland. There was no shortage of material well suited for the poet's glorification: studies and tributes to Dante abounded between the 1820s and the 1860s, culminating in May 1865 with three days of national festivities. Hailed as the prophet of the new united Italy, the figure of Dante galvanized the popular imagination throughout the country.[6] Critics like Bartoli and D'Ancona wrote on Dante, at least in part, in a nationalistic spirit. D'Ancona's interest in the poet, for example, was initially inspired by Francesco De Sanctis's impassioned Dante lectures in Turin (1854–55) during his exile from Naples. "La prima ventura che mi è stata concessa," wrote D'Ancona, "e della quale giorno per giorno, ora per ora, ringrazio la Provvidenza, è l'esser nato e vissuto nei tempi del Risorgimento italiano" ["The first fortune that has been conceded to me, for which day by day, hour by hour, I thank Providence, is to have been born and to have lived in the time of the Italian Risorgimento"].[7] The figure of Dante exemplified the political commitment to rebirth and national unity which pervaded the scholarly and civic activities of patriotic critics like D'Ancona and De Sanctis.

De Sanctis's lectures on Dante are shot through with nationalistic statements. His essay on *Inferno* x is a monument to the spirit of the Risorgimento. Its focus is Farinata degli Uberti, the great captain of the Ghibellines whom Dante encounters among the heretics. The essay's revolutionary spirit is evident from the first page: De Sanctis recalls the passions which brought about the French Revolution, in an effort to reproduce the sentiments underlying Dante's "concezione colossale"—Farinata. For De Sanctis, the canto's overriding theme is "amor della patria", a sentiment which Dante himself embodied: "Fatto parte per se stesso, alzatosi sopra amici e nemici, le ire e le ingiustizie partigiane sono in lui temperate da un sentimento piú nobile: dall'amor della patria" ["Having made a party unto himself, having risen above friends and enemies, the anger and partisan injustices in him were tempered by a more noble sentiment: by the love of his homeland"].[8] Who could better exemplify the transcendence of partisan feelings than Dante? It is difficult to imagine how D'Ancona could not have been moved by such rousing statements.

Besides the influences of positivism and nationalism, antiquarianism also played an important part in the move from commentary to criticism of the commentaries. A significant number of the nineteenth-century editions were made possible by the English Dantophile George, Lord Vernon, who provided the funds for the publication of the commentaries of Pietro Alighieri (1845), Jacopo Alighieri, Graziolo Bambaglioli and the "falso" Boccaccio. After Vernon's death, his son William Vernon paid for the publication of J. P. Lacaita's five-volume edition of Benvenuto da Imola.[9] By the turn of the century the majority of Dante's fourteenth- and fifteenth-century commentaries were available in modern editions.[10] Given this remarkable output, it comes as little surprise that in a review of an edition of Graziolo Bambaglioli one critic describes this period as being imbued with a "fervore di studi sugli antichi commentatori."[11] Many of the men who were involved in the production of these editions were friends, and this community exemplifies the mutual reliance of amateur and scholar. George Vernon, for example, numbered among his friends J. P. Lacaita, editor of Benvenuto da Imola, and Vincenzo Nannucci, editor of Pietro Alighieri.

Vernon's son William shared his father's fascination with Dante.[12] He too numbered many scholars among his friends, including Edward Moore, Paget Toynbee and Charles Eliot Norton. The extent of the community inhabited by the younger Vernon is remarkable. His acquaintance with Norton's work, for instance, was largely conducted through correspondence. Vernon's and Norton's interest in commentaries is evident in their correspondence: in a letter of 1888 Norton lists among the books "indispensable" to a student of Dante the commentaries of "Boccaccio, Buti, Benvenuto and [...] Landino".[13]

By the end of the nineteenth century these forces had combined to produce a steady interest in the commentaries. The positivist studies of scholars such as Bartoli and D'Ancona, the bibliographical data and initial evaluations furnished by Colomb de Batines, Carducci and Witte,[14] the elevation of Dante to a figure of national unity, the publication of critical editions of the early commentaries, and the antiquarian interests of a variety of scholars and aristocratic connoisseurs had all contributed to this development. But the different impulses underlying these activities bequeathed a varied and somewhat fragmented legacy. The studies of Carducci and Witte, for example, sought to distinguish the different critical contributions of the earliest commentators, while the work of D'Ancona and Bartoli provided the basis for a historico-philological approach to literature. Nevertheless, the sudden availability of critical editions provided new opportunities for scholars: a shift in focus from the poem itself to the nature of its interpretative legacy was now possible.

The continuation of interest in the commentaries at the turn of the century was largely due to the personal legacy of critics such as D'Ancona and Bartoli. Projects envisaged by these scholars were subsequently realized by some of their students. At Bartoli's instigation, Luigi Rocca undertook a detailed examination of Dante's earliest commentators. Michele Barbi wrote a dissertation on the poet's reception in the Renaissance under D'Ancona's supervision. Rocca's *Di alcuni commenti composti nei primi vent' anni dopo la morte di Dante* (1891) and Barbi's *Dante nel Cinquecento* (1890) are among the first book-length studies of, respectively, Dante's medieval and Renaissance commentators.[15] Somewhat later, another of Bartoli's students, Guido Biagi, helped to realize perhaps the most ambitious of his teacher's ideas, the compilation of an anthology of the commentaries. Biagi's massive undertaking, *La "Divina commedia" nella figurazione artistica e nel secolare commento* (1921), was an attempt to fulfil Bartoli's vision of a "supercommentary" that would contain, in Barbi's words, "il meglio di tutti gli espositori antichi e moderni, cronologicamente ordinato" ["the best of all the early and modern commentators, chronologically ordered"].[16] Such a project has had an enduring appeal. In the eighteenth century Francesco Cionacci had envisaged a similar but far larger project: one hundred volumes, one for each canto, which would include all the commentary written to date.[17] Some twenty years after the publication of Biagi's work Michele Barbi emphasized the importance of a compilation of commentaries for Dante criticism by calling for "uno spoglio giudizioso che raccogliesse quello che veramente giovi alla critica odierna" ["a judicious culling that would gather together what would be genuinely useful to criticism of the present day"]. A selection, Barbi added, was especially desirable with respect to the earliest commentaries, many of which were perceived to be "minori o troppo abbondanti".[18] Cionacci's idea, though in the form of Biagi's more manageable project, was finally realized, then, in the *Secolare commento*. In three volumes this "Dantone", to use Biagi's term, amassed illustrations from early manuscripts and selections from six centuries of *lecturae Dantis*.[19]

Published in 1921 to commemorate the sixth centenary of the poet's death, the first volume was dedicated to Vittorio Emanuele III, "che dié all'Italia i termini auspicati da Dante" ["who gave to Italy the aims augured by Dante"]. Once again, after the War, the nationalism which had inspired so many of the nineteenth-century studies of Dante surfaced in patriotic sentiments.

Hailed as "splendida e importantissima",[20] the *Secolare commento* represents a major milestone in Dante studies. Few libraries, especially outside Italy, could boast copies of all the commentaries included in this edition. The *Secolare commento* enabled students everywhere to consult the contributions of twenty-three of the poem's commentators ranging from Jacopo Alighieri to Raffaele Andreoli. Yet although Biagi's work was truly a boon to scholarship, attention should be paid to the nature of the passages which were omitted. There is a pattern to these omissions, one which has in turn subtly determined our understanding of the commentaries' content. The omissions are most readily discernible in the commentaries of the Middle Ages and Renaissance, many of which feature long discussions on philosophical, theological or mythological points. While many of these discussions were considerably abbreviated, the editors still took pains to retain passages from the commentators' doctrinal and allegorical explications. What tended to be omitted, for example in the commentaries of Jacopo della Lana, the Ottimo commentator, Boccaccio and Benvenuto da Imola, were passages in which myths were recounted, anecdotes concerning fictional and historical personages mentioned by Dante, lists of authorities, and observations of a more personal nature. Also excluded were the general *proemi* to the commentaries and the prefaces to individual cantos—features commonly employed by the fourteenth-century commentators. Generally, doctrinal and allegorical readings were retained at the expense of more informal or less analytic glosses. The result was a flattening of perspective: that which had previously been uneven, varied and heteroglot became univocal and homogenous. The omission of the often elaborate framing prefaces also contributed to this uniformity.

Although a few brief examples cannot do justice to the issue of selection, they can help to typify the editors' procedures. For instance, in his discussion of Dante's condemnation of Brutus and Cassius, Cristoforo Landino, wishing to distance himself from Dante's judgement, goes to considerable lengths to temper the poet's presentation. He attributes Dante's decision to his imperial sympathies, a position which Landino, a staunch Guelf, considers misguided. Landino further suggests that others would place Brutus in Paradise.[21] In the excerpt from Landino's reading in the *Secolare commento* there is no trace of this disagreement with Dante. The passage, which has clear relevance to an understanding of Landino's critical disposition, was perhaps too personal for the analytical bias of the *Secolare commento*.

Another example of the kind of cut made may be found in the excerpts from Jacopo della Lana's discussion of the "ciance" ["idle stories"] of preachers alluded to in *Paradiso*, XXIX. 110. In the midst of his lengthy disquisition on the qualities of angels, Lana suddenly interrupts his analysis to provide two examples of the long-winded speeches of contemporary clerics. The abrupt shift in tone and subject-matter is remarkable: an amusing anecdote is woven into a dry technical exposition.[22] Such striking shifts are common in the Trecento commentators' move from scholastic expositions to narratives about mythical and historical figures. This plurality of voices reflects different rhetorical and intellectual orientations. The editors' omission of such passages in the *Secolare commento*, however, tended to homogenize the variety of discourses present in the medieval commentaries. The excerpts they included rarely provide a glimpse of this interplay of narrative and analysis. Such omissions stemmed largely from a somewhat limited view of commentary, which prevented the editors from seeing it as a complex response to the poem which can encompass many styles of discourse: narrations, scholastic analysis, personal anecdote, didactic retelling of myth or history.

Despite such omissions, however, the *Secolare commento* constitutes the first concerted effort to provide scholars with a sense of the range and variety of the commentary tradition. It was a monumental project, which, in the absence of widely accessible critical editions, made it possible for students everywhere to consult previous readings of a passage. The editors of the *Secolare commento* deserve much credit for drawing attention to commentaries as an important part of the *Commedia*'s remarkable fortune. But in weighting the selections in favour of the more analytical glosses, the *Secolare commento* also conditioned perceptions of the texts themselves.

We may see many of the same impulses as conditioned work on commentary in the nineteenth century in more recent studies of commentary. I do not wish to suggest that no critical work has been done on commentary between the end of the nineteenth century and the present; I have examined the phenomenon more thoroughly elsewhere.[23] My intention here, however, is to compare the scholarship on commentary in the nineteenth and twentieth centuries, as a consideration of the similar projects undertaken in the two periods is instructive.

Recently, a wide range of scholarly activities has contributed much towards a more detailed reading of commentary. This resurgence of interest in commentary has taken a number of forms: new critical editions or reissues of medieval and Renaissance commentaries (Jacopo Alighieri, Filippo Villani, the Anonimo Lombardo, the Chiose Ambrosiane, Francesco da Buti, and Bernardino Daniello); overviews of particular periods of commentary; surveys of the sources employed by Trecento commentators; investigations of medieval poetics; and examinations of Dante as a commentator on his own work.[24] The most ambitious undertaking is undoubtedly the Dartmouth Dante Project, which will make available through a database roughly sixty of the poem's major commentaries. As this range of activity attests, commentary is being explored on a number of levels: editorial, rhetorical, historical, and theoretical.

Recent work by Alastair Minnis has offered an important conceptual advance in the study of commentary. By treating commentary as a genre Minnis focuses attention on it as an object of study in its own right. For Minnis, commentary is a productive mode of medieval criticism which has important ramifications for later periods like the Renaissance. Minnis's work bespeaks a more inclusive approach, one which sees commentary as a European phenomenon. While most of Minnis's work has focused on commentaries on the Bible and ancient works, a recent anthology which he helped to edit includes excerpts from fourteenth-century commentaries on the *Commedia*.[25] By addressing the larger issue of commentary in general, this anthology provides a revealing perspective on critical treatments of Dante commentators and commentaries. It is in this way that attention to Minnis's work can be useful: not primarily as a model, but as a guide to producing a model suited to the particular requirements and problems of studying the commentary tradition generated by the *Commedia*. Specialized studies on dating, sources and attribution are important, but they are often carried out in isolation from larger theoretical concerns. Such investigations would benefit from a more comprehensive view of the range and force of medieval commentary.

Most of the recent work, however, has focused on production and representation: on what the text, considered from a formal standpoint, means. I believe we might profitably turn to the related issues of reception and influence. Two theorists, one recent and one whose work has recently come to light, serve as cogent reminders of concerns less often addressed in criticism of the commentaries. Critics have often remarked on the frequent absence of a unifying perspective in the Trecento and Quattrocento commentaries. Such statements, however, tell us more about the preconceptions of scholars than they do about the manner in which Dante's first readers approached the text. Medieval textual meaning is essentially pluralistic; a wide range of voices—theological, philosophical, popular, legal and analytic—is often prominent. What is needed is a way of gauging the social force and ultimately the meaning of these different registers of writing. For example, Bakhtin's sociohistorical method, which sees all utterances as phenomena marked with their concrete origins and history, is helpful here. In Bakhtin's "dialogical" analysis, words have particular inflections, that is, their meanings vary according to their different social environments and historical moments. Each word, for Bakhtin, becomes a locus of competing forces, and criticism must take account of this vital ideological struggle for meaning. Hence a given word or phrase in a commentary is soaked with meanings, some particular to the commentary tradition, some oriented towards a current philosophical question, some imbued with political overtones, but all present in the word simultaneously.[26]

This account of language has a diachronic element as well. Such concepts as dialogism ultimately lead to a consideration of the dialectic between a work's original moment and its point of reception. Future treatments of the commentaries would also benefit from a consideration of Hans Robert Jauss's theories of reception, which would do much to promote a more historical understanding of medieval modes of reading. For Jauss, literary history is formed, at least in part, by previous readings and valuations. The *Commedia* does not exist in a static world of universal values presenting one unchanging face through time. Jauss's work on reception stresses the importance of attending to the manner in which a work is successively transformed and redefined at the hands of various readers or receivers.[27] Since commentaries tend to reflect the socio-historical and cultural circumstances of the time of their composition, they provide an excellent view of the *Commedia*'s historicity and its productive potential. Attention to recent studies of medieval exegesis and poetics, Bakhtin's notion of dialogism, and Jauss's emphasis on the historicity of a work might just slow us down enough to appreciate the inflections of commentaries, that is, the social function of Dante's poem at a given time.

Future evaluations of the commentaries will need to take account of the entire complex of influences which inform medieval and Renaissance commentaries. This may best be achieved through a heightened awareness of the critical tradition which has come to shape our present views. Only through an understanding of our own, perhaps unconscious, formation as critics can we hope to understand the way in which commentary functions as a genre, as a flexible, at times creative, response to Dante's poem. This awareness, in my view, must be accompanied by a self-conscious and self-critical stance if we are to avoid the reification which has accompanied the less reflexive historical criticism of the past.

Such caution and deliberation are especially desirable at this moment. Criticism of the commentaries, as the foregoing examination shows, has approximated to a periodic form. The current resurgence of interest, which follows a period of relative inactivity between 1960 and 1975, resembles the late nineteenth-century fascination with commentary.[28] A similar complex of influences and investments informs the study of commentary both then and now. While the parallels are necessarily inexact, there are enough repetitions for a careful consideration of the features of the earlier moment to assist in directing studies on commentary today. Forms of patronage, for example, are important to the circulation of commentaries in both moments. While it would be easy to dismiss the activities of George and William Vernon as those of amateurs and dilettantes, especially since few would praise the precision or scholarship of the editions they subsidized, this would be to mistake the effect of the Vernons' intervention. By reproducing and circulating commentaries long unavailable or inaccessible, the Vernons helped to amass a kind of scholarly capital on which critics could draw. Today, in the United States of America, the National Endowment for the Humanities has contributed over half a million dollars to the creation of the Dartmouth Dante Project, and this action is a modern equivalent of the financial backing of figures like the Vernons. I have taken liberties in drawing this analogy, but the effects of the Vernons' philanthropy and the NEH's grants are similar: both are preconditions that facilitate the diffusion and further study of the commentaries.

Parallels between our moment and the end of the nineteenth century may also be discerned in the kind of projects envisaged. The periodic nature of interest in commentaries is perhaps best seen in the conceptions of massive compilations and distribution of the commentaries. In the nineteenth century, as we have seen, Adolfo Bartoli conceived of an anthology "che avrebbe voluto contenere il meglio di tutti gli espositori antichi e moderni" ["that would contain the best of all the early and modern commentators"]. In 1982, Robert Hollander was "struck by the idea that a computerized database of the commentaries" would alleviate the inadequate holdings of libraries everywhere.[29] In broad terms, the Dartmouth Dante Project is the computer counterpart of Bartoli's and Cionacci's earlier conceptions.

The explosion of information that a database brings with it will require careful thought. After all, the Dartmouth Dante Project does not come with instructions for critical use. When we address commands to the database, we are making, albeit surreptitiously, methodological choices. This aspect needs careful consideration, because the particular form in which the Project offers commentaries encourages, unconsciously and unintentionally, certain kinds of interpretation. Its very strengths will carry with them certain weaknesses. For example, it will be tempting for anyone discussing a given passage simply to call up the information from the commentaries on the lines in question. This is not, however, a neutral activity: boundaries are drawn in the very specifications. It will be easy, given the wealth of information that will appear, to lose oneself in what is basically a formalism and a textualism whose thickness may well serve to insulate the interpreter from other questions. What is easily occluded by the power of the Dartmouth Dante Project is historical context. Commentaries, like all texts, are social products whose social dimensions are reflected in their physical constitutions.[30] The introduction of this new set of material conditions for the study of commentary must be accompanied by a critical self-consciousness that it will take some pains to develop.

Put another way, one must be sensitive to the difference in form between manuscripts or books and a database. This is a drastic change in bibliographic coding. In manuscript or book form, a version or an edition of a commentary reminds us with relentless particularity that commentary is a social act, that each text is imbued with cultural, social and historical specificity. The physical form of the version testifies to these conditions. Only by attending to the social and cultural circumstances that conditioned the responses of each commentator can we begin to understand the complex of material presented in them. While the Dartmouth Dante Project contains the complete texts of the commentaries included in it, in practice one will read selections from many commentaries. Using the Dartmouth Dante Project as it is designed will allow the user to produce a personal text—essentially one's own book, a highly subjective version which suggests that commentary is one large text, rather than a collection of books. When we avail ourselves of the Olympian overview provided by the database, it is important to remember that our perspective can mislead us. The Dartmouth Dante Project is a re-presentation of commentary, and it should be handled as such. Using the Project is like viewing the ground from a great height, and we must bear in mind that what looks like a number of indistinguishable ants is in fact a number of individual authors. For it is only when we have a clear sense of the contents and omissions of a project, of what it foregrounds and what it occludes, of what choices are implicit in the act of constructing a method, that we can begin to use a given critical apparatus effectively.

Such considerations, while important, only hint at the methodological questions that the Dartmouth Dante Project will raise. For instance, we shall have to come to terms with issues of coverage, since it is not reasonable, nor perhaps even possible, to have more than a cursory familiarity with all the commentaries. We may have to develop reliable sampling techniques in order to map the face of the commentary tradition. Perhaps cartography may be taken as the leading metaphor for our new relation to the commentaries: they represent a largely uncharted continent, and we shall need shrewd scholarly strategies to open up this new world. But unlike the brave new world discovered by Miranda, this continent is "new to us" less out of innocence than because of the need for a systematic rethinking of our relation to the past—one that displaces the positivist scholarship of the nineteenth century in favour of a different and more demanding hermeneutic.

NOTES

1 In tracing the history of criticism about the commentaries on the *Commedia* it is important to bear in mind the difference between the commentary tradition and the critical tradition. By the commentary tradition I mean commentaries on the *Commedia*, criticism of an interpretative nature whose object is the poetic text. In this essay I use the expression "the critical tradition" to refer to studies of a metacritical nature—scholarly work which has as its object the commentaries themselves.

2 For recent discussions of the sources employed by Dante's medieval and Renaissance commentators, see Emilio Bigi's two essays, "Dante e la cultura fiorentina del Quattrocento" and "La tradizione esegetica della *Commedia* nel Cinquecento", in his *Forme e significati nella "Divina commedia"* (Bologna, Cappelli, 1981), pp. 145–72 and 173–209; A. M. Caglio, "Materiali enciclopedici nelle *Expositiones* di Guido da Pisa", *Italia medioevale e umanistica*, 24 (1981), 213–56; G. De Medici, "Le fonti dell'Ottimo commento alla *Divina commedia*", *Italia medioevale e umanistica*, 26 (1983), 71–123; L. Caricato, "Il *Commentarium* all'*Inferno* di Pietro Alighieri", *Italia medioevale e umanistica*, 26 (1983), 124–50. For recent attempts to date medieval and Renaissance commentaries, see S. Bellomo, "Primi appunti sull'*Ottimo commento* dantesco: II, Il codice palatino 313, primo abbozzo dell'*Ottimo commento*", *Giornale storico della letteratura italiana*, 157 (1980), 533–40; L. Pertile, "Le edizioni dantesche del Bembo e la data delle *Annotationi* di Trifone Gabriele", *Giornale storico della letteratura italiana*, 160 (1983), 393–402. On the dating of Landino's lectures on Dante for the Florentine Studio, see A. Field, "Cristoforo Landino's First Lectures on Dante", *Renaissance Quarterly*, 39 (1986), 16–48. Recent book-length studies include A. Canal, *Il mondo morale di Guido da Pisa interprete di Dante* (Bologna, Patron, 1981); D. Pietropaolo, *Dante Studies in the Age of Vico* (Ottawa, Dovehouse, 1989); C. Paolazzi, *Dante e la "Comedìa" nel Trecento* (Milan, Università Cattolica, 1989).

3 See A. D'Ancona, *La Beatrice di Dante* (Pisa, Nistri, 1865) for D'Ancona's view of Beatrice. On Bartoli's response to Rocca's discovery, see R. Renier, "Adolfo Bartoli", in *Dante e la Lunigiana*, by various authors (Milan, Hoepli, 1909), pp. 465–66. On Bartoli's critical legacy, see F. Neri, "La scuola del Bartoli", *Rivista d'Italia*, 2 (1913), 673–92.

4 R. Renier, "Adolfo Bartoli", p. 465.

5 For discussions of the figure of Beatrice in the eighteenth century, see D. Pietropaolo, *Dante Studies in the Age of Vico*, pp. 263, 357–71.

6 For a discussion of Dante's immense popularity in the nineteenth century, see C. Dionisotti, "Varia fortuna di Dante", in his *Geografia e storia della letteratura italiana* (Turin, Einaudi, 1967), pp. 222–42.

7 Quoted in L. Russo, *Alessandro D'Ancona e la scuola storica italiana* (Bologna, Zanichelli, 1936), p. 18.

8 F. De Sanctis, "Il Farinata di Dante" [1869], in his *Saggi critici*, edited by L. Russo, 3 vols (Bari, Laterza, 1952), II, 281–308 (pp. 281, 285).

9   For an account of George Vernon's life, see the *Dictionary of National Biography*, edited by L. Stephen and S. Lee (reissue), 22 vols (London, Smith and Elder, 1908–09), xx, 275–76. Editions of the commentaries and of the *Commedia* made possible by George Vernon include: *Le prime quattro edizioni della "Divina commedia" letteralmente ristampate*, edited by G. G. Warren, Lord Vernon (London, Boone, 1858); *L'"Inferno" di Dante Alighieri disposto in ordine grammaticale e corredato di brevi dichiarazioni di G. G. Warren, Lord Vernon*, 3 vols (London, Boone, 1858–65); *"Inferno" secondo il testo di B. Lombardi con ordine e schiarimento per uso di forestieri di Lord Vernon* (Florence, Piatti, 1841); *Petri Allegherii super Dantis Ipsius Genitoris Comoediam Commentarium*, edited by V. Nannucci (Florence, Garinei, 1846); *Chiose sopra Dante, testo inedito, ora per la prima volta pubblicato* (Florence, Piatti, 1846), commonly known as the "falso Boccaccio". William Vernon provided the funds for the printing of *Benevenuti de Rambaldis de Imola Comentum super Dantis Aldigherij Comoediam*, edited by J. P. Lacaita, 5 vols (Florence, Barbèra, 1887).

10 Besides the editions made possible by patronage, a number of other critical editions appeared: *L'Ottimo commento della "Divina commedia", testo inedito di un contemporaneo di Dante*, edited by A. Torri, 3 vols (Pisa, Capurro, 1827–29); *Lo "Inferno" della "Commedia" di Dante Alighieri col comento di Guiniforto delli Bargigi*, edited by G. Zac[c]heroni (Marseille, Mossy; Florence, Molini, 1838); *Commento di Francesco da Buti sopra la "Divina commedia" di Dante Allighieri*, edited by C. Giannini, 3 vols (Pisa, Nistri, 1858–62); *Chiose anonime alla prima cantica della "Divina commedia" di un contemporaneo del Poeta*, edited by F. Selmi (Turin, Stamperia Reale, 1865); *Il codice cassinese della "Divina commedia", per cura dei monaci benedettini della badia di Monte Cassino* (Monte Cassino, Tipografia di Monte Cassino, 1865); *"Commedia" di Dante Allaghieri col Commento di Jacopo della Lana bolognese*, edited by L. Scarabelli, 3 vols (Bologna, Tipografia Regia, 1866–67); *Commento alla "Divina commedia" d'anonimo fiorentino del secolo XIV*, edited by P. Fanfani, 3 vols (Bologna, Romagnoli, 1866–74); Filippo Villani, *Il commento al primo canto dell'"Inferno"*, edited by G. Cugnoni (Città di Castello, Lapi, 1896); *Fratris Iohannis de Serravalle Ord. Min. Episcopi et Principus Firmani Translatio et Comentum Totius Libri Dantis Aldigherii*, edited by M. Da Civezza and T. Domenichelli (Prato, Giachetti, 1891); *La "Commedia" di Dante Alighieri, col commento inedito di Stefano Talice da Ricaldone*, edited by V. Promis and C. Negroni (Turin, Bona, 1886). The impact of these editions may be seen in the commentaries of Scartazzini (1874) and Tommaso Casini (1921), both of whom refer extensively to the fourteenth- and fifteenth-century commentators. Unfortunately, however, most of the nineteenth-century editions are seriously flawed: they are frequently based on only one or two manuscripts; editors did not identify the patristic and classical sources cited by the commentators; and they occasionally omitted glosses they considered irrelevant. Notwithstanding such editorial shortcomings, the availability of these editions did much to facilitate evaluation of the medieval commentaries by specialists. A notorious example of loose editorial procedures is Scarabelli's justifiably maligned edition of Jacopo della Lana. The edition's deficiencies include a failure to consult all the existing manuscripts, the absence of any consistent criteria in the determination of readings, arbitrary emendations and reordering of glosses, and careless transcription of material throughout.

11 "Cronaca", *Giornale storico della letteratura italiana*, 19 (1892), 214.

12 Further evidence of William Vernon's interest in the early commentaries may be found in his own studies on Dante: see W. W. Vernon, *Readings on the "Inferno" of Dante Chiefly Based on the Commentary of Benvenuto da Imola* (London–New York, Macmillan, 1894). Vernon's readings of *Purgatorio* (1889–97) and *Paradiso* (1900–09) were also based on Benvenuto.

13 "Correspondence between Charles Eliot Norton and the Honorable William Warren Vernon, 1869–1908", edited by W. C. Lane, *Annual Report of the Dante Society of America*, 47–48 (1930), 25. Benvenuto, in particular, is frequently mentioned in the two men's correspondence. Norton had once proposed that the Dante Society of America print an edition of Benvenuto.

14 P. Colomb de Batines, *Bibliografia dantesca*, 2 vols (Prato, Tipografia Aldina, 1845–46); G. Carducci, "Della varia fortuna di Dante", in his *Opere* [Edizione nazionale], 30 vols (Bologna, Zanichelli, 1935–44), x, 253–420; K. Witte, *Essays on Dante*, translated and edited by C. M. Lawrence and P. H. Wicksteed (London, Duckworth, 1898).

15 L. Rocca, *Di alcuni commenti della "Divina commedia" composti nei primi vent' anni dopo la morte di Dante* (Florence, Sansoni, 1891); M. Barbi, *Dante nel Cinquecento* (Pisa, Scuola Normale, 1890; reprinted Rome, Polla, 1975). For a largely negative review of Rocca's study, see F. Roediger in *Rivista critica della letteratura italiana*, 7 (1891), 99–114.

16 Quoted by R. Renier, "Adolfo Bartoli", p. 471.

17 A modern equivalent of Cionacci's project may be identified in the *Lectura Dantis Americana*, which is being published by the University of Pennsylvania Press; the general editor of the project is Robert Hollander. The first two volumes are now available: see A. K. Cassell, *Inferno I* and R. Jacoff and W. A. Stephany, *Inferno II* (both Philadelphia, University of Pennsylvania Press, 1989).

18 M. Barbi, "Un cinquantennio di studi danteschi (1866–1936)", in his *Problemi fondamentali per un nuovo commento della "Divina commedia"* (Florence, Sansoni, 1955), p. 141.

19 *La "Divina commedia" nella figurazione artistica e nel secolare commento*, edited by G. Biagi, G. L. Passerini and E. Rostagno, 3 vols (Turin, UTET, 1921–39). (Biagi, Passerini, and Rostagno edited the first two volumes; volume III was edited by the same scholars and Umberto Bosco.) Biagi refers to Cionacci's and Bartoli's earlier conceptions on p. ix of his preface. See also P. Colomb de Batines, *Bibliografia dantesca*, I, 3–4 for a description of Cionacci's project. The twenty-three commentaries excerpted in the *Secolare commento* are Jacopo Alighieri, Graziolo Bambaglioli, the Selmi *Chiose anonime*, Jacopo della Lana, the *Ottimo commento* [Andrea Lancia], Pietro Alighieri, Guido da Pisa, Boccaccio, the "false" Boccaccio, Benvenuto da Imola, Francesco da Buti, the Anonimo Fiorentino, Giovanni Serravalle, Cristoforo Landino, Alessandro Vellutello, Bernardino Daniello, Lodovico Castelvetro, Lorenzo Magalotti, Pompeo Venturi, Baldassare Lombardi, Antonio Cesari, Niccolò Tommaseo and Raffaello Andreoli.

20 M. Barbi, "Notizie sulla '*Divina commedia*' nella figurazione artistica e nel secolare commento", *Studi danteschi*, 5 (1922), 135. For further testimony of the nationalistic sentiments underlying Biagi's project, see Vittorio Cian's review of it in *Giornale storico della letteratura italiana*, 84 (1924), 112–13.

21 *Comedia del divino poeta Dante Alighieri, con la dotta & leggiadra spositione di Cristoforo Landino* (Venice, Stagnino, 1536), p. 192^v.

22 *"Commedia" col Commento di Jacopo della Lana*, III, 444. Significantly, in his edition of Lana, Scarabelli sets the two anecdotes apart from the more didactic portion of the commentary. Francesco Mazzoni suggests that this digression shows Lana's sensitivity to his audience of students, in that the anecdotes serve to alleviate the dryness of his doctrinal exposition: see F. Mazzoni, "Jacopo della Lana e la crisi nell'intepretazione della *Divina commedia*", in *Dante e Bologna nei tempi di Dante* (Bologna, Commissione per i testi di lingua, 1967), pp. 265–306 (pp. 301–02).

23 See my *Commentary and Ideology: Dante in the Renaissance* (Durham, North Carolina, Duke University Press, 1993), pp. 3–24.

24 For studies of the sources employed by the Trecento commentators, see n. 2 above.

25 *Medieval Literary Theory and Criticism, c.1100–c.1375: The Commentary Tradition*, edited by A. J. Minnis and A. B. Scott with the assistance of D. Wallace (Oxford, Oxford University Press, 1988). See also A. J. Minnis, *Medieval Theory of Authorship*, second edition (Aldershot, Wildwood House, 1988).

26 For Mikhail Bakhtin's views on language, see the chapter "Discourse in the Novel", in his *The Dialogic Imagination*, translated by C. Emerson and M. Holquist (Austin, University of Texas Press, 1981), pp. 259–422.

27 See H. R. Jauss, "Literary History as a Challenge to Literary Theory", in his *Toward an Aesthetic of Reception*, translated by T. Bahti (Brighton, Harvester, 1982), pp. 3–45.

28 I list below only some of the more notable studies published between the late 1950s and the 1970s. One of the most illuminating is C. Dionisotti, "Dante nel Quattrocento", in *Atti del Congresso internazionale di studi danteschi*, 2 vols (Florence, Sansoni, 1965–66), I, 333–78. Other studies on medieval and Renaissance commentaries published in the same period include G. Padoan, *L'ultima opera di Giovanni Boccaccio: le Espositioni sopra il Dante* (Padua, Cedam, 1959); F. Tateo, *Retorica e poetica fra medioevo e Rinascimento* (Bari, Adriatica, 1960); A. Ciotti, "Il concetto della 'figura' e la poetica della 'visione' nei commentatori trecenteschi della *Commedia*", *Convivium*, 30 (1962), 405–16; G. Fallani, *Pietro Alighieri e il suo commento al "Paradiso"* (Florence, Le Monnier, 1965); R. Hollander, *Allegory in Dante's "Commedia"* (Princeton, Princeton University Press, 1969); G. Ronconi, *Le origini delle dispute umanistiche sulla poesia* (Rome, Bulzoni, 1976); L. La Favia, *Benvenuto da Imola, dantista* (Madrid, Porrúa Turanzas, 1977); F. Caliri, "Guido da Montefeltro nel commento di Benvenuto", in *Dante nel pensiero e nella esegesi dei secoli XIV e XV*, edited by A. and P. Borraro (Florence, Olschki, 1975), pp. 319–41; A. Ciotti, "Fra Dolcino, Dante e i commentatori trecenteschi della *Commedia*", in *Psicoanalisi e strutturalismo di fronte a Dante*, edited by E. Guidubaldi, 3 vols (Florence, Olschki, 1972), I, 429–42; G. Messori, "Il *Commentarium* di Pietro Alighieri" and D. Bertocchi, "Le oscillazioni dell'Ottimo commento", both in *Lectura Dantis Mystica*, edited by D. Bertocchi (Florence, Olschki, 1969), pp. 169–79 and 227–44; P. Rigo, "Il Dante di Guido da Pisa", *Lettere italiane*, 29 (1977), 196–207; S. Bellomo, "Tradizione manoscritta e tradizione culturale delle *Expositiones* di Guido da Pisa (prime note e appunti)", *Lettere italiane*, 31 (1979), 153–75; V. Cioffari, "Problems Concerning the Earliest Dante Commentaries", *Forum Italicum*, 13 (1979), 496–500; *Giovanni Boccaccio editore e interprete di Dante* (Florence, Olschki, 1979). See also the following volumes for some general studies: *Dante e Bologna nei tempi di Dante*; *Dante nel pensiero e nella esegesi dei*

secoli XIV *e* XV. A new edition of Pietro Alighieri's commentary on *Inferno* also appeared: *Il Commentarium di Pietro Alighieri*, edited by R. Della Vedova and M. T. Silvotti (Florence, Olschki, 1978).

29 R. Hollander, "The Dartmouth Dante Project", *Quaderni d'italianistica*, 10 (1989), 287–98 (p. 287).

30 I have here adapted a passage of J. J. McGann's "Some Forms of Critical Discourse", in his *Social Values and Poetic Acts* (Cambridge, Massachusetts–London, Harvard University Press, 1988), pp. 132–51 (pp. 137–38).

INDEX OF REFERENCES TO DANTE'S WORKS

This index does not include the list of liturgical references in the *Commedia* presented as an appendix to the essay by John C. Barnes, "Vestiges of the Liturgy in Dante's Verse" (pp. 264–69).

Commedia 21, 33, 60, 104, 109, 111, 112, 120, 124, 126, 133, 141, 142, 149, 151, 153, 156, 157, 159, 163, 164, 166, 174, 179, 180, 181, 194, 195, 198, 203, 211, 212, 215, 217, 219, 224, 226, 228, 231, 232, 233, 235, 241, 243, 247, 257, 271, 272, 274, 275, 276, 279, 282, 283, 288, 293, 294, 295, 296, 299

Inferno 12, 216, 219, 234, 235, 239, 272, 273, 277, 301
Limbo 219, 221, 228

I	60, 213, 216, 218, 241, 301
II	179, 214, 215, 217, 223, 225, 301
III	214, 215
IV	218–19, 220, 241
V	84, 219, 278, 279, 280, 283, 286
VI	
VII	233
VIII	223
IX	60, 63, 226
X	13, 41, 186, 203, 212, 289
XI	109, 110
XII	
XIII	38, 186, 187, 203
XIV	
XV	14
XVI	12, 221–22
XVII	273
XVIII	33, 60, 190
XIX	
XX	152, 221, 222, 228
XXI	15, 273
XXII	15
XXIII	186, 232
XXIV	
XXV	
XXVI	
XXVII	297
XXVIII	
XXIX	13
XXX	190
XXXI	91, 234
XXXII	
XXXIII	223
XXXIV	234, 284, 292

Purgatorio 12, 142, 157, 202, 203, 213, 216, 219, 229, 233, 236, 238, 240, 253, 254, 255, 256, 272, 301
Ante-Purgatory 110, 202, 236, 239, 240, 241, 242, 243, 246
cornice of sloth 182
cornice of pride 262
Terrestrial Paradise 224, 228
Valley of the Princes 241, 242

I	
II	35, 190, 209, 236, 240, 264
III	148, 189–97, 200–02, 207, 209
IV	
V	136, 240
VI	28
VII	194, 220, 241, 261
VIII	36, 226, 232, 241, 242, 243, 262
IX	179, 237, 239, 244, 252, 263
X	173, 183, 236

XI	173, 237, 260	XVI	39, 60, 136
XII	173, 242, 259	XVII	23, 225, 229, 241, 251
XIII	37, 237, 260	XVIII	38, 41, 145, 146, 150, 181, 183
XIV		XIX	194, 250
XV	254	XX	150, 181, 221, 250
XVI	132, 237	XXI	229, 250
XVII		XXII	111, 131, 250
XVIII	203	XXIII	38, 247, 248, 251, 257
XIX	237, 247	XXIV	212, 239, 250, 252
XX	188, 240, 255, 272	XXV	13, 35, 52, 163, 212, 226, 251, 252, 263, 264
XXI	240, 272		
XXII	38, 218	XXVI	212, 242, 252, 253
XXIII	133, 237	XXVII	50, 111, 133, 197, 229, 251, 252, 253
XXIV	44		
XXV	132, 237, 255	XXVIII	173
XXVI		XXIX	173, 293
XXVII	224, 236, 244, 254	XXX	28, 39, 215, 225, 246, 263
XXVIII		XXXI	36, 246, 262–63
XXIX	146, 224, 235, 238, 239	XXXII	219, 241, 246
XXX	173, 222, 228, 235, 238, 239, 254, 261	XXXIII	164, 166, 173, 178, 229, 247, 248, 263
XXXI	136, 173, 238		
XXXII	146, 147, 148		
XXXIII	35, 139–80, 226, 236, 261		

Convivio 13, 14, 21, 26, 35, 60, 84, 133, 185, 186, 191, 193, 203, 204, 209, 211, 217, 226, 227, 228, 260

Paradiso 13, 60, 157, 162, 163, 164, 166, 216, 219, 225, 226, 229, 233, 245, 246, 253, 254, 256, 262, 282, 286, 301

Celestial Rose 212, 246

Empyrean 110, 245, 246, 262

Heaven of the Fixed Stars 111, 250, 251, 264

Heaven of Jove/Jupiter 145, 181, 250

Heaven of Mars 181, 249

Heaven of Mercury 249

Heaven of the Moon 184, 247, 248, 249

Heaven of Saturn 250

Heaven of Venus 248, 249

Primum Mobile 111

De Vulgari Eloquentia 13, 29, 144, 170, 171, 185, 203, 289

Epistolae

I	30
V	31
VI	53, 226, 229
VII	30
XII	30, 38
XIII	209, 227

I	150, 163, 164, 165, 179
II	173, 211
III	178, 182, 184, 247
IV	159, 164, 173, 179, 246
V	
VI	50, 118, 135, 181, 204, 205
VII	117–37, 173, 249
VIII	248
IX	38, 60
X	136, 173, 226, 253, 263
XI	158, 173, 177
XII	158, 173, 174, 177
XIII	173, 249
XIV	173, 249, 263
XV	12, 61, 78, 84, 181, 212, 231

Monarchia 51, 147, 170, 185, 212, 217, 218, 227, 228

Questio de Aqua et Terra 157

Rime

"Amor che ne la mente mi ragiona" 264

Vita nuova 15, 35, 36, 212

INDEX OF NAMES

This index does not include the list of liturgical references in the *Commedia* presented as an appendix to the essay by John C. Barnes, "Vestiges of the Liturgy in Dante's Verse" (pp. 264–69). An asterisk (*) before an entry indicates a character or place in the *Commedia*.

*Abbot of San Zeno 182, 203
Abulafia, D. 206, 207
Acheron (beast) 114
Adam 242, 252
Adam of Clermont 189, 194, 207, 208
Adolf of Nassau 182
Adrastus 193
Aeneas 179, 217, 223, 228
Aeneid: see Virgil
Affò, I. 55
Agnes, Saint 77, 91
Agresti, A. 118, 134, 135
Ahern, J. 175
Alan of Lille 159, 170
Albert of Habsburg 182
Albert of Stade 206
Albertus Magnus 178, 212
Albornoz, Cardinal 278, 286
Alcuin 101
    De Fide Sanctae Trinitatis 101
Alderotti: see Taddeo Alderotti
Alexander 188
Alexander III, Pope 182
Alexander IV, Pope 202
Alighieri: see Jacopo Alighieri; Pietro Alighieri
Altopascio 17, 46
Amauri of Narbonne 17
Amaury of Saint Amand 278
Ambrogio Sansedoni, Blessed 42
Ambrose, Saint 48
Amos (prophet) 225
Anagni 209
Anchises 222, 223, 254, 264
Ancient Mariner (Coleridge) 261
Ancona 16

Andreoli, R. 292, 301
Angela of Foligno 37
Angevin dynasty 19, 40, 50, 188, 278
Annals of Genoa 198, 208
Anne, Saint 246
Anonimo Fiorentino (commentator) 195, 301
Anonimo Lombardo (commentator) 294
Anonymus Vaticanus 206
Ansanus, Saint 40, 43
Anselm, Saint 117–37
    Cur Deus Homo 117–37
Antichrist 186, 196
Antonio "the Pilgrim", Saint 34
Antony, Saint 34
Apollinaris, Saint 46, 47
Apollo 162, 223, 229
Apollonio, M. 260
Apulia 189, 196, 200
Aquinas: see Thomas Aquinas
Arabs 85
Aragon 193, 194
Ardissino, E. 259
Arezzo 15, 18, 21, 23, 37, 49
Argenti: see Filippo Argenti
Aristotle 60, 65, 66, 67, 68, 70, 71, 72, 76, 80, 81, 82, 86, 89, 142, 151, 157, 159, 162, 174, 177, 185, 212
    De Longitudine et Brevitate Vitae 71, 72
    Economics 71
    Parva Naturalia 60, 68, 71
    Physics 86
    Politics 66, 67, 71, 72, 73, 78, 81, 82, 88, 185
Armagh 275

Index of Names

Armour, P. 53, 175, 227, 236, 259, 260, 261, 262
Arnaut de Pellegrue, Cardinal 49
Artamendi, P. 171
Ashworth, E. J. 172
Assunto, R. 246, 262
Attila the Hun 49
Auerbach, E. 263, 264
Augustine, Saint 63, 73, 98, 99, 100, 103, 105, 113, 114, 115, 139, 141, 147, 150, 151, 157, 160, 170, 172, 176, 177, 178, 227
    Aliquando (De Nuptiis et Concupiscentia) 73
    Confessions 160, 177
    De Civitate Dei 105
    De Dialectica 170
    De Doctrina Christiana 139, 140, 141, 147, 160, 169, 170, 172, 176, 178
    De Genesi ad Litteram 177
    De Magistro 160, 170
    De Trinitate 160
    Enchiridion 73
    In Johannis Evangelium Tractatus 156, 160, 176, 177, 178
Augustinian Canons 96, 97
Augustus, Emperor 182, 222, 282
Austria 284
Averroes 66, 71
Avicenna 68, 87
    Canon of Medicine 68, 87
Avignon 49, 152, 279

Babylon 199
Bacchus 249
Bacon, R. 169, 170
Baghdad 69, 87
Bakhtin, M. 295, 296, 302
Balboni, D. 261, 263
Balfour, M. 208
Bambaglioli: see Graziolo Bambaglioli
Bamberg 182
Barański, M. 168
Barański, Z. G. 139–80, 170, 173, 174, 175, 177, 178, 179, 180
Baratin, M. 169
Barbarossa: see Frederick I
Barbi, M. 291, 301
Bari 34, 278
Barkan, L. 172
Barlow, H. C. 203, 209
Barnabas, Saint 49, 50
Barnes, J. C. 167, 231–69, 261, 262
Barolini, T. 175, 177, 179
Barraclough, G. 184
Bartholomaeus Anglicus 77, 78, 91
    De Rerum Proprietatibus 77, 91

Bartholomew of Parma 68, 85
Bartoli, A. 287, 288, 289, 290, 291, 297, 299, 301
Bartolomeo Pignatelli, Archbishop of Cosenza 198, 208
Basinio of Parma 282, 286
Battaglia, S. 168
Battistini, A. 175
Baudot, Dom 258
Beatrice 14, 35, 288; *Beatrice 35, 37, 117, 120, 121, 125–28, 139–80, 215, 216, 222, 223, 225, 226, 228, 238, 239, 288, 299
Beaujouan, G. 115
Beccari: see Nicholas Beccari
Becker, E. J. 115
Bede, The Venerable 99, 103, 105, 113
Beierwaltes, W. 171
Bell, R. 53
Bellincione (Dante's grandfather) 13
Bellomo, S. 299
Bembo, P. 299
Benedetto of Cesena 282, 286
Benedict XI, Pope 19
Benedictine Order 114, 232
Benevento 188, 189, 197, 198, 199, 209
Benvenuto da Imola 195, 208, 214, 227, 256, 290, 292, 300, 301, 302
Bergin, T. G. 227
Bernard of Clairvaux, Saint 36, 95, 97, 151; *Bernard of Clairvaux 36, 247, 248, 262
Bernard of Parma 70
Bernard Gui 69, 227
Bernard, R. W. 169
Bernardino of Siena, Saint 79
Bernardus Silvestris 159, 170
Beroul 281, 286
Bertocchi, D. 302
Bertolini, L. 285
Bettini, S. 257
Biagi, G. 291, 292, 301
Bianca Lancia, Marchioness 193
Bible 62, 81, 83, 134, 139, 145, 160, 162, 171, 191, 192, 205, 207, 223, 224, 225, 235, 238, 249, 253, 255, 294
    Epistles 207, 243; see also Paul
    Exodus 92, 240
    Gospels 136, 153, 154, 155, 156, 176, 207, 229, 235, 238, 246, 248, 254, 260
    Jeremiah 207
    Numbers 92
    Psalms 209, 227, 235, 236, 237, 238, 240, 241, 242, 243, 244, 246, 251, 252, 261, 263, 264
    Revelation 273
    Samuel 208
    Song of Songs 254
    Wisdom 145, 162

Index of Names

Bieler, L. 115
Bigi, E. 299
Biller, P. 57–92, 84, 89, 91
Binni, W. 208
Blaise, A. 170
Bloch, M. 206
Boccaccio, G. 213, 227, 231, 290, 292, 301, 302
Boethius 14, 150
   De Consolatione Philosophiae 14
Bologna 20, 22, 24, 34, 64, 65, 67, 68
Bona of Pisa 34
Bonafedi: see Noffo di Guido Bonafedi
*Bonagiunta of Lucca 44
Bonaventure, Saint 36, 71, 73, 89, 90, 91, 150, 151, 155, 157, 162, 163, 164, 165, 174, 176, 177, 178; *Bonaventure, Saint 158
   Sermons 174
     Commentaria in Quatuor Libros Sententiarum 178
     Commentarius in Evangelium S. Ioannis 176
     Collationes in Hexaëmeron 177
Boniface VIII, Pope 19, 197, 204, 209, 215
Bonvesin della Riva 12
Bosco, U. 134, 152, 162, 169, 175, 176, 178, 259, 301
Boso (character in *Cur Deus Homo*) 123, 124, 125, 129
Boswell, C. S. 105, 114
Bottin, F. 170
Bowsky, W. M. 31, 53, 54, 228
Boyde, P. 170, 174
Braccini, M. 259
Bran (*Voyage of Bran*) 107
Branca, V. 175
Brandeis, I. 175
Bredero, A. H. 94, 95, 112
Brendan, Saint 277
Britain 65–66
Broglio: see Gaspare Broglio
Brownlee, K. 264
Brunetto (Dante's uncle) 13
Brunetto Latini 14, 19, 64, 65, 66, 67, 72, 85, 86, 184, 196, 206, 208
   Li Livres dou tresor 65, 66, 67, 86, 184, 206, 208
Bruni, Leonardo 25
*Brutus 292, 293
Buondelmonte de' Buondelmonti 18
Burci: see Salvo Burci
Burr, D. 89, 90
Burrow, J. A. 84
Buti: see Francesco da Buti
Butler, C. 114, 115

*Cacciaguida 12, 13, 38, 60, 61, 181, 182, 183, 212
Caetani family 19
Caglio, A. M. 299
Calabria 189
Caliri, F. 302
Camelot, P. T. 171
Campaldino 15, 16, 17, 48
Campana, A. 286
Campania 200
Canal, A. 299
Can Grande della Scala 22, 23, 28, 226
Canterbury 135
Capasso, B. 206
Capella: see Martianus Capella
Capet: see Hugh Capet
Capetian dynasty 203
Capua 187
Caramello, P. 262
Carducci, G. 290, 301
Caricato, L. 299
*Casella 190
Cashel 104, 275
Casini, T. 281, 286, 300
Cassell, A. K. 301
*Cassius 292
Castelvetro, L. 301
Castruccio Castracani 22, 23, 25, 46
Catalonia 16
Cathars 58, 68, 69, 75, 76, 82
Catherine, Saint 88
Catto, J. 29
*Cavalcante Cavalcanti 213
Cavalcanti: see Cavalcante Cavalcanti; Guido Cavalcanti
Cecco Meletti 279
Celestine V, Pope 214, 215, 216, 227, 228
Ceprano 200
*Cerberus 247
Cerchi family 19
Cervigni, D. S. 261
Cesari, A. 301
Chanson de Roland 192
Charlemagne 189, 204, 205
Charles of Anjou 16, 18, 48, 188, 189, 197, 198, 199, 200, 209
Charles of Calabria 43
Charles of Valois 19, 25
Chartres 151
Chenu, M-D. 168, 170, 171, 172, 176, 177, 178
Cherchi, P. 114
China 82
Chiose ambrosiane (commentary) 294

Index of Names

Chollet, A. 172
Christ 90, 119, 120, 121, 123, 124, 128, 133, 134, 145, 153, 214, 217, 219, 220, 222, 226, 235, 240, 244, 248, 258, 272
Christendom 82, 94, 197, 206
Christians 220
Chronica de Origine Civitatis 61
Chrysostom: see John Chrysostom
Church Militant 233, 237, 251
Church Suffering 233, 237
Church Triumphant 233, 237, 244, 246, 250
Chydenius, J. 169, 170
Cian, V. 301
Cicero 14
    De Amicitia 14
Cilicia 183
Cioffari, V. 226, 302
Cioffi, C. 261
Cionacci, F. 291, 297, 301
Ciotti, A. 179, 302
Cistercian Order 93, 95, 97, 207, 262
Clare of Montefalco 37
Clement IV, Pope 188, 197, 198, 199, 209
Clement V, Pope 49
Clogher 277
Cloyne 275
*Cocytus 234
Coens, M. 54
Colasanti, G. 200, 209
Colish, M. 170, 171, 175
Colle Val d'Elsa 49
Colomb de Batines, P. 290, 301
Colombo, M. 175
Colonna family 19
Coluccio Salutati 24
Come san Brandano andoe al paradiso dilitiano 277
Compagni: see Dino Compagni
Comparetti, D. 228
Compostela 34, 36, 43
Conrad III, Emperor 13, 181, 182, 183, 206
Conrad IV, Emperor 186, 187, 188, 196, 203, 208
Conradin 187, 196, 203
Consoli, D. 175
Constance, Empress 85, 184, 193, 194, 195, 202, 204, 205, 209
Contini, G. 177
Cork 104, 272
Cormac, King of Cashel (*Vision of Tnugdal*) 276
Corso Donati 18, 19, 25, 35
Corti, M. 174, 175, 178
Cosenza 197, 198, 209
Cosmo, U. 177, 264

Coulter, J. A. 172
Council of Lyons 186
Courcelle, P. 228
Cremona 187
Crescentius, Saint 40
Cristiani, M. 173
Croagh Patrick 96, 97
Croatia 36
Crusades 181, 183
Curtius, E. 171
Cytherea: see Venus

d'Alverny, M-T. 87, 171
D'Ancona, A. 260, 287, 288, 289, 290, 291, 299
Daniello, B. 294, 301
Daniels, D. E. 169
Dartmouth Dante Project 294, 296, 297, 298, 303
Dati, A. 54, 55
David, King 63, 192, 241
Davidsohn R. 29, 30
Davis, C. T. 39, 69, 75, 84, 87, 88, 89, 90, 179
d'Avray, D. 69, 70, 83, 87, 88, 89, 90
Debenedetti, S. 29
De Bonfils Templer, M. 173
Deely, J. 171
De Honore Mulierum 282
Delcorno, C. 86, 88
Delehaye, H. 55
Del Giudice, G. 208
Della Terza, D. 286
della Torre dynasty 27
Del Lungo, I. 287
de Lubac, H. 172, 173
Demaray, J. G. 175
De Medici, G. 299
de Pontfarcy, Y. 93–115, 113, 115, 283
De Sanctis, F. 289, 299
Desbordes, F. 169
Dido 228
Dino Compagni 12, 24, 53
    Cronica 12, 53
Dionisotti, C. 299, 302
Dis 223
Di Zenzo, S. F. 118, 134
Dolcino (heretic leader) 63, 76, 302
Dombroski, R. 168
Domenico di Bandino 279, 286
Dominic, Saint 36, 90, 158
Dominican Order 58, 59, 63, 64, 66, 69, 72, 76, 79, 88, 90
Donati: see Corso Donati; Forese Donati; Gemma Donati; Manente Donati; Piccarda Donati

Index of Names

Donegal, County 95, 271
donna gentile (Lady Philosophy) 14
D'Ovidio, F. 228, 236, 259
Down 275
Dronke, P. 173, 174
Duccio di Buoninsegna 40, 41
Dunbabin, J. 86, 88
Dunbar, H. F. 175
Durandus, Bishop 202, 209
*DXV 225

*Eagle of Justice 38
Earthly Paradise 95, 96, 102, 103, 104, 110; *Earthly Paradise 145, 146, 148
Easter 251
Easting, R. 95, 112, 113
Eco, U. 59, 84, 171
Egypt 209, 240, 244
Eisenhofer, L. 258, 260, 262, 263, 264
Eisenstein, E. 71, 88
Elijah 223
Elisha 223, 225
Elsa (river) 147, 152
Elucidarium 272
Elwert, W. T. 134
Elysian Fields (*Aeneid*) 228
Emery, K. 171, 177
Emilia 16
Emmen, A. 90
Empire, Holy Roman 186, 188, 203, 204, 205, 206
Empire, Roman 216, 217, 218
Enciclopedia dantesca 117, 134
Engelbert of Admont 68
Engels, J. 169
England 22, 80, 95, 111, 189, 199, 279, 282, 286, 290
Enrico Sandei 22
Epicureans 186, 213
Erodatus 91
Esau 214, 215, 227
Espurgatoire Seint Patriz 98
Este dynasty 24, 48, 51
*Eunoè (river) 141
Europe 57, 62, 63, 78, 79, 82, 188, 283
Evans, J. 171
Eve 241–42
Ezechiel (prophet) 225

Fabricius 255–56
Faenza 23, 34
Fair Welcome (personification) 214
Faitinelli: see Pietro Faitinelli
Faitinelli family (Lucca) 45

Fallani, G. 259, 302
False Shame (personification) 214
"Falso Boccaccio" (commentary) 290, 300, 301
Far East 69
Farinata degli Uberti 19, 21, 23; *Farinata degli Uberti 13, 213, 289, 299
Farris, G. 175
Fay, T. A. 171
Fazio of Cremona 34
Fazio degli Uberti 24
Féret, H. M. 169
Ferrara 24, 49, 278
Ferri, F. 281, 286
Fiatarone, J. J. 259
Field, A. 299
Filippo of Langusco 27
*Filippo Argenti 221, 223
Filippo Villani 294, 300
Fiocco, G. 257
Fioravanti, J. 54
FitzRalph: see Richard FitzRalph
Fiumi, E. 29, 84
Flanders 22, 279, 282, 286
Florence 11–31, 38, 39, 40, 41, 43, 44, 47, 49, 52, 53, 59, 60, 61, 62, 63, 64, 67, 68, 69, 70, 71, 73, 74, 75, 77, 78, 79, 82, 83, 85, 89, 90, 179, 183, 184, 186, 206, 211, 214, 216, 226, 231, 232, 284, 285, 287, 288, 289, 299
    Baptistery (San Giovanni) 11, 37, 49, 50, 63, 74
    Benedictine Abbey 231
    Duomo 11
    La nazione 288
    Palazzo del Podestà 11
    Palazzo della Signoria 11
    Ponte Vecchio 38
    Santa Croce 11, 14, 64, 69, 70, 72, 73, 74, 88
    Santa Maria Novella 14, 64, 69, 74, 75, 79, 83
Forese Donati 18; *Forese Donati 133
Forlí 23, 279
Foscolo, U. 201, 205, 210
    Discorso sul testo della "Divina commedia" 201
    Dei sepolcri 205, 210
Foster, K. 55, 174, 177
Fowler, G. B. 87
France 16, 33, 34, 58, 64, 74, 78, 111, 189, 199, 214, 257, 283, 289
Francesca of Rimini 279, 283; *Francesca of Rimini 219, 221, 222, 279
Francesco of Garbagnate 27
Francesco da Buti 195, 208, 227, 260, 290, 294, 300, 301

Index of Names

Francesco Sforza 282
Francis, Saint 26, 158
Franciscan Order 58, 64, 69, 74, 77, 79, 88, 232, 256, 257
Frankl, P. 257
Frati, L. 284
Freccero, J. 168, 173, 174, 179
Frederick I (Barbarossa), Emperor 48, 182, 183, 184, 185, 203, 204, 205, 206
Frederick II, Emperor 48, 184, 185, 186, 187, 188, 189, 193, 194, 200, 203, 204, 205, 206, 207
Frederick II, King of Sicily 194, 204
Frediano, Saint 44, 45, 47
Friedman, J. B. 171
Frisians 77, 78, 91
Frugoni, A. 84
Fursa (Irish monk) 277

Gabriel, Angel 246, 248
Gabriele: see Trifone Gabriele
Galeotto Malatesta 278, 279
Gallehault 280
Garden of Eden 242
Gardner, E. G. 175, 227
Garigliano (river) 199
Gaspare Broglio 281–82, 286
Gaudemus in Domino: see Gregory IX, *Decretals*
Geminianus, Saint 48, 51
Gemma Donati 14, 24
Genoa 23, 24, 284
George, Saint 41, 42, 54
George Grissaphan 277, 278, 285
Gerard of Prato 69, 71, 72, 73, 74
  Breviloquium 74, 88
*Geri del Bello 13
*Gerione 273
Germania 77, 78
Germany 58, 62, 64, 101, 104, 111, 196, 203, 205
Ghibelline Party 188, 213, 289
Ghiberto of Correggio 28
Ghisalberti, A. 173
Giacalone, G. 207
Giles of Rome 65, 66, 67, 72, 73, 84, 86
  De Regimine Principum 65, 66, 67, 84
Gilles, Saint 34
Gilson, E. 173, 174, 179
Giordano of Pisa 63, 64, 73, 79, 83, 85, 86, 88, 89, 90, 91, 92
Giovanni Bertoldi da Serravalle 300, 301
Giovanni Boccaccio: see Boccaccio, G.
Giovanni de' Cerchi 27
Giovanni de Nono 12

Giovanni "Gianciotto" Malatesta 279, 280
Giovanni Pisano 257
Giovanni Villani 12, 14, 33, 37, 43, 46, 47, 49, 50, 61, 62, 63, 64, 65, 68, 74, 76, 78, 83, 85, 182, 184, 196, 198, 199, 206, 207, 208
  Nuova cronica 12, 14, 33, 37, 43, 46, 48, 49, 50, 61, 62, 63, 64, 65, 85, 87, 182, 184, 196, 199, 206, 207, 208
Giraldus Cambrensis 96, 113
  Topographia Hibernica 96, 113
Glossa Ordinaria 176
Gmelin, H. 134
Godefroy de Bouillon 183
Godfrey of Viterbo 206
Golubovich, G. 84
Gorni, G. 175, 258
Grabmann, M. 69, 87, 172
Graf, O. 259
Gratian 70, 88
  Decretum 70, 72, 73, 88
Graziolo Bambaglioli 290, 301
Green, L. 30, 31
Gregory the Great, Saint and Pope 150
Gregory VII, Pope 200
Gregory IX, Pope 70, 72, 88, 200
  Decretals 70, 72, 73, 88
Gregory X, Pope 19
Greyhound: see *Veltro*
Grissaphan: see George Grissaphan
Guala, Cardinal 46, 47
Gubbio 23
Guelf Party 182, 183, 184, 186, 203, 206, 213, 293
Gui: see Bernard Gui
Guidi, P. 55
Guido, Bishop 47
Guido Cavalcanti 18, 19, 20, 35
*Guido da Montefeltro 302
Guido Minore da Polenta 279
Guillaume de Lorris: see *Roman de la rose*
Guiniforto delli Bargigi 300
Guiscard: see Robert Guiscard
Gurevich, A. J. 94, 95, 112
Guy, J-C. 114
Gwynn, A. 101

H. of Saltrey 95, 96, 98, 102, 103, 271, 272, 274, 275, 277
Hagman, E. 174
Hammerich, L. L. 285, 286
Hankey, A. T. 211–29, 222, 286
Haren, M. 285
*Harpies 247
Hatzfeld, H. A. 259, 263

Index of Names

Hazelden Walker, J. 258, 260
Heaven 71, 72, 93–115, 133, 144, 155, 189, 194, 198, 220, 233, 236, 241, 271, 272, 293
Hector 206
Heers, J. 29, 30
Hell 93–115, 194, 198, 212, 219, 223, 228, 233, 234, 235, 236, 241, 247, 271, 272, 282
Henry III, King of England 199
Henry V, Emperor 181
Henry VI, Emperor 47, 184, 203
Henry VII, Emperor 21, 23, 26, 27, 28, 39, 49, 50, 51, 183, 214, 228
Herlihy, D. 92
Herod 206
Hesperis 282, 286
Hilary, Saint 48, 50; see also Society of St Hilary
Hippocrates 87
   Aphorisms 87
Hippodamus 81
Hirsch-Reich, B. 229
Hohenstaufen dynasty 40, 181–210
Hollander, R. 168, 175, 177, 178, 179, 261, 297, 301, 302, 303
Holmes, G. 29, 30, 53, 64, 67, 68, 69, 86, 87, 89
Holy Land 34, 35, 64, 82
Holy See: see Papacy
Holy Spirit 151, 172
Honorius of Autun 272
Honorius II, Pope 181
Honorius IV, Pope 209
Housley, N. 55, 207, 208
Hugh of St Victor 103, 109, 113, 115
   Summa de Sacramentis Christianae Fidei 103
   De Scripturis et Scriptoribus Sacris Prenotatiunculae 115
Hugh Capet 255
Huguccio of Pisa 70, 71, 72, 73, 88
   Magnae Derivationes 71
Huillard-Bréholles, J-L-A. 206
Hungary 277, 282, 285
Huntingdonshire 95
Hyde, J. K. 29, 31, 84

Iannucci, A. A. 262
Imola 23
Innocent IV, Pope 48, 188, 199, 207
Innocent VI, Pope 279
Ireland 93–115, 271–86
Irvine, M. 176, 177
Isaiah (prophet) 225
Islam 82
Israel 244

Istoria di Tugdalo d'Ibernia 277
Italy 57, 58, 65, 68, 78, 111, 182, 188, 238, 257, 278, 280, 283, 287

Jackson, B. D. 169
"Jacobipeta" 34
Jacobus de Varagine 111, 115, 274
   Golden Legend 111, 115, 274, 284
Jacoff, R. 229, 301
Jacopo Alighieri 290, 292, 301
Jacopo da Acqui, Fra 195
   Imago Mundi 195
Jacopo della Lana 227, 232, 256, 260, 264, 292, 293, 300, 301, 302
James, Saint 34, 36, 43, 49; *James, Saint 212
James II, King of Aragon 194, 209
Jauss, H. R. 295, 296, 302
Javelet, R. 168–69, 171
Jealousy (personification) 214
Jenaro-McLennan, L. 226
Jeremiah 229
Jerusalem 49, 125, 183, 222, 240
Jesus: see Christ
Jews 197, 202, 209, 240
Joachim of Fiore, Abbot 184, 225, 229
Jocelin of Furness 96, 97, 113
Johannitius 87
   Isagoge 87
John of Pian di Carpine 69
John of Vicenza 59
John the Baptist, Saint 37, 38, 39, 40, 44, 48, 49, 50, 52, 226, 229
John the Evangelist, Saint 36, 176, 212
John Chrysostom 176
   Homiliae in Iohannem 176
John de Courcy 96
John de Frowick 277
John Scotus Eriugena 151
Johnson, W. R. 228
Jones, P. J. 285
Jordan, E. 55, 207
Joseph II, Emperor 215
Jove 217, 222
Judas 206
*Justinian, Emperor 50, 120, 181

Kilmainham 277
Kilwardby: see Pseudo-Robert Kilwardby
Klapisch-Zuber, C. 86, 92
Klauser, T. 258
Kurze, D. 84

Index of Names

Lacaita, J. P. 290, 300
Ladner, G. B. 169, 171
La Favia, L. 201, 209, 259, 302
Lambertazzi family 24
Lampe, G. W. H. 135
Lancelot du Lac 280
Lanci, A. 175, 259
Lancia: see Bianca Lancia
Land of the Women (*Voyage of Bran*) 107
Landino, C. 209, 290, 292, 293, 299, 301
Landor, W. S. 256
Lang, B. 263
Lanzoni, F. 55
Larner, J. 285
Latini: see Brunetto Latini
Latino Malabranca, Cardinal 25
La Turbia: see Turbia
Laurent, J. K. 30
Lawlor, F. X. 257
Lazio 200
Lebanon 254
Lechner, J. 258, 260, 262, 263, 264
Lefèvre, Y. 284
Le Goff, J. 93, 94, 95, 98, 99, 100, 101, 102, 112, 113, 115, 231, 256, 283
Leonardo of Pisa 58, 59
Leopardi, G. 204, 210
Lepschy, G. 168
Lerici 189
Lesnick, D. R. 87, 88, 89
*Lethe (river) 139, 238
Lewis of Bavaria, Emperor 46
Liber de Pomo 193, 195
Liber de Tribus Habitaculis Animae 114
Liri (river) 199, 200
Liver, R. 259
Livi, G. 30
Livy 218, 228
Lombardi, B. 300, 301
Lombards 14
Lombardy 15, 16, 27, 189, 199, 278
Loreto, Litany of 251, 263
Lough Derg 95, 96, 97, 271, 277, 278, 279, 283
Louis of Auxerre (*Vision of Louis d'Auxerre*) 276, 277, 279, 285
Louis of Toulouse, Saint 50
Louis the Great, King of Hungary 278
Louis IX, King of France 188, 199
Luard, H. R. 206
Lucan 208
Lucca 21, 22, 23, 25, 28, 34, 37, 44, 46, 47, 52, 53
    San Frediano (church) 45, 52

San Martino (cathedral) 45
San Paolino (church) 46
Sant' Antonio (church) 46
Serchio (river) 44
Volto Santo 34, 43, 44, 45, 52, 53
Lucifer: see Satan
Lucrezi, B. 203, 209
*Lucy, Saint 37, 53, 225
Lugarini, E. 175
Lyons 66; see also Council of Lyons
Lyttkens, H. 171

Macbeth 261
Mac Cathasaigh: see Nicholas Mac Cathasaigh
Machiavelli, N. 288
Macrobius 105, 106, 107, 114, 150
    Commentary on the Dream of Scipio 105, 106, 107, 114
Mac Tréinfhir, N. 284
Magalotti, L. 301
Mahomet 85
Mahoney, J. F. 260
Maierù, A. 170, 171
Mainardo da Susinana 16
Malabranca: see Latino Malabranca
Malachy, Saint 97, 275
Malaspina: see Saba Malaspina
Malaspina, D. R. 259
Malatesta: see Galeotto Malatesta; Giovanni "Gianciotto" Malatesta; Pandolfo Malatesta; Paolo "il Bello" Malatesta; Sigismondo Pandolfo Malatesta
Malatesta dynasty 277ff, 285
Malatesta da Verrucchio 279
Malatesta "Guastafamiglia" 278
Malatesta Ungaro 277, 278, 279, 280, 281, 282, 283, 286
*Malebolge 33
Malispini: see Ricordano Malispini
Manente Donati 14
Manetti, G. 170
Manfred of Sicily, King 41, 185, 186, 188, 189, 192, 193, 195, 196, 197, 198, 199, 200, 206, 207, 209; *Manfred of Sicily, King 191, 192, 193, 194, 195, 196, 197, 201, 202, 204, 205
Manichaeanism 90
Marcellus 222, 254
Marches (Italy) 278, 279
*Marco Lombardo 132, 237
Marco Polo 68, 87
Marcus (author of *Vision of Tnugdal*) 104, 105, 107, 108, 109, 110, 111, 114, 272
Margaret of Cortona, Saint 53

Index of Names

Marie de France 98
Marigo, A. 175
Markus, R. A. 169
Marmo, C. 171
Mars (god) 38, 41, 200
Martianus Capella 105, 106, 114
 The Marriage of Philology and Mercury 105, 106, 114
Martimort, A-G. 258, 260
Martin of Tours, Saint 43, 44, 45, 46
Martin of Troppau 183, 206
Martin, C. 83, 88
Martindale, A. 54
Martini: see Simone Martini
Mary, Blessed Virgin 39, 40, 41, 42, 44, 46, 48, 49, 51, 52, 54, 237, 241, 246, 247, 248, 263, 264; *Mary, Blessed Virgin 37, 225, 251
Masciandaro, F. 168
Massa Trabaia 22
Massèra, A. F. 281
Mastrobuono, A. 174, 261, 262
*Matelda 141, 238
Mattalia, D. 169, 176
Matthew Paris 206, 207
Mayo, County 96
Mazzantini, P. 208
Mazzeo, J. A. 169, 173, 179
Mazzoni, F. 175, 286, 302
Mazzotta, G. 151, 173, 180
McCracken, A. 262
McDannell, C. 263
McGann, J. J. 303
McGrade, S. 168
McNair, P. M. J. 202, 208, 209
McVaugh, M. 91
Meath (province of Ireland) 109
Medici, Cosimo de' 24
Meek, C. 11–31, 30
Mégier, E. 112
Meletti: see Cecco Meletti
Mellone, A. 173, 175, 179
Mengaldo, P. V. 206
Messiah 225
Messori, G. 302
Michael, Saint 237
Michael, A. 170
Milan 12, 25, 27, 48, 182, 183, 205, 206, 278, 286
Mineo, N. 171
Miniato, Saint 49
Minio-Paluello, L. 69, 86, 87, 88, 89
Minnis, A. 294, 302
Miranda (*The Tempest*) 298
Modena 34, 48, 51, 53, 55
Mone, F. J. 264

Moneta of Cremona 75, 90
Mongols 62, 69
Monneret de Villard, U. 87
Montalcino 41
Montano, R. 257–58
Montaperti 16, 20, 21, 39, 41, 47, 49, 52
Montauri: see Paolo di Tommaso Montauri
Mont Cenis Pass 34
Montecatini 17, 25
Monza 27
Moore, E. 86, 264, 290
Moses 83, 209
Mourning Fields (*Aeneid*) 229
Mtega, N. W. 172
Munich 101
Murray, A. 58, 83, 209

Najemy, J. M. 29
Nannucci, V. 290, 300
Naples 50, 58, 188, 199, 278, 289
Napoleone Orsini, Cardinal 49
Nardi, B. 173, 174, 208, 228
Narducci, E. 87
National Endowment for the Humanities 296, 297
Nello della Pietra de' Pannocchieschi 16
Nemias, Bishop of Cloyne 275
Neri del Giudice 19
Neri, F. 299
Nero 206
Niccolo de Jamsilla 192, 199, 207
Nicholas (*Golden Legend*) 274, 275
Nicholas of Butrinto 27
Nicholas of Clairvaux 95
Nicholas, Saint 34
Nicholas III, Pope 19, 25, 89
Nicholas Beccari 278
Nicholas Mac Cathasaigh 277
Nicodemus 53
Nimrod 233
Noffo di Guido Bonafedi 19
Noonan, J. T., Jr 79, 89, 91
Normans 204
Norton, C. E. 290, 301
Novati, F. 195, 208
Nuttall, A. D. 229

O'Brien, W. J. 264
Ó Cuilleanáin, C. 86, 261
Odoricus Raynaldus 209
Oedipus 193
Oerter, H. L. 29
Ohly, F. 171
Oliger, L. 89, 90, 91

Index of Names

Olivi: see Peter Olivi
Orderic Vitalis 112
Ó Riain, P. 115
Orsini: see Napoleone Orsini
Orvieto 18
Othlo 95, 112
Ottimo commento 227, 292, 299, 300, 301
Otto of Freising 112
Ottone Visconti, Archbishop 25
Ovid 153, 176, 227
    Ovide moralisé 153, 176
    Metamorphoses 153, 227
Owein (*Tractatus de Purgatorio Sancti Patricii*) 95, 102, 103, 104, 112, 271, 272, 275, 277
Oxford English Dictionary 80, 83
Ozanam, A. F. 257

Padoan, G. 118, 134, 302
Padua 12, 27, 34, 68, 284
Palermo 184, 209
Palgen, R. 173, 174
Pandolfo Malatesta 278
Pandulf, Cardinal 47
Paolazzi, C. 299
Paolini, L. 87
Paolino Minorita 227
Paolo di Tommaso Montauri 53
Paolo "il Bello" Malatesta 278, 280, 282, 283; *Paolo Malatesta 221, 222, 279
Papacy 183, 186, 188, 196, 206, 209, 214
Papal States 199, 278
Paradise: see Heaven
Paris (city) 14, 57, 64, 69, 70, 93
Paris (prince) 206
Paris: see Matthew Paris
Parker, D. 287–303, 302
Parma 18, 28, 33, 34, 48
Parodi, E. G. 262
Passau Anonymous 84
Passerini, G. L. 301
Passion Sunday 252
Patarines 90
Patrick, Bishop 113, 114
Patrick, Saint 96, 97, 111, 274, 275, 276
Paul, Prior of Lough Derg 277
Paul, Saint 38, 49, 105, 107, 150, 160, 161, 162, 171, 172, 176, 179, 217
    Epistles 150, 160, 161, 162, 171, 172, 176, 178, 179
    Visio Pauli 179
Paulinus, Saint 46, 47, 50
Pavia 27
Pears, E. 84

Pelikan, J. 135
Pellegrue: see Arnaut de Pellegrue
Pelster, F. 88
Pentecost 251, 252
Pépin, J. 172, 175, 178
Peraldus: see William Peraldus
Pertile, L. 151, 168, 173, 176, 179, 299
Peter of Auvergne 72, 88
Peter, Saint 36, 38, 46, 47, 49, 237; *Peter, Saint 50, 212, 252
Peter III of Aragon, King 194
*Peter Damian, Saint 250
Peter Lombard 71, 73, 163, 178, 179
    Sentences 71, 73, 75, 80, 82, 163, 169, 170, 178, 179
Peter Olivi 14, 70, 74, 75, 79, 80, 89, 92
    De Perfectione Evangelica 92
Peters, E. 29
Petrarch 24, 231
Petrus Comestor 93, 95
Peyer, H. 53
Pézard, A. 170, 173
Pezzana, A. 55
Pharaoh 48
Philip, Saint 49, 50
Piacenza 34, 58
Pia de' Tolomei 16
Picard, J-M. 115, 271–86, 283
*Piccarda Donati 247
Piccioni, L. 282, 286
Pier della Vigna 187, 207; *Pier della Vigna 187
Pier Pettinaio, Saint 37, 42
Pietro Alighieri 208, 227, 288, 290, 299, 300, 301, 302, 303
Pietro d'Abano 68
Pietro Faitinelli, Ser 20
Pietropaolo, D. 299
Pignatelli: see Bartolomeo Pignatelli
Pilate: see Pontius Pilate
Piramus 147
Pisa 12, 22, 23, 27, 37, 62, 85, 257
Pisano: see Giovanni Pisano
Pistoia 18, 23, 43
Plato 142, 150, 151, 159, 160, 173
    Timaeus 150, 159
Poitiers 48, 234
Polynices 193
Pontieri, E. 208
Pontius Pilate 214
Prato 23
Promised Land: see Israel
Provence 16, 198
Pseudo-Dionysius 150
Pseudo-Robert Kilwardby 169, 170

Purgatorio di san Patrizio 277
Purgatory 93–115, 186, 191, 195, 201, 208, 233, 236, 271
Pusterla, Archbishop 181

Quintavalle, A. C. 53

Raimondi, E. 259
Raimondo "the Palmer", Saint 34
Rainier Sacconi 75, 84, 91
Ravenna 28, 279
Rees, A. & B. 114
Reeves, M. 226, 229
Reggio Emilia 34
Reggio, G. 118, 134, 163, 169, 175, 176, 178, 259
Regnum: see Sicily, Kingdom of
Regulus, Saint 44, 45
Remigio de' Girolami 12, 14, 70, 74, 75, 76, 84, 89, 90, 91
    Contra Falsos Ecclesie Professores 75, 89
Renier, R. 288, 299, 301
Reparata, Saint 39, 40, 49, 50
Rheinfelder, H. 259, 260, 263
Riccardo of Camino 28
Riccobaldo of Ferrara 61
Richard, Saint 45
Richard FitzRalph 277
Ricoldo of Monte Croce 69, 87
Ricordano Malispini 198, 208
Rigo, P. 262, 302
Rimini 34, 277, 279, 280, 281, 282, 283, 285, 286
*Ripheus 220, 221
Ristoro of Arezzo 65, 66, 68, 85
Robert of Naples, King 50
Robert Guiscard 183
Robertson, D. W., Jr. 168
Rocca, L. 288, 291, 299, 301
Roediger, F. 301
Roger Bacon: see Bacon, R.
Roland 208
Romagna 15, 25, 278, 282
Roman de la rose 213–14
Roman liturgy 236, 248, 253, 258
"Romans, King of the" 205, 206
Rome 13, 14, 33, 34, 35, 43, 78, 81, 182, 278, 284, 286; see also Empire; Papacy
    Ponte Sant' Angelo 33
    St Peter's 33
    Veronica (relic) 36
Romena 16

Ronconi, G. 302
Roques, R. 135
Rostagno, E. 301
Rubinstein, N. 85
Rudolf of Habsburg 182, 261
Ruef, H. 169
Runciman, S. 209
Russell, J. C. 29
Russo, L. 299
Russo, P. F. 208
Rutebeuf 189, 207
Ryan, C. 117–37

Saba Malaspina 192, 199, 207
St Bernard Pass 34
St Emmeram 95
St Patrick's Purgatory 95, 102, 103, 111, 114, 272, 274, 276, 277, 278, 279, 281, 282, 283, 286
St Victor (school) 151
Sacconi: see Rainier Sacconi
Salef (river) 183
Salimbene de Adam 59, 69, 83, 84, 87, 187, 207
Salmon, P. 258
Salmoneus 223
Salome 38
Salutati: see Coluccio Salutati
Salvetti, G. 259
Salvo Burci 76, 90
Samain (boundary of Celtic year) 107, 115
Sanarica, M. 174
Sandei: see Enrico Sandei
San Germano, Peace of 200
San Gimignano 34
San Godenzo 23
Sansedoni: see Ambrogio Sansedoni
Sansovino, F. 209
Sant'Adriano, Cardinal of 199
Sapegno, N. 173, 175, 176, 177, 179, 214
*Sapia 37, 42
Sapori, A. 84
Saracens 62, 63, 64, 67, 69, 85, 197, 208
Sarah (Biblical figure) 63, 66, 85
Sardanapalus 61, 66, 84, 86
Sarolli, G. R. 261
Sarri, F. 174
Sarteano 16
Sarzana 20
Satan 93, 110, 114, 186, 234, 258, 273, 274
Savinus, Saint 40
Scarabelli, L. 300, 302
Scartazzini-Vandelli edition of *Commedia* 118, 134, 300

Index of Names

Schmaus, M. 174
Schmitt, F. S. 117
Selmi, F. 301
Seneca 206
Serravalle: see Giovanni Bertoldi da Serravalle
Servasanto of Faenza 70, 74, 75, 76, 77, 78, 79, 88, 89, 90, 91
    Liber de Exemplis Naturalibus 75, 77
    Summa de Poenitentia 75
    Antidotarium Animae 91
Seymour, M. C. 91
Seymour, St J. D. 101, 113, 114
Sforza: see Francesco Sforza
Sibyl of Cumae 223, 224, 225, 229
Sichaeus 228, 229
Sicily 184, 188, 189, 193, 194, 198, 209
Sicily, Kingdom of 188, 196, 196, 199, 200
Siena 12, 16, 20, 21, 22, 37, 39, 40, 41, 42, 43, 44, 49, 51, 52, 62, 85, 257, 275, 282
Sigismondo Pandolfo Malatesta 282
Simone Martini 40, 41
Simone, R. 169
Sinclair, J. D. 131
Singleton, C. S. 131, 168, 170, 227, 260, 263
Siriasi, N. 67, 86, 87
Slander (personification) 214
Smalley, B. 172
Smith, R. 83, 92
Soave-Bowe, C. 181–210
Society of St Hilary 48
Solinus 65
Solomon 145
*Sordello 243
Southern, R. W. 94, 112, 135
Sparta 81
Speier 27
Spicq, C. 172
Starn, R. 20, 30, 31
Station Island 96
*Statius 216, 221, 237, 239, 240
Stäuble, A. 263
Stefano Talice da Ricaldone 300
Stephany, W. A. 301
Stephens, J. N. 87
Stopani, R. 53
Storia di Furseo monaco 277
Strasbourg 58
Strata Claudia 33, 53
Strayer, J. R. 207
Strecker, K. 284
Strnad, A. A. 286
Strubel, A. 172
"Sultan of Lucera": see Manfred of Sicily
Swabia, House of: see Hohenstaufen dynasty

Syria 39
Syrus, Saint 46, 47

Tacitus 77, 210
    Agricola 210
    Germania 77
Taddeo Alderotti 67, 68, 87
Talice: see Stefano Talice
Tartars 68, 87
Tateo, F. 302
Temperini, L. 173, 174
Terrestrial Paradise: see Earthly Paradise
Thaddeus of Suessa 187
Themis 153
Thomas of Tuscany 183, 196, 206, 208
Thomas Aquinas, Saint 36, 50, 72, 75, 81, 88, 89, 136, 137, 155, 170, 176, 178, 212;
    *Thomas Aquinas 157, 158, 159
    Catena Aurea in Quatuor Evangelia 176
    De Regimine Principum 75, 81
    Summa Theologica 136, 137, 169, 170, 177
    Super Epistolam ad Corinthios Lectura 178
    Super Epistolam ad Romanos Lectura 178
Tintaguel 281
Titus, Emperor 125
Tityus 223
Tnugdal (*Vision of Tnugdal*) 104, 105, 106, 107, 110, 271, 272, 275, 277
Tocco, F. 228
Todi 111, 275, 276, 284
Todorov, T. 171
Tolomeo of Lucca 46, 47, 54, 70, 74, 75, 81, 89, 90
    De Regimine Principum Continuatio 81, 82
    Examaeron 75, 81
Tommaseo, N. 301
Took, J. F. 173
Torraca, F. 118
Toynbee, P. J. 290
Tractatus de Purgatorio Sancti Patricii 95–98, 102–05, 111–12, 271–72, 274, 275
Trajan, Emperor 220
Trani 278
Treviso 28
Trifone Gabriele 299
Tripartite Life of St Patrick 96, 113
Tristan 281
Trompeo, P. P. 257
Troy 220, 221
Tucker, D. J. 260, 262
Turbia 189

Turin 289
Tuscany 16, 25, 28, 34, 39, 41, 43, 44, 47, 65, 74, 83, 189
Tyerman, C. 83, 90
Tyrer, J. W. 258
Tyrrhenian Sea 189

Ubertino da Casale 14
Ugolino da Vico 27
Uguccione of Pisa: see Huguccio of Pisa
Uguccione della Faggiuola 16, 21, 22, 23, 25
Uisnech (navel of Ireland) 109
Ulster 96, 113
Umbria 16
Umiliati 12
United States of America 296
Urban IV, Pope 48, 188, 189, 199, 207, 208
Usher, J. 84

Valerius Maximus 264
Valesio, P. 286
Vallese, G. 208
Vallone, A. 185, 203, 206, 209, 259, 263
Van Cleve, T. C. 207
Vandelli, G. 287
Van den Eynde, D. 170
Van Dijk, S. J. P. 258, 260
Vanni Rovighi, R. 174, 179
Vasoli, C. 173, 174
Vauchez, A. 34, 42, 53, 54, 55
Vellutello, A. 209, 301
Veltro 223, 225, 226
Venantius Fortunatus 234
Venice 22, 49, 68, 284
Venturi, P. 301
Venus 282, 286
Verde (river) 197, 199, 209
Vermiglio degli Alfani 21, 27
Vernon, Lord George 290, 296, 297, 300
Vernon, William Warren 290, 296, 297, 301
Verona 22, 182
Via Emilia 34
Via Francigena 34
Vicenza 27
Vico, G. B. 204, 209, 299
Victor, Saint 40
Vienna 284
Vieri de' Cerchi 18, 21
Vigevano 27
Vigo, P. 30

Villani: see Filippo Villani; Giovanni Villani
Villari, P. 271, 284
Viola Novella 280, 281, 282, 283, 286
Virgil 191, 200, 211–29, 253, 282, 283; *Virgil 43, 189, 190, 191, 192, 215, 234, 244, 258, 272, 273
    Aeneid 200, 217, 218, 219, 220, 222, 228, 229, 264, 282
    Eclogues 191, 217, 218, 222
Virgin Mary: see Mary, Blessed Virgin
Visconti: see Ottone Visconti
Visconti dynasty 278
Visione di Tundale 277
Vision of Drycthelm 99, 100–02, 107–08
Vision of Louis d'Auxerre 276, 277, 279, 282, 284
Vision of Tnugdal 104, 106–11, 114–15, 271–76, 284
Visio Pauli: see Paul, Saint
Vita Sancti Patricii 96
Vittorio Emanuele III, King of Italy 292
Voyage of Bran 107, 115

Waldensians 76
Waley, D. 29, 30
Warnke, K. 112, 113, 114
Webb, D. M. 33–55, 53, 54
Westra, H. J. 169
Wetherbee, W. 170, 172
White, J. 29, 54
Whitman, J. 172
William of Auxerre 71, 72, 74, 89
    Summa Aurea 71, 72, 74, 89
William of Moerbeke 73, 89
William Peraldus 66
Witte, K. 290, 301
Worcester 114
World of Darkness (*Vision of Tnugdal*) 105, 106, 108
World of Light (*Vision of Tnugdal*) 105, 106, 107
Wulfstan, Saint 114

Yseut 281

Zama, P. 285
Zdekauer, L. 54
Zeno, Saint 43
Zenobius, Saint 39, 40, 43, 49
Zita, Saint 37, 44, 45, 46, 54